UGC NET ECONOMICS

Previous Years Questions
Solved with Explanations

SIMRANJIT KAUR

Published by :

Invincible Publication Pvt. Ltd.

INVINCIBLE
Publication Private Limited

Published by
Invincible Publication Pvt. Ltd.
201A, SAS Tower, Sector 38, Gurugram – 122003

www.invinciblepublishers.com

UGC NET Economics By Simranjit Kaur

Updated Edition
This edition can be exported from India only by Invincible Publication.

ISBN- 978-9358866858

Invincible Publication Pvt. Ltd.

Sales Office : 4760-61/23, Basement, Pratap Street, Ansari Road,
Daryaganj, New Delhi - 110002
Email: invinciblepublishers@gmail.com

Note:- For Video lectures follow MS Study Guru

★UGC NET Economics Previous Year Questions★

1. **The 15th Finance Commission (FC) has recommended that the States be given what percent of the divisible tax pool of the Centre during the period 2021-2022 to 2025-26?**
(Year 2021)

(a) 31 (b) 41

(c) 51 (d) 61

Answer: b

Solution:

15th Finance Commission :- Article 280 of the Constitution requires that FC to be constituted. To recommend the distribution of the net proceeds of taxes between the centre and states and among the states.

Centre ↓ Vertical Distribution ↓ State

State ⟷ State — Horizontal Distribution

NK Singh → Chairman of 15th FC

→ The formula for sharing revenues is decided by the FC every 5 years.

→ The time, however the 15th FC will decide the formula for six years.

→ The 15th FC was required to submit two reports.

First Report	**Final Report**
Recommendations for the FY 2020-21 was tabled in Parliamenton 1 February. 2020	With recommendations for the 2021-26 period

Key Recommendations :-

Devolution of taxes to states :-

The share of taxes to states decreased form 42% to 41 [Vertical Devolution].

→ Horizontal Devaluation→	14th FC	15th FC
Income distance [States with higher average income will get less share]	50	45
Population 1971	17.5	-
Population 2011	10.0	15.0
Area	15.0	15.0
Forest Cover	7.5	-
Forest and Ecology	-	10
[share of dense forest of each state in the aggregate dense forest of all states]		
Demographic Performance	-	12.5
[States with lower fertility ratio will bescored higher]		
Tax effort [Reward States with higher tax collection efficiency	-	2.5
Total	100	100

2. **Arrange the following business cycles in ascending order in terms of their approximate duration.**

(Year 2021)

A. Kondratiev cycle
B. Kitchin cycle
B. Juglar cycle
D. Kuznets cycle

Choose the correct answer from the options given below

(a) A, C, B, D,
(b) B, C, D, A,
(c) C, B, A, D,
(d) D, A, C, B,

Answer : (b)

Solution:

The business cycles can be arranged in ascending order based on their approximate durations:

1. Kitchin cycle: Discovered by Joseph Kitchin in the 1920s, it is a short-term cycle lasting around 40 months. It is attributed to delays in information flow affecting decision-making by businesses.
2. Juglar cycle: Identified by Clément Juglar in 1862, it is a fixed investment cycle lasting between 7 to 11 years. It involves fluctuations in investments specifically into fixed capital, rather than just changes in employment levels.
3. Kuznets cycle: Proposed by Simon Kuznets in 1930, it is a medium-range economic wave with a period of 15 to 25 years. It is characterized by fluctuations in long-term investments, particularly in infrastructure and major construction projects.
4. Kondratiev cycle: Also known as Kondratiev waves, they are hypothesized cycle-like phenomena in the modern world economy. They are closely linked to the life cycle of technology and are the longest business cycles, lasting approximately 40 to 60 years. Kondratiev waves encompass broad economic trends, including major innovations, technological advancements, and international trade and finance shifts.

3. Which of the following is NOT a Commercial Bank? *(Year 2021)*

(a) Co-operative Bank
(b) Private Sector Bank
(c) Public Sector Bank
(d) Regional Rural Bank

Answer : (a)

Solution: → Co-operative Bank

Commercial banks are those which are included in the 2nd schedule of RBI Act 1934.

Cooperative Banks :- (established on the cooperative principles of cooperation, self help and mutual help and is engaged in the normal banking activities)

- Their interest rate is high on Savings and low on credit.
- State Cooperative Banks
- District cooperative banks
- Primary Agricultural credit societies

4. In the context of investments, which of the following statement(s) is/are CORRECT? *(Year 2021)*

A. According to the accelerator model, investment demand is proportional to change in income

B. The higher the real interest rate, the higher is the rental cost of capital

C. Investment is a stock variable

D. The real rate of interest is equal to the nominal rate of interest plus the inflation rate

Choose the correct answer from the options given below:

(a) A and B only/ (b) A and D only/

(c) B and C only/ (d) C and D only

Answer : (a)

Solution

A. According to the accelerator model, investment demand is directly proportional to changes in income. When income increases, investment demand tends to increase, and when income decreases, investment demand decreases accordingly.

B. The rental cost of capital rises with higher real interest rates. This is because a higher real interest rate implies higher borrowing costs, leading to increased rental fees for utilizing capital goods.

C. Investment is a flow variable, not a stock variable. It represents the expenditure on acquiring capital goods over a specific period, such as annual investment spending.

D. The real interest rate is determined by subtracting the inflation rate from the nominal interest rate. It reflects the adjusted interest rate after accounting for the impact of inflation on the purchasing power of money.

5. The total population of city 'X' in 2011 was 28 lakhs and the total number of live births was 50 thousand. Find out crude birth rate per 1000 population. *(Year 2021)*

(a) 0.17857 (b) 1.7857

(c) 17.857 (d) 178.57

Answer : (c)

Solution: To calculate the crude birth rate per 1000 population, the formula is: Crude Birth Rate = (Number of live births / Total population) x 1000

Given that the total population of city 'X' in 2011 was 28 lakhs and the total number of live births was 50,000.

Crude Birth Rate = (50,000 / 28,00,000) x 1000 Calculating this expression:

Crude Birth Rate = (0.017857) x 1000

Crude Birth Rate $\approx$ 17.857

Therefore, the crude birth rate per 1000 population is approximately 17.857.

6. Given below are two statements, one is labelled as Assertion A and the other is labelled as Reason R

Assertion A: There is no incentive for a profit maximizing producer to supply public goods.

Reason R: If he produces it, he is unable to exclude people from consuming it and hence he cannot charge a price.

In light of the above statements, choose the most appropriate answer from the options given below *(Year 2021)*

(a) A is correct but R is not correct

(b) A is not correct but R is correct

(c) Both A and R are correct and R is the correct explanation of A

(d) Both A and R are correct but R is NOT the correct explanation of A

Answer : (c)

Solution: The assertion given, "There is no incentive for a profit-maximizing producer to supply public goods", is true as producer is profit maximizing and property of public good is non excludable and non-rivalrous.

Non excludable : if it can be consumed by anyone.

Non-rivalrous : if no one has an exclusive right over its consumption.

Hence, both assertion and reason are correct and R is correct explanation of A.

7. **Which of the following are relevant conditions assumed by the Factor Price Equalization theorem?** *(Year 2021)*

(A) The countries are characterized by different factor endowments

(B) The countries are characterized by different production functions

(C) The industries are characterized by different factor intensities

(D) Each country will export the commodity which uses its abundant factor

Choose the correct answer from the options given below:

(a) A, B and C only/ (b) A, B and D only

(c) A, C and D only/ (d) B, C and D only

Answer : (c) Solution :

Modern theory of trade (factor proportion theory/ factor endowment theory) Heckscher ohlin

The countries are characterized by different factor endowments

"Countries which are rich in labour will export labour intensive growth and countries which are rich in capital will export capital intensive goods. The basis of trade is difference in availability of resources.

The industries are characterized by different factor intensities

The countries should export the good which makes intensive use of abundant factor and import the good which makes intensive use of cheap factor. Commodity Y is capital intensive if Capital labour ratio (K/L)used in production of Yis greater than K/L ratio used in production of X. Y is Capital intensive and L is labour intensive in following case.

(K/L)Y > (K/L)X

Assumptions:-

1. 2×2×2 model
2. Perfect competition
3. Full employment
4. Constant returns to scale
5. Perfectly mobility with the nation and perfect in mobility between Nations.
6. The countries are characterized by same production function for same commodity. i.e. commodity X will be labour intensive in both Countries and commodity Y will be capital intensive in both countries.

8. Zero Based Budgeting (ZBB) lays emphasis on:

(A) Allocation of resources based on cost-benefit terms

(B) Unlimited deficit financing

(C) Preparing a new budget right from the scratch

(D) Preparing the budget, neglecting the history of expenditure

Choose the correct answer from the options given below: (Year 2021)

(a) A, B and C only/ (b) A, B and D only/

(c) A, C and D only/ (d) B, C and D only/

Answer : (c)

Solution:

Zero based budgeting :- Budget starting from the scratch [from zero] [Developed by Peter Phyrr in 1970]. Zero-based budgeting (ZBB) is an approach where every expense must be justified and approved from scratch for each budgeting period. It breaks away from traditional methods that use previous budgets as a baseline. ZBB requires departments to justify their budget requests based on value and necessity, aiming to eliminate unnecessary expenses and improve resource allocation. It involves identifying decision packages, evaluating them based on goals, allocating resources accordingly, and continuously monitoring and reviewing the budget. ZBB promotes fiscal discipline and efficiency but can be time-consuming. Organizations should consider its benefits and costs before implementing it.

9. Given below are two statements, one is labelled as Assertion A and the other is labelled as Reason R

Assertion A: A lumpsum tax imposed on a monopolist cannot be shifted to the consumers.
Reason R: The lumpsum tax becomes a part of his fixed cost and it does not affect the marginal cost of production.

In light of the above statements, choose the most appropriate answer from the options given below (Year 2021)

(a) A is correct but R is not correct/(,

(b) A is not correct but R is correct

(c) Both A and R are correct and R is the correct explanation of A

(d) Both A and R are correct but R is NOT the correct explanation of A

Answer : (c)

Solution : Both A and R are correct, and R is the correct explanation of A.

Assertion A states that a lumpsum tax imposed on a monopolist cannot be shifted to the consumers. This means that the monopolist cannot pass on the burden of the tax to the consumers in the form of higher prices.

Reason R provides an explanation for Assertion A by stating that the lumpsum tax becomes a part of the monopolist's fixed cost and does not affect the marginal cost of production. Since the tax is not directly tied to the quantity produced, it does not influence the monopolist's pricing decisions. The lumpsum tax, being a fixed cost, does not affect the monopolist's marginal cost of production. Consequently, the tax cannot be transferred to consumers through increased prices since it does not influence the pricing decisions of the monopolist.

10. With reference to the programme 'NIDHI' which of the following statement(s) is/are CORRECT? *(Year 2021)*

(A) The programme of 'NIDHI' was started for students to begin startups

(B) Its aim is to financially support 20 students for startups each year

(C) Its aim is to financially support 200 students for startups each year

(D) Its aim is to financially support only students of backward classes to start up each year

Choose the correct answer from the options given below:

(a) A, C and D only/ (b) A and B only/

(c) A and D only (d) C and D only/

Answer : (b)

Solution:- The National Initiative for Developing and Harnessing Innovations (NIDHI) is a program initiated by the Department of Science & Technology (DST), Government of India. It aims to provide initial funding, known as ignition funding, to startups. This program is referred to as Startup-NIDHI. In short, NIDHI is a program that provides ignition funding to startups, known as Startup-NIDHI. It supports 20 student startups each year with Rs 10.00 lakhs as an ignition grant. The selection process is conducted through a national-level competition, and the startups must be associated with IEDC/New Gen IEDC.

11. Arrange the following committees appointed for the Banking sector in India in chronological order: *(Year 2021)*

(A) Urjit Patel Committee **B. Goiporia Committee**

C. Narasimham Committee-I **D. Chakravarty Committee**

Choose the correct answer from the options given below

(a) A, C, D, B, (b) C, B, D, A,

(c) D, B, C, A (d) D, C, B, A,

Answer : (c)

Solution:

D. Chakravarty Committee (1985) - to review the working of monetary policy

B. Goiporia Committee (1990) - focus on prudential norms and accounting standards,

C. Narasimham Committee-I (1991) - focus on banking sector reforms, and

A. Urjit Patel Committee (2013) - focus on monetary policy framework and RBI effectiveness.

12. General Economic Equilibrium is NOT related to which one of the following problems? *(Year 2021)*

(a) Existence problem (b) Moral Hazard problem

(c) Stability problem (d) Uniqueness problem

Answer : (b)

Solution:

A. Existence problem: General Economic Equilibrium theory addresses the question of whether an equilibrium exists in an economy or not, where supply and demand are balanced across all markets.

B. Moral Hazard problem: The Moral Hazard problem is a concept related to asymmetric information in contract situations, where one party may take risks knowing that the consequences will be borne by another party.

C. Stability problem: General Economic Equilibrium theory examines the stability of equilibrium states and whether they are prone to disturbances or fluctuations.

D. Uniqueness problem: The Uniqueness problem refers to the question of whether there is only one possible equilibrium in an economy or if multiple equilibria can exist.

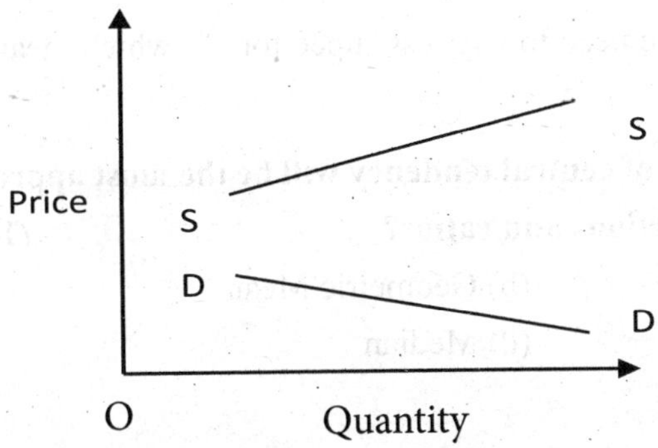

a) Zero production case [price which consumers are willing to pay for the good is not enough to cover the cost of the producers.

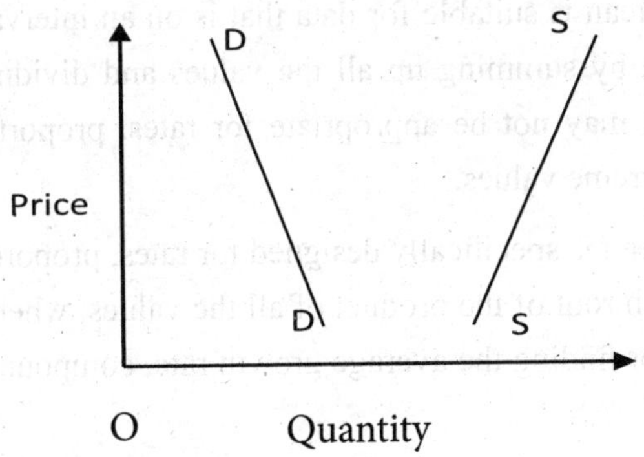

b) Free Good Case Available in abundance that MC of production of them is zero i.e. Air and Water

QS > QD

Stability of Equilibrium :-

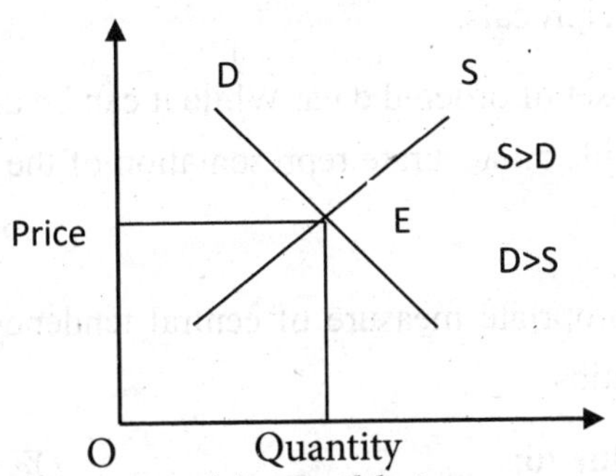

Stable equilibrium

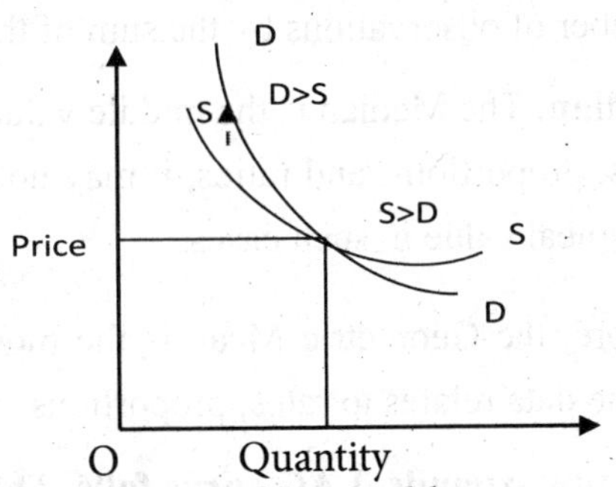

Unstable equilibrium

13. When the exchange rate changes from 1$ = Rs. 72 to 1$ = Rs. 68, then the:

A. Rupee has depreciated
B. Dollar has depreciated
C. Rupee has appreciated
D. Dollar has appreciated

Choose the correct answer from the options given below:

(a) A and B only/
(b) A and D only/
(c) B and C only
(d) C and D only

Answer – c

Solution: In the above question, now we need to pay less rupee for 1$, which means that the value of the rupee has appreciated.

14. Which one of the following measures of central tendency will be the most appropriate to use if the data relates to rates, proportions and ratios? *(Year 2021)*

(a) Arithmetic Mean/ (b) Geometric Mean

(c) Harmonic Mean (d) Median

Answer – b

Solution:

(a) **Arithmetic Mean:** The Arithmetic Mean is suitable for data that is on an interval or ratio scale and is used to find the average by summing up all the values and dividing by the number of observations. However, it may not be appropriate for rates, proportions, and ratios as they can be influenced by extreme values.

(b) **Geometric Mean:** The Geometric Mean is specifically designed for rates, proportions, and ratios. It is calculated by taking the nth root of the product of all the values, where n is the number of observations. It is useful for finding the average growth rate, compound interest rate, or other multiplicative factors.

(c) **Harmonic Mean:** The Harmonic Mean is suitable for data that involves rates or ratios, particularly when dealing with average rates or speeds. It is calculated by dividing the number of observations by the sum of their reciprocals.

(d) **Median:** The Median is the middle value in a set of ordered data. While it can be used with rates, proportions, and ratios, it may not provide an accurate representation of the average or typical value in such cases.

Therefore, the Geometric Mean is the most appropriate measure of central tendency to use when the data relates to rates, proportions, and ratios.

15. As output expands, LAC curve falls. This is due to: *(Year 2021)*

(a) Diseconomies of scale/ (b) Economies of scale

(c) Law of diminishing returns/ (d) Law of variable proportions

Answer – b

Solution:

L – Shaped Long Run Average Cost Curve

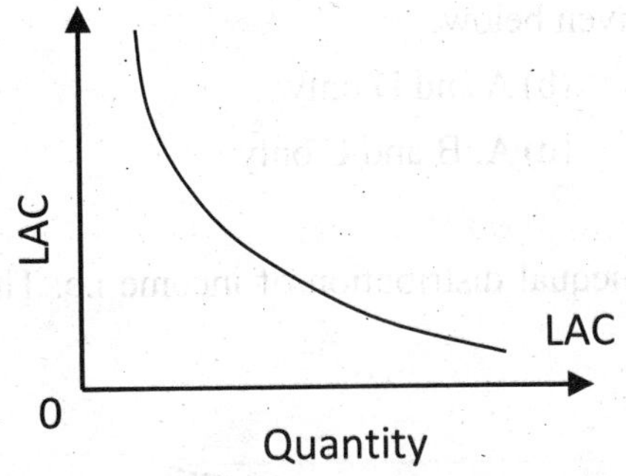

Reasons:-

(a) Economies of Scale

(b) Learning Effect

(c) Technological Progress

16. Arrange the following Committees of poverty estimation in chronological order: *(Year 2021)*

(A) Alagh Committee

(B) Lakdawala Committee

(C) Tendulkar Committee

(D) Rangarajan Committee

Choose the correct answer from the options given below

(a) A, B, C, D,
(b) A, C, B, D,
(c) B, A, C, D,
(d) B, C, A, D,

Answer – a

Solution:

A. **Alagh Committee :** The Alagh Committee was formed in 1979 to reassess and revise the poverty line and measurement methods in India.

B. **Lakdawala Committee :** The Lakdawala Committee was established in 1993 to review and revise the existing poverty line and estimation methods in India.

C. **Tendulkar Committee :** The Tendulkar Committee was set up in 2005 to review and update the methodology for poverty estimation in India, including the determination of poverty lines and measurement techniques (Submitted report in 2007)

D. **Rangarajan Committee :** The Rangarajan Committee was constituted in 2012 to review and update the methodology for poverty estimation in India, including the calculation of poverty lines and measurement approaches (It Submitted its report in 2014)

17. Inequalities in income are measured by which of the following? *(Year 2021)*

A. Lorenz Ratio
B. Theil's Index
C. Palma Ratio
D. Deprivation Ratio

Choose the correct answer from the options given below:

(a) A and B only (b) A and D only/

(c) A only (d) A, B and C only

Answer : (d)

Solution : The greater this ratio, the more unequal distribution of income i.e. The more the Lorenz curve falls below the 45° line.

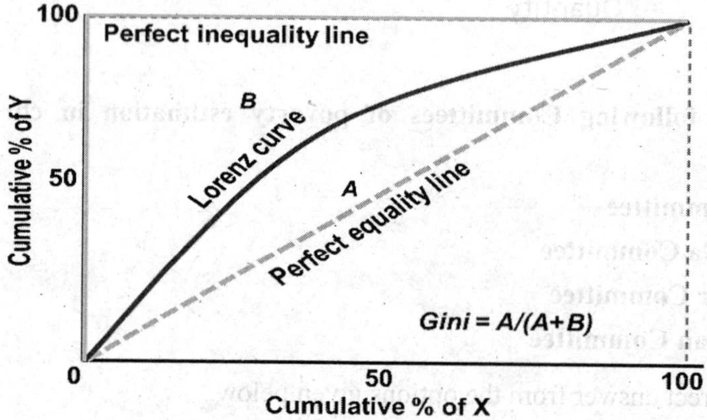

Income inequality falls with an increase in per capita income. Reason of increase in inequality in UDCs – Dualism

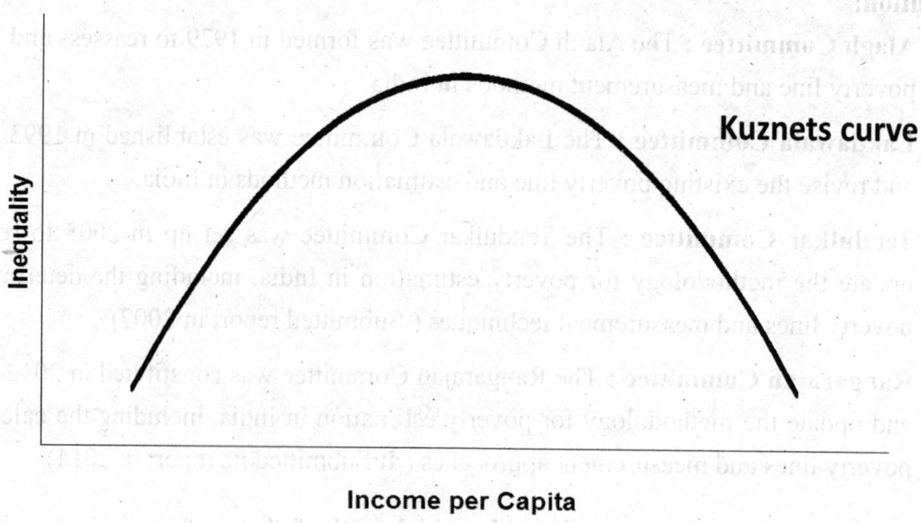

Reason of reduction in inequality DC's → Trickledown effect/ spread effect (Gradually benefit the poorest as a result of the increasing wealth of the richest).

- The Palma ratio is an alternative to the Gini index, and focuses on the differences between those in the top and bottom income brackets. The ratio takes the richest 10% of the population's share of gross national income (GNI) and divides it by the poorest 40% of the population's share.

Theil's Index: Theil's Index is a numerical measure of income inequality. It quantifies the relative dispersion of incomes within a population. The index takes into account both within-group income inequality (inequality among individuals within groups) and between-group inequality (inequality among different groups).

Deprivation Ratio," is not specifically used to measure income inequality. The Deprivation Ratio generally refers to a measure of poverty or deprivation, which assesses the proportion of the population lacking access to certain basic needs or resources. While poverty and inequality are related, they are distinct concepts with different measurement approaches.

18. Which of the following would reduce the credit creation capacity of a Commercial Bank?

(Year 2021)

(A) Time and Demand deposits

(B) Loans

(C) Deposits with the Central Bank

(D) Cash in hand

Choose the correct answer from the options given below:

(a) A and B only
(b) A and D only
(c) B and C only
(d) C and D only

Answer – d

Solution: As we can clearly identify that deposits with central banks and cash in hand cannot be used by commercial banks for credit creation.

19. Which of the following are true for the Environmental Kuznets Curve (EKC)?

(Year 2021)

(A) The relationship between Income and Environmental damages takes the shape of an inverted U

(B) EKC is applicable in case of irreversible environmental damage

(C) EKC holds true for global pollutants

(D) EKC hypothesis intends to represent a long-term relationship between economic growth and pollution

Choose the correct answer from the options given below:

(a) A and B only/
(b) A and D only
(c) A, B, C and D
(d) C and D only

Answer – b

Solution: The Environmental Kuznets Curve (EKC) shows the relationship between income and environmental damages following an inverted U-shape, indicating that pollution levels initially increase with economic development and then start to decline. The EKC hypothesis represents a long-term relationship between economic growth and pollution. However, it does not specifically address irreversible environmental damage, and its applicability may vary for different pollutants and at the global level.

20. According to Ronald Coase, which of the following statements is CORRECT for pollution control? *(Year 2021)*

(a) Providing property rights to polluters and pollutees/
(b) Providing property rights to the legal institutions
(c) Providing property rights to the state/
(d) Providing property rights to Trade Unions/

Answer – a

Solution:

Property Rights and Coase Theorem:- If property rights are clearly defined, the affected parties will adopt policies to internalize the externality. In other words, if property rights and liability are properly defined and there are no transaction cost, then people can be held responsible for any negative Externalities they impose on others and market transactions will produce an efficient outcome.

21. Which one of the following correctly describes the concept of 'Super Multiplier'? *(Year 2021)*

(a) Employment multiplier/
(b) Interaction between multiplier and accelerator/
(c) Investment multiplier
(d) Money multiplier

Answer – b

Solution: The concept of the 'Super Multiplier' involves the combined effect of the multiplier and accelerator in an economy, where changes in investment or spending amplify economic output. It refers to the interaction between the multiplier effect and the accelerator effect, leading to larger-than-expected increases in output and income.

22. The sampling distribution of mean based on a sample of 13 units selected without replacement shows a variance of 5 units. If the population consists of 49 units, estimate the variance of the population. *(Year 2021)*

(a) 80.67 (b) 84.87

(c) 86.67 (d) 86.87

Answer – c

Solution:

If the **population is finite** with mean μ and standard deviation σ or **the sampling is without replacement**, use the following:

mean	*variance*	*standard deviation**
$\mu_{\bar{X}} = \mu$	$\sigma_{\bar{X}}^2 = \frac{\sigma^2}{n}\left(\frac{N-n}{N-1}\right)$	$\sigma_{\bar{X}} = \frac{\sigma}{\sqrt{n}} \cdot \sqrt{\frac{N-n}{N-1}}$

σ_x = sample standard deviation

σ = Population standard deviation

With replacement, formula is

$$\sigma_{\bar{X}} = \frac{\sigma}{\sqrt{n}}$$

23. Which of the following measures are used by a risk-averse person to minimize risk? *(Year 2021)*

(A) Diversification of resources

(B) Insurance of risk event

(C) Total cost of resources

(D) Value of information of risk event

Choose the correct answer from the options given below:

(a) A, B and C only (b) A, B and D only/

(c) A, C and D only (d) B, C and D only

Answer – b

Solution:

A. **Diversification of resources:** Risk-averse individuals can minimize their risk exposure by diversifying their resources or investments, and spreading their resources across different assets or investments to reduce the potential impact of a single risk event.

B. **Insurance of risk event:** Risk-averse individuals often opt for insurance as a means to mitigate potential losses from specific risk events. Insurance transfers the risk from the individual to an insurance provider, providing financial protection against unforeseen events.

C. **Total cost of resources:** This option is not directly related to risk mitigation. The total cost of resources refers to the overall cost incurred in acquiring and maintaining resources, but it does not specifically address risk management.

D. **Value of information of risk event:** The value of information regarding risk events is crucial for risk management. Having accurate and relevant information allows risk-averse individuals to make informed decisions and take appropriate actions to minimize risk.

24. Which of the following conditions hold true for factor pricing when factor market is perfectly competitive and product market is monopolistic? *(Year 2021)*

(A) VMP > MRP

(B) Both VMP and MRP decreasing

(C) VMP < MRP

(D) MRPL = W

(a) A, B and C only (b) A, B and D only

(c) A, C and D only (d) B, C and D only/

Answer – b

Solution

Monopolistic exploitation is difference between VMP (Value of marginal product) and MRP(marginal revenue product.

Demand for labour curve in perfect competition is VMP curve of labour that is downward sloping and VMP is equal to MRP curve. Equilibrium is supply curve of labour(W*) tangent with Demand curve of labour (VMP) at e point.

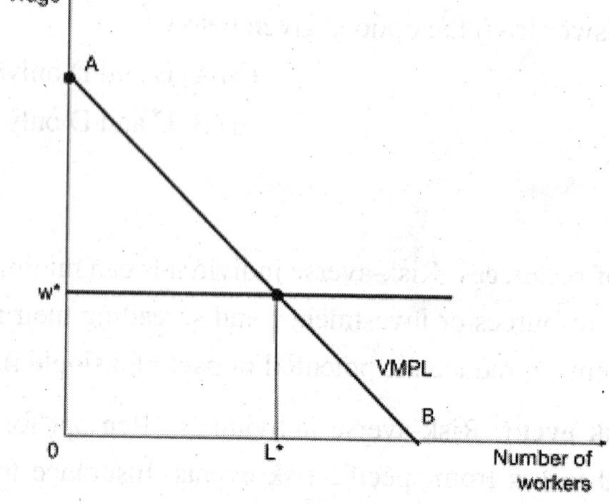

Demand for labour curve in imperfect competition is MRP curve of labour. It is also downward sloping. Here VMP is greater than MRP curve.

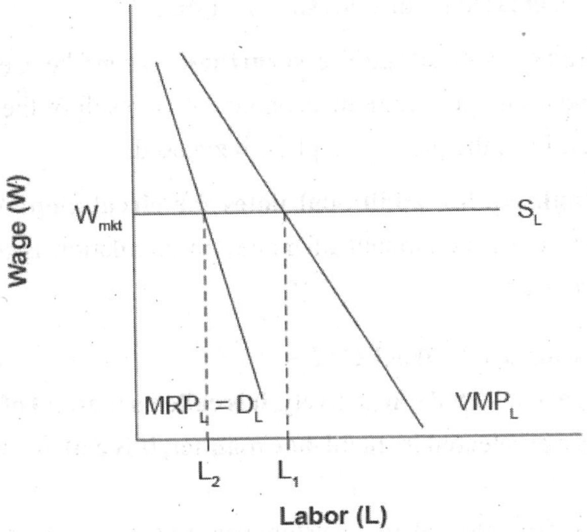

25. Which of the following measures would result in an increase in the money supply in the economy? *(Year 2021)*

(A) Purchase of government securities from the public by Central Bank

(B) Deposit of currency in Commercial Banks by the public

(C) Borrowing by the government from the Central Bank

(D) Sale of government securities to the public by the Central Bank

(E) Minting of more money by the Central Bank for circulation

Choose the correct answer from the options given below:

(a) A, B and C only
(b) A, C and E only
(c) B, C and D only
(d) B, D and E only

Answer – b

Solution:

A. **The Central Bank's purchase of public government assets:** The Central Bank injects cash into the economy when it buys public government securities. Because the public receives cash in return for the securities, this expands the money supply.

B. **Public currency deposits in commercial banks:** Deposits made by the general public in commercial banks do not directly enhance the money supply. Instead, it causes a rise in bank reserves, which may allow banks to boost their lending and overall money supply by using the money multiplier effect. The act of depositing money does not, however, directly increase the amount of money in circulation.

C. **Government borrowing from the Central Bank:** The government obtains monies in the form of newly created money when it borrows from the Central Bank. The economy's money supply is increased by this infusion of cash.

D. **The Central Bank's sale of public securities:** When the Central Bank sells public securities, it removes money from the economy. As a result of the public paying money to purchase the securities, the money supply is decreased.

E. **The Central Bank issuing additional notes for circulation:** When the Central Bank issues additional notes, the amount of money in circulation is directly increased as the notes go into circulation.

26. Which of the following are CORRECT? *(Year 2021)*

(A) If observations are selected purposively, it is called a method of non-random sampling

(B) If observations are selected in an ad-hoc manner, it is called a method of non-random sampling

(C) If observations are selected in a systematic manner, it is called a method of non-random sampling

(D) If observations are selected on the basis of judgment, it is called a method of non-random sampling

Choose the correct answer from the options given below:

(a) A, B and C only
(b) A, B and D only
(c) A, C and D only
(d) B, C and D only

Answer – b

Solution:

A. When observations are selected with a specific goal or target in mind, frequently based on the researcher's experience or judgment, it is said that they were chosen with purpose. Non- random sampling is the term used to describe this way of choosing observations.

B. If observations are selected ad hoc, it means that they were not chosen according to a set strategy or method; rather, they were selected as they seemed necessary at the time. Non-random sampling also covers this situation.

C. Observations that are selected in a systematic way are those that follow a predetermined method or pattern, such as choosing every nth observation from a list. But this approach of systematic sampling is a type of random sampling, not non-random sampling. As a result, statement C is untrue.

D. When observations are selected based on judgement, it signifies the researcher's expert or subjective judgement was used to make the decision. Non-random sampling refers to the subjective process of this type of selection.

In conclusion, option A, B, and D are correct, but option C is incorrect.

27. Which of the following statement(s) is/are CORRECT for environmental evaluation?

(A) Travel cost method measures the recreational values of Environmental Resources

(B) Hedonic pricing is used for environmental amenities associated with property values

(C) Replacement cost method is used by substituting natural resources with a man-made equipment

(D) Defensive expenditure deals with preventive measures

Choose the correct answer from the options given below: *(Year 2021)*

(a) A and B only (b) A, B, C and D

(c) B and C only, (d) C only

Answer – b

Solution:

Travel cost method: - This approach is used to value the recreational benefits of public parks and other natural areas. This method seeks to determine the demand for recreational site (i.e. number of visits per year to a park) as a function of variables like price, visitor's income and socioeconomic characteristics. The price is sum of entry fees, cost of travel and opportunity cost of time spent.

Hedonic price method: - Price of property is related to stream of benefits derived.

Replacement cost method: - Measure the potential expenditure that would be required to replace or restore a productive asset that would be damaged by some development.

The term "defensive expenditure" refers to costs made by people, businesses, or governments in an effort to prevent or reduce possible losses or harm. It means taking actions to guard against a number of hazards and threats. These actions are intended to lessen the possibility or effect of unwanted situations or incidents.

28. What type of relationship the Phillips curve postulates between the rate of unemployment and the rate of increase of money wages? *(Year 2021)*

(a) Direct and proportional (b) Direct

(c) Inverse and proportional (d) Inverse

Answer – d

Solution: Phillips curve suggests that there is an inverse relationship between the rate of unemployment and the rate of increase of money wages. When unemployment is low, wage increases tend to be higher, and when unemployment is high, wage increases tend to be lower.

It's important to note that the relationship depicted by the Phillips curve is primarily applicable in the short run. In the long run, other factors, such as inflation expectations and changes in productivity, can influence the relationship between unemployment and wage growth.

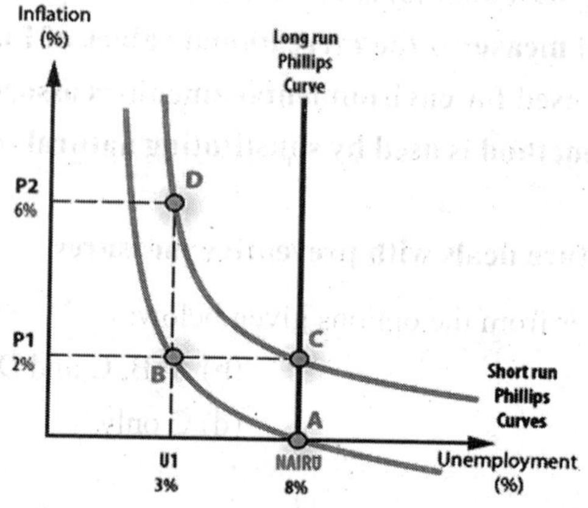

29. Which of the following statements are CORRECT for welfare economics? *(Year 2021)*

(A) Any competitive equilibrium leads to a Pareto efficient allocation of resources

(B) Competitive equilibrium does not lead to Pareto efficient allocation of resources

(C) Any efficient allocation can be attained by a competitive equilibrium given the market mechanism leading to Redistribution

(D) There will be no Pareto efficient allocation of resources in the society

Choose the correct answer from the options given below:

(a) A and C only
(b) A, B and C only
(c) B and C only
(d) C and D only,

Answer – a

Solution :

First Fundamental Theorem :-

1. General competitive equilibrium is Pareto optimal.
2. Ensures Pareto efficiency but not Social Justice.

Requirements:- Pareto optimality

Second order conditions

Externalities in production and consumption do not exist.

Second Fundamental Theorem:-

✧ For every Pareto-optimal situation, there is a competitive equilibrium, given the initial income distribution.

30. Demand pull inflation may be caused by?

(a) An increase in costs

(b) A reduction in interest rate

(c) A reduction in government spending

(d) An outward shift in aggregate supply

Answer – b

Solution: Demand pull inflation AD >AS, When interest rates reduces, AD becomes more than AS.

31. According to the Phillips curve unemployment will return to the natural rate when?

(a) Nominal wages are equal to expected wages

(b) Real wages are back at the equilibrium level

(c) Nominal wages are growing faster than inflation

(d) Inflation is higher than the growth of nominal wages

Answer – a

Solution: Long-Run PC: - Given by Milton Friedman. (Augmented Phillips curve /Adaptive Expectations Philip curve) The natural rate of unemployment: - Given by Friedman.

Tobin has given it a new name "non-accelerating inflation rate of unemployment" It is the rate at which actual inflation and expected inflation are equal. In the long run, no trade-off exists between inflation and unemployment. People are rational. There is no possibility for the actual rate of unemployment to differ from the natural rate in long run, according to Friedman.

32. An increase in costs will?

(a) Shift aggregate demand

(b) Shift aggregate supply

(c) Reduce the natural rate of unemployment

(d) Increase the productivity

Answer –b

Solution: An increase in cost, such as raw materials, labor, or energy, can impact the cost of production. An increase in cost would decrease supply, shifting the supply curve to the left, while a decrease in input prices would increase supply, shifting the supply curve to the right.

33. An increase in the marginal propensity to consumer (MPC)?

(a) Raises the value of the multiplier

(b) Has no impact on the value of the multiplier?

(c) Rarely occurs because the MPC is set by congressional legislation

(d) Lowers the value of the multiplier

Answer – a

Solution: M = 1 / (1 - MPC).

When MPC will increase, multiplier will also increase.

34. If the nominal interest rate is 7 percent and the inflation rate is 3 percent, what is the real interest rate?

(a) 4 percent
(b) 10 percent
(c) 5 percent
(d) 3 percent

Answer – a

Solution: The real interest rate can be calculated by subtracting the inflation rate from the nominal interest rate. In this case:

Real interest rate = Nominal interest rate - Inflation rate Real interest rate = 7% - 3% Real interest rate = 4%

Therefore, the real interest rate is 4%.

35. The initial impact of an increase in government spending is to shift?

(a) An aggregate demand to the right
(b) aggregate demand to the left
(c) aggregate supply to the right
(d) aggregate supply to the left

Answer – a

Solution: When the government increases its spending, it injects more money into the economy. This increase in government spending leads to an increase in aggregate demand, which is the total spending on goods and services in an economy. Hence, it will shift demand to the right.

36. The initial effect of an increase in the money supply is to?

(a) increase the interest rate
(b) increase the price level
(c) decrease the price level
(d) decrease the interest rate

Answer – b

Solution: There is more money accessible in the economy when the money supply rises. As aggregate demand rises as a result of the increased money supply, the level of prices in the economy as a whole may also rise.

The purchasing power of people and businesses increases when more money is in circulation. As a result, they have the ability to bid up the cost of goods and services, which raises the overall price level. The quantity theory of money, which suggests that changes in the money supply have a direct impact on the level of prices in the economy, explains this relationship.

37. Which of the following statements is/are correct about normal profit? *(December 2018)*

(a) It is earned over a long period only.

(b) It is earned in a short period only.

(c) It is earned in both the long period and the short period.

(d) It is earned only in perfect competition.

Answer – (c)

Solution:

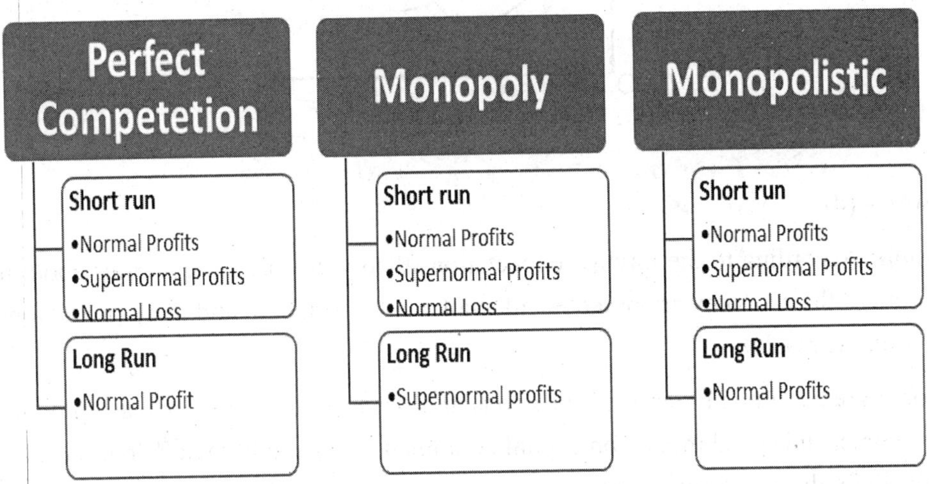

38. Which one of the statements about Pareto optimality is incorrect? *(December 2018)*

(a) Consumers maximize their satisfaction.

(b) All the factors are used in the production of all the commodities.

(c) There is perfect competition in the factor and commodity markets.

(d) Consumers have cardinal utility functions.

Answer = (d)

Solution: It is an ordinal measure of utility.

39. An economic region of production consists of *(December 2018)*

(a) The positively sloped portions of all isoquants

(b) The negatively sloped portions of all isoquants

(c) The middle of all isoquants

(d) The highest points of all isoquants

Answer = (b)

Solution:

Ridge Lines : - Are the locus of points where Marginal productivity of at least one factor is zero.

The optimum stage of production is the region between the two ridge lines and hence is called the region of economic production.

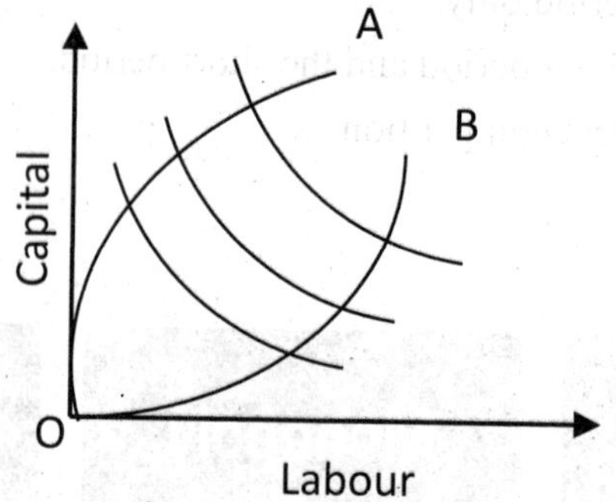

Answer – (d)

Solution: According to the rational expectations theory, people's predictions about the future condition of the economy are based on all available information, and these predictions have an impact on the results.

If people predict a rise in demand for goods and services, they may increase production, hire more people, and spend money on capital equipment. This might then help to boost economic growth and reduce unemployment.

Similarly in the example before, if people expect that demand will diminish, they may reduce output, lay off workers, and limit investment, which can lead to a decline in economic activity and increased unemployment. Therefore, changes in predicted demand may significantly affect employment and other economic outcomes.

Hence, unexpected changes in demand have long-lasting effect on both unemployment and price level is false for rational expectation theory.

40. Who amongst the following economists treated nature to be niggardly? *(December 2018)*

i. J. S. Mill

ii. David Ricardo

iii. Karl Marx

iv. Thomas Robert Malthus

Choose the correct answer from the code given below:

Code:

(a) (i), (ii) and (iii)
(b) (ii) and (iv)
(c) (iii) and (iv)
(d) (ii) and (iii)

Answer – (b)

Solution: David Ricardo and Thomas Robert Malthus treated nature as niggardly. While Malthus believed that nature's resources were limited and would lead to scarcity, Ricardo, in his theory of rent, emphasized that as the population increased and more land was brought into cultivation, diminishing returns would occur, indicating a limited capacity of nature to provide abundant resources.

41. **Which amongst the following is/are correct for the Keynesian model?** *(December 2018)*
   (a) It assumes full employment of resources.
   (b) It ignores the money market.
   (c) It is supply determined.
   (d) None of the above

   Answer – (d)

   Solution: The Keynesian model assumes less than full employment of resources. In fact, one of the central insights of Keynesian economics is that economies can experience persistent unemployment and underutilization of resources, particularly during economic downturns.

   The Keynesian model does not ignore the money market. It recognizes the importance of the money market and the role of monetary policy in influencing aggregate demand and economic activity.

   The Keynesian model is demand determined rather than supply determined. It emphasizes the role of aggregate demand in driving economic output and employment levels. Keynesian economics suggests that changes in aggregate demand, particularly through fiscal policy and monetary policy, can have significant effects on economic performance.

42. **According to New Classical Economics, Real Business Cycles are the result of which of the following?** *(December 2018)*
   (i) Innovations
   (ii) Bad Weather
   (iii) Tax Policy
   (iv) Debt Policy

   Choose the correct answer from the code given below:

   (a) (i) and (ii) (b) (i) and (iii)
   (c) (iii) and (iv) (d) (ii) and (iv)

   Answer – (a)

   Solution: According to the principles of New Classical Economics, Real Business Cycles (RBC) occur as a result of two factors: **technological innovations and adverse weather conditions.**

Innovations and productivity shocks drive shifts in economic activity, while extreme weather events disrupt sectors like agriculture and transportation, causing fluctuations in output and employment. Tax policy and debt policy are not typically considered as primary drivers of RBC according to this theory.

43. Consider the following diagram and the statements: *(December 2018)*

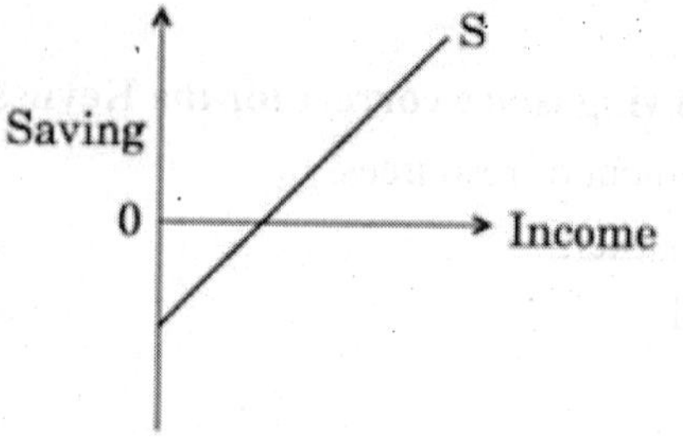

(i) Saving is positively related to income.

(ii) Marginal propensity to save is positive, but less than 1.

Choose the correct answer from the code given below:

(a) Only (i)
(b) Both (i) and (ii)
(c) Only (ii)
(d) Neither (i) nor (ii)

Answer – (b)

Solution: Both statement 1 and 2 are correct as proportion of savings increase with the increase in income and MPS+MPC = 1, hence MPS is positive and less than 1.

44. An increase in the level of government spending, other things being equal, will in the IS-LM model *(December 2018)*

(a) Increase interest rates, shifting the LM curve to the left

(b) Increase the level of equilibrium income at all interest rates, shifting the IS curve right

(c) Lower interest rates, shifting the LM curve to the right

(d) Always move an economy to full employment

Answer – (b)

Solution: In the IS-LM model, an increase in government spending leads to an upward shift of the IS (Investment-Saving) curve. This shift occurs because higher government spending increases aggregate demand, leading to a higher level of equilibrium income at all interest rates. The IS curve represents the combinations of interest rates and income levels that achieve equilibrium in the goods market.

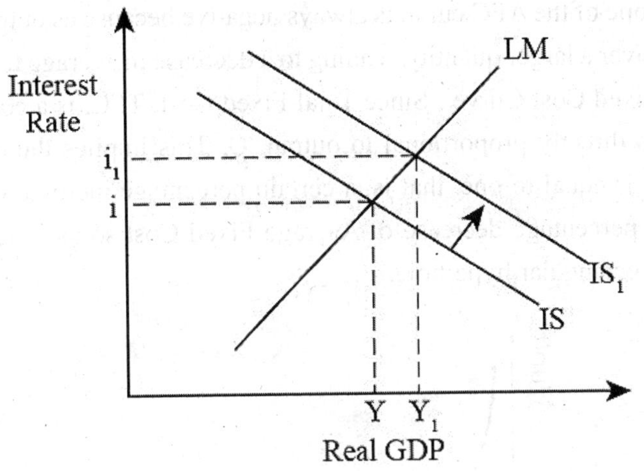

45. The price elasticity of a linear supply curve through the origin is *(December 2018)*

(a) Zero
(b) Unity
(c) Infinite
(d) Less than unity

Answer – (b)

Solution: When a supply curve is linear and passes through the origin, it implies that the quantity supplied is directly proportional to the price. In such a case, the price elasticity of supply (PES) is constant and equal to 1, which means it is unitary elastic.

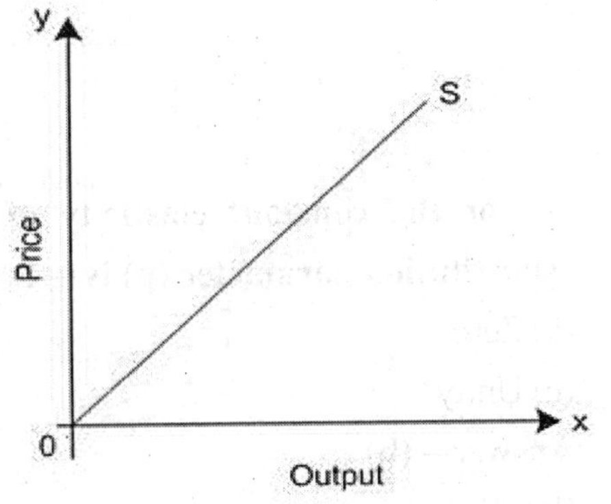

46. Consider the following statements about the Average Fixed Cost of a firm: *(December 2018)*

(i) Its slope is always negative.

(ii) Its slope is always greater than one.

(iii) Its slope is always equal to one.

(iv) Elasticity with respect to output is equal to one.

Choose the correct answer from the code given below:

(a) Only (i)
(b) (ii) and (iii)
(c) (i) and (iv)
(d) Only (iii)

Answer – (c)

Solution: The slope of the AFC curve is always negative because as output increases, the fixed costs are spread over a larger quantity, leading to a decrease in average fixed cost. At each point of the Average Fixed Cost Curve , Since Total Fixed Cost, TFC, is a constant, Average Fixed Cost turns out as directly proportional to output, Q. This implies the curve's elasticity with respect to output is equal to one, that is, a certain percentage increase in output brings about an exactly equal percentage decrease of Average Fixed Cost so as to leave Total Fixed Cost unchanged. It is rectangular hyperbole.

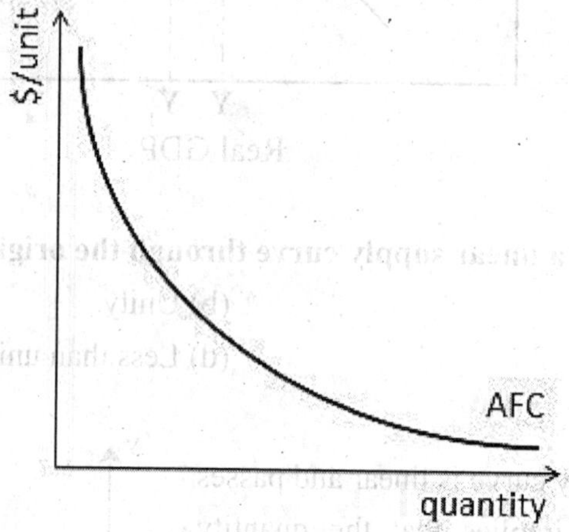

47. If for the constant elasticity of substitution production function, the value of the substitution parameter (p) is =-1, the elasticity of substitution will be *(December 2018)*

(a) Zero
(b) Infinite
(c) Unity
(d) Indeterminate

Answer – (b)

Solution:

CES Production Function: - 1961 **Arrow, Minhas, Chenery, Solow**

$$Q = \gamma\left[\alpha L^{-\beta} + (1-\alpha)K^{-\beta}\right]^{-\frac{1}{\beta}}$$

γ = Coeff. Of Technical Efficiency.

α = Distribution Parameter.

β = Substitution Parameter.

$$E_S = \frac{1}{1+\beta}$$

Es= 1/1+(p)

=1/1+(-1)

=1/0

$= \infty$

48. The problem of adverse selection arises due to *(December 2018)*

(a) Asymmetric information

(b) No information

(c) Full information

(d) Wrong information

Answer – (a)

Solution: Asymmetric Information: - Pareto optimality assumes that Producers and Consumers have perfect information regarding market behavior but in real world, due to a asymmetric information on the part of buyers and sellers, they are unable to equate social and private benefits and costs

49. Consider the following statements about the law of variable proportions: *(December 2018)*

(i) Input ratio remains unchanged.

(ii) Ultimately the marginal and average product of variable input becomes negative.

(iii) Effect of technological change is visible on output.

Choose the correct answer from the code given below:

(a) (i) and (ii) are correct

(b) Only (ii) is correct

(c) (ii) and (iii) are correct

(d) None of the above option is correct

Answer – (d)

Solution:

(a) Input ratio changes as more and more variable factors are combined with fixed factors.

(b) MP becomes negative but AP does not.

(c) Technology is fixed.

Production Function

Law of Variable Proportion	Law of Returns to scale
[Short Run Law]	[Long Run Law]
[1 factor Variable, others fixed]	[All factors Variable]

Law of variable proportions/ Returns to a factor:-

It is short run theory in which there is at least one factor which is fixed. Beyond a certain point, the MP of the factor would diminish.

Assumptions

1. Technology is fixed.
2. One factor is variable others are fixed.

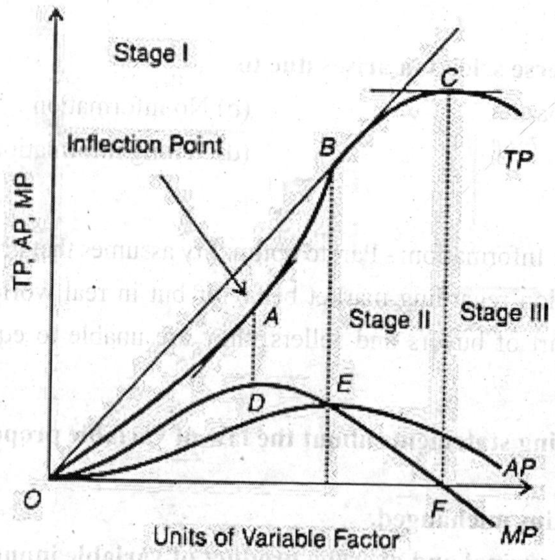

50. The Inada conditions are applicable to *(December 2018)*

(A) A well-behaved investment function

(B) A well-behaved consumption function

(C) A well-behaved production function

(D) A well-behaved technical progress function

Answer: C

Solution

Inada conditions:-

Assumptions about the shape of production function that guarantee the stability of an economic growth path in a Neo-classical growth model. A production function satisfies these conditions are referred to as well behaved production function.

1. No output can be produced without any capital i.e. f (0) =0
2. Marginal product of capital is positive for all levels of capital - labour ratio

   f'(K) >0 for all k
3. Marginal product of capital diminishes as capital for laborer increases

   f'' (K) < 0for all k

51. Monetary policy instruments are *(December 2021 and June 2022)*

(A) Changes in public expenditure

(B) Changes in taxation:

(C) Open market operations

(D) Bank reserve requirement

(E) Interest rate policy

Choose the most appropriate answer from the options given below:

(A), (B) only | (b) (A), (B), (C) only

(c) (C), (D), (E) only | (d) (B), (D), (E) only

Answer - (c)

Solution: Credit control measures adopted by Central Bank of a country.

Instruments:- Quantitative measures to control credit

- Bank Rate
- Open market operations
- Liquidity adjustment facility (LAF)
- Repo Rate
- Reverse Repo Rate
- Cash reserve Ratio
- Statutory liquidity
- Marginal standing facility (MSF)
- Standing Deposit Facility

Qualitative Measures of credit control

- Rationing of credit
- Margin requirements
- Moral Suasion
- Direct Action

52. Basic characteristics of an underdeveloped economy. *(December 2021 and June 2022)*

(A) A low level of technology and poor human capital.

(B) Higher level of GDP and per capita income

(C) A high proportion of the labour force engaged in agriculture and low agriculture productivity

(D) A high proportion of domestic expenditure on food

(E) Higher incidence of poverty

Choose the most appropriate answer from the options given below:

(a) (A), (C), (D) (E) only

(b) (A), (C), (B), (E) only

(B), (D), (E) only

(B) only

Answer - a

Solution: Features of underdeveloped economies include:

- Low GDP per capita.
- High poverty rates.
- Limited industrialization.
- Limited access to healthcare and education.
- High dependency on primary commodities.
- Limited infrastructure.
- Political instability and institutional weaknesses.
- Limited technological advancement.
- High income inequality.

These features are often observed in underdeveloped economies.

53. Given below are two statements: One is labelled as Assertion A and the other is labelled as Reason R

Assertion A: The Endogenous growth theory examines production function that shows increasing returns.

Reason R: Increasing returns in Endogenous growth theory is due to specialization and investment in knowledge capital and learning by doing.

(December 2021 and June 2022)

In the light of the above statements, choose the most appropriate answer from the given below:

(a) Both (A) and (R) are correct and (R) is the correct explanation of (A)

(b) Both (A) and (R) are correct but (R) is NOT the correct explanation of (A)

(c) (A) is correct but (R) is not correct

(d) (A) is not correct but (R) is correct

Answer - (a)

Solution: The assertion "The Endogenous growth theory examines production function that shows increasing returns" is correct.

The reason "Increasing returns in Endogenous growth theory is due to specialization and investment in knowledge capital and learning by doing" is also correct.

In the context of endogenous growth theory, the focus is on explaining long-term economic growth as an endogenous outcome of the economic system rather than relying solely on exogenous factors like capital accumulation and technological progress. In this theory, increasing returns to scale play a crucial role in sustaining long-term economic growth.

The reason provided further explains that increasing returns in endogenous growth theory result from factors such as specialization, investment in knowledge capital (including research and development), and learning by doing. These factors contribute to the accumulation and diffusion of knowledge and skills, leading to productivity gains and positive feedback loops that drive economic growth.

Hence, both the assertion and the reason are correct, and the reason provides a valid explanation for the assertion.

54. The change in welfare due to change in environmental quality is measured by

(December 2021 and June 2022)

(a) Hedonic price function
(b) Marginal implicit function
(c) Marginal Willingness to Pay (WTP) function
(d) Offer function

Answer - (c)

Solution: The change in welfare due to a change in environmental quality is typically measured by the Marginal Willingness to Pay (WTP) function. The Marginal Willingness to Pay (WTP) function measures the additional amount of money an individual is willing to pay for a small improvement in environmental quality. It reflects the change in welfare or utility that individuals experience as a result of a change in the environment.

The Hedonic price function (option A) is used to estimate the implicit prices of different characteristics or attributes of a good, including environmental quality. It is often used in hedonic pricing models to assess the value individuals place on environmental amenities.

The Marginal Implicit Function (option B) is not specifically used to measure changes in welfare due to environmental quality. It refers to the derivative of an implicit function with respect to one of its variables.

The Offer function (option D) is not directly related to measuring changes in welfare due to environmental quality. It is a concept used in game theory to represent the possible actions or strategies available to a player in a game.

Therefore, the correct answer is C. Marginal Willingness to Pay (WTP) function.

55. Match List I with List II: *(December 2021 and June 2022)*

List I	List II
(A) Reverse repo rate	**(I) RBI provides loan to commercial banks for short term**
(B) Bank rate	**(II) RBI provides loan to commercial banks for long term**
(C) Repo rate	**(III) RBI borrows money from commercial banks**
(D) Cash reserve ratio	**(IV) Commercial banks have to deposit minimum ratio of their net total liabilities in RBI**

Choose the correct answer from the options given below:

(a) (A)-(I) (B)-(III) (C)-(II) (D)-(IV)

(b) (A)-(III) (B)-(II) (C)-(I) (D)-(IV)

(c) (A)-(III) (B)-(I) (C)-(II) (D)-(IV)

(d) (A)-(I) (B)-(II) (C)-(III) (D)-(IV)

Answer: (b)

Solution

- **Bank Rate :-**To reduce money supply, bank rate is increased. RBI charges bank rate to commercial banks for long term loans.
- **Repo Rate :-**RBI charges to commercial banks for short term loans.↑ in repo rate ↓ in money supply. Repo rate is technically a repurchase agreement in which the commercial banks offer securities such as Treasury Bills to the RBI in return for short term funds.
- **Reverse repo :-**RBI borrows from banks short term loans at reverse repo rate.
- **Cash reserve Ratio :-** It is percentage of money, which a bank has to keep with RBI in the form of cash.
- SLR>CRR>BR>REPO>REVERSE REPO

56. Which of the following holds good for Lewis model of development

(December 2021 and June 2022)

(A) Unlimited supply of labour

(B) Marginal productivity of labour in the subsistence sector is equal to, or less than. subsistence wage

(C) Dual economy with a modern sector and a subsistence sector

(D) Agricultural sector subject to increasing returns

(E) Model that explains the crucial role of capitalist surplus in the development process

Choose the more appropriate answer from the options given below:

(a) (A), (B), (C), (E) only (b) (A), (B), (D), (E) only

(c) (B), (C), (D), (E) only (d) (A), (C), (D), (E) only

Answer – (a)

Solution:

Structural transformation models:-

Lewis theory of development :- given by Arthur Lewis in 1954. Also known as "Model of unlimited supply of labour." It states that with the movement of labour from rural to urban sector, the traditional society transforms into Modern society.

Assumptions :-

1. Dual economy that is coexistence of agriculture/ subsistence/ traditional sector and Industrial /manufacturing modern sector.
2. Development in an economy takes place due to transfer of labour from agriculture to industrial sector. As a result of movement of labour from traditional to modern sector, the capital in the latter accumulates and output expands, thus leading this economy towards development.
3. No capital accumulation in the agriculture sector.
4. The number of workers in rural sector are more as compared to that in the industrial sector.
5. There are diminishing returns to labour.

Growth process :- If some workers are withdrawn from the primary sector and prepared to work in the capitalist sector at there prevailing wage rate, the Marginal productivity of these workers should be higher than their paid out wages, so that profits are expected to rise. Capitalist are expected to reinvest their surplus which would stimulate the process of capital formation. It would cease at a point when the workers are prepared to work only at capitalistic wage rate equal to their productivity. Capitalist can stimulate their capital through bank credit.

Analysis:

The Lewis model of development includes the following characteristics:

A. **Unlimited supply of labor:** This is one of the key assumptions of the Lewis model. It posits that there is a large pool of surplus labor available in the traditional subsistence sector that can be absorbed into the modern industrial sector without affecting wages.

B. **Marginal productivity of labor in the subsistence sector is equal to, or less than, the subsistence wage:** The model assumes that the productivity of labor in the subsistence sector is low and that wages in that sector are at or near subsistence levels.

C. **Dual economy with a modern sector and a subsistence sector:** The Lewis model describes an economy with a traditional subsistence sector and a modern industrial sector. The subsistence sector is characterized by low productivity and low wages, while the modern sector experiences higher productivity and wages.

D. **Agricultural sector subject to increasing returns:** This statement is not specifically mentioned in the characteristics of the Lewis model. The model primarily focuses on the transition of surplus labor from the subsistence sector to the modern industrial sector, rather than specifically addressing the agricultural sector.

E. **Model that explains the crucial role of capitalist surplus in the development process:** This statement accurately describes the Lewis model. It highlights the role of the capitalist surplus generated in the modern sector, which is reinvested in industrialization and drives the development process.

Therefore, the correct statements that hold true for the Lewis model of development are:

(A) Unlimited supply of labor

(B) Marginal productivity of labor in the subsistence sector is equal to, or less than, the subsistence wage

(C) Dual economy with a modern sector and a subsistence sector

(E) Model that explains the crucial role of capitalist surplus in the development process.

57. Which of the followings are correct? *(December 2021 and June 2022)*

(A) The market is a system that works with price mechanism

(B) Market failure refers to the divergence of market equilibrium from pareto optamality

(C) Market fails to efficiently supply public goods and the same makes a case for govt intervention

(D) Market efficiently works in the presence of positive externalities

(E) Market efficiently works in the presence of negative externalities

Choose the correct answer from the options given below:

(a) (A), (B), (C) and (D) only

(b) (A), (B) and (C) only

(c) (C), (D) and (E) only

(d) (B) and (E) only

Answer - (b)

Solution:

A. The market is a system that works with price mechanism. This statement is correct as the market system relies on the price mechanism to allocate goods and services based on supply and demand.

B. Market failure refers to the divergence of market equilibrium from Pareto optimality. This statement is correct as market failure occurs when the allocation of resources in a market economy is not efficient and does not achieve the Pareto optimality condition, where no one can be made better off without making someone else worse off.

C. Market fails to efficiently supply public goods, and the same makes a case for government intervention. This statement is correct as public goods, such as national defense or public infrastructure, are not efficiently provided by the market due to their non-excludability and non-rivalrous nature. Government intervention is often required to ensure their provision.

D. Market efficiently works in the presence of positive externalities. This statement is incorrect. In the presence of positive externalities, such as education or research and development, the market may underprovide these goods or services as the private market actors do not capture the full social benefits. Government intervention, such as subsidies or public funding, is often needed to address this market failure.

E. Market efficiently works in the presence of negative externalities. This statement is incorrect. Negative externalities, such as pollution or congestion, lead to overproduction or consumption of goods that generate harmful effects on third parties. In the presence of negative externalities, the market fails to achieve efficiency, and government intervention, such as taxes or regulations, is necessary to internalize these external costs.

In summary, the correct statements are A, B, and C.

58. Tools of expansionary Fiscal policy include *(December 2021 and June 2022)*

(A) Raising Government expenditure

(B) Reducing Government expenditure

(C) Increasing tax rate

(D) Reducing tax rate

(E) Increasing money supply

Choose the correct answer from the options given below

(a) (A), (D) only (b) (B), (C) only

(c) (A), (D), (E) only (d) (B), (C), (E) only

Answer - (a)

Solution:

Fiscal Policy :-It is the revenue and expenditure policy of the government.

Instruments are government expenditure, taxes

During inflation/ Boom :- expenditure ↓ taxes ↑

Surplus Budget :-Government Revenue > Government Expenditure

Borrow more from the public also reduce money supply

During deflation/ depression :- expenditure↑Taxes ↓

Deficit budget Government revenue < Government expenditure

Crowding out effect :-Reduction in private expenditure caused by an increase in government expenditure through deficit budget.

Government expenditure ↑ AD ↑ rate of interest ↑ private investment ↓

Three forms of discretionary fiscal policy :-

1. Change tax, constant government expenditure.
2. Change government expenditure, constant taxes.
3. Variations in both.

59. Match List I with List II: *(December 2021 and June 2022)*

List I	List II
(A) FEMA	**(I) 1969**
(B) MRTP Act	**(II) 2002**
(C) Competition Act	**(III) 1978**
(D) FERA	**(IV) 1999**

Choose the correct answer from the options given below:

(a) (A)-(I), (B)-(II), (C)-(IV), (D)-(III)

(b) (A)-(III), (B)-(I), (C)-(II), (D)-(IV)

(c) (A)-(IV), (B)-(II), (C)-(I), (D)-(III)

(d) (A)-(IV), (B)-(I), (C)-(II), (D)-(III)

Answer - (d)

A. **FEMA (Foreign Exchange Management Act) :** - Enacted in 1999, it governs foreign exchange transactions and external trade in India.

B. **MRTP Act (Monopolies and Restrictive Trade Practices Act) :** - Enacted in 1969 to prevent monopolistic and restrictive trade practices.

C. **Competition Act :** - Enacted in 2002 to promote competition, protect consumer interests, and ensure fair trade practices.

D. **FERA (Foreign Exchange Regulation Act) :** - Enacted in 1973 to regulate foreign exchange transactions, replaced by FEMA in 1999.

60. The binomial distribution can be used under the following conditions

(December 2021 and June 2022)

(A) n the number of trials is finite and independent

(B) n the number of trials is infinite and independent

(C) Each trial results in two mutually exclusive and exhaustive outcomes, terms as success and failure

(D) P. the probability of success is constant for each trial

(E) The probability of failure does not remain same for each trial

Choose the correct answer from the options given below:

(a) (A), (C) and (E) only

(b) (B), (C) and (D) only

(c) (A), (C) and (D) only

(d) (B), (C) and (E) only

Answer - (c)

Solution:

(a) **Binomial distribution :** it is given by James Bernoulli. It is a kind of discrete probability

distribution where we have only two cases.

Either a success or a failure.

$$^{n}C_{r}\, p^{r}\, q^{n-r}$$

n = no. of trials

p = probability of success q = probability of failure r = no. of success

BD is also called a limiting case of normal distribution Mean = n*p

SD =√npq

Variance= npq

Analysis:

(A) n, the number of trials, is finite and independent: This condition means that there is a fixed number of trials conducted, and the outcome of one trial does not affect the outcome of another trial. The binomial distribution is commonly used to model a fixed number of independent Bernoulli trials.

(C) Each trial results in two mutually exclusive and exhaustive outcomes, termed as success and failure: The binomial distribution assumes that each trial has two possible outcomes, which are mutually exclusive (they cannot both occur at the same time) and exhaustive (one of the outcomes must occur). These outcomes are typically labeled as success and failure, but they can represent any two distinct outcomes.

(D) The probability of success, denoted as P, is constant for each trial: In a binomial distribution, the probability of success remains the same for each trial. This means that the probability of obtaining a success or a failure does not change from trial to trial.

Therefore, the correct conditions for using the binomial distribution are:

(A) n, the number of trials, is finite and independent. (C) Each trial results in two mutually exclusive and exhaustive outcomes, termed as success and failure. (D) The probability of success is constant for each trial.

61. What are the practical consequences of multicollinearity in CLRM?

(December 2021 and June 2022)

(A) R2 the overall measure of goodness of fit can be very high

(B) OLS estimators are not BLUE

(C) OLS estimators have small variance and covariances

(D) t ratio of one or more coefficients is statistically insignificant

(E) The OLS estimators and their standard errors can be sensitive to small changes in the data

Choose the correct answer from the options given below:

(a) (A), (B) and (C) only
(b) (A), (B) and (D) only
(c) (A), (D) and (E) only
(d) (B), (C) and (E) only

Answer - C

Solution

The practical consequences of multicollinearity in the Classical Linear Regression Model (CLRM) include:

(A) R2, the overall measure of goodness of fit, can be very high: Multicollinearity can lead to an inflated R-squared value in the regression model. This is because highly correlated independent variables can collectively explain a large proportion of the variation in the dependent variable, leading to a high R-squared. However, it is important to note that multicollinearity itself does not directly cause a high R-squared; it is the correlation between independent variables that can result in this consequence.

(D) The t ratio of one or more coefficients is statistically insignificant: Multicollinearity can increase the standard errors of the coefficient estimates, making it difficult to establish statistical significance for individual coefficients. As a result, the t-ratios associated with these coefficients may become statistically insignificant.

(E) The OLS estimators and their standard errors can be sensitive to small changes in the data: Multicollinearity can cause instability in the coefficient estimates and their standard errors. This means that even small changes in the data can lead to large changes in the estimated coefficients and their standard errors, making the regression results sensitive to minor variations in the data.

Option (B) is not included because multicollinearity does not directly impact whether OLS estimators are Best Linear Unbiased Estimators (BLUE). Multicollinearity affects the precision of the coefficient estimates, but OLS estimators can still be unbiased even in the presence of multicollinearity.

Therefore, the correct answer is C. (A), (D), and (E) only.

62. Which of the following is correct? *(December 2021 and June 2022)*

(A) The gross barter terms of trade uses quantity index for imports and exports

(B) Both gross barter terms of trade and net barter terms of trade make use of the price index for imports and exports

(C) The net barter terms of trade uses price index for imports and export

(D) Both gross barter terms of trade and net barter terms of trade make use of the quantity index for imports and exports

(E) The gross barter terms of trade uses price index but the net barter terms of trade uses quantity index for imports and exports

Choose the correct answer from the options given below:

(a) (A) and (B) only

(b) (B) and (C) only

(c) (C) and (E) only

(d) (A) and (C) only

Answer - (d)

Solution:

Terms of Trade

$$= \frac{\text{Index of exports prices}}{\text{Index of imports prices}} \times 100$$

<u>Net Barter TOT</u> :- The concept was given by Taussing.

$$T_C = \frac{P_{x1}/P_{xo}}{P_{m1}/P_{mo}}$$

Price of export/Price of import.

More the ratio, more favourable are the TOT.

<u>Gross Barter TOT</u> :- Taussing

$$T_g \rightarrow \frac{Q_{m1}}{Q_{mo}} / \frac{Q_{x1}}{Q_{xo}} \qquad \left[\frac{\text{Quantity Imported}}{\text{Quantity Exported}}\right]$$

63. The irrelevance of money for real variables in the classical system is called

(December 2021 and June 2022)

(a) Fiscal neutrality
(b) Monetary neutrality
(c) Exchange rate neutrality
(d) Technological neutrality

Answer - (b)

Solution: Monetary neutrality, in the classical system, refers to the idea that changes in the money supply have no long-term impact on real variables like output and employment. It suggests that real economic outcomes are determined by factors other than monetary factors.

64. The total revenue (R) and total cost (C) function of a firm are given by $R = 30Q - Q^2$, $C = 20 + 4Q$. Where Q is output. find the equilibrium output of the firm

(December 2021 and June 2022)

(a) 4
(b) 13
(c) 15
(d) 10

Answer - (b)

Solution: To find the equilibrium output of the firm, we need to determine the quantity where total revenue (R) is equal to total cost (C). In other words, we need to find the value of Q where R = C.

Given: $TR = 30Q - Q^2$ $TC = 20 + 4Q$

Equilibrium is MR = MC

$MR = d(TR)/dQ$

$= 30 - 2Q$

$MC = d(TC)/dQ$

$=4$

$30-2Q = 4$

$-2Q = -26$

$Q=26/2$

$Q=13$

65. Which of the followings are assumptions of ordinal utility analysis?

(December 2021 and June 2022)

(A) Consumers are consistent in their preferences

(B) Consumer can measure the total utility received from any given basket of goods

(C) Consumer preferences follow transitivity

(D) Consumers are non-satiated with respect to goods they confront

(E) Consumers are irrational

Choose the correct answer from the options given below:

(a) (B), (C), (D) only
(b) (C), (D), (E) only
(c) (A), (C), (D) only
(d) (A), (B), (C) only

Answer - (c)

Solution:

Consistency :- It means if anyone time he will prefer A from B, then at any other time, when both are available then he will again prefer A from B.

Transitivity :- If he prefers A from B and B from C, then he will also prefer A from C.

The concept of non-satiation implies that consumers do not reach the saturation level in the consumption of any good and always want to consume more of a good and not less. This concept of non-satiation is a major assumption of ordinal utility.

66. Which of the following are correct with respect to IS-LM model?

(December 2021 and June 2022)

(A) The LM schedule slopes upward to the right.

(B) The LM schedule will shift to the left with an increase in quantity of money

(C) The LM schedule gives equilibrium in the money market

(D) The IS schedule will shift to the left when these is an increase in government expenditure

(E) The IS schedule will shift to the right when taxes are reduced

Choose the most appropriate answer from the options given below:

(a) (A), (C), (E) only
(b) (A), (B), (C), (D) only
(c) (A), (C) only
(d) (B), (D), (C), (E) only

Answer - (a)

Solution:

(A) The LM schedule slopes upward to the right: Correct. The LM curve represents the equilibrium in the money market, showing that as income increases, the demand for money also increases, leading to higher interest rates.

(B) The LM schedule will shift to the left with an increase in the quantity of money: Incorrect. An increase in the quantity of money would shift the LM curve to the right.

(C) The LM schedule gives equilibrium in the money market: Correct. The LM curve shows combinations of interest rates and income levels where the money market is in equilibrium.

(D) The IS schedule will shift to the left when there is an increase in government expenditure: Incorrect. An increase in government expenditure would shift the IS curve to the right.

(E) The IS schedule will shift to the right when taxes are reduced: Correct. A reduction in taxes increases disposable income, leading to higher consumption and shifting the IS curve to the right.

Therefore, the correct statements are:

(A) The LM schedule slopes upward to the right.

(C) The LM schedule gives equilibrium in the money market.

(E) The IS schedule will shift to the right when taxes are reduced.

IS - LM Model :- Given by Hicks and Hansen

Product Market :- IS curve shows equilibrium in the product market.

↓in rate of interest→ ↑in investment→ ↑in AD→ ↑in income.

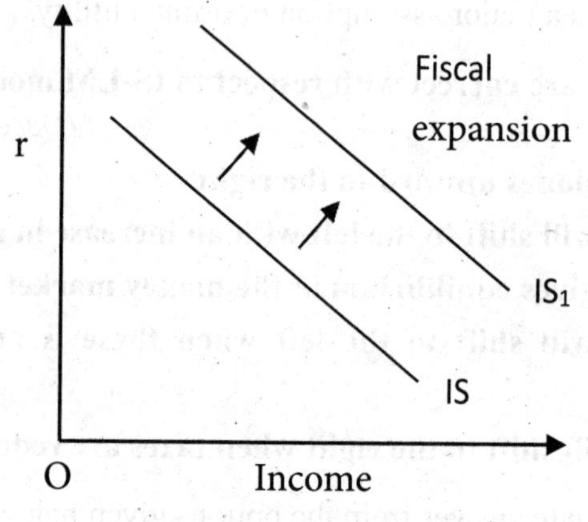

Slope of IS curve depends on

1) **Interest elasticity of investment Demand** Higher the elasticity of demand, flatter will be the IS curve and vice versa.

2) **Size of the Multiplier** More the size of the multiplier, flatter will be theIS curve and vice versa.

Money market :- Money market equilibrium is represented by LM curve

↑increase in income→MD ↑ →r↑

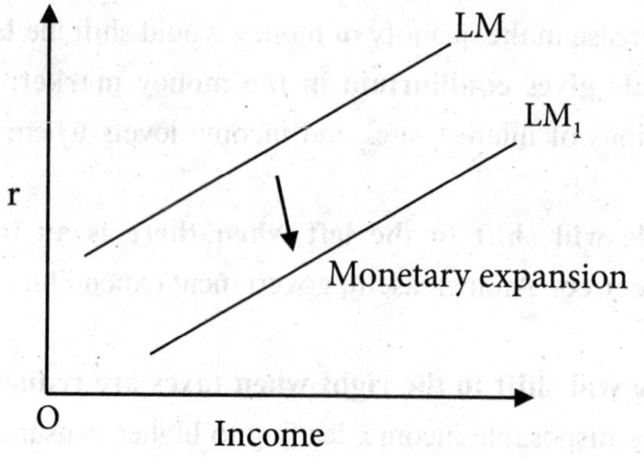

Slope of LM curve depends on

Income elasticity of demand for money :- More the income elasticity of demand for money, steeper will be the LM curve and vice versa.

Interest elasticity of demand for money :- →Lesser the interest elasticity of demand for money, steeper the LM curve and vice versa

67. Arrange the following events in sequence (the oldest one being first)

(December 2021 and June 2022)

(A) The Tokyo Round
(B) The Uruguay Round
(C) The Annecy Round
(D) The Dillon Round
(E) The Torquay Round

Choose the correct answer from the options given below:

(a) (C), (E), (D), (B), (A)
(b) (E), (C), (A), (D), (B)
(c) (C), (E), (D), (A), (B)
(d) (E), (C), (D), (A), (B)

Answer - (c)

Solution: GATT[General Agreement on Tariffs and Trade]

Formed in 1947

Headquarters in Geneva (Switzerland).

Principles of GATT:- Non Discrimination

Objective -promotes free trade.

Uruguay round replaced GATT with WTO.

WTO- World Trade Organisation-(1995)-

Geneva Round 1947

Annecy round 1949

Torquay round 1951

Geneva round 1955-56

Dillon round 1960-62

Kennedy round 1962-67

Tokyo round 1973-79

Uruguay round 1986-94

Doha round 2001

Bali 2013

68. Which of the followings are correct? *(December 2021 and June 2022)*

(A) M1 =C+DD+OD

(B) M2 = M1 + saving deposits with post office saving banks

(C) M3 = M2 + net time deposits of banks

(D) M3 = M1 + net time deposits of banks

(E) M4 = M1 + total deposits with the post office savings

Choose the correct answer from the options given below:

(a) (A), (B) and (C) only
(b) (A), (B) and (D) only
(c) (A), (C) and (D) only
(d) (B), (D) and (E) only

Answer - (b)

Solution : Money supply [Amount of money in circulation] Measures of money supply: -

M1 = C + DD + other deposits [Narrow def.]

M2 = M1 + Demand Deposits with the post office

M3 = M1 + Time deposits [Broader def.]

M4 = M3 + All deposits with post office [Excluding NSC]

69. What will be the aggregate Domestic Income NDP (FC) of the economy for 2022-23; if GDP (Market Price) = 27,654 crores

Depreciation =2847 crores

Indirect taxes less subsides = 2160 crores

(December 2021 and June 2022)

(a) 24,807
(b) 22,647
(c) 26,967
(d) 28,467

Answer – (b)

Solution: NDP FC =?

GDP (MP) – Depreciation - NIT = 27654 – 2847 – 2160

NDP(FC) = 22647

National income:-

Monetary value of all final goods and services produced by the residents of a country. It is a flow concept.

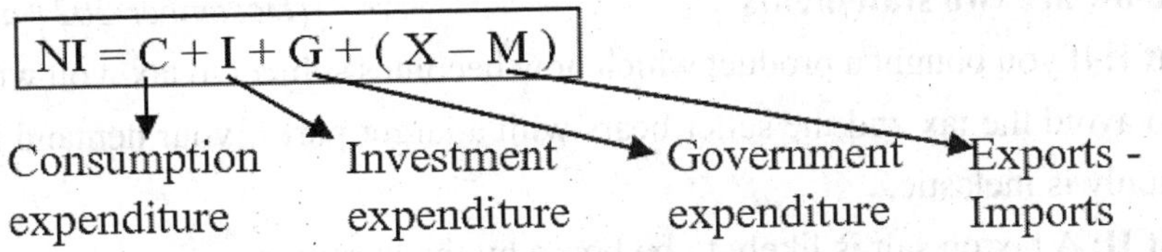

Depreciation is deducted from the gross value to get net value. Net factor income from abroad (NFIA) is added to the domestic product to get national income.

GDP → monetary value of all final goods and services produced in a country in a period of one year

NDP → GDP - Depreciation GNP → GDP +NFIA

NNP → GNP - Depreciation

NNP_{FC} → (National Income) [Value of G & S is taken at production point]

$NNP_{MP} = NNP_{FC}$ + Indirect taxes - Subsidies

70. Match List I with List II *(December 2021 and June 2022)*

List I	List II
(A) Pure Public good	**(I) Non rival but excludable**
(B) Pure Private good.	**(II) Non-excludable but rivalry**
(C) Open access resources	**(III) Non-rival and non-excludable**
(D) Congestible resource	**(IV) Excludable and rival**

Choose the correct answer from the options given below:

(a) (A)-(III), (B)-(IV), (C)-(I), (D)-(II)

(b) (A)-(III), (B)-(IV), (C)-(II), (D)-(I)

(c) (A)-(I), (B)-(II), (C)-(III), (D)-(IV)

(d) (A)-(III), (B)-(II), (C)-(I), (D)-(IV)

Answer - (b)

Solution: The matching between List I and List II is as follows:

(A) Pure Public good (III) Non-rival and non-excludable (Defence)

(B) Pure Private good (IV) Excludable and rival (Washing Machine)

(C) Open access resources (II) Non-excludable but rivalry (Fishing in Lake)

(D) Congestible resource (I) Non-rival but excludable (Congestion on road)

71. Given below are two statements *(December 2021 and June 2022)*

Statement I: If you bought a product which now becomes subject to tax, you will be in a better position to avoid the tax and the seller bears with a larger part if your demand is elastic while seller's supply is inelastic.

Statement II: A tax on salt is likely to be borne by the consumer.

In the light of the above statements, choose the most appropriate answer from the options given below:

(a) Both Statement I and Statement II are correct

(b) Both Statement I and Statement II are incorrect

(c) Statement I is correct but Statement II is incorrect

(d) Statement I is incorrect but Statement II is correct

Answer – (a)

Solution: If you bought a product which now becomes subject to tax, you will be in a better position to avoid the tax, and the seller bears a larger part if your demand is elastic while the seller's supply is inelastic. This statement is correct. When the demand for a product is elastic (responsive to price changes), and the supply by the seller is inelastic (not responsive to price changes), the burden of a tax on the product is more likely to be shifted onto the seller. In this case, consumers have the ability to avoid the tax by reducing their demand for the product, while the seller may not be able to adjust their supply easily, leading to a larger portion of the tax burden falling on the seller.

A tax on salt is likely to be borne by the consumer : Salt is considered a necessity, which means that even with a tax imposed on it, consumers are likely to continue purchasing it. As a result, the burden of the tax is more likely to be passed on to the consumer through higher prices, as the demand for salt is relatively inelastic. Therefore, a tax on salt is expected to be borne by the consumer.

Hence, both the statements are correct.

72. In Harrod Domar Model, if the growth rate of income is 8% and the capital output ratio is 4% then the saving rate must be *(December 2021 and June 2022)*

(a) 32%

(b) 2%

(c) 36%

(d) 1/2%

Answer - (a)

Growth Rate = Saving/Capital Output Ratio

8 = Saving/4

32% must be the saving rate.

73. Which of the followings conditions prevail in the long run equilibrium of industry for achieving optimal resource allocation *(December 2021 and June 2022)*

(A) The output is produced at the minimum feasible cost

(B) consumer pays the minimum possible price which just covers the marginal cost of the product

(C) Plants are used at full capacity in long run

(D) Firms earn supernormal profits

(E) Perfect competitive firms and price mechanism operates

Choose the correct answer from the options given below:

(a) (A), (B), (C) and (E) only
(b) (C), (D) and (E) only
(c) (B), (D) and (E) only
(d) (A), (B) and (E) only

Answer - (a)

Solution: In the long run equilibrium of an industry for achieving optimal resource allocation, the following conditions prevail:

(A) The output is produced at the minimum feasible cost: This condition ensures that resources are allocated efficiently, and production is carried out with the lowest possible cost.

(B) Consumer pays the minimum possible price which just covers the marginal cost of the product: This condition ensures that consumers pay a price that reflects the actual cost of producing the product, promoting efficiency and preventing monopolistic pricing.

(C) Plants are used at full capacity in the long run: This condition means that firms are operating at their optimal level of output, utilizing all available resources efficiently.

(E) Perfect competitive firms and price mechanism operate: Perfect competition implies that there are many small firms in the market, none of which can individually influence the market price. The price mechanism operates to balance supply and demand, ensuring efficiency.

Therefore, the correct answer should be A. (A), (B), (C), and (E) only.

74. Real and nominal income is calculated respectively at *(December 2021 and June 2022)*

(a) Current and constant prices
(b) Constant and current prices
(c) Constant and constant prices
(d) Current and current prices

Answer - (b)

Solution: Nominal income is calculated at current prices, while real income is calculated at constant prices. Constant prices are the prices that existed in a base year. By comparing nominal income to real income, we can see how much purchasing power has changed over time.

75. If the demand function is: P = 35 - 2x - x^2 and the demand x0 is 3. What will be the consumer's surplus? *(December 2021 and June 2022)*

(a) 27
(b) 25
(c) 60
(d) 20

Answer - (a)

Solution: Can be solved in a similar manner

Consumer surplus

3. *Demand function*( ) p=20-2x. find CS at p=4

4=20-2x

4-20=-2x

X=8

$$CS = \int_0^x f(x)dx - px = \int_0^x (20-2x)dx - 4 \times 8 = \left[20x - \frac{2x^2}{2}\right] - 32$$

$$= \left[20 \times 8 - \frac{2(8)^2}{2}\right] - \left[20(0) - 2\left(\frac{(0)^2}{2}\right]\right)\text{-}32$$

= 160-64-32 =64

=64

76. What does the result of the first empirical test of the Heckscher Ohlin model by Wassily Leontief find? *(December 2021 and June 2022)*

(a) U.S. exports were less capital-intensive than U.S. imports

(b) U.S. exports were more capital intensive than U.S. imports

(c) U.S. exports were more human capital-intensive than U.S. imports

(d) All the above

Answer - (a)

Solution: The first empirical test of the Heckscher-Ohlin model was conducted by Wassily Leontief, and it is known as the Leontief Paradox. The test aimed to analyze the factor proportions theory, which suggests that countries will export goods that use their abundant factors of production and import goods that use their scarce factors of production.

Leontief analyzed the U.S. input-output tables and examined the relationship between the capital and labor used in U.S. exports and imports. Contrary to the predictions of the Heckscher-Ohlin model, Leontief found that U.S. exports were less capital-intensive than U.S. imports. This result was unexpected since the United States was considered a capital-abundant country at that time.

77. Hari's score in the statistics in the first year is 76, whereas the class average is 68 with standard deviation of 5. What is Hari's Z-score? *(December 2021 and June 2022)*

(a) 1.5 (b) 1.6

(c) 1.2 (d) 1.4

Answer - (b)

Solution: To calculate Hari's Z-score, we can use the formula:

$Z = (X - \mu) / \sigma$

Where:

X is Hari's score

μ is the mean (class average)

σ is the standard deviation

Given:

Hari's score (X) = 76

Class average (μ) = 68

Standard deviation (σ) = 5

Plugging in the values into the formula, we have:

$Z = (76 - 68) / 5$

$Z = 8 / 5$

$Z = 1.6$

Therefore, Hari's Z-score is 1.6.

78. The hypothesis of cumulative causation as an explanation of the backwardness of developing nations is associated with *(December 2021 and June 2022)*

(a) Ragnar Nurkse (b) Gunnar Myrdal

(c) Arthus Lewis (d) Fes and Ranis

Answer - (b)

Solution: The theory of cumulative causation, proposed by economist Gunnar Myrdal, suggests that developing nations experience a cycle of poverty and underdevelopment that reinforces itself. Initial disadvantages result in low investment and productivity, perpetuating the cycle. To break this cycle, specific policies and investments are needed to foster inclusive growth.

79. Two factors of production, say A and B have the same price. The least cost combination of A and B for producing given level of output will be achieved at a point where the Iso-

quant has slope equal to *(December 2021 and June 2022)*

(a) 0 (b) 1

(c) -1 (d) 2

Answer – (c)

Solution: The answer is **C. -1.**

The slope of an isoquant represents the marginal rate of technical substitution (MRTS) between two inputs. The MRTS is the amount of one input that can be substituted for another input without changing the output level.

When the price of two inputs is the same, the firm will minimize its costs by using the inputs in the same proportion. This means that the MRTS will be equal to 1.

The slope of an isoquant is negative because the inputs are substitutes. As the firm uses more of one input, it will need to use less of the other input in order to keep the output level constant.

Therefore, the least cost combination of A and B for producing a given level of output will be achieved at a point where the isoquant has a slope of -1.

80. Match List I with List II *(December 2021 and June 2022)*

List I	List II
(A) Testing of overall significance	**(I) Chi-square test**
(B) Testing the independence of attributes	**(II) Jarque Bera test**
(C) Testing the significance of regression coefficients	**(III) F-test**
(D) Normality test	**(IV) t-test**

Choose the correct answer from the options given below:

(a) (A)-(I), (B)-(II), (C)-(III), (D)-(IV) (b) (A)-(III), (B)-(I), (C)-(IV), (D)-(II)

(c) (A)-(I), (B)-(IV), (C)-(III), (D)-(II) (d) (A)-(I), (B)-(III), (C)-(IV), (D)-(II)

Answer - (b)

Solution:

(A) Testing of overall significance - (III) F-test: Determines if a regression model is statistically significant as a whole.

(B) Testing the independence of attributes - (I) Chi-square test: Tests if two categorical variables are independent or related.

(C) Testing the significance of regression coefficients - (IV) t-test: Assesses if individual regression coefficients are significantly different from zero.

(D) Normality test - (II) Jarque Bera test: Tests the normality of a distribution based on skewness and kurtosis.

81. One of the various qualitative instruments used by the central bank during inflation is *(December 2021 and June 2022)*

a. Raise margin requirement

b. Remove margin requirement

c. Reduce margin requirement

d. Fix margin requirement

Answer - (a)

Solution: Margin requirement is a qualitative instrument used by the central bank to control the amount of credit that banks can extend to their customers. When the central bank raises the margin requirement, it forces banks to hold more collateral against loans. This makes it more expensive for banks to lend money, which in turn reduces the amount of money in circulation. This can help to slow down inflation.

82. In the Mundell-Fleming model. under floating exchange rate, which policy is more effective to influence aggregate income? *(December 2021 and June 2022)*

(a) Fiscal policy

(b) Monetary policy

(c) Exchange rate policy

(d) None of the above

Answer – (b)

Solution: Mundell Fleming model -IS-LM-BP model

→In case of fixed exchange rate, expansionary fiscal policy more effective.

→In case of fixed exchange rate, monetary policy is not effective.

→In case of flexible exchange rate, fiscal policy ineffective.

→In case of flexible exchange rate, monetary policy is effective.

83. In the context of the transaction demand for money, the square root rule was developed by *(December 2021 and June 2022)*

(a) Kydland Prescott

(b) Friedman Sewartz

(c) Boumol Tobin

(d) J. M. Keynes

Answer - (c)

Solution: The square root rule, developed by William J. Baumol and James Tobin, states that the optimal amount of money for transactions is proportional to the square root of income. The rule suggests an inverse relationship between money demand and interest rates, as higher rates reduce the opportunity cost of holding money.

Square root formula

$$M_D = \sqrt{\frac{2by}{r}}$$

84. A bag contains 20 tickets marked with numbers 1 to 20. One ticket is drawn at random. Find the probability that will be multiple of 2 or 3. *(December 2021 and June 2022)*

(a) 0.7 (b) 0.9

(c) 0.6 (d) 0.3

Answer - (c)

Solution: The probability that a ticket drawn at random from a bag containing 20 tickets will be a multiple of 2 or 3 is 65%.

There are 10 multiples of 2 in the bag (2, 4, 6, 8, 10, 12, 14, 16, 18, 20) and 6 multiples of 3 (3, 6, 9, 12, 15, 18). However, there are 3 numbers that are multiples of both 2 and 3 (6, 12, 18), so we need to subtract these once to avoid double counting.

This means that there are 10 + 6 - 3 = 13 numbers in the bag that are multiples of 2 or 3. The probability of drawing one of these numbers is 13/20 = 0.65 = 65%.

85. If time deposit is not included, then the money multiplier will be (Cr currency deposit ratio. rr= reserve deposit ratio) *(December 2021 and June 2022)*

(a) (Cr+rr)/(1+Cr) (b) (Cr+rr)/(rr+1)

(c) Cr/rr (d) (Cr+1)/(rr+Cr)

Answer - (d)

Solution: You are correct, the answer is D. (Cr+1)/(rr+Cr).

The money multiplier formula is:

Money Multiplier = (1 + Currency Deposit Ratio)/(Reserve Requirement Ratio + Currency Deposit Ratio)

In this case, the currency deposit ratio is Cr and the reserve requirement ratio is rr. Therefore, the money multiplier is:

Money Multiplier = (1 + Cr)/(rr + Cr)Z

86. Which of the following strategy is not correct in order to have expansionary impact of fiscal policy? *(December 2021 and June 2022)*

(a) Public expenditure must be financed by borrowing

(b) Public expenditure must be financed through increased taxes only

(c) Compensatory spending for public investment

(d) Cut in taxes

Answer - (b)

Solution: Expansionary fiscal policy is a macroeconomic policy that involves increasing government spending or decreasing taxes to stimulate the economy. This can be done through a variety of methods, including borrowing, printing money, or a combination of both.

However, increasing taxes is not an expansionary fiscal policy. In fact, it can have the opposite effect by decreasing aggregate demand. This is because when taxes are increased, people have less money to spend, which reduces the amount of goods and services that are demanded. As a result, businesses produce less, and employment falls.

87. Provide proper chronological order of different schemes launched in India

(December 2021 and June 2022)

(A) Pradhan Mantri Jan Aushadhi Yojana

(B) Pradhan Mantri Ujjwala Yojana

(C) Atal Pension Yojana

(D) PM Jan Dhan Yojana

(E) Ayushman Bharat Yojana

Choose the correct answer from the options given below:

(a) (C), (B), (A), (D), (E) (b) (C), (D), (B), (A), (E)

(c) (D), (A), (B), (C), (E) (d) (D), (C), (A), (B), (E)

Answer - (d)

Solution:

(D) PM Jan Dhan Yojana (2014): This scheme was launched by Prime Minister Narendra Modi on August 28, 2014. It aims to provide financial services to the poor, including bank accounts, insurance, and credit.

(C) Atal Pension Yojana (2015): This scheme was launched by Prime Minister Narendra Modi on May 9, 2015. It is a voluntary, defined contribution pension scheme for the unorganized sector.

(A) Pradhan Mantri Jan Aushadhi Yojana (2015): This scheme was launched by Prime Minister Narendra Modi on June 1, 2015. It aims to provide affordable generic medicines to the poor.

(B) Pradhan Mantri Ujjwala Yojana (2016): This scheme was launched by Prime Minister Narendra Modi on May 1, 2016. It aims to provide free LPG connections to poor families.

(E) Ayushman Bharat Yojana (2018): This scheme was launched by Prime Minister Narendra Modi on September 25, 2018. It is a health insurance scheme for poor families.

88. Which of the following is correct? *(December 2021 and June 2022)*

(A) Current account includes merchandise export

(B) Current accounts do not include merchandise export

(C) Current account includes invisible export

(D) Current accounts do not include invisible export

(E) Current account includes both merchandise exports and imports and invisible exports and imports

Choose the correct answer from the options given below:

(a) (A), (B) and (C) only (b) (A), (C) and (E) only

(c) (A), (D) and (E) only (d) (C), (D) and (E) only

Answer - (b)

Solution:

Balance of payments:-It is a systematic record of all economic transactions of a country with outside world in a given year.

Trade in goods - Balance of visible trade

Trade in services - Balance of invisible trade

Credit (Receipts)	Debits (Payment)
1) Current account Export - goods and services →Unilateral Receipts →Interest, profits, Dividend received	1) current account Imports - Goods and services →Unilateral payments →Interest, profits, dividend paid.
2) Capital Account →Borrowing from foreign countries → investments by foreigncountries	2) Capital Account →Lending to foreign countries →Investments in foreign countries

89. The provision for social goods or the process by which total resource use is divided between private and social goods and by which the mix of social goods is chosen is known as:

(December 2021 and June 2022)

(a) Allocation function (b) Distribution function

(c) Stabilization function (d) Normalization function

Answer - (a)

Solution : The allocation function is the process by which a government decides how to allocate its resources between private and social goods. The government must decide how much to spend on things like national defense, education, and healthcare, and how much to leave to the private sector.

The distribution function is the process by which a government decides how to distribute its resources among its citizens. The government must decide how much to tax its citizens, and how to spend the tax revenue.

The stabilization function is the process by which a government tries to stabilize the economy. This includes things like trying to keep inflation under control and trying to prevent the economy from going into a recession.

The normalization function is not a term that is used in economics.

90. Here is given sex ratio for different states of India for 2011.

(December 2021 and June 2022)

(A) Gujarat: 942

(B) Madhya Pradesh: 931

(C) Odisha: 979

(D) Tamil Nadu: 996

(E) Haryana: 862

Choose the correct answer from the options given below:

(a) (B), (C) and (D) only
(b) (A) and (B) only
(c) (C) and (D) only
(d) (C), (D) and (E) only

Answer – (a)

91. The strategy of choosing the policy which has the best possible outcome is known as

(December 2021 and June 2022)

(a) Dominant strategy
(b) Maxi max
(c) Mini max
(d) Maxi min

Answer - (2)

Solution: The strategy of choosing the policy with the best possible outcome is referred to as the "maxi max" strategy. This approach involves maximizing the maximum possible payoff or benefit among all available alternatives. It aims to identify the option that provides the highest potential gain or advantage, regardless of the associated risks or potential losses. The maxi max strategy focuses on maximizing the potential upside, even if it means accepting higher risks or potential downsides.

Game Theory:-Game is a strategic situation given by Neumann - Morgan Stein in 1944

Pay off :- Utility that a player gets given a certain outcome of the game.

Pay off Matrix :- shows players, their actions and their pay offs in a game.

Pure strategy :-The player will surely follow a particular action.

Mixed strategy :-The player will indifferent between several pure strategies and he will select the strategy according to the probability distribution.

Dominant Strategy	Nash equilibrium
Firm A will adopt best strategy regardless of firm B will do.	Firm A will adopt best strategy, given other's strategy.

Optimal strategy :- is the course of plan which puts the player into the most favourable situation, irrespective of the other strategies.

Zero Sum Game :-when the gain of one competitor is the loss of the other, then it is a zero-sum game.

Minimax: - Minimum loss out of maximum losses.

Maximin: - Maximum out of Minimum profits.

Fair Game :-It is the point where minmax and maximin are equal to zero.

92. In which stage of the product cycle model, the imitating country starts producing the product for domestic consumption? *(December 2021 and June 2022)*

(a) Stage III (b) Stage II

(c) Stage I (d) Stage V

Answer - (a)

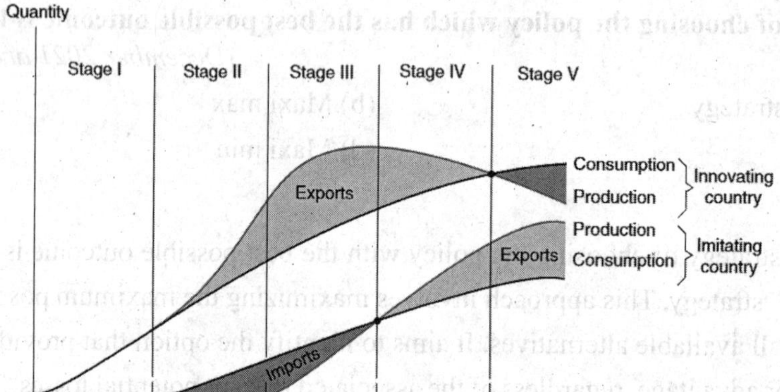

In stage I (time OA), the product is produced and consumed only in the innovating country. In stage II (AB), production is perfected in the innovating country and increases rapidly to accommodate rising demand at home and abroad. In stage III (BC), the product becomes standardized and the imitating country starts producing the product for domestic consumption. In stage IV (CD), the imitating country starts underselling the innovating country in third markets, and in stage V (past point D) in the latter's market as well.

93. Pradhan Mantri Jan Dhan Yojana (PMJDY) has been a flagship programme of the Government of India. *(December 2021 and June 2022)*

(A) Beneficiaries of this scheme are eligible for accident insurance cover of Rs. 1 lakh now

(B) PMJDY is helpful in inclusive development

(C) PMJDY beneficiaries should not be given other benefits like benefits under MUDRA scheme

(D) It is leading to women empowerment

(E) More than 45 crore people have benefitted so far under PMJDY

Choose the most appropriate answer from the options given below:

(a) (A), (B) and (C) only
(b) (B), (C) and (D) only
(c) (B), (D) and (E) only
(d) (A), (D) and (E) only

Answer - (c)

Solution: Pradhan Mantri Jan Dhan Yojana (PMJDY) is a financial inclusion program of the Government of India open to Indian citizens, that aims to expand affordable access to financial services such as bank accounts, remittances, credit, insurance and pensions. The scheme was launched on 28th August 2014 by Prime Minister Narendra Modi.

The scheme has been very successful in achieving its objectives. As of March 2023, more than 45 crore people have opened bank accounts under PMJDY. The scheme has also helped to increase financial literacy and awareness among the poor and marginalized sections of society.

The following are the statements that are most appropriate for the question:

(B) PMJDY is helpful in inclusive development. This is because the scheme provides access to financial services to people who previously did not have access to them. This helps to reduce poverty and inequality.

(D) It is leading to women empowerment. This is because more women than men have opened bank accounts under PMJDY. This gives women more control over their finances and helps to improve their economic status.

(E) More than 45 crore people have benefitted so far under PMJDY. This shows that the scheme has been very successful in reaching its target population.

94. Given below are two statements: *(December 2021 and June 2022)*

Statement I: Devaluation always correct a chronic balance of payments deficit.

Statement II: An expected devaluation leads speculative, capital outflows from domestic country.

In the light of the above statements. choose the correct answer from the options given below:

(a) Both Statement I and Statement II are true

(b) Both Statement I and Statement II are false

(c) Statement I is true but Statement II is false

(d) Statement I is false but Statement II is true

Answer - (d)

Solution: Statement I is false. Devaluation can help to correct a chronic balance of payments deficit, but it is not always effective. In some cases, devaluation can actually make the deficit worse. This is because devaluation can lead to inflation, which can make exports more expensive and imports cheaper. This can lead to a decrease in exports and an increase in imports, which can worsen the balance of payments deficit.

Statement II is true. When there is an expected devaluation, investors may start to sell their assets in the domestic country and move their money to other countries where the currency is not expected to devalue. This can lead to capital outflows, which can further worsen the balance of payments deficit.

95. Find the rank of

$$A = \begin{vmatrix} 6 & 3 & 5 \\ -10 & 2 & 8 \\ 5 & 2 & 3 \end{vmatrix}$$

(December 2021 and June 2022)

(a) 3
(b) 2
(c) 1
(d) 0

Answer - (b)

Solution:

Rank of matrix is order of largest square sub matrix whose determinant is non-zero.

Determinant of 3x3 matrix is 0.

So we take 2x2 matrix $= \begin{vmatrix} 6 & 3 \\ -10 & 2 \end{vmatrix}$

Its determinant will be non zero

$|A| = 12 + 30 = 42$

So the rank is 2

96. Which of the followings is not a marginal condition of pareto optimality criteria?

(December 2021 and June 2022)

A. $MRS^{A}_{x,y} = MRS^{B}_{x,y} = \frac{P_x}{P_y}$

B. $MRTS^{x}_{L,K} = MRTS^{y}_{L,K} = \frac{w}{r}$

C. $MRS^{A}_{x,y} = MRS^{B}_{x,y} = MRPT_{x,y}$

D. $MRPT^{K}_{x,y} = MRPT^{L}_{x,y} = \frac{w}{r}$

Answer - (d)

Solution: (A) MRSAx,y, MRSBx,y = Px / Py: This condition states that the marginal rate of substitution between goods x and y for consumer A must equal the marginal rate of substitution between goods x and y for consumer B. This is necessary for Pareto optimality, as it ensures that no one consumer can be made better off without making another consumer worse off.

(B) MRTSxL,K = MRTSyL,K = w / r: This condition states that the marginal rate of technical substitution between labor and capital in the production of good x must equal the marginal rate of technical substitution between labor and capital in the production of good y. This is necessary for Pareto optimality, as it ensures that no one input can be used more efficiently in the production of one good without making it less efficient in the production of another good.

(C) MRSAx,y=MRSBx,y=MRPTx,y: This condition states that the marginal rate of substitution between goods x and y for consumer A must equal the marginal rate of transformation between goods x and y. This is necessary for Pareto optimality, as it ensures that no one consumer can be made better off by consuming more of good x without making someone else worse off by consuming less of good y. The condition in (D) is not a marginal condition of Pareto optimality criteria, as it does not take into account the preferences of consumers. It only considers the costs of production.

97. Integrate: x^2 / x+2 *(December 2021 and June 2022)*

(a) $4x / (x + 2)^2 + c$

(b) $x^2 / 2 + 2x + 4\log (x + 2) + c$

(c) $x^2 / 2 - 2x + 4\log (x + 2) + c$

(d) $x^2 / 2 - 2x + c$

Answer – (c)

Solution:

X+2) X² (X-2
X² +2X
\- \-
-2X
-2X - 4
\+ \+
4

$$=\int\left((x-2)\frac{4}{x+2}\right)dx$$

$$=\int\left(\frac{(x-2)(x+2)+4}{x+2}\right)dx$$

$$=\int\left(x-2+\frac{4}{x+2}\right)dx$$

$$=\frac{x^2}{2}-2x+4\log(x+2)+c$$

98. When an increase in government purchases raises incomes shifts money demand to the right raises the interest rate, and lowers investment we have seen a demonstration of?

(a) supply-side economics
(b) None of these answers
(c) The crowding-out effect
(d) The multiplier effects

Answer : (c)

Solution: Crowding out effect :-Reduction in private expenditure caused by an increase in government expenditure through deficit budget.

Government expenditure ↑ AD ↑ rate of interest ↑ private investment ↓

99. An increase in the marginal propensity to consumer (MPC)?

(a) raises the value of the multiplier
(b) has no impact on the value of the multiplier?
(c) rarely occurs because the MPC is set by congressional legislation
(d) Lowers the value of the multiplier

Answer: (a)

Solution: Multiplier = 1/1-MPC or 1/MPS

The marginal propensity to consume (MPC) is the fraction of an increase in income that is spent on consumption. A higher MPC means that people will spend more of their income on consumption, which will lead to a larger increase in aggregate demand. The multiplier effect is the idea that a small increase in spending can lead to a larger increase in output and income. The size of the multiplier is determined by the MPC. A higher MPC will lead to a larger multiplier.

100. Which of the following best describes how an increase in the money supply shift the aggregate demand curve?

(a) The money supply shifts right prices fall A spending increases and the aggregate demand curve shifts right
(b) The money supply shifts right the interest rate rises investment decreases and the aggregate demand curve shifts left
(c) The money supply shifts right the interest rate falls, investment increases, and the aggregate demand curve shifts right
(d) The money supply shifts right, prices rise, the demand curve shifts left

Answer: c

Solution: An increase in the money supply will shift the aggregate demand curve to the right. This is because an increase in the money supply will lead to a decrease in the interest rate. A lower interest rate will make it cheaper for businesses to borrow money, which will lead to an increase in investment. An increase in investment will lead to an increase in aggregate demand.

101. The initial effect of an increase in the money supply is to?

(a) increase the interest rate
(b) increase the price level
(c) decrease the price level
(d) decrease the interest rate

Answer: b

Solution: There is more money accessible in the economy when the money supply rises. As aggregate demand rises as a result of the increased money supply, the level of prices in the economy as a whole may also rise.

The purchasing power of people and businesses increases when more money is in circulation. As a result, they have the ability to bid up the cost of goods and services, which raises the overall price level. The quantity theory of money, which suggests that changes in the money supply have a direct impact on the level of prices in the economy, explains this relationship.

102. Indices of income distribution measure?

(a) absolute poverty
(b) economic growth
(c) relative poverty
(d) standard of living

Answer: c

Solution: Absolute poverty is the state of being extremely poor, lacking basic necessities such as food, water, shelter, clothing, and healthcare. Economic growth is the increase in the inflation-adjusted market value of the goods and services produced by an economy over time. Standard of living is the level of wealth, comfort, and material goods available to a certain socioeconomic class in a particular place.

Relative poverty is the state of having less income than the average person in a society. Indices of income distribution measure the degree of inequality in the distribution of income within a society. They can be used to compare the income distribution of different societies or to track changes in the income distribution over time.

103. The difference between a country's merchandise exports and its merchandise imports is the?

(a) balance of payments
(b) capital account
(c) current account
(d) balance of trade

Answer: d

Solution: The balance of trade is the difference between the value of a country's exports and imports of goods and services. A positive balance of trade, also known as a trade surplus, occurs when a country exports more goods and services than it imports. A negative balance of trade, also known as a trade deficit, occurs when a country imports more goods and services than it exports.

Balance of payments:-It is a systematic record of all economic transactions of a country with outside world in a given year.

Trade in goods - Balance of visible trade

Trade in services - Balance of invisible trade

Credit (Receipts)	Debits (Payment)
1) Current account Export - goods and services →Unilateral Receipts →Interest, profits, Dividend received	1) current account Imports - Goods and services →Unilateral payments →Interest, profits, dividend paid.
2) Capital Account →Borrowing from foreign countries → investments by foreigncountries	2) Capital Account →Lending to foreign countries →Investments in foreign countries

104. The Vicious circle theory indicates that?

(a) country is poor because it has lower productivity but high savings

(b) as countries grow richer they save less

(c) poverty perpetuates itself in mutually reinforcing circles on supply and demand sides

(d) market size is large in LDCS

Answer: (c)

Solution:

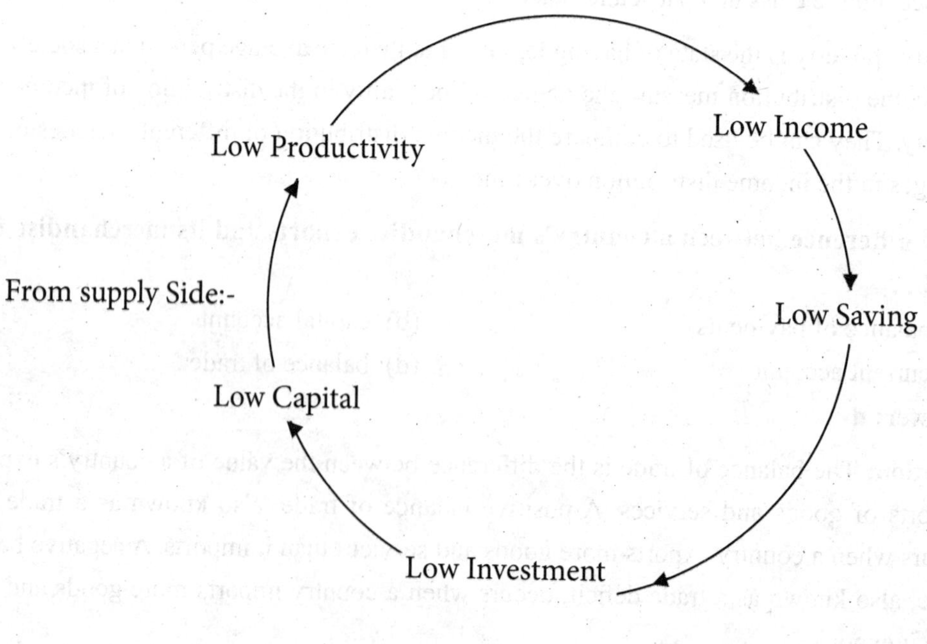

Vicious circle of poverty :-Nurkse, Gunar Myrdal "A country is poor because it is poor"

From Demand Side:-

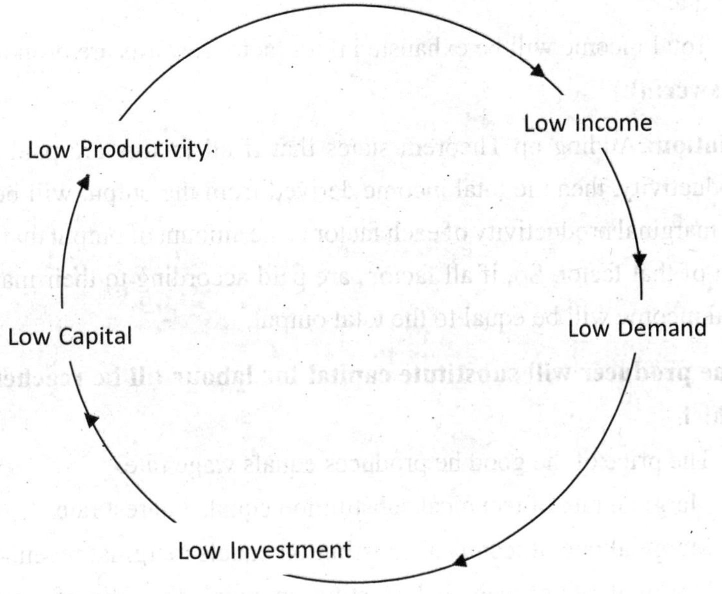

105. A short-run Phillips curve?

(a) a higher rate of inflation is associated with a lower unemployment rate

(b) a higher rate of growth in output is associated with a lower unemployment rate

(c) a higher rate of inflation is associated with a higher unemployment rate

(d) a higher rate of growth in output is associated with a higher unemployment rate

Answer: (a)

Solution: The Phillips curve shows an inverse relationship between inflation and unemployment.

So the answer is (a).

A higher rate of inflation is associated with a lower unemployment rate in the short run. This is because when inflation is high, wages tend to rise, which leads to higher spending and economic growth. This, in turn, leads to lower unemployment. However, in the long run, inflation expectations adjust, and wages and prices rise in li ne with inflation. This means that the Phillips curve becomes vertical, and there is no longer any trade-off between inflation and unemployment.

106. Select the correct statement of Adding up Theorem.

(a) If income generated by the given output produced during the given period is distributed according to average productivity of all factors, total income will be exhausted.

(b) Total income derived from the output will be exhausted if all factors are paid according to their marginal productivity.

(c) Total income derived from the output will be exhausted if all factors are paid at the same rate.

(d) Total income will be exhausted if all factor rewards are proportional to commodity prices.

Answer: (b)

Solution: Adding up Theorem states that if all factors are paid according to their marginal productivity, then the total income derived from the output will be exhausted. This is because the marginal productivity of each factor is the amount of output that is produced by an additional unit of that factor. So, if all factors are paid according to their marginal productivity, then the total income will be equal to the total output.

107. The producer will substitute capital for labour till he reaches that point of isoquant at which

(a) The price of the good he produces equals wage rate.

(b) Marginal rate of technical substitution equals interest rate.

(c) Marginal rate of technical substitution equals marginal revenue

(d) Marginal rate of technical substitution equals the ratio of marginal productivity of labour and capital.

Answer: (d)

Solution:

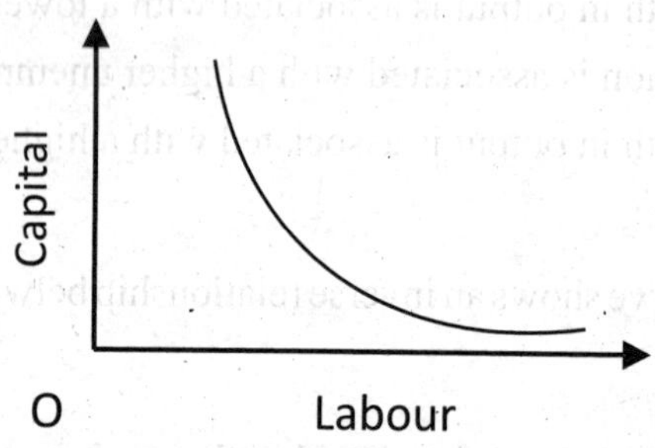

Slope of isoquants: - Marginal rate of Technical substitution [MRTS]

(No. of units of capital gives up to get one unit of labour).

It is Diminishing in nature.

MRTSLK = MPL / MPK

108. Terms of Trade of the developing countries are unfavourable due to the fact that whenever income in developed countries increases the demand for primary goods reduces because

(a) Income elasticity of demand for primary goods is high.

(b) Income elasticity of demand for primary goods is low.

(c) Income elasticity of demand is neutral towards primary goods.

(d) None of the above

Answer: (b)

Solution: Perbisch - singer hypothesis (1958):-It states that there will be a long term deterioration of TOT in developing countries due to long-term decline in the prices of primary goods which were exported by developing countries in comparison to the prices of manufactured goods imported by the developing countries.

Income elasticity of demand measures the responsiveness of demand to changes in income. A low income elasticity of demand means that demand for a good does not change significantly when income changes. In the case of primary goods, such as agricultural products and minerals, the demand is relatively low. This is because primary goods are often used as inputs in the production of other goods, and as incomes increase, people tend to demand more of the final goods and services, and less of the inputs.

109. Assertion (A) : Non-collusive model of Chamberlin asserts that a stable equilibrium can be reached if each firm charges Monopoly price and equally shares the market demand for their products.

Reason (R): Reasoning is that the firms recognize mutual interdependence in terms of action and reaction with regard to price decision with the objective of profit maximization which will be realized if prices are determined at a level which equals marginal cost.

(a) Both (A) & (R) are correct and (R) is the correct explanation of (A).

(b) (A) is correct, but (R) is not correct

(c) Both (A) & (R) are correct but (R) IS not the correct explanation of (A).

(d) (R) is correct, but (A) is incorrect.

Answer: (a)

Solution: Chamberlin Model (small group model)

- ✧ Two firms, homogeneous goods
- ✧ Chamberlin assumes that monopoly solution can be achieved with out collusion.
- ✧ One firm recognise the interdependence and will predict the action of other firm and set its output.
- ✧ At the end, each firm to acts as monopoly and 1/2 of the output is produced.

110. The revealed preference approach to the derivation of indifference curve

(a) Assumes stability over time of an observed person's tastes.

(b) Assumes that all people have identical tastes

(c) Relies repeated observations of the market behaviour of a single person

(d) Is correctly described by both (A) and (C)

Answer: (d)

Solution: The revealed preference approach assumes that a person's tastes are stable over time and that they can be inferred from their market behavior. It relies on repeated observations of the market behavior of a single person to infer their indifference curves.

The revealed preference approach does not assume that all people have identical tastes. It is possible for two people to have different indifference curves even if they have the same market behavior.

The revealed preference approach is a useful tool for economists because it allows them to infer people's preferences without having to ask them directly. This is important because people may not be able to accurately describe their own preferences, or they may be unwilling to do so.

111. Which of the following statements does not hold true in case of the Keynesian Economics?

(a) Velocity of money is an unstable function determinants

(b) Labour is subject to money illusion.

(c) Aggregate supply function tends to become flat at levels of output well below full employment and to become steeper as full capacity is reached.

(d) Aggregate supply schedule is vertical, and output and employment are completely supply determined.

Answer: (d)

Solution:

Keynesian's theory :-

1) Full employment not possible [under employment equilibrium].

2) Workers suffer from money illusions.

3) D_L =f (w/p). D_L is function of real wages

S_L = f (w). S_L is function of nominal wages because workers cannot estimate the effect of price levels on their income.

4) Money also act as a store of value

5) Short-run analysis

Classicals focused on supply side
Keynesian's focused on demand side

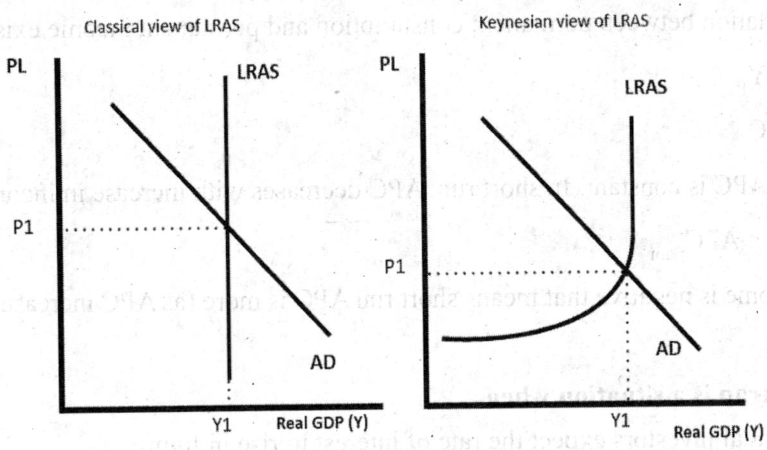

112. When current income includes negative transitory component relating consumption with current income will produce

(a) an average propensity to consume that is lower than the long run average propensity to consume.

(b) an average propensity to consume that is higher than the average long run propensity to consume.

(c) an average propensity to consume that equals the long run average propensity to consume.

(d) None of the above

Answer: (b)

Solution:

Permanent income hypothesis :- given by Milton Friedman in 1957 in his book "A theory of consumption function.

Income

↙ ↘

Permanent (X_P) Transitory (Y_t)

Consumption :-

Permanent (C_P) Transitory (C_t)

Assumptions:-

1) No covariance between permanent income and transitory income.

2) No covariance between transitory income and transitory consumption.

3) No covariance between permanent consumption and transitory con sumption

4) Only relation between permanent consumption and permanent income exists.

$C_P = K.Y_P$

$K = APC$

In long run APC is constant. In short run, APC decreases with increase in income.

$APC_{rich} < APC_{poor}$

Current income is negative that means short run APC is more (as APC increases with decrease in income.)

113. Liquidity trap is a situation when

(a) all potential investors expect the rate of interest to rise in future

(b) all potential investors expect the rate of interest to fall in future

(c) natural rate of interest is above the critical rate of interest

(d) demand for money for speculative purpose is interest inelastic

Answer: (a)

Solution:

Liquidity trap :- Interest rate is so low that the demand for money becomes infinitely elastic.

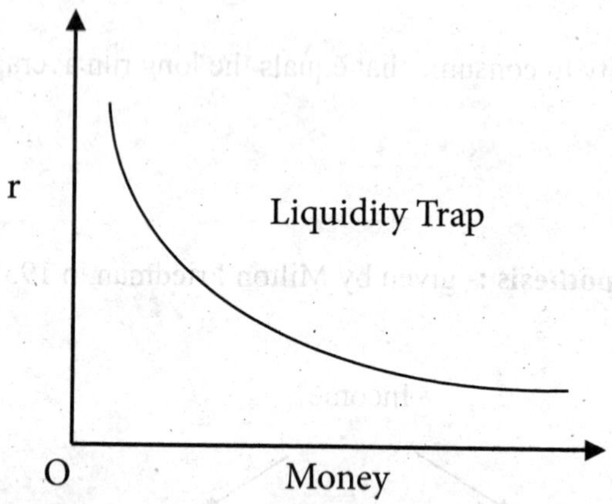

114. In Harrod's model of economic growth, if warranted rate is below the natural rate of growth then it is possible to maintain steady state growth at the warranted rate with

(a) continually increasing unemployment

(b) a constant rate of unemployment

(c) continually decreasing unemployment

(d) None of the above

Answer: (a)

Solution:

Knife-edge equilibrium :- If G =$G_W = G_n$

There can be deviations from the steady path.

Case 1 → G < G_W - depression

C > C_r - depression

Case2 → G > G_W - Inflation

C< C_r - Inflation

If $G_n > G_W$ →Inflation/Boom

If $G_W > G_n$ →depression

For steady state growth Gw has to increase, that means increasing unemployment as rising Gw leads to depression and depression leads to unemployment.

115. Which of the following is not a feature of the A.W. Phillip's inflation unemployment trade-off relation?

(a) A non-linear inverse relationship between unemployment rate and the rate of change in wage rate.

(b) There is a loop in the anti-clockwise around the Phillip's curve,

(c) The wage-inflation unemployment relationship is predictable.

(d) Philip's curve shifts when expected rate of inflation shifts

Answer: (d)

Solution: Phillips curve (1958)

It is stated that there is a negative relationship between wages and unemployment.

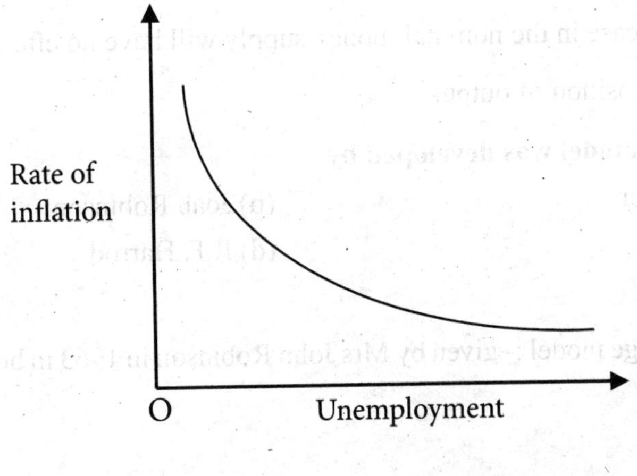

Later on, Phillips curve was established showing a negative relationship between rate of inflation and rate of unemployment.

Assumptions :-

1) PC is a short run curve and static in nature.
2) Downward-sloping and take the shape of a rectangular hyperbola.
3) Non - linear relationship.
4) Price expectations are static

116. Suppose there is full employment and vertical aggregate supply schedule. An increase in the nominal money supply

(a) reduces the rate of interest and changes the composition of output
(b) causes a proportional increase in real output
(c) has no effect on the real money supply or the composition of output
(d) causes the real money supply to increase, which changes composition of output

Answer: (c)

Solution: In a situation where there is full employment and a vertical aggregate supply schedule, an increase in the nominal money supply will have no effect on real output. This is because the economy is already at full employment, so there is no spare capacity to produce more output.

The increase in the nominal money supply will only lead to an increase in the price level. This is because the aggregate demand curve is horizontal at full employment, so an increase in the nominal money supply will lead to a proportional increase in the price level.

The real money supply is the nominal money supply divided by the price level. In this case, the increase in the nominal money supply will be offset by the increase in the price level, so the real money supply will remain unchanged.

Therefore, the increase in the nominal money supply will have no effect on the real money supply or the composition of output.

117. The Golden Age model was developed by

(a) Nicholas Kaldor
(b) Joan Robinson
(c) J.R. Hicks
(d) R.F. Harrod

Answer: (b)

Solution: Golden age model :- given by Mrs John Robinson in 1963 in book" The accumulation of capital"

Assumptions :-

→ laissez-faire

→ Two factors - labour, capital

→ Perfect competition

→ Constant returns to scale

→ fixed capital - labour ratio

→ National income is sum of wages and profits.

Desired rate:-[Harrodian warranted rate] Rate which makes the firm satisfied with the situation in which they find themselves.

Possible rate :- [Harrodian natural rate] depends on physical conditions i.e. population growth and technical knowledge.

Golden age → Desired rate = Possible rate

In other words, Growth rate of labour = Growth rate of capital Static state where Growth rate is zero and Profit rate is zero. State of economic bliss when consumption is at maximum level.

118. Given below are two statements, one labelled as Assertion (A) and other labelled as Reason (R):

Assertion (A) : Information Technology (IT) industry is a "high knowledge" based industry that has developed rapidly, mainly on its own merits in India.

Reason (R): Industry that is based on high knowledge does not need any significant support from the Government nor there is much scope for outside interference.

Choose the correct combination of codes given below:

(a) (A) is correct, but (R) is wrong.

(b) Both (A) and (R) are correct.

(c) (A) is wrong, but (R) is correct.

(d) Both (A) and (R) are wrong.

Answer: (b)

Solution: The IT industry in India is a high-knowledge based industry that has developed rapidly, mainly on its own merits. The industry has benefited from a number of factors, including a large pool of skilled workers, a favorable business environment, and government support. However, the industry has also grown without much outside interference.

The reason (R) is also correct. Industries that are based on high knowledge do not need as much government support as other industries. This is because the knowledge base of these industries is constantly evolving, and the government is often not able to keep up with the latest developments.

119. Match 'SEBI' with the appropriate item among the following:

(a) Regulation of Money market

(b) Regulation of Capital market

(c) Regulation of Commodity market

(d) All the above

Answer: (b)

Solution: SEBI - Securities and Exchange Board of India

→1988 – formed

→ 1992 - Statutory status

Functions :-

- Promote interest of investors
- Promote development and to regulate securities market
- To prevent insider trading and of unfair practices.
- Investor's education and training

SEBI is responsible for regulating and overseeing the functioning of the capital market in India. It aims to protect the interests of investors and promote the development and regulation of securities markets in the country. SEBI sets rules and regulations for various entities involved in the capital market, such as stock exchanges, brokers, merchant bankers, and other intermediaries. It ensures transparency, fairness, and efficiency in capital market transactions and promotes investor education and awareness.

120. In the presence of Heteroscedasticity, which of the following is not a correct statement?

(a) Heteroscedasticity does not alter the unbiasedness and consistency properties of OLS estimators.

(b) OLS estimators are of minimum variance or efficient

(c) BLUE estimators are provided by the method of weighted least squares.

(d) T and F tests based on standard assumptions of classical linear regression model may not be reliable.

Answer: (b)

Solution:

Heteroscadasticity

A regression model in which disturbance variance change from observation to observation is known as Heteroscadasticity.

Regression Model

i.e. Var (ui) = σ^2 u (Homoscedasticity)

Var (ui) = σ^2 ui (Heteroscadisticity)

Consequences : OLS estimates have large variance but remain unbiased and linear.

Tests : Spearman Rank Correlation Test

Gold Fed Quandt Test

Glejer Test

Park Test

The correct answer is (b).

Heteroscedasticity refers to the situation where the variance of the error term is not constant. This means that the error term is not evenly spread out around the regression line, but rather is more spread out in some areas than in others.

When heteroscedasticity is present, the OLS estimators are still unbiased and consistent. However, they are not of minimum variance, which means that there are other estimators that have a smaller variance.

The BLUE estimators (Best Linear Unbiased Estimators) are provided by the method of weighted least squares. This method takes into account the heteroscedasticity of the error term and weights the observations accordingly.

The T and F tests based on the standard assumptions of the classical linear regression model may not be reliable in the presence of heteroscedasticity. This is because these tests assume that the error term is homoscedastic, which is not the case when heteroscedasticity is present.

121. Correlation coefficient between X and Y is 0.3 and correlation coefficient between P and Q is 0.6, then the strength of correlation between P and Q is higher than between X and Y by

(a) two times
(b) three times
(c) four times
(d) five times

Answer : (c)

Solution:

rxy = 0.3

rpq = 0.6

r^2xy = 0.09

$r^2pq = 0.36$

0.36/ 0.09

= 36/9

= 4 times

122. WTO agreement on Agriculture consists of

I. Domestic support

II. Export subsidies

III. Market access

IV. Input subsidies

(a) I and IV are correct.
(b) II and IV are correct.
(c) I, II and III are correct.
(d) I, II and IV are correct.

Answer : c

Solution: AOA (Agreement on Agricultures)-

- **Agriculture Subsidies:-**
  - **(1) Green box:**-No or minimum trade distorting effects.
  - **(2) red box:** - All agricultural subsidies which are considered to distort trade and production fall.
  - **(3) Blue box:**-red Box subsidies with conditions.
- **Domestic support:**-Reduction of Agricultural subsidies.
- **Export subsidies:**-Abolish
- **Market access :**-Reduction in tariff and non tariff barriers of agriculture products

123. In Harrod's growth model, neutral technical progress implies technical progress as

(a) Capital augmenting
(b) Labour augmenting
(c) Both labour and augmenting
(d) Productivity increasing capital

Answer : (b)

Solution:

Technical progress :- inventing a new technology or improving existing through innovations.

Neutral :-Produce more output with increase in capital and labour in same proportion.

Capital savings :- same amount of output can be produced with lesser amount of capital.

Labour saving :- same amount of output can be produced with lesser amount of labour.

Hicks neutral technical progress :- both labour and capital augmenting.

Harrod's technical progress :- labour augmenting, i.e labour efficiency improves. Marginal productivity of labour increases with constant K/L ratio.

Hicks vs Harrod neutral technical progress :- Technical progress, in the per-worker production function, is said to be Harrod-neutral if, at any constant value of the capital-output ratio, the marginal product of capital remains unchanged. Harrod's classification compares points at which the capital output ratio is constant as opposed to the Hicks procedure which compares points at which the capital-labour ratio is constant

Solow's :- Capital augmenting. Marginal product of capital increases with constant K/L ratio.

124. Which are the two gaps affecting growth process of an economic system in the two gap model of growth?

(a) Saving gap and investment gap

(b) Income gap and consumption gap

(c) Foreign exchange gap and domestic saving gap

(d) Export gap and import gap

Answer : c

Solution: The correct answer is (c) Foreign exchange gap and domestic saving gap.

The two gap model of growth is a development economics model that was developed in the 1950s. The model argues that the growth of an economic system is constrained by two gaps: the foreign exchange gap and the domestic saving gap.

The foreign exchange gap is the difference between the amount of foreign exchange needed to finance imports and the amount of foreign exchange earned from exports. The domestic saving gap is the difference between the amount of savings needed to finance investment and the amount of savings generated domestically.

If either of these gaps is too large, it will constrain the growth of the economic system.

125. Assertion (A) The new endogenous growth theory examines the production function that shows increasing returns

Reason (R) Because that shows increasing returns of specialization and investment in knowledge capital.

(a) (A) is true, but (R) is false.

(b) (R) is true, but (A) is false.

(c) Both (A) and (R) are correct, but (R) is not the correct explanation of (A).

(d) Both (A) and (R) are correct and (R) is the Correct explanation of (A)

Answer :

(d) Solution:

The new endogenous growth theory examines the production function because it shows increasing returns of specialization and investment in knowledge capital. In other words, the new endogenous growth theory argues that the output of an economy can increase more than proportionately to the inputs, and this is because of specialization and investment in knowledge capital.

Specialization allows workers to focus on the tasks they are best at, which can lead to productivity gains. Investment in knowledge capital can lead to the development of new technologies, which can also lead to productivity gains.

The combination of specialization and investment in knowledge capital can lead to sustained economic growth. This is because the productivity gains that result from specialization and investment in knowledge capital can be spread throughout the economy, which can lead to an increase in the overall output of the economy.

126. Assertion (A): Financial inclusion is desirable to help weaker sections of society in the country.

Reason (R): Investment activity needs to be promoted to facilitate access to development benefits to masses.

(a) Both (A) and (R) are correct and (R) is not the correct explanation of (A).

(b) Both (A) and (R) are correct and (R) is the correct explanation of (A).

(c) (A) is not correct, but (R) is correct.

(d) (A) is correct, but (R) is not correct.

Answer : (b)

Solution:

Assertion (A) : states that financial inclusion is desirable to help weaker sections of society in the country. This is because financial inclusion can help people to access financial services, such as savings accounts, loans, and insurance. These services can help people to improve their financial situation and to invest in their businesses or education.

Reason (R) : states that investment activity needs to be promoted to facilitate access to development benefits to masses. This is because investment can help to create new jobs and to generate economic growth. When people have access to financial services, they are more likely to invest in their businesses or education. This can lead to increased investment activity, which can in turn lead to economic growth.

Therefore, both (A) and (R) are correct. Assertion (A) states the benefit of financial inclusion, and Reason (R) explains how financial inclusion can help to achieve that benefit.

127. Assertion (A): Stationary state is the end of the process of capital formation.

Reason (R): Scarcity of natural resources as also capital leads the economy to the stationary state.

(a) Both (A) and (R) are correct and (R) is not the correct explanation of (A).

(b) Both (A) and (R) are correct and (R) is the correct explanation of (A).

(c) (A) is correct, but (R) is not correct

(d) (A) is not correct, but (R) is correct

Answer : (b)

Solution:

Assertion (A) : states that a stationary state is the end of the process of capital formation. This is because in a stationary state, the economy is no longer growing, and therefore there is no need to accumulate more capital.

Reason (R) : states that scarcity of natural resources as also capital leads the economy to the stationary state. This is because when natural resources and capital are scarce, it becomes more difficult to produce goods and services. This can lead to a slowdown in economic growth, and eventually to a stationary state.

128. Assertion (A): Investment has also a supply effect.

Reason (R): Because it raises capacity to produce. Codes:

(a) Both (A) and (R) are correct and (R) is not the correct explanation of (A).

(b) Both (A) and (R) are correct and (R) is the correct explanation of (A).

(c) (A) is correct, but (R) is not correct.

(d) (A) is not correct, but (R) is correct.

Answer : (b)

Solution: Assertion (A) states that investment has also a supply effect. This is because investment increases the amount of capital in the economy, which can lead to an increase in the output of goods and services.

Reason (R) states that investment raises capacity to produce. This is because investment can be used to build new factories, purchase new equipment, and train new workers. All of these things can lead to an increase in the capacity of the economy to produce goods and services.

129. Assertion (A): Gold standard was finally given up after the Second World War.

Reason (R): Countries had different rates of inflation.

(a) Both (A) and (R) are correct and (R) is the correct explanation of (A).

(b) Both (A) and (R) are correct and (R) is not correct explanation of (A).

(c) (A) is correct, but (R) is not correct.

(d) (A) is not correct, but (R) is correct.

Answer : (a)

Solution: The gold standard is a monetary system in which the value of a currency is directly linked to the value of gold. This means that a country's central bank must hold gold reserves equal to the value of its currency in circulation.

After the Second World War, many countries abandoned the gold standard. This was because the war had caused a lot of economic disruption, and countries were no longer able to maintain their gold reserves. Additionally, the different rates of inflation between countries made it difficult to maintain a fixed exchange rate under the gold standard.

Therefore, both Assertion (A) and Reason (R) are correct. Reason (R) is the correct explanation of Assertion (A) because it explains why countries abandoned the gold standard after the Second World War.

130. Assertion (A) Disguised unemployment is present in Indian agriculture. Reason (R): Marginal productivity of agriculture is close to zero.

(a) Both (A) and (R) are correct and (R) is the correct explanation of (A).

(b) Both (A) and (R) are correct and (R) is not the correct explanation of (A).

(c) (A) is correct, but (R) is not correct.

(d) (A) is not correct, but (R) is correct.

Answer : (a)

Solution: The correct answer is (a), both (A) and (R) are correct and (R) is the correct explanation of (A).

Disguised unemployment is a type of unemployment where people are employed, but they are not actually contributing to output. This can happen in agriculture when there are more workers than needed to produce a given level of output. The marginal productivity of these workers is close to zero, which means that their output is very small.

131. Arrange the following in chronological order:

I. CES production function.
II. Cobb-Douglas production function
III. Translog production function
IV. The law of variable proportions

(a) III, I, IV, II
(b) I, IV, II, III
(c) IV, II, I, III
(d) II, III, I, IV

Answer : (c)

Solution: The correct chronological order of the production functions is:

1. The law of variable proportions
2. Cobb-Douglas production function
3. CES production function
4. Translog production function

The law of variable proportions was first proposed by economists in the early 19th century. It states that as more and more of a single input is added to a production process, the marginal product of that input will eventually decline.

The Cobb-Douglas production function was developed in the early 20th century. It is a simple but powerful model of production that is still widely used today.

The CES production function was developed in the 1960s. It is a more general model of production than the Cobb-Douglas production function, and it can be used to represent a wider range of production relationships.

The Translog production function was developed in the 1970s. It is a more flexible model of production than the CES production function, and it can be used to represent a wider range of production relationships.

132. Arrange the origin of money in a sequential order

I. Cheque

II. Metallic money

III. Commodity money

IV.Paper money

(a) IV, I, III, II
(b) I, III, II, IV
(c) III, II, IV, I
(d) II. IV. I, III

Answer : c

Solution:

- Commodity money is the earliest form of money, and it is made of a valuable good, such as gold, silver, or copper.
- Metallic money is a type of commodity money that is made of metal.
- Paper money is a type of money that is made of paper and is backed by a government or central bank.
- Cheques are a type of paper money that is used to transfer money from one account to another.

133. Arrange the following theories in the chronological order:

I. Restatement of Quantity Theory

II. Income Theory

III Quantity Theory

IV. Cash Balance Approach

Select the correct answer from the given codes:

(a) I, II, IV, III (b) III, I, II, IV

(c) IV, III, I, II (d) III. IV. II. I

Answer : (d)

Solution:

- Quantity Theory
- Cash Balance Approach
- Income Theory (1936)
- Restatement of Quantity Theory (1956)

134. Identify the correct chronological order of the following classical economists:

(a) Adam Smith, Malthus, Ricardo, J.S. Mill

(b) Adam Smith, Ricardo, Malthus, J.S. Mill

(c) Adam Smith, J.S. Mill, Ricardo, Malthus

(d) Adam Smith, Malthus, J.S. Mill, Ricardo

Answer: (a)

Solution:

✧ Adam Smith (1723-1790) is considered the father of classical economics. His book The Wealth of Nations is one of the most influential books in the history of economics.

✧ Thomas Malthus (1766-1834) was a demographer and economist who is best known for his theory of population growth. He argued that population growth would eventually outstrip the ability of the economy to provide food, leading to widespread poverty and misery.

✧ David Ricardo (1772-1823) was an economist who is best known for his theory of comparative advantage. He argued that countries should specialize in the production of goods that they have a comparative advantage in producing, even if they do not have an absolute advantage in producing those goods.

✧ John Stuart Mill (1806-1873) was an economist and philosopher who is best known for his work on utilitarianism. He argued that the best way to organize society is to maximize the happiness of the greatest number of people.

135. The sequencing process of Schumpeter model of development is

(a) Swarm like Clusters, Innovation, Bank credit, Breaking circular flow

(b) Breaking circular flow, Innovation, Bank credit, Swarm like Clusters

(c) Innovation. Bank credit. Breaking circular flow, Swarm like Clusters

(d) Bank credit, Innovation, Swarm like Clusters, Breaking circular flow

Answer : (b)

Circular flow breaks with innovation. For innovation, innovator needs credit from the banks. Then others also follows this innovation like swarn like clusters.

Solution

Schumpeter theory of development:-

Schumpeter ideas about economic development first appeared in his book "The theory of economic development" in 1911. According to him, Development is a spontaneous and discontinuous change in the flow channels which cause a disturbance in equilibrium and hence to alters and displaces the equilibrium state forever. According to Schumpeter, "development will happen only when circular flow is disturb. The circular flow can only be disturbed through innovation.

Five kinds of innovations :-

a. New product

b. New method of production

c. New source of raw material

d. New industrial organization

e. New market

Qualities of innovator :-

1) He should have a technical know how

2) Must able to manage funds

→Through the process of development, old things are replaced by new things - Primary wave of expansion will be followed by secondary waves.

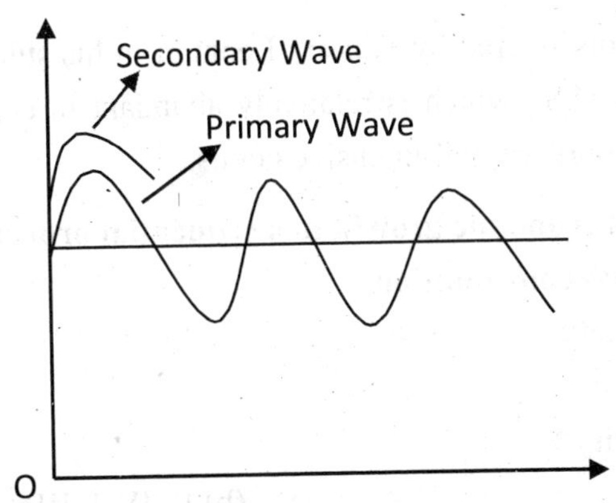

136. Arrange the following theories in order in which they appeared:

I. Comparative Cost Advantage Theory

II. Absolute Cost Advantage Theory

III. Leontief Paradox

IV.Factor Endowment Theory

Codes:

(a) I, III, II, IV
(b) II, III, IV, I
(c) II, I, IV. III
(d) I. IV. II, III

Answer : (c)

Solution:

- Absolute Cost Advantage Theory (1776)
- Comparative Cost Advantage Theory (1817)
- Factor Endowment Theory (1933)
- Leontief Paradox (1953)

Absolute Cost Advantage Theory was proposed by Adam Smith in his book The Wealth of Nations. The theory states that a country should specialize in the production of goods that it can produce at a lower cost than other countries.

Comparative Cost Advantage Theory was proposed by David Ricardo in his book On the Principles of Political Economy and Taxation. The theory states that a country should specialize in the production of goods that it has a comparative advantage in producing, even if it does not have an absolute advantage in producing those goods.

Factor Endowment Theory was proposed by Eli Heckscher and Bertil Ohlin in their book Interregional and International Trade. The theory states that a country's pattern of trade is determined by the factors of production that the country is abundant in.

Leontief Paradox was discovered by Wassily Leontief in his study of the U.S. economy. The paradox states that the U.S., which is relatively abundant in capital, actually exports labor-intensive goods and imports capital-intensive goods.

137. Arrange the stages of economic growth in a sequential order:

I. The age of high mass consumption

II. The traditional society

III. The take-off stage

IV.The drive to maturity

(a) I, III, IV, II
(b) II, IV. I, III

(c) III, I, II, IV (d) II, III, IV, I

Answer : (d)

Solution:

The stages of economic growth are as follows:

- **Traditional society:** This is the first stage of economic growth, and it is characterized by a low level of technology and a subsistence economy.
- **Preconditions for take-off:** This is the second stage of economic growth, and it is characterized by the development of certain preconditions for economic growth, such as a rise in savings and investment, and the development of a modern infrastructure.
- **Take-off:** This is the third stage of economic growth, and it is characterized by a rapid increase in economic growth.
- **Drive to maturity:** This is the fourth stage of economic growth, and it is characterized by
- a continued increase in economic growth, but at a slower pace than in the take-off stage.
- **Age of high mass consumption:** This is the fifth and final stage of economic growth, and it is characterized by a high level of consumption and a focus on the production of consumer goods.

138. Identify the sequence of implementation of the following taxes.

Select the correct answer from the given codes:

I. Land Revenue

II. Sales tax

III. MODVAT

IV.Service tax

Codes:

(a) I, II, III, IV (b) II, IV, I, III

(c) III, II, IV. I (d) IV, II, I, III

Answer : (a)

Solution:

- Land revenue is the oldest tax in India, and it has been in existence since the Mughal Empire.
- Sales tax was introduced in the early 1900s,
- MODVAT (Modified Value Added Tax) was introduced in the 1980s.
- Service tax was introduced in the 1990s.

139. Identify the correct chronology of the following:

I. Fisher's test of significance of differences between means of three or more samples.

II. Kendal's partial rank correlation

III. Gossest's T test of significance between means of two samples.

IV.Chy square test of goodness of fit of the curve and randomness of the sample values.

Codes:

(a) III, I, II, IV
(b) I. II. III. IV
(c) IV, III, II, I
(d) I. II. IV. III

Answer : (a)

140. Which among the following is not correctly matched?

(a) Golden age : Mrs. Joan Robinson
(b) Golden rule of accumulation : Edmund Phelfs
(c) Steady state growth : Robert Solow
(d) Low income equilibrium trap : T.R. Malthus

Answer : (d)

Solution: Low level equilibrium trap :-given by Nelson in his work "Theory of Low level equilibrium trap". It is based on Malthusian theory of population. Population and per capita income are positively related only till some point, beyond which rise in per capita income would not have much effect on Population levels

141. Who among the following economists is not associated with the Dependency Theory?

(a) S. Amin
(b) P. Baron
(c) Raul Prebisch
(d) A. G. Frank

Answer : (c)

Solution: Raul Prebisch was an Argentine economist who is considered to be one of the founders of dependency theory. However, he is not associated with the theory because he is not a neoclassical economist.

Neoclassical economists believe that markets are generally efficient and that government intervention should be limited. Dependency theory, on the other hand, argues that government intervention is necessary to break the cycle of dependency.

Other economists who are associated with dependency theory:

- Andre Gunder Frank
- Samir Amin
- Theotonio dos Santos

- Fernando Henrique Cardoso
- Enzo Faletto
- Ruy Mauro Marini
- Paul Baran
- Paul Sweezy

142. Which one of the following is not a feature of neoclassical economics?

(a) Flexible wages and interest rates

(b) Capital in physical and financial form

(c) Perfect Competition

(d) Neutrality of money

Answer : (b)

Solution: Capital in physical and financial form is a feature of Keynesian economics, not neoclassical economics. Neoclassical economics is a school of thought in economics that emphasizes the role of markets in allocating resources and determining prices. Neoclassical economists believe that markets are generally efficient and that government intervention should be limited.

143. Renewed focus to control increasing population is required from the viewpoint of women because:

(a) Family planning programme needs to be reoriented keeping in view the reproductive health rights of women.

(b) Increased budget needed to provide quality services to women.

(c) Increased number of women councellers needed for health and youth friendly services.

(d) All of the above.

Answer : (d)

Solution: Population control is a complex issue with a variety of factors to consider. However, from the viewpoint of women, there are three key reasons why renewed focus is needed:

Family planning programs need to be reoriented to keep in view the reproductive health rights of women. This means that women should have access to a variety of family planning methods, including safe and effective contraception, and that they should be able to make informed decisions about their own fertility.

Increased budget is needed to provide quality services to women. This includes funding for family planning programs, as well as funding for other services that are important to women's health, such as maternal and child health care.

Increased number of women counselors are needed for health and youth friendly services. This is because women often feel more comfortable talking to other women about their reproductive health needs. Counselors can provide information and support to women, and they can also help women to access the services that they need.

All of these factors are important to consider when designing and implementing population control programs. By taking into account the needs and rights of women, we can create programs that are more effective and that have a greater impact on reducing population growth.

144. Match List - I with List - II and select the correct answer: *(December 2020-june 2021)*

List - I	List - II
(A) Supply side of international trade	**(i) David Ricardo**
(B) Demand side of international trade	**(ii) Bastable and Alfred Marshall**
(C) Opportunity cost of international trade	**(iii) G. Haberler**
(D) Real cost theory of International trade	**(iv) Alfred Marshall and Edgeworth**

Codes:

	(A)	(B)	(C)	(D)
(a)	(i)	(iv)	(ii)	(iii)
(b)	(i)	(iv)	(iii)	(ii)
(c)	(iv)	(i)	(ii)	(iii)
(d)	(iv)	(i)	(iii)	(ii)

Answer : (b)

Solution:

(A) Supply side of international trade (i) David Ricardo

(B) Demand side of international trade (iv) Alfred Marshall and Edgeworth

(C) Opportunity cost of international trade (iii) G. Haberler

(D) Real cost theory of International trade (ii) Alfred Marshall and Bastable

145. Justice in taxation is best ensured by applying the principle of:

(a) Equal marginal sacrifice

(b) Equal proportional sacrifice

(c) Equal absolute sacrifice

(d) None of the above.

Answer : (a)

Solution: Theories of Distribution of Tax - Burden

1. **Benefit Principal :-** Given by Lindahl

   Taxes should be charged in proportion of the benefits received.ie toll tax

2. **Ability to Pay Theory :-** Seligman

   Taxes charged should be according to the 'ability to pay' of the tax payer.

- The principle of equal marginal sacrifice states that the tax burden should be distributed in such a way that the marginal utility of income is the same for all taxpayers. This means that taxpayers with a higher income should pay a higher tax rate, but only to the extent that the marginal utility of income is lower for them.
- The principle of equal proportional sacrifice states that the tax burden should be distributed in such a way that the proportion of income paid in taxes is the same for all taxpayers. This means that taxpayers with a higher income should pay a higher tax rate, but only in proportion to their income.
- The principle of equal absolute sacrifice states that the tax burden should be distributed in such a way that the total amount of sacrifice (in terms of utility) is the same for all taxpayers. This means that taxpayers with a higher income should pay a higher tax rate, but only to the extent that the total amount of sacrifice is the same for them.
- Of the three principles, the principle of equal marginal sacrifice is considered to be the most equitable, as it takes into account the diminishing marginal utility of income. However, it is also the most difficult to implement, as it requires information about the marginal utility of income for all taxpayers.

146. All the funds which belong to Government go to:

(a) Public Account
(b) Consolidated fund
(c) Contingency fund
(d) Revenue Account

Answer : (b)

Solution:

1. The Consolidated Fund is the most important of all government accounts. It is constituted under Article 266 (1) of the Constitution of India. All revenues received by the government by way of direct taxes and indirect taxes, money borrowed and receipts from loans given by the government flow into the Consolidated Fund of India.
2. The Public Account is a separate account that is used to hold money that is not part of the Consolidated Fund. This money may include money that is received by the government from loans, grants, or other sources. The Public Account is also used to hold money that is set aside for specific purposes, such as the repayment of loans or the funding of social welfare programs.

3. The Contingency Fund is a small fund that is used to meet unforeseen expenses. The Contingency Fund is not part of the Consolidated Fund, but it is controlled by the government. The government can use the Contingency Fund to meet expenses that are not covered by the Consolidated Fund, such as natural disasters or military operations.
4. The Revenue Account is an account that is used to record the government's revenue and expenditure. The Revenue Account is not part of the Consolidated Fund, but it is closely linked to it. The Revenue Account is used to record the government's income from taxes and other sources, as well as its expenditure on programs and services.

147. 'Gender budgeting' means:

(a) a separate budget for women (b) a tool for gender empowerment

(c) a tool for gender discrimination (d) a separate budget for men and women.

Answer : (b)

Solution: Gender budgeting is a process of analyzing government budgets from a gender perspective. It involves identifying the different ways in which government spending and revenue collection affect women and men, and using this information to make recommendations for how the budget can be more gender-equitable.

148. Which sector in India has developed breaking the Colin Clark sequence of development?

(a) Export Sector (b) Primary Sector

(c) Secondary Sector (d) Service Sector

Answer : (d)

Solution: Colin Clark's sequence of development states that countries typically develop through the following stages:

- The primary sector, which is based on agriculture and natural resources.
- The secondary sector, which is based on manufacturing.
- The tertiary sector, which is based on services.

However, India has developed by breaking this sequence. The service sector in India has grown rapidly, even though the primary and secondary sectors have not developed as quickly. This is due to a number of factors, including the rise of the IT industry and the growth of the tourism sector.

149. Match List - I with List - II by selecting correct codes given below:

List - I	List - II
(A) Liquidity trap	**(i) M. Friedman**
(B) Demonstration effect	**(ii) A. C. Pigou**
(C) Permanent Income Hypothesis	**(iii) J. Duesenberry**
(D) Wealth Effect	**(iv) J. M. Keynes**

	(A)	(B)	(C)	(D)
(a)	(iv)	(iii)	(i)	(ii)
(b)	(i)	(ii)	(iv)	(iii)
(c)	(iv)	(ii)	(i)	(iii)
(d)	(i)	(iii)	(iv)	(ii)

Answer : (a)

Solution:

(A) Liquidity trap (iv) J. M. Keynes

(B) Demonstration effect (iii) J. Duesenberry

(C) Permanent Income Hypothesis (i) M. Friedman

(D) Wealth Effect (ii) A. C. Pigou

1. **Liquidity trap:** The term was first used by economist John Maynard Keynes. Liquidity trap refers to a situation where the interest rates in an economy are at extremely low levels, and individuals prefer to hold their money in cash or cash equivalent form as they are uncertain about the performance of a nation's economy. Liquidity traps occur when a country is trying to recover from a recession, and the government aims to boost investment in the nation by reducing interest rates to facilitate borrowing.
2. **Demonstration Effect:** Duesenberry (1949) gave "demonstration effect" .Demonstration effects are effects on the behavior of individuals caused by observation of the actions of others and their consequences. The term is particularly used in political science and sociology to describe the fact that developments in one place will often act as a catalyst in another place.
3. **Permanent Income Hypothesis:** The permanent income theory was developed by Milton Friedman in 1957. It is an economic theory that suggests that people's consumption patterns are determined by their long-term, or permanent, income, rather than their current income level.
4. **Wealth Effect:** In a 1943 article the economist Arthur Pigou coined the phrase "the Wealth Effect", to measure the changes in consumption based on the change in the values of housing and financial assets. The wealth effect is a behavioral economic theory suggesting

that people spend more as the value of their assets rises. The idea is that consumers feel more financially secure and confident about their wealth when their homes or investment portfolios increase in value. They are made to feel richer, even if their income and fixed costs are the same as before.

150. An over-valued currency will have which of the following effects:

(a) Make exports and imports equally costly

(b) Make exports and imports equally cheaper

(c) Make imports relatively more costly

(d) Make imports relatively cheaper.

Answer : (d)

Solution: When a currency is overvalued, it means that its exchange rate is higher than its fundamental value. In this case, the domestic currency has stronger purchasing power compared to other currencies.

As a result, an overvalued currency makes imports relatively cheaper for domestic buyers.

This is because domestic buyers can exchange their overvalued currency for more units of the foreign currency, allowing them to purchase more goods and services from other countries at a lower cost.

151. According to Prebisch-Singer thesis which of the following is true?

(A) International trade has increased international inequalities and has retarded the development of developing countries.

(B) The strategy of import substitution has resulted in misallocation of resources within a developing country.

(a) Both (A) and (B) are true.

(b) Only (A) is true.

(c) Only (B) is true

(d) Both (A) and (B) are not true.

Answer: (b)

Solution: Perbisch - singer hypothesis (1958):-It states that there will be a long term deterioration of TOT in developing countries due to long-term decline in the prices of primary goods which were exported by developing countries in comparison to the prices of manufactured goods imported by the developing countries.

152. Assertion (A) : Marshall-Lerner condition should be fulfilled if devaluation is to successful.

Reason (R) : Devaluation makes exports costly and imports cheaper.

(a) Both (A) and (R) are correct

(b) Both (A) and (R) are not correct

(c) (A) is correct but (R) is not correct

(d) (A) is correct and (R) is the correct reason of (A)

Answer: (c)

Solution:

Elasticity Approach

Marshall- lerner condition :-Devaluation of a currency can be successfuldepending on the elasticities of demand of exports(e_x) and of demand for imports(e_m).

If $e_x + e_m > 1$ Devaluation Successful.

If $e_x + e_m = 1$ Devaluation has no effect on BOP

If $e_x + e_m < 1$ Devaluation will worsen the BOP

Devaluation :- Decline in the value of currency in terms of foreign currency. [Done by government]

Depreciation : - same as devaluation but it occurs as a result of forces of demand and supply(in flexible exchange rate).

153. Productivity changes in domestic export industry are incorporated in which types of terms of trade?

(a) Income terms of trade

(b) Single factoral terms of trade

(c) Gross barter terms of trade

(d) None of the above.

Answer: (b)

Solution: Terms of Trade

$$= \frac{\text{Index of exports prices}}{\text{Index of imports prices}} \times 100$$

Net Barter TOT :- The concept was given by Taussing.

$$T_C = \frac{P_{x1}/P_{xo}}{P_{m1}/P_{mo}}$$

Price of export/Price of import.

More the ratio, more favourable are the TOT.

Gross Barter TOT :- Taussing

$$T_g \rightarrow \frac{Q_{m1}}{Q_{mo}} / \frac{Q_{x1}}{Q_{xo}} \qquad \left[\frac{\textit{Quantity Imported}}{\textit{Quantity Exported}}\right]$$

Income Terms of Trade :- Dorrance

$T_y = T_c . Q_x$ $\quad$ Q_x = Quantity index of export.

$= \frac{P_x}{P_m} \times Q_x$

Single factorial TOT :- (Viner) $T_c . F_x$

F_x = productivity index of export industries. $T_S = \frac{P_x}{P_m} . F_x$

Double factoral terms of trade (Viner)

$T_d = P_x / P_m . F_x / F_m$

Real factoral terms of trade

$T_r = T_S . R_x$

R_x =Disutility per unit of Factors Of Production engaged in country's exports.

Utility TOT →Tu =Tr. U

U = relative utility of imports and domestically forgone commodities. Robinson called it Real TOT.

154. The proposed GST bill will subsume:

(a) Entertainment tax

(b) Value-added tax

(c) Union excise duty

(d) All of the above.

Answer: (d)

Solution: The proposed GST bill will subsume a number of indirect taxes, including entertainment tax, value-added tax, and union excise duty. These taxes will be replaced by a single tax, which will be called the Goods and Services Tax (GST).

The GST is a destination-based tax, which means that the tax is paid in the state where the goods or services are consumed. This is in contrast to the current system, where taxes are paid in the state where the goods or services are produced.

The GST is expected to simplify the tax system and reduce the cost of doing business in India. It is also expected to increase tax revenue for the government.

The GST bill was passed by the Parliament of India in 2017 and was implemented on July 1, 2017.

155. Select the pair of economists, who first gave the canons of taxation and public expenditure:

(a) R. N. Bhargav and R. A. Musgrave

(b) Adam Smith and Findlay Shirras

(c) A. C. Pigou and David Ricardo

(d) A. R. Prest and Ursula K Hicks

Answer: (b)

Solution:

Canons of Taxation:-Given by Adam Smith

Canon of Equality : Burden of tax is equally shared.

Canon of economy :cost of collecting tax should be the minimum

Canon of Certainty :-The contributor should be clear of all the information regarding the time of payment, amount to be paid etc.

Canon of convenience :-People should not face inconvenience while paying taxes.

Canons of Public Expenditure :- given by Findlay Shirras

Canons of Benefit :- It should benefit maximum number of people

Canon of economy :- should not be overspending

Canon of sanction :- It can be done only up to a certain limit without sanction from higher authorities.

Canon of surplus :- Budget should be in balance or surplus but not deficit budget.

156. Following are some of the effects of parallel economy in India:

(A) Loss of revenue to the Government

(B) Greater burden on honest tax-payers

(C) Results in equitable distribution of wealth and income

(D) Encouragement to non-essential items of conspicuous consumption. Find the correct combination from the codes given below:

(a) (A), (B) and (C)

(b) (A), (B) and (D)

(c) (B), (C) and (D)

(d) (A) and (D)

Answer: (b)

Solution: The parallel economy is a part of the economy that is not recorded or regulated by the government. It is also known as the black market or the underground economy. The parallel economy exists in all countries, but it is more prevalent in developing countries like India.

Some of the effects of the parallel economy in India include:

Loss of revenue to the government: The parallel economy results in a loss of revenue to the government because it does not pay taxes. This can lead to a decrease in government spending on essential services, such as education and healthcare.

Greater burden on honest taxpayers: The parallel economy puts a greater burden on honest taxpayers because they have to pay more taxes to compensate for the loss of revenue to the government. This can lead to tax evasion and other forms of avoidance.

Encouragement to non-essential items of conspicuous consumption: The parallel economy can encourage the consumption of non-essential items, such as luxury goods and services. This can lead to inflation and a decrease in the savings rate.

The parallel economy does not result in equitable distribution of wealth and income. In fact, it can lead to increased inequality because it allows wealthy individuals and businesses to avoid paying taxes.

157. Reference period for the Neonatal Mortality Rate in India is:

(a) Three months after birth (b) One month after birth

(c) 28 days after birth (d) None of the above.

Answer: (c)

Solution: The reference period for the Neonatal Mortality Rate (NMR) in India is the first 28 days of life. This is in accordance with the World Health Organization (WHO) definition of the neonatal period. The NMR is a measure of the number of deaths that occur in the first 28 days of life per 1,000 live births.

158. Recently launched "Indradhanush" programme is related with:

(a) Production of medicines

(b) Vaccination against fatal diseases

(c) Multivocational training for adolscent girls.

(d) None of the above.

Answer : (b)

Solution: The recently launched "Indradhanush" programme is related to immunization. It is the fourth phase of the Mission Indradhanush, which was launched in 2014 by the Government of India to improve immunization coverage in the country. The main goal of the programme is to reach all children up to the age of 2 years with all available vaccines, and to ensure that pregnant women are also vaccinated.

The Intensified Mission Indradhanush 4.0 (IMI 4.0) was launched on February 9, 2023, by the Union Minister of Health and Family Welfare, Dr. Mansukh Mandaviya. The programme aims to reach 110 million children and 30 million pregnant women with all available vaccines by the end of 2023.

159. Identify the proper sequence in the traditional econometric methodology of conducting research

(A) Data collection **(B) Policy prescription**

(C) Testing of hypothesis **(D) Formulation of hypothesis**

Choose the correct answer from the options given below

(a) A, B, C, D, (b) A, D, B, C,

(c) D, A, B, C, (d) D, A, C, B,

Answer : (d)

Solution:

Formulation of hypothesis (D): The first step in conducting research is to formulate a hypothesis or a research question that will guide the study.

Data collection (A): After formulating the hypothesis, researchers gather the necessary data through various methods, such as surveys, experiments, or secondary data sources.

Testing of hypothesis (C): Once the data is collected, researchers apply statistical techniques and econometric models to analyze the data and test the formulated hypothesis.

Policy prescription (B): Based on the results obtained from testing the hypothesis, researchers can make policy recommendations or draw conclusions about the relationships between variables.

Therefore, the correct answer is option (d) D, A, C, B.

160. Which one of the following measures of central tendency will be the most appropriate to use if the data relates to rates, proportions and ratios? *(December 2020 and June 2021)*

(a) Arithmetic Mean (b) Geometric Mean,

(c) Harmonic Mean (d) Median

Answer : (b)

Solution:

(a) **Arithmetic Mean:** The Arithmetic Mean is suitable for data that is on an interval or ratio scale and is used to find the average by summing up all the values and dividing by the number of observations. However, it may not be appropriate for rates, proportions, and ratios as they can be influenced by extreme values.

(b) **Geometric Mean:** The Geometric Mean is specifically designed for rates, proportions, and ratios. It is calculated by taking the nth root of the product of all the values, where n is the number of observations. It is useful for finding the average growth rate, compound interest rate, or other multiplicative factors.

(c) **Harmonic Mean:** The Harmonic Mean is suitable for data that involves rates or ratios, particularly when dealing with average rates or speeds. It is calculated by dividing the number of observations by the sum of their reciprocals.

(d) **Median:** The Median is the middle value in a set of ordered data. While it can be used with rates, proportions, and ratios, it may not provide an accurate representation of the average or typical value in such cases.

Therefore, the Geometric Mean is the most appropriate measure of central tendency to use when the data relates to rates, proportions, and ratios.

161. Assuming the probability of a male birth as 0.5, find the chances that a family of 3 children will have two boys and one girl. *(December 2020 and June 2021)*

(a) 1/8 (b) 2/8 (c) 3/8 (d) 4/8

Answer : (c)

Solution: There are 8 possible outcomes for a family of 3 children, all equally likely (if we assume each gender is equally likely). There are 3 ways to have 2 boys and 1 girl:

- BGB
- BBG
- GBB

Therefore, the probability of having 2 boys and 1 girl is 3/8. Here is the calculation:

Probability of 2 boys and 1 girl = (Probability of boy) * (Probability of boy) * (Probability of girl) = 0.5 * 0.5 * 0.5 = 0.125 = 3/8

162. For a firm with the following total cost and demand

$C = 1/3 \times Q^3 - 7Q^2 + 111Q + 50$

$Q = 100 - P$

The profit maximising level of output Q is:

(a) 11 (b) 9

(c) 10 (d) 12

Answer: (a)

Solution:

Profit Maximizing rule

MR = MC

For this find TR first,

Q = 100 - P

P = 100 - Q

$TR = PQ$

$TR = (100 - Q)Q$

$TR = 100Q - Q^2$

New MR = 100 - 2Q

and $TC = 1/3Q^3 - 7Q^2 + 111Q + 50$ (Given)

$MC = 3Q^2/3 - 14Q + 111$

$MR = MC$

$100 - 2Q = Q^2 - 14Q + 111$

$Q^2 - 14Q + 111 + 2Q - 100 = 0$

$Q^2 - 12Q + 11 = 0$

$Q^2 - 11Q - Q + 11 = 0$

$Q (Q - 11) -1 (Q - 11) = 0$

$\boxed{Q = 11,1}$

Now for profit max, slope of MR < Slope of MC

$-2 < 2Q - 14$

Put Q = 1 $\boxed{-2 < -12}$ Not Satisfied

Put Q = 11 $\boxed{-2 < 8}$ Satisfied

$\boxed{\therefore Q = 11}$

163. Given the following total cost and demand functions of a firm, find the price at which profits would be maximised

$C = 5Q^2 + 20Q + 10$

$P = 100 - 3Q$

Where C = Total cost

Q = Output

P = Price

(a) 95 (b) 85

(c) 100 (d) 5

Answer: (b)

Solution:

Profit Max

MR = MC

Find TR first

TR = PQ

= (100-3Q) Q $\boxed{P = 100 - 3Q}$

$TR = 100Q - 3Q^2$

$MR = 100 - 6Q$

$MC = 100 + 2Q$

New MR = MC

$100 - 60 = 10Q + 20$

$- 60 - 10Q = 20 - 100$

$- 16Q = - 80$

$Q = 80/16$

Now $P = 100 -3\ (80/16)$

$= 100 - 3\ (5)$

$= 100 - 15 = 85$

164. Marginal product of CES production function is always

(a) negative
(b) cubic
(c) positive
(d) Square

Answer: (c)

Solution: The marginal product of CES production function is always positive.

The CES production function is a type of production function that is used to model the relationship between inputs and outputs in a production process. The marginal product of a CES production function is the additional output that is produced when one additional unit of input is added to the production process.

The marginal product of a CES production function is always positive because the production function is assumed to be increasing in all inputs. This means that as more and more inputs are added to the production process, the output will also increase.

165. Horizontal merger

(a) is a merger across firms that produces same type of products.
(b) is a merger across firms that produces intermediate and final products.
(c) is a merger across firms that produces both homogenous and non-homogenous products.
(d) is a merger across firms that produces only intermediate products

Answer : (a)

Solution: Horizontal merger is a type of merger that occurs between firms that operate in the same industry. This means that the firms produce the same or similar products. Horizontal mergers are often motivated by the desire to increase market share or to achieve economies of scale.

The other options are incorrect. Horizontal mergers do not necessarily involve firms that produce intermediate and final products, both homogenous and non-homogenous products, or only intermediate products.

166. The spirit of Engel's Law is that with an increase in family income:

(a) Proportion of income spent on luxuries decline.

(b) The savings rate increases.

(c) The proportion of income spent on food declines.

(d) Expenditure on food declines.

Answer: (c)

Solution:

Engel Curve : - Engel Curve describes how household expenditure onparticular group of good or service varies with household income.

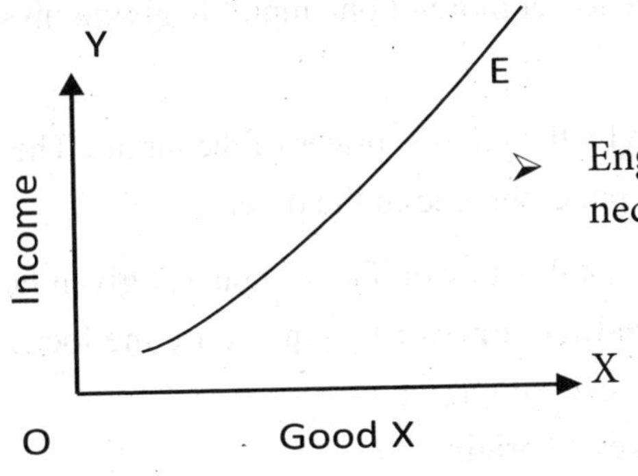

➢ Engel Curve in case of necessities

167. Match List-I with List-II

List-I	List-II
(A) Oligopoly	**(i) Identical price**
(B) Monopoly	**(ii) Price discrimination**
(C) Bilateral monopoly	**(iii) Collective bargaining**
(D) Perfect competition	**(iv) Sales maximisation**

(A) (B) (C) (D)

(a) (iv) (ii) (iii) (i)

(b) (i) (ii) (iii) (iv)

(c) (iv) (iii) (ii) (i)

(d) (ii) (iii) (iv) (i)

Answer : a

Solution:

(A) Oligopoly (iv) Sales maximisation

(B) Monopoly (ii) Price discrimination

(C) Bilateral monopoly (iii) Collective bargaining

(D) Perfect competition (i) Identical price

168. A given total outlay on factor inputs at given factor prices is reflected by

(a) Iso-revenue curve.
(b) Iso-cost curve.
(c) Isoquant.
(d) Production possibility curve

Answer: (b)

Solution: An isocost curve is a line that shows all combinations of inputs that cost the same amount. It is a graph that depicts potential input (labor and capital) combinations that can be acquired at an estimated total cost.

In economics, the isocost curve is used to show the combinations of inputs that a firm can purchase with a given budget. The isocost curve is also used to show the tradeoff between inputs, as the firm can move along the curve to get more of one input by giving up some of the other input.

The slope of the isocost curve is determined by the relative prices of the inputs. The steeper the slope, the higher the relative price of one input compared to the other.

Therefore, the isocost curve reflects a given total outlay on factor inputs at given factor prices.

Isoquants /Equal product curves/Iso- Product curves :-I so quant are the locus of various combinations of inputs producing the same level of output.

Properties : -Down ward sloping and Convex to origin.

Two isoquants never intersect.

Higher isoquant means higher level of production.

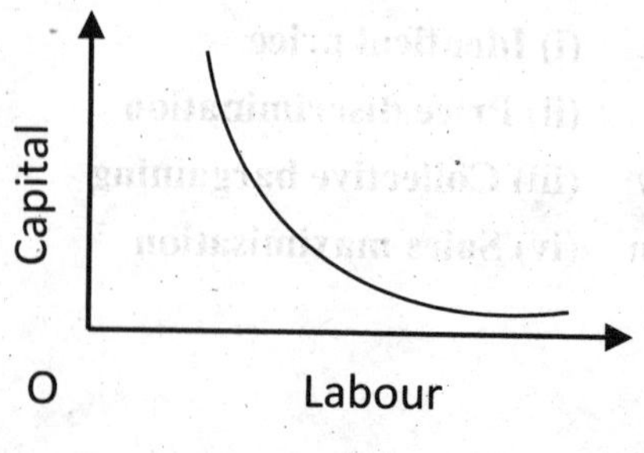

Slope of isoquants: - Marginal rate of Technical substitution [MRTS]

(No. of units of capital gives up to get one unit of labour).

It is Diminishing in nature.

$MRTS_{LK} = MP_L / MP_K$

Multi Product Firm:-

PPC Production possibility frontiers :- Combination of two goods which can be produced given the technology.

ISO – Revenue Line: - It is the locus of points of Combination of two goods produced which generate equal revenue

Producer Equilibrium:-

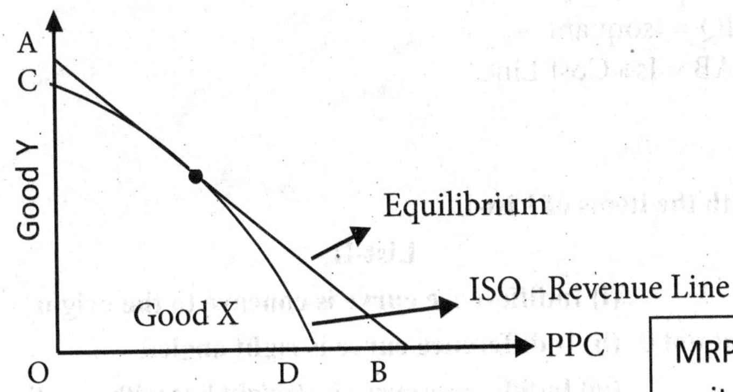

MRPT – Ratio of number of units of a good is sacrificed to produce one more unit of another good.

Slope of PPC is Marginal rate of product transformation (MRPT) whichis increasing.

$$MRPT_{XY} = \frac{MC_X}{MC_Y}$$

$$\underline{\text{Equilibrium}}: - MRPT_{XY} = \frac{P_X}{P_Y}$$

PPC is concave in shape as more and more of one good is produced, factors producing it become less and less productive. Hence more units are sacrificed. Therefore, MRPT is increasing.

For a firm producing single output, equilibrium will occur at the point of tangency of isoquant and the iso cost line.

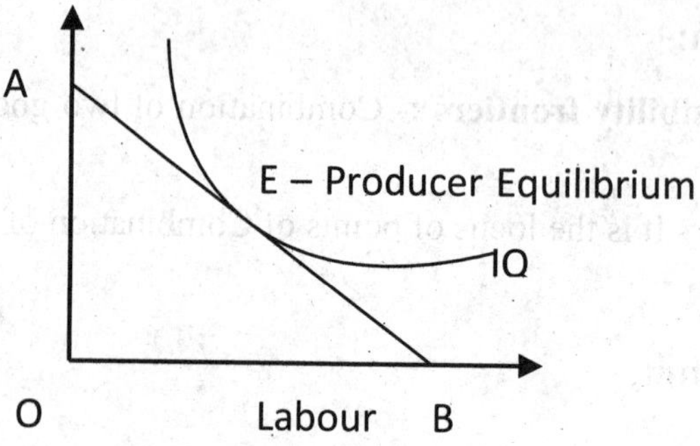

IQ = Isoquant
AB = Iso Cost Line

169. Match items of List-II with the items of List-I.

List-I	List-II
(A) MRSxy = 0	**(i) Indifference curve is concave to the origin**
(B) MRSxy is constant but not 0	**(ii) Indifference curve is right angled**
(C) MRSxy is decreasing	**(iii) Indifference curve is straight line with negative slope**
(D) MRSxy is increasing	**(iv) Indifference curve is convex to the origin**

Codes:

	(A)	(B)	(C)	(D)
(a)	(ii)	(iii)	(iv)	(i)
(b)	(i)	(iii)	(ii)	(iv)
(c)	(i)	(iv)	(ii)	(iii)
(d)	(iv)	(iii)	(i)	(ii)

Answer: a

Solution:

When MRSxy = 0, shape of curve is right angled, and goods are complementary whereas when MRSxy is constant but not 0, goods are substitute ad IC is straight line with negative slope.

Shapes of IC's : -

(a) Substitutes

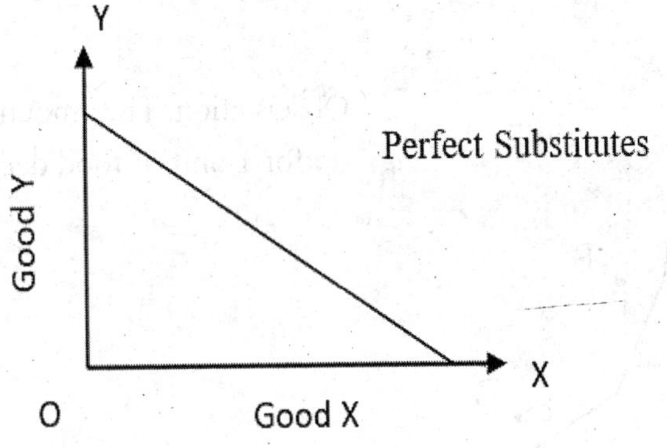

(b)Complements

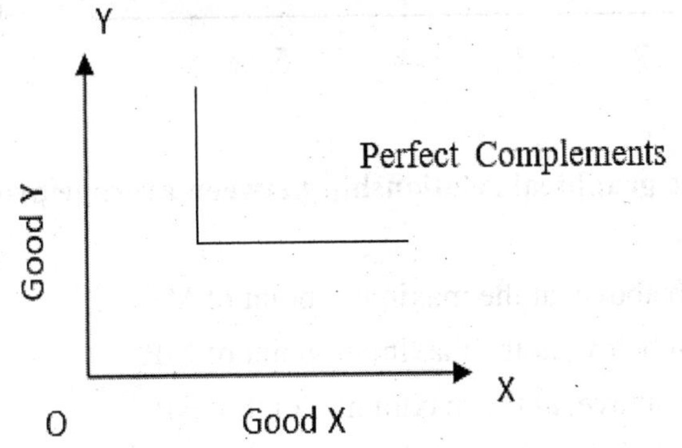

Increasing Marginal Rate Of Substitution

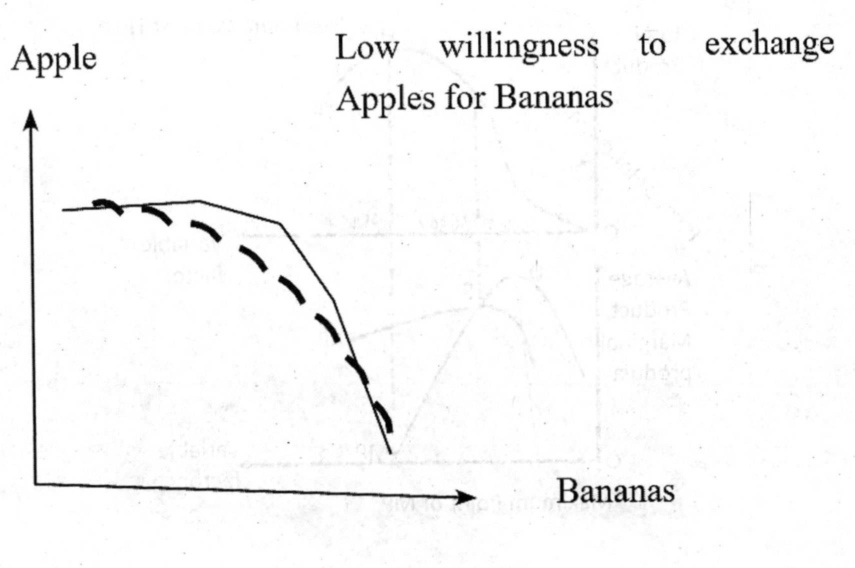

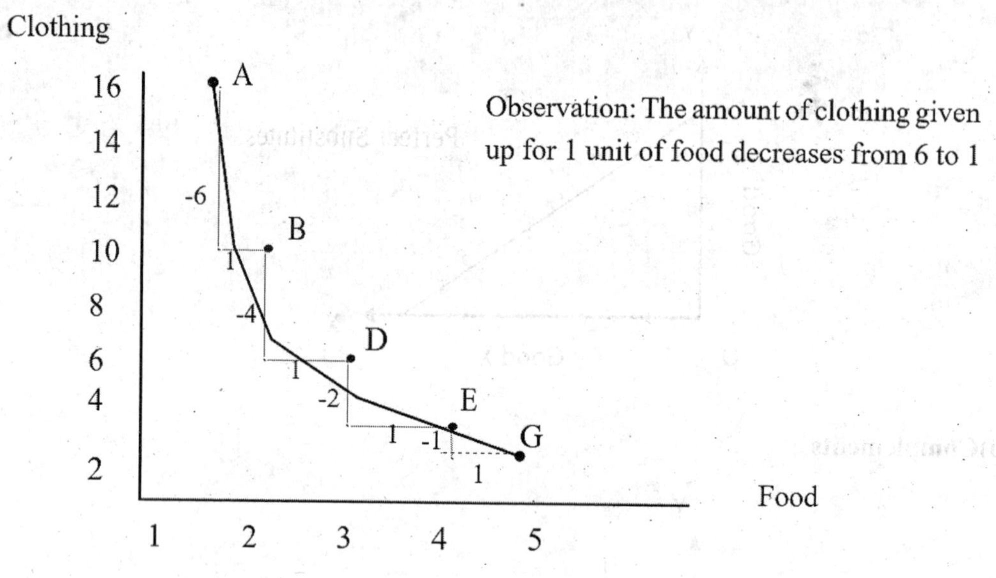

170. What describes the graphical relationship between average product (AP) and marginal product (MP)?

(a) AP cuts MP from above, at the maximum point of MP.

(b) AP cuts MP from below, at the maximum point of MP.

(c) MP cuts AP from above, at the maximum point of AP.

(d) MP cuts AP from below, at the maximum point of AP.

Answer: (c)

Solution:

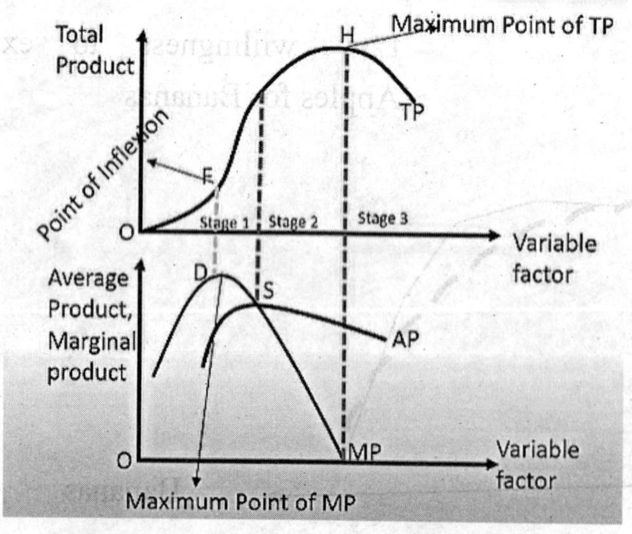

Stage 1:-

Increasing returns to a factor

Under this stage the MP increases, reaches maximum and starts decreasing. This stage ends where the AP reaches maximum.

Reasons:-

1) Indivisibility of factors.
2) Specialisation increases.
3) Fixed factor is effectively utilised.

Stage2:-

Diminishing returns to a factor

Under the stage, MP and AP decrease.

Stage ends where MP becomes zero.

Reasons : -

1) Scarcity and indivisibility of a fixed factor.
2) Imperfect substitutability of factors.

Stage3:-

Negative returns to a factor MP becomes negative TP starts falling.

Reason :-Variable factor is in excess of fixed factor.

Most optimal stage of production is stage 2 where Total product is Maximum.

171. For Giffen good

(a) income elasticity of demand is positive and price effect is positive.
(b) income elasticity of demand is negative and price effect is negative.
(c) income elasticity of demand is negative and price effect is positive.
(d) income elasticity of demand is positive and price effect is negative.

Answer: (c)

Solution: Giffen Goods :- According to Robert Giffen, for Giffen goods there is a positive relation between price and quantity demanded.

Goods	PE	IE	SE
Normal	Negative.	Positive	Negative
Inferior	Negative. (IE<SE)	Negative	Negative
Giffen	Positive. (IE>SE)	Negative	Negative

172. Limit Pricing is also termed as

(a) entry preventive pricing.
(b) entry encouraging pricing.
(c) competition enhancing pricing.
(d) maximum profit generating pricing.

Answer: (a)

Solution: Limit pricing is a pricing strategy that is used by a firm to deter entry into a market. The firm sets a price that is below its profit-maximizing price, but still high enough to prevent new firms from entering the market. This is because if the new firms enter the market, they will not be able to make a profit at the limit price.

Limit pricing is a type of predatory pricing, which is a pricing strategy that is used to drive out competitors. $P_c < P_L < P_m$

More than competitive price and less than monopolist price.

173. Social welfare is

(i) equal to deadweight loss.

(ii)maximum under perfect competition.

(iii) what the consumer is willing to pay minus the cost of production.

(iv) equal to consumer's surplus plus producer's surplus.

(a) Only (i) is true
(b) Only (i) and (ii) are true
(c) (ii), (iii) and (iv) are true
(d) Only (iii) is true

Answer : c

Solution:

1. Deadweight loss refers to the economic inefficiency arising in markets when price distortions, such as monopolies or taxes, prevent the allocation of resources to their most efficient use. It represents a decrease in social welfare compared to a hypothetical ideal state. Therefore, social welfare cannot be equal to deadweight loss.
2. Perfect competition, a theoretical economic model with numerous buyers and sellers, perfect information, and identical goods, tends to achieve allocative efficiency. This means resources are allocated to their most valuable uses, maximizing total economic surplus (consumer surplus + producer surplus). Under perfect competition, the market

price is equal to the marginal cost of production. This means that there is no deadweight loss, and social welfare is maximized.

3. Social welfare is a measure of the well-being of a society. It is typically measured as the sum of consumer surplus and producer surplus.

Consumer surplus is the difference between what a consumer is willing to pay for a good or service and what they actually pay. Producer surplus is the difference between what a producer is willing to sell a good or service for and what they actually sell it for. SW = CP+PS

SW= consumer willing to pay – actually paid + price received - cost of production

Here, the price paid by the consumer is equal to what received by the producer

So, social welfare is = a consumer willing to pay - cost of production.

Hence, from here statements 2, 3 and 4 are correct.

174. In case income elasticity of demand for good Y be zero, the income-consumption curve for good X will be

(a) parallel to horizontal axis.
(b) parallel to vertical axis.
(c) positively sloped straight line.
(d) negatively sloped straight line.

Answer : (a)

Solution: The income elasticity of demand for a good measures the responsiveness of the demand for that good to changes in income. If the income elasticity of demand for a good is zero, then the demand for that good does not change as income changes. This means that the income-consumption curve for that good will be parallel to the horizontal axis.

Income Consumption Curve (ICC) shows the changes in consumer equilibrium with changes in income.

175. Marginal revenue is the when output is?

(a) Change in average revenue, increased
(b) Change in total revenue, increase by one unit
(c) change in average revenue, increased by one unit
(d) change in total revenue increased

Answer: (b)

Solution: Marginal revenue is the change in total revenue that results from the sale of one additional unit of output. So, the answer is a change in total revenue, increased by one unit.

176. When a country has a trade deficit it?

(a) purchases more stocks and bonds from the rest of the world than it sells
(b) purchases more goods from the rest of the world than it sells

(c) sells more goods to the rest of the world than it purchases

(d) sells more stocks and bonds to the rest of the world than it purchases

Answer: (b)

Solution : When a country has a trade deficit, it means that it is importing more goods than it is exporting. So the correct answer is the option that says it purchases more goods from the rest of the world than it sells.

177. When money demand is expressed in a graph with the interest rate on the vertical axis and the quantity of money on the horizontal axis an increase in the interest rate?

(a) None of these answers

(b) decrease the quantity demanded of money

(c) increase the quantity demanded of money

(d) decreases the demand for money

Answer: (b)

Solution: When money demand is expressed in a graph with the interest rate on the vertical axis and the quantity of money on the horizontal axis, an increase in the interest rate will decrease the quantity demanded of money. This is because a higher interest rate means that people have more incentive to hold their money in interest-bearing assets, such as bonds or savings accounts. As a result, they will hold less money in cash, which decreases the quantity demanded of money.

178. The elasticity of pro-poor growth is?.

(a) the percentage increase in the consumption growth of the poor divided by the percentage increase in the consumption growth of the non-poor

(b) the percentage increase in the poor times percentage increase in the non-poor

(c) the percentage increase in the poverty of the poor divided by the percentage increase in the poverty of the non-poor

(d) the percentage increase in the poor people in the Urban divided by the percentage increase in the non-poor in the urban

Answer: (a)

Solution: The elasticity of pro-poor growth is the percentage increase in the consumption growth of the poor divided by the percentage increase in the consumption growth of the non-poor. It is a measure of how much the poor benefit from economic growth relative to the non-poor.

179. In a regressive tax system?

(a) The amount of tax paid increases with income

(b) The marginal rate of tax decrease with more income

(c) The average rate of tax falls as income increase

(d) The average rate of tax is constant as income increases

Answer: (c)

Solution: In a regressive tax system, the average rate of tax falls as income increases. This means that the poor pay a higher proportion of their income in taxes than the rich.

Regressive taxes are often flat taxes, meaning that the tax rate is the same for everyone, regardless of income. This type of tax system is often seen as unfair because it disproportionately burdens the poor.

180. The initial impact of an increase in government spending is to shift.

(a) aggregate demand to the right

(b) aggregate demand to the left

(c) aggregate supply to the right

(d) aggregate supply to the left

Answer: (a)

Solution: The initial impact of an increase in government spending is to shift aggregate demand to the right. This is because government spending is a component of aggregate demand, and an increase in government spending will increase aggregate demand.

181. If your income doubles and the prices of the goods you buy double then your demand for these goods will likely?

(a) increase

(b) not change

(c) decrease

(d) shift

Answer : (b)

Solution: If your income doubles and the prices of the goods you buy double, then your purchasing power will remain the same. This means that you will be able to afford to buy the same amount of goods as you could before. Therefore, your demand for these goods will not change.

182. Which of the following statements regarding taxes is correct?

(a) Most economists believe that in the short run the greatest impact of a change in taxes is on aggregate supply, not aggregate demand

(b) An increase in taxes shifts the aggregate demand curve to the right

(c) A decrease in taxes shifts the aggregate supply curve to the left

(d) A permanent change in taxes has a greater effect on aggregate demand than a temporary change in taxes.

Answer : (d)

Solution: A permanent change in taxes tends to have a greater effect on aggregate demand compared to a temporary change. When taxes are permanently reduced, it provides individuals and businesses with a sustained increase in disposable income. This increase in disposable income leads to higher consumption and investment over the long term, resulting in a larger shift in aggregate demand.

On the other hand, a temporary change in taxes, such as a temporary tax cut or tax credit, may provide a short-term boost to aggregate demand. However, since it is temporary, the effect on spending and investment is often less significant than a permanent change. Individuals and businesses may be less likely to make long-term adjustments to their behavior in response to a temporary tax change.

183. In a regressive tax system?

(a) The amount of tax paid increases with income

(b) The marginal rate of tax decrease with more income

(c) The average rate of tax falls as income increase

(d) The average rate of tax is constant as income increases

Answer: (c)

Solution: In a regressive tax system, the average rate of tax falls as income increases. This means that the poor pay a higher proportion of their income in taxes than the rich.

Regressive taxes are often flat taxes, meaning that the tax rate is the same for everyone, regardless of income. This type of tax system is often seen as unfair because it disproportionately burdens the poor.

184. For Rosentein Rodan a major indivisibility is in?

(a) Supply
(b) infrastructure

(c) agriculture
(d) services

Answer: (b)

Solution: Rosenstein-Rodan's big push theory argues that economic development requires a simultaneous investment in a number of industries, including infrastructure. This is because infrastructure provides a foundation for other industries to grow, and it can be difficult or expensive to build infrastructure piecemeal.

Theory of Big Push:- Given by Rosenstein Rodan in 1943.

The theory talks about indivisibilities generated through external economies which will result from wide scale production and hence cheap raw materials and a wide extent of markets.

1) **Production indivisibilities :**-The theory states that initial capital requirements should be high. Greater level of output would result in decreased cost and thus capital output ratio decreases.
2) **Demand Indivisibilities:**-Investment in a number of ventures at the same time would be profitable. Rodan gave example of shoe making industry. If capital of the country is invested in shoe making industry. All the people will not spend all their income on shoes, but will spend on buying other goods. If no increase in production of other sectors then income of other people has not gone up.They will not be able to buy shoes. Thus shoe making industry will come to a halt
3) **Supply Indivisibilities :**- Usage of saving should be in profitable ventures.

Main elements of theory. a) Government role b) Savings c) Foreign capital d) Foreign trade

185. As the required reserve ratio is decreased the money multiplier?

(a) could either increase or decrease

(b) decrease

(c) increase

(d) remain the same, as long as bank hold no excess reserves

Answer: (c)

Solution: The answer is (c), increase.

The money multiplier is the amount of money that the banking system can create with each dollar of reserves. The required reserve ratio is the percentage of deposits that banks are required to hold in reserve. A lower required reserve ratio means that banks can lend out more of their deposits, which in turn increases the money supply.

So, as the required reserve ratio is decreased, the money multiplier will increase. This is because banks will be able to lend out more of their deposits, which will increase the amount of money in circulation.

186. The opportunity cost of a student

(a) Course fees and rent

(b) A loan from the bank

(c) What the student could have earned in the best job available by not studying

(d) What the student will earn after graduation

Answer: (c)

Solution: what the student could have earned in the best job available by not studying.

Opportunity cost is the value of the next best alternative that is foregone when a choice is made. In the case of a student, the opportunity cost is the best job that the student could have gotten if they had not chosen to study.

187. Sen's welfare theory relies on?

(a) individuals' accomplishments (b) individuals' capabilities

(c) individuals' wealth. (d) individuals' education

Answer: (b)

Solution: Amartya Sen's welfare theory is based on the idea that people should be able to achieve their goals and live a life that they value. This means that welfare is not just about having money or possessions, but also about having the ability to do things that are important to you.

Sen's theory is called the capability approach to welfare. It focuses on the capabilities that people have, rather than on their resources or achievements. This means that two people with the same amount of money or possessions could have different levels of welfare, depending on their capabilities.

For example, a person who is blind may have the same amount of money as a person who is not blind, but the blind person may have fewer capabilities. This is because the blind person may not be able to drive, read, or see the world around them.

Sen's capability approach to welfare is a valuable tool for measuring welfare. It allows us to compare the welfare of people who have different resources or achievements, and it helps us to focus on the things that are important to people's well-being.

188. The role of..............is to direct one nation's savings into investments of another nation?

(a) merchandise trade flows (b) services flows

(c) current account flows (d) capital flows

Answer: (d)

Solution: Capital flows are the movement of money between countries for the purpose of investment. They can be used to finance the purchase of assets, such as stocks, bonds, and real estate. They can also be used to finance the construction of new businesses or infrastructure projects.

Capital flows can help to direct one nation's savings into investments of another nation. This can help to promote economic growth in both countries. For example, if a country has a lot of savings but not enough investment opportunities, capital flows can help to bring those savings to where they are needed.

189. The extra utility from consuming one more unit of a good is called?

(a) Marginal utility (b) Additional utility

(c) Surplus utility (d) Bonus utility

Answer : (a)

Solution: Marginal utility is the additional satisfaction that a consumer gets from consuming one more unit of a good or service. It is the change in total utility that results from consuming one more unit of a good

190. When all of the debit or credit items in the balance of payments are combined?

(a) merchandise imports equal merchandise exports

(b) capital imports equal capital exports

(c) services exports equal services imports

(d) the total surplus or deficit equals zero

Answer: (d)

Solution: The balance of payments is a record of all the economic transactions between a country and the rest of the world. It is divided into two main components: the current account and the capital account. The current account records the flow of goods, services, and income between countries. The capital account records the flow of financial assets between countries.

In theory, the balance of payments should always balance. This means that the total surplus or deficit on the current account should be equal to the total surplus or deficit on the capital account. In practice, however, this is not always the case. There can be temporary imbalances in the balance of payments, but these imbalances should eventually be corrected.

So, when all of the debit or credit items in the balance of payments are combined, the total surplus or deficit should equal zero.

191. Income inequalities are often shown on?

(a) production possibility curve

(b) marginal inequality curve

(c) sen curve

(d) Lorenz curve

Answer : (d)

Solution:

Kuznets hypothesis

→ Size distribution of income was more unequal in LDC's than in DC's. It was in his 1963 study that Kuznets developed his inverted U-shaped hypothesis. He constructed Lorenz curve for DC's and LDC's and derived their Gini Coefficients. It was 0.37 for DC's and 0.44 for LDC's.

The greater this ratio, the more unequal distribution of income i.e. The more the Lorenz curve falls below the 45° line.

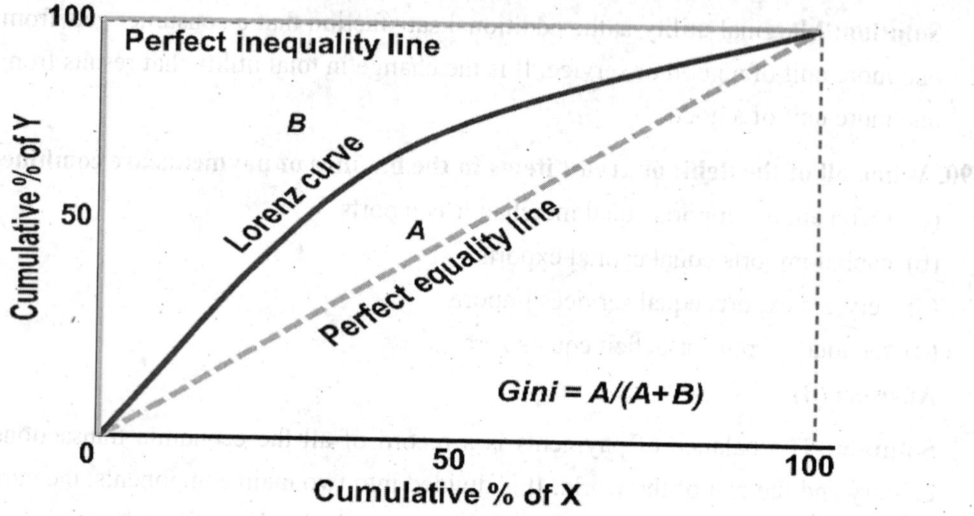

192. Which of the following act as an instrument to help in the borrowing by the government? *(December 2018)*

i. Repo rate

ii. Reverse Repo rate

iii. CRR

iv. SLR

Choose the correct answer from the code given below:

(a) iii & iv

(b) only iv

(c) i & iii

(d) i & iv

Answer - (b)

Solution: SLR is a requirement imposed by the central bank on commercial banks, mandating them to maintain a certain percentage of their deposits as liquid assets, such as government securities. The primary objective of SLR is to ensure that commercial banks have enough liquid assets to meet their obligations in case there is a sudden surge in withdrawal demands.

To fund its expenses, the government utilizes a method of borrowing that involves issuing treasury bills and other government securities, which are made available for purchase by both individuals and institutions through commercial banks. By selling these securities, the government is able to raise the necessary funds to support its expenditures.

193. Consider the following statements

i. Minimum support price (MSP) policy of India covers only wheat, paddy and coarse cereals

ii. Minimum Support Price (MSP) for Grade A paddy is always higher than that of the

common paddy. *(December 2018)*

Choose the correct answer from the code given below:

Code:

(a) Both i & ii (b) Only i

(c) Only ii (d) Neither i nor ii

Answer - (c)

Solution: Statement i is incorrect. The MSP policy of India covers a wider range of crops, including wheat, paddy, coarse cereals, pulses, oilseeds, and sugarcane.

Statement ii is correct. The MSP for Grade A paddy is always higher than that of the common paddy. This is because Grade A paddy is of a higher quality and has a higher market value.

194. On which of the following do Keynesians and Monetarists agree? *(December 2018)*

(a) When there is recessionary gap, flexible wages will retrieve the labour market to equilibrium quickly

(b) The most important cause of demand shock is changes in supply

(c) Output deviates at times from the potential output because of demand shocks

(d) The demand for money is interest elastic

Answer - (d)

Solution: Keynesians and Monetarists agree that the demand for money is interest elastic. This means that an increase in interest rates will lead to a decrease in the demand for money.

195. Which one of the statements about Pareto optimality is incorrect? *(December 2018)*

(a) Consumers maximize their satisfaction

(b) There is perfect competition in the factor and commodity market

(c) Consumers have cardinal utility functions

(d) All the factors are used in production of all the commodities

Answer - (c)

Solution: It is an ordinal measure of utility.

196. Which of the following will result in the crowding effect in the economy?

i. Public borrowings to finance spending on infrastructure

ii. Public borrowings to finance spending on salaries and wages

iii. Public borrowings to finance spending on health and education

iv. Public borrowings to finance spending on skill development

(December 2018)

Choose the correct answer from the code given below:

(a) i & ii
(b) iii & iv
(c) i, ii & iii
(d) i, iii & iv

Answer - (d)

Solution: Crowding out effect :-Reduction in private expenditure caused by an increase in government expenditure through deficit budget.

Government expenditure ↑ AD ↑ rate of interest ↑ private investment ↓

197. The concept of Universal Banking in India was recommended by which of the following committee? *(December 2018)*

(a) Y H Malegam committee
(b) S Padmanabhan committee
(c) R H Khan committee
(d) Abid Hussain committee

Answer - (c)

Solution: The Khan Working Group was set up by the Reserve Bank of India (RBI) in 1995 to review the financial system in India. The group recommended that the concept of universal banking should be introduced in India. This would allow banks to undertake a wider range of financial activities, such as insurance and investment banking.

198. Consider the following diagram and the statements *(December 2018)*

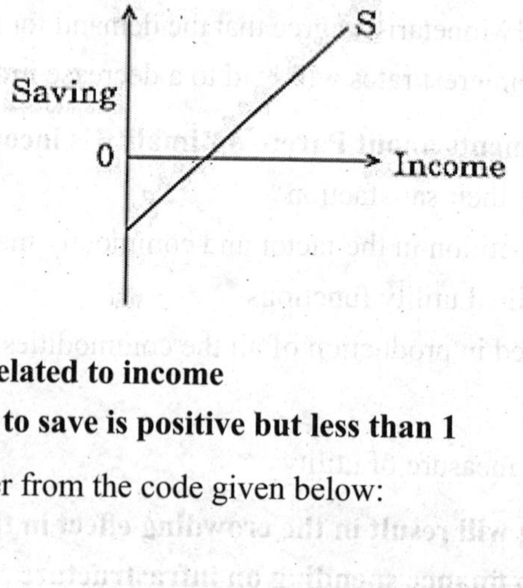

i. Saving is positively related to income

ii. Marginal propensity to save is positive but less than 1

Choose the correct answer from the code given below:

Code:

(a) Both i & ii
(b) Neither i & ii
(c) Only i
(d) Only ii

Answer – (a)

Solution: Saving is positively related to income. This means that as income increases, so does saving. This is because people have more money to save when their income increases.

Marginal propensity to save is positive but less than 1. This means that when income increases, the amount of income that is saved increases, but at a slower rate. This is because people tend to spend some of their increased income on consumption, and only save the rest.

MPS+MPC=1

The marginal propensity to save (MPS) is the proportion of an increase in income that is saved. It is calculated as the change in saving divided by the change in income.

199. In an economy with a linear homogeneous Cobb Douglas production function, the share of capital and labour in total output are respectively, 40% and 60%. The capital stock and labour force are growing, respectively at 8% and 3% per annum. If the rate of growth of output is recorded as 7% per annum, then the rate of growth of Total Factor Productivity will be *(December 2018)*

(a) 2%
(b) 10%
(c) 4%
(d) 11%

Answer – (a)

Solution:

$Q = AL^{\alpha}K^{\beta}$

$7 = A(3)^{0.6}(8)^{0.4}$

$\log_e 7 = \log_e A + 0.6\log_e 3 + 0.4\log_e 8$

$7 = A + 0.6*3 + 0.4*8$

$7 = A + 1.8 + 3.2$

$7 = A + 5$

$A = 7-5$

$\mathbf{A = 2}$

200. Which of the following is not a macroeconomic challenge before Indian Economy as of now? *(December 2018)*

(a). Widening current account deficit
(b) Rising protectionism in the world
(c) High imports of gold
(d) Depreciation of Indian rupee

Answer – (c)

201. Which of the following are the objectives of the Commission for Agricultural costs and prices (CACP)? *(December 2018)*

i. To ensure meaningful real income levels to the farmers

ii. To stabilize agricultural prices

iii. To protect the interest of the consumers

Choose the correct answer from the code given below:

Code:

(a) All of the above (b) ii & iii

(c) i & iii (d) i & ii

Answer - (a)

Solution: The Commission for Agricultural Costs and Prices (CACP) is an autonomous body under the Ministry of Agriculture, Government of India. It was established in 1965 to advise the government on agricultural prices and costs.

The objectives of the CACP are to:

- Assure fair and remunerative prices to farmers.
- Stabilize agricultural prices.
- Protect the interests of consumers.
- Promote efficient use of resources.
- Induce technological change.

202. According to the New classical economics, Real Business Cycles are the result of which of the following? *(December 2018)*

i. Innovations

ii. Bad weather

iii. Tax policy

iv. Debt policy

Choose the correct answer from the code given below:

(a) i & ii (b) ii & iv

(c) iii & iv (d) i & iii

Answer - (a)

Solution: Real business cycles (RBC) are a theory of economic fluctuations that emphasizes the role of real shocks, such as technological shocks, in causing economic fluctuations. RBC theory is a subset of new classical economics, which is a school of thought in macroeconomics that emphasizes the role of rational expectations in economic decision-making.

According to RBC theory, real shocks are exogenous, meaning that they are not caused by economic policy. This means that tax policy and debt policy do not play a role in causing real business cycles. However, innovations and bad weather can play a role in causing real business cycles.

203. Who amongst the following economists treated nature to be niggardly? *(December 2018)*

i. J S Mill

ii. David Ricardo

iii. Karl Marx

iv. Thomas Robert Malthus

Choose the correct answer from the code given below:

(a) iii & iv (b) i, ii & iii

(c) ii & iii (d) ii & iv

Answer - (d)

Solution: David Ricardo and Thomas Robert Malthus treated nature as niggardly. While Malthus believed that nature's resources were limited and would lead to scarcity, Ricardo, in his theory of rent, emphasized that as the population increased and more land was brought into cultivation, diminishing returns would occur, indicating a limited capacity of nature to provide abundant resources.

204. Why are indirect taxes are regressive? *(December 2018)*

(a) None of the above are correct

(b) They are charged at higher rates than direct tax

(c) They are charged at the same rate for all income groups

(d) Both above are correct

Answer – (c)

Solution: Indirect taxes are regressive because they are charged at the same rate for all income groups. This means that a poor person who spends a large proportion of their income on consumption will pay a higher proportion of their income in indirect taxes than a rich person who spends a smaller proportion of their income on consumption.

205. According to Bent Hansen which amongst the following were treated as factors enhancing effective demand? *(December 2018)*

i. Public expenditure

ii. Rising population

iii. Banking and financial system

Choose the correct answer from the code given below:

(a) i & ii (b) i, ii & iii

(c) ii & iii (d) i & iii

Answer - (a)

Solution: Bent Hansen was a Danish economist who is known for his work on inflation. He argued that inflation can be caused by a number of factors, including excess demand, cost-push, and structural factors. Hansen also argued that the banking and financial system can play a role in exacerbating inflation.

However, Hansen also argued that public expenditure and rising population can be factors that enhance effective demand. Effective demand is the amount of goods and services that people are willing and able to buy. When effective demand is high, it can lead to economic growth.

Therefore, according to Bent Hansen, public expenditure and rising population are two factors that can enhance effective demand.

206. Match the List I with List II and choose the correct answer from the code given below

List I	List II
(a) absorptive capacity of capital	**i. M Kalecki**
(b) technological dualism	**ii. A O Hirschman**
(c) physical quality of life index	**iii. D Morris**
(d) permissive and compulsive sequence of expanding industries.	**iv. B Higgins**

(December 2018)

Codes:

(a) a- ii, b- iv, c-iii, d-i (b) a-I, b-iv, c-iii, d-ii

(c) a-iv, b-iii, c-ii, d-i (d) a-i, b-ii, c-iii, d-iv

Answer - (b)

Solution:

- Absorptive capacity pertains to a company's ability to effectively utilize external knowledge for creating value, and it is influenced by firm-specific investments, particularly past relevant R&D efforts. M Kalecki was a Polish economist who developed the theory of effective demand. He argued that the level of economic activity is determined by the level of effective demand, which is the sum of planned investment and consumption.
- Technological dualism, as proposed by Benjamin Higgins, explains unemployment in developing economies, where both advanced and traditional sectors coexist.
- The Physical Quality of Life Index (PQLI) developed by M. D. Morris in the 1970s assesses individuals' well-being based on indicators such as literacy rates, infant mortality, and life expectancy.

- Hirschman's perspective suggests that growth driven by excess available capacity allows for orderly development, while growth driven by shortages leads to a disorderly and compelled sequence of events.

207. Historically the terms of trade of the developing countries have been unfavorable due to the fact that when income in developed countries rises, the demand for primary goods declines because *(December 2018)*

(a) income elasticity of demand for primary goods is high

(b) income elasticity of demand for primary goods is low

(c) income elasticity of demand for primary goods is zero

(d) price elasticity of demand for primary goods is high

Answer - (b)

Solution: The income elasticity of demand measures how much the demand for a good or service changes when income changes. A low income elasticity of demand means that the demand for a good or service does not change much when income changes.

When income in developed countries rises, the demand for primary goods does not rise as much. This is because consumers in developed countries can afford to buy more of a variety of goods, including manufactured goods. This leads to a decline in the terms of trade for developing countries, which export primary goods.

Perbisch - singer hypothesis (1958):-It states that there will be a long term deterioration of TOT in developing countries due to long-term decline in the prices of primary goods which were exported by developing countries in comparison to the prices of manufactured goods imported by the developing countries.

208. The National Rural Health Mission was launched in the year *(December 2018)*

(a) 1991 (b) 1998 (c) 2005 (d) 2009

Answer - (c)

Solution: The National Rural Health Mission (NRHM) was launched in India on 12 April 2005. It was a government initiative to provide accessible, affordable, and quality health care to the rural population, especially the vulnerable groups. The NRHM was merged with the National Urban Health Mission (NUHM) in 2013 to form the National Health Mission (NHM).

The NRHM had a number of goals, including:

- Reducing maternal and child mortality
- Improving access to essential drugs and diagnostics
- Strengthening the public health infrastructure

- Promoting community participation in health care

The NRHM was a significant step forward in the government's efforts to improve the health of the rural population. It has helped to improve access to health care for millions of people, and has made a significant contribution to reducing maternal and child mortality.

209. If for the constant elasticity of substitution production function, the value of the substitution parameter is -1, the elasticity of substitution will be *(December 2018)*

(a) Indeterminate (b) Infinite

(c) Zero (d) Unity

Answer - (b)

Solution:

CES Production Function : - 1961 Arrow, Minhas, Chenery, Solow

$$Q = \gamma\left[\alpha L^{-\beta} + (1-\alpha)K^{-\beta}\right]^{-\frac{1}{\beta}}$$

γ = Coeff. Of Technical Efficiency.

α = Distribution Parameter.

β = Substitution Parameter.

$$E_S = \frac{1}{1+\beta}$$

E_s= 1/1+(p)

=1/1+(-1)

=1/0

= ∞

210. The statements, 'Too much money chasing too few goods' is based on which of the following theoretical concepts? *(December 2018)*

(a) Real balance effects

(b) Inventory theoretic approach to the demand for money

(c) Quantity theory of prices

(d) Quantity theory of money

Answer - (d)

Solution: The statement "Too much money chasing too few goods" is based on the quantity theory of money. The quantity theory of money states that the price level is directly proportional to the money supply. This means that if the money supply increases, the price level will increase, and vice versa.

The quantity theory of money is based on the idea that the demand for money is proportional to the level of economic activity. This means that when the economy is growing, the demand for money will increase, and when the economy is shrinking, the demand for money will decrease.

If the money supply increases but the demand for money does not increase, then there will be too much money chasing too few goods. This will lead to inflation, as people will bid up the prices of goods and services in order to get their hands on the limited supply of goods. Therefore, the correct answer is 4.

211. Given below are two statements, one labeled as assertion (A) and the other labeled as Reason (R). read the statements and choose the correct answer using the code given below. *(December 2018)*

Assertion (A): In an oligopolistic market, there is price rigidity

Reason(R): Rival firms match price decrease but no price increase

Code:

(a) Both A and R are true, and R is the correct explanation of A

(b) A is false but R is true

(c) A is true but R is false

(d) Both A and R are true, but R is not the correct explanation of A

Answer – (a)

Solution:

Kinked Demand Curve:-Sweezy 1939

If a firm raises price, then others will not rise their prices. If a firm reduces price, others will also reduce it.

- ✧ Prices and quantities are rigid at Kink
- ✧ Decline in costs; keep the prices stable but the gap in elasticities increase. As a result, the break in MR curve increases.
- ✧ Decline in demand keep the prices stable.
- ✧ Due to kink in demand curve, MR is discontinuous.
- ✧ Discontinuity of MR implies the range within costs may change with out affecting equilibrium price and quantity.

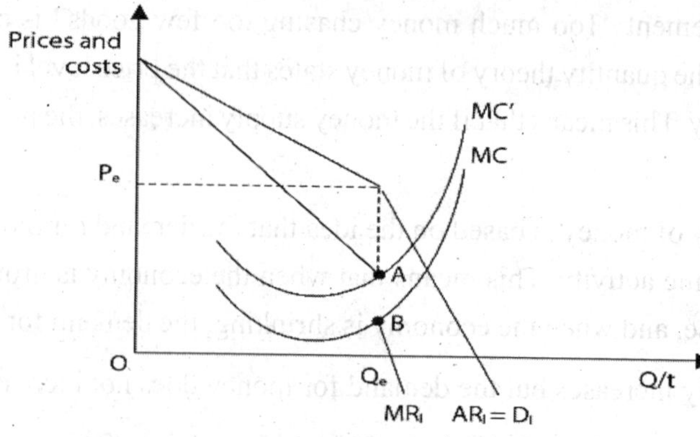

212. Given below are two statements, one labeled as assertion (A) and the other labeled as Reason (R). read the statements and choose the correct answer using the code given below.

Assertion (A): In the P.N. Rosenstein Rodan model the positive role of indivisibilities in production has been analysed

Reason(R): Removal of indivisibilities leads to constant returns to scale in production

(December 2018)

Code:

(a) A is true but R is false

(b) A is false but R is true

(c) Both A and R are true, and R is the correct explanation of A

(d) Both A and R are true, but R is not the correct explanation of A

Answer – (a)

Solution: Rosenstein-Rodan's big push theory argues that economic development requires a simultaneous investment in a number of industries, including infrastructure. This is because infrastructure provides a foundation for other industries to grow, and it can be difficult or expensive to build infrastructure piecemeal.

Theory of Big Push:- Given by Rosenstein Rodan in 1943.

The theory talks about indivisibilities generated through external economies which will result from wide scale production and hence cheap raw materials and a wide extent of markets.

1) **Production indivisibilities** :-The theory states that initial capital requirements should be high. Greater level of output would result in decreased cost and thus capital output ratio decreases.

2) **Demand Indivisibilities:**-Investment in a number of ventures at the same time would be profitable. Rodan gave example of shoe making industry. If capital of the country is

invested in shoe making industry. All the people will not spend all their income on shoes, but will spend on buying other goods. If no increase in production of other sectors then income of other people has not gone up. They will not be able to buy shoes. Thus, shoe making industry will come to a halt

3) **Supply Indivisibilities :-** Usage of saving should be in profitable ventures.

Main elements of theory. a) Government role b) Savings c) Foreign capital d) Foreign trade

The reason states that: Removal of indivisibilities leads to constant returns to scale in production Indivisibilities refer to situations where certain inputs or factors of production cannot be easily divided or scaled down without significantly impacting the production process's efficiency. For instance, specialized machinery might be designed to work optimally at a certain scale, and reducing that scale could lead to inefficiencies.

Removing or reducing indivisibilities can have different effects on returns to scale depending on the specific circumstances. If the removal of indivisibilities allows for better flexibility in adjusting inputs and achieving economies of scale, it might lead to increasing returns to scale. On the other hand, if the removal of indivisibilities eliminates specialized advantages at larger scales, it might lead to constant or even decreasing returns to scale.

213. Given below are two statements, one labeled as assertion (A) and the other labeled as Reason (R). Read the statements and choose the correct answer using the code given below. *(December 2018)*

Assertion(A): a progressive income tax is based on equi-marginal sacrifice

Reason(R): Higher the income, lower will be the marginal utility of money for the tax payer

(a) A is false but R is true

(b) Both A and R are true, but R is not the correct explanation of A

(c) Both A and R are true, and R is the correct explanation of A.

(d) A is true but R is false

Answer - (b)

Solution: Assertion (A) states that a progressive income tax is based on equi-marginal sacrifice. This means that the tax rate should be higher for people with higher incomes, as they can afford to pay more in taxes without experiencing as much of a loss of utility.

Reason (R) states that the marginal utility of money decreases as income increases. This means that the additional utility that a person gets from an extra unit of money decreases as their income increases.

The reason R is not the correct explanation of assertion A is because it does not explain why a progressive income tax is based on equi-marginal sacrifice. The correct explanation is that the marginal utility of money decreases as income increases. This means that a higher tax rate will have a smaller impact on the utility of a person with a higher income than it will on the utility of a person with a lower income.

214. Below are two statements, one labeled as assertion (A) and the other labeled as Reason (R). read the statements and choose the correct answer using the code given below.

(December 2018)

Assertion(A): India is a service sector driven economy

Reason(R): Share of the service sector in total employment is highest

(a) A is true but R is false

(b) A is false but R is true

(c) Both A and R are true, but R is not the correct explanation of A

(d) Both A and R are true, and R is the correct explanation of A

Answer – (a)

Solution: Service sector has highest share in GDP of India and agriculture sector has highest share in employment.

215. Below are two statements, one labeled as assertion (A) and the other labeled as Reason (R). read the statements and choose the correct answer using the code given below. Assertion(A): Business cycles according to new classical economics are monetary in nature Reason(R): These are the results of the fall in the real wage rates

(December 2018)

(a) A is false but R is true

(b) Both A and R are true, but R is not the correct explanation of A

(c) A is true but R is false

(d) Both A and R are true, and R is the correct explanation of A

Answer - (a)

Solution: Assertion (A) states that business cycles according to new classical economics are monetary in nature. This means that business cycles are caused by changes in the money supply. Reason (R) states that these are the results of the fall in the real wage rates. This means that business cycles are caused by changes in the real wage rate, which is the wage rate adjusted for inflation.

The New Classical Economics school of thought argues that business cycles are not caused by monetary factors, but by real factors such as changes in technology, productivity, and preferences. They argue that people and businesses have rational expectations and change their behavior in response to knowledge, including the expected effects of governmental policy.

Therefore, assertion A is false, but reason R is true. Business cycles are not caused by monetary factors in the New Classical Economics framework.

216. In the context of simultaneous equations econometric models, consider the following statements *(December 2018)*

i. Both order and rank conditions for identification are to be satisfied before estimation

ii. Order conditions is a necessary but not a sufficient condition of identification

iii. Two stage least squares method is suitable for over identified equations

Which of the above statements is/are correct?

Choose the correct answer from the codes below:

(a) Only ii (b) i & iii (c) i, ii & iii (d) Only i

Answer – (c)

Solution: The order conditions for identification are a necessary but not sufficient condition for identification. This means that if the order conditions are not satisfied, then the equation is not identified, but if the order conditions are satisfied, then the equation may or may not be identified.

The rank conditions are a sufficient condition for identification, which means that if the rank conditions are satisfied, then the equation is identified.

Two stage least squares (2SLS) method is suitable for over identified equations, but it can also be used for just identified.

Order Conditions

K - M	G -1
K - M< G -1	Underidentified
K - M = G -1	just identified
K - M > G -1	Over identified

K = Total no. of variables

M = No. of endogeneous and exogenous variables in a particular condition.

G = Total no. of equations in a model.

For eg.

$Y1 = \alpha0 + \alpha1y2 + \alpha3y3 + \alpha4x1 + \alpha5x2 + u1$

$Y2 = \beta0 + \beta1y3 + \beta2y1 + \beta2x2 + u2$

$Y3 = \gamma0 + \gamma1x1 + \gamma2x2 + \gamma3x3 + u3$

According to order condition, the first eq. is

a) Unidentified b) Exact identified c) Over identified

K = (y 1, y2 , y3, x1,x2, x3) = 6

M = (y1,y2,y3,x1,x2) = 5

G = 3

K - M G - 1

6 - 5 3 – 1

1 < 2] – Unidentified

Methods of SEM

(a) Reduced form method or Indirect least square

- Appropriate for exactly identified equations.

(b) Instrumental variables

- Applied at over identified equations

(c) Two Stage least square

- Applied in just identified and over identified equations.

217. In a two variable regression, the correlation coefficient between dependent and independent variables Y and X is 0.7. what is the percentage of variations in Y explained by X?

(December 2018)

(a) 49% (b) 7% (c) 0.7% (d) 70%

Answer - (a)

Solution: The percentage of variations in Y explained by X can be determined by squaring the correlation coefficient (r) and multiplying by 100.

In this case, the correlation coefficient (r) between Y and X is given as 0.7.

Percentage of variations explained = $(r^2) * 100$

$= (0.7^2) * 100$

$= 0.49 * 100$

= 49%

218. A series of index numbers is given as follows

Year :	2014	2015	2016
Index number:	100	120	126

If the base year is shifted to 2015 the value of index number in the year 2016, in the new series will be *(December 2018)*

(a) 151.2 (b) 106 (c) 95.2 (d) 105

Answer - (d)

Solution: To calculate the value of the index number in the year 2016 in the new series, where the base year is shifted to 2015, we need to adjust the index numbers accordingly.

In the original series, the base year is 2014, and the index number for 2016 is given as 126. To find the corresponding value in the new series, we need to adjust it based on the new base year of 2015.

To do this, we divide the index number for 2016 in the original series (126) by the index number for 2015 in the original series (120) and multiply it by 100, as the base year in the new series is set to 2015.

(126 / 120) * 100 = 105

Therefore, the value of the index number in the year 2016 in the new series will be 105.

219. By autocorrelation we mean that *(December 2018)*

(a) The square of the residuals of a regression model are not equally spread

(b) The variance of the residuals of a regression model is not constant for all observations

(c) The residuals of a regression model are related with one more of the regressors

(d) The residuals of a regression models are not independent

Answer - (d)

Solution:

Autocorrelation

Correlation between successive values of same variable. In other words, correlation between different values of disturbance term is zero. i.e. E(uiuj) = 0. If this assumption is violated then there is Autocorrelation.

Consequences: Variance of OLS estimates becomes large but remain unbiased. Invalid test of significance and misleading confidence internals.

Tests :

1. Durbin - watson Test (for small samples) d =2[1-ê]

d = d - w statistic

ê = coeff. Of Autocorrelation

d lies between 0 to 4

2. Non - Neuman Ratio Test (for large samples)

220. Consider the following statements about a time series of annual observations on sales of a firm for ten years *(December 2018)*

i. The series will have seasonal variations

ii. The series will have a secular trend

iii. The series will have cyclic variations

Choose the correct answer from the codes given below:

(a) ii & iii (b) i, ii & iii

(c) i & iii (d) i & ii

Answer - (d)

Solution: A time series of annual observations on sales of a firm for ten years will have seasonal variations and secular trend.

Seasonal variations are regular and predictable patterns that repeat themselves within a year, such as higher sales during the holiday season.

Secular trend is a long-term movement in the data, such as an upward or downward trend in sales over the past ten years.

Cyclical variations, on the other hand, are irregular and unpredictable patterns that may occur over a period of years. It is unlikely that a time series of annual observations will have cyclical variations, unless the firm is cyclically affected by external factors such as the economy.

221. Harrod' s growth model is given as under *(DECEMBER 2019)*

St = aYt **0 < a < 1**

It = b(Yt – Yt-1) **b>0**

St = It

In the model, growth condition is

(a) b/(b-a) > 0 (b) b/(b-a) < 0

(c) a/b-a > 0 (d) a/b-a < 0

Answer – (A)

Solution:

St = It

$\alpha Y_t = \beta (Y_t - Y_{t-1})$

$\alpha Y_t = \beta Y_t - \beta Y_{t-1}$

$\beta Y_{t-1} = \beta Y_t - \alpha Y_t$

$\beta Y_{t-1} = Y_t (\beta - \alpha)$

$\frac{\beta}{\beta-\alpha} (Y_{t-1}) = Y_t$

$\left[\frac{\beta}{\beta-\alpha}\right]$ should be positive for economic growth

222. A monopolist faces a linear demand curve p=100-4q, while his cost functions is C= 50+20q. *(December 2018)*

The profit maximizing output for this monopolist is

(a) 20 (b) 5 (c) 40 (d) 10

Answer – (d)

Solution:

For Profit Maximisation

MR = MC

now, TR = PQ

=(100 - 4Q) Q

$TR = 100Q - 4Q^2$

MR = 100 - 8Q

MC = 20

Now

100 - 8Q =20

$\frac{80}{8} = Q$

$\boxed{10 = Q}$

2nd Condition of profit max. is slope of MR should be less than slope of MC i.e.

MR = 100 - 8Q

= - 8 $\boxed{-8 < 0}$

223. A box contains 10 bulbs, 4 of which are defective. If 3 of the bulbs are drawn randomly without replacement what is the probability that all 3 bulbs are defective.

(December 2018)

(a) 8/10 (b) 8/4

(c) 4/10 (d) 1/30

Answer - (d)

Solution:

$$\frac{4c_3}{10c_3}$$

$$\frac{\frac{4\times3\times2}{3\times2\times1}}{\frac{10\times9\times8}{1\times2\times3}}$$

$$\frac{24}{720}$$

$$=\frac{1}{30}$$

224. The price elasticity of demand for a good with the demand function q = kpr, (where p is the price, q is the quantity demanded, k and r are positive constants) is

(December 2018)

(a) 1

(b) R

(c) Not constant as the function is non linear

(d) 1/r

Answer: (a)

Solution:

With the demand function q= kpr, where p is the price, q is the quantity demanded, and k and r are positive constants.

$$\text{Price elasticity of demand} = \frac{\%\Delta in\text{QD}}{\%\Delta in\text{P}}$$

To find the percentage change in quantity demanded, we differentiate the demand function with respect to price p, and then multiply it by the price and quantity demanded:

dq/dp=kr

Now, we'll find the percentage change in quantity demanded by multiplying the derivative by p/q

$$\%\Delta \text{ in QD} = \frac{dq}{dp} \times \frac{p}{q}$$

$$\%\Delta \text{ in QD} = kr \times \frac{p}{kpr}$$

$$\%\Delta \text{ in QD} = r \times \frac{1}{r} = 1$$

Thus, the price elasticity of demand for the given demand function is 1, indicating unitary elasticity, meaning a 1% change in price leads to a 1% change in quantity demanded. This implies that the demand for the good is perfectly elastic.

225. Though two time series are individually non stationary, the linear combination is stationary. This is an example of *(December 2018)*

(a) Random walk
(b) Cointegration
(c) Trend stationarity
(d) Spurious regression

Answer - (b)

Solution: Cointegration is a statistical property of a collection of time series variables. It occurs when two or more nonstationary time series:

- Have a long-run equilibrium.
- Move together in such a way that their linear combination results in a stationary time series.
- Share an underlying common stochastic trend.

In other words, cointegration means that even though two time series may be individually nonstationary, they may still be related to each other in a meaningful way. This relationship can be captured by a linear combination of the two series, which will be stationary.

Random walk is a stochastic process that is characterized by the fact that its future values cannot be predicted from its past values. Trend stationarity means that a time series has a constant trend, but its variance may change over time. Spurious regression is a regression model that appears to be significant, but is actually not due to the presence of a spurious correlation between the independent and dependent variables.

226. For the diagram given below which of the following is correct in terms of derivatives? *(December 2018)*

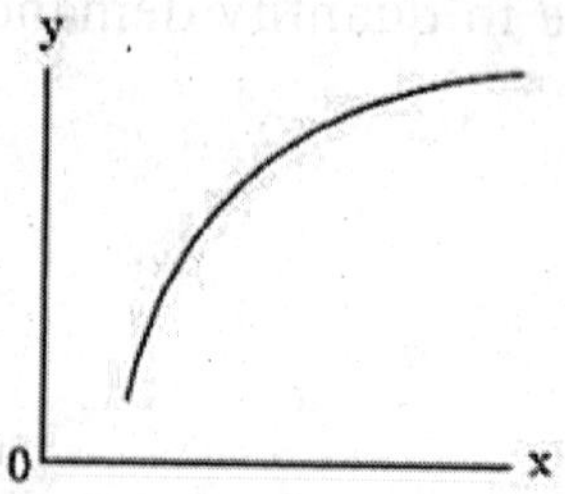

1. $\frac{dy}{dx} > 0, \frac{d^2y}{dx^2} > 0$

2. $\frac{dy}{dx} < 0, \frac{d^2y}{dx^2} < 0$

3. $\frac{dy}{dx} < 0, \frac{d^2y}{dx^2} > 0$

4. $\frac{dy}{dx} > 0, \frac{d^2y}{dx^2} < 0$

Answer – (d)
Solution:

For maxima second derivative is negative and for minima second derivative is positive

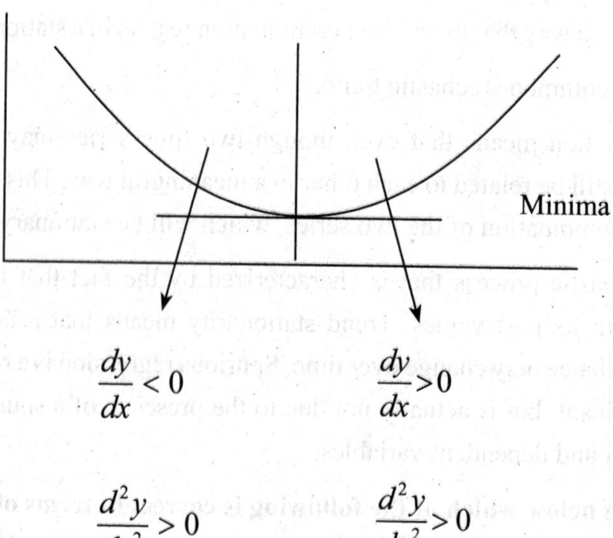

Maxima

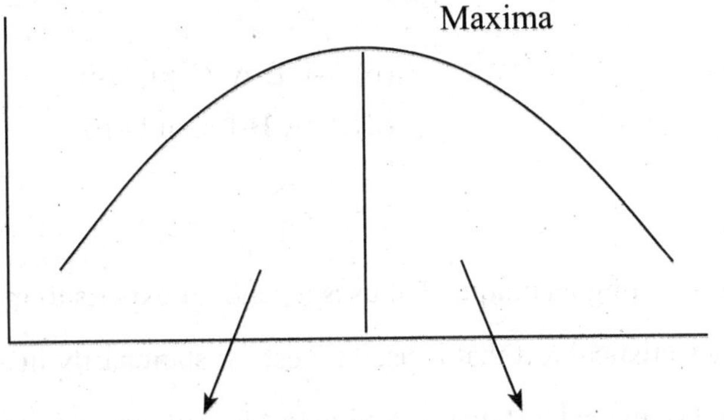

$$\frac{dy}{dx}>0 \qquad \frac{dy}{dx}<0$$

(as slope is -ve)

$$\frac{d^2y}{dx^2}<0 \qquad \frac{d^2y}{dx^2}<0$$

(as there is maxima)

227. If demand for a consumer is given by the function p =27-3x-x2 (where x= quantity demanded, p = price), the consumers surplus at x = 3 is *(December 2018)*

(a) 50.5 (b) 49.5

(c) 31.5 (d) 32.5

Answer - (c)

Solution:

$$cs = \int_0^x f(x)dx - Px$$

$$p = 27 - 3x - x^2$$

$$(x = 3,\ P = 27 - 3x - x^2)$$

$$P = 27 - 9 - 9$$

$$\boxed{P = 9}$$

$$cs = \int_0^x (27 - 3x - x^2)dx - 27$$

$$= 27x - \frac{3x^2}{2} - \frac{x^3}{3} - 27$$

$$= 81 - \frac{27}{2} - \frac{27}{3} - 27$$

$$= 81 - 13.5 - 9 - 27$$

$$= \boxed{31.5}$$

228. Match List I with List II and choose the correct answer from the code given below

List I	List II
(A) Delphi method	**i. Stationarity**
(B) Dickey Fuller test	**ii. Autocorrelation**
(C) Durbin Watson test	**iii. Testing significant of a regression coefficient**
(D) Students t test	**iv. Forecasting**

(December 2018)

Codes:

(a) A- iv, B-ii, c-i, D-iii
(b) A-i, B-iv, C-iii, D-ii
(c) A-i, B-ii, C-iii, D-iv
(d) A-iv, B-I, C-ii,D-iii

Answer - (d)

Solution:

- Delphi method is a forecasting technique that uses a panel of experts to make predictions.
- Dickey Fuller test is a statistical test that is used to test for stationarity in a time series.
- Durbin Watson test is a statistical test that is used to test for autocorrelation in a time series.
- Students t test is a statistical test that is used to test for the significance of a regression coefficient.

229. In regression analysis if a quantitative variable has ''m'' categories, one can introduce

(December 2018)

(a) only m-1 dummy variables
(b) only m+1 dummy variables
(c) only 2m variables
(d) only m dummy variables

Answer – (a)

Solution: If a quantitative variable has m categories, then we can introduce m-1 dummy variables to represent the categories. This is because we can use one of the categories as the reference category, and then create dummy variables for the other m-1 categories.

For example, if we have a variable for the gender of a person, and the categories are "male" and "female", then we can create two dummy variables. One dummy variable will be equal to 1 if the person is male, and 0 if they are female. The other dummy variable will be equal to 1 if the person is female, and 0 if they are male.

We cannot introduce m dummy variables, because this would result in perfect multicollinearity. Perfect multicollinearity occurs when two or more independent variables are perfectly correlated. This means that the two variables are measuring the same thing, and they cannot be used to explain the dependent variable independently.

230. Match List I with List II and choose the correct answer from the code given below

List I	List II
(A) Hawkins Simon conditions	**i. Theory of games**
(B) Saddle point	**ii. Non linear programming**
(C) Simplex method	**iii. Input output analysis**
(D) Kuhn Tucker conditions	**iv. Linear programming**

(December 2018)

Codes:

(a) A-ii, B-i, C-iii, D-iv
(b) A-iii, B-i, C-iv, D-ii
(c) A-iii, B-ii, C-I, D-iv
(d) A-i, B-ii, C-iv, D-iii

Answer – (b)

231. Harrod' s growth model is given as under *(DECEMBER 2019)*

St = aYt **0 < a < 1**

It = b(Yt – Yt-1) **b>0**

St = It

In the model, growth condition is

(a) b/(b-a) > 0
(b) b/(b-a) < 0
(c) a/b-a > 0
(d) a/b-a < 0

Answer – (A)

Solution:

St = It

$\alpha Y_t = \beta (Y_t - Y_{t-1})$

$\alpha Y_t = \beta Y_t - \beta Y_{t-1}$

$\beta Y_t - 1 = \beta Y_t - \alpha Y_t$

$\beta Y_{t-1} = Y_t (\beta - \alpha)$

$\frac{\beta}{\beta - \alpha} (Y_{t-1}) = Y_t$

$\left[\frac{\beta}{\beta - \alpha} \right]$ should be positive for economic growth

232. Arrange in chronological order the following economists in relation to their contribution to the theory of consumer behaviour. Choose the correct answers *(DECEMBER 2019)*

(a) A. Marshall , R Stone, P Samuelson, J R Hicks, and R G D Allen
(b) R Stone, P Samuelson, J R Hicks and R G D Allen and A Marshall
(c) P Samuelson, J R Hicks and R G D Allen, R Stone and A Marshall
(d) A Marshall, J R Hicks, R G D Allen, P Samuelson and R Stone

Answer - (d)

Solution:

1. A.Marshall (1842-1924)
2. R. G. D. Allen (1906-1983)

3. J. R. Hicks (1904-1989)
4. P. A. Samuelson (1915-2009)
5. R. Stone (1913-1991)

- Alfred Marshall developed the concept of marginal utility, which is the additional satisfaction that a consumer gets from consuming one more unit of a good. He also developed the indifference curve, which is a graphical representation of the consumer's preferences between two goods.
- R. G. D. Allen and J. R. Hicks developed the indifference curve analysis, which is a more formal way of representing the consumer's preferences. They also developed the budget constraint, which is a graphical representation of the consumer's income and the prices of the goods that they can purchase.
- Paul A. Samuelson developed the modern theory of consumer behavior, which is based on the indifference curve analysis and the budget constraint. He also developed the revealed preference theory, which is a way of testing the consumer's preferences based on their actual behavior.
- Richard Stone developed the social accounting matrix, which is a way of summarizing the economic transactions in an economy. He also developed the input-output model, which is a way of analyzing the interdependencies between different sectors of an economy.

233. Assertion : For certain goods, the expenditure by the consumer decreases.
Reason: For such goods, the income elasticity of demand is high

(DECEMBER 2019)

(a) Both (A) and (R) are true and (R) is the correct explanation of (A)
(b) Both (A) and (R) are true, (R) is not the correct explanation of (A)
(c) (A) is true but (R) is false
(d) (A) is false but (R) is true

Answer - (c)

Solution: Assertion states that for certain goods, the expenditure by the consumer decreases. This is true for inferior goods. Inferior goods are goods whose demand decreases as income increases. For example, if a person's income increases, they may be able to afford to buy a car instead of taking public transportation. As a result, their expenditure on public transportation will decrease.

Reason states that for such goods, the income elasticity of demand is high. This is false. The income elasticity of demand measures how responsive the demand for a good is to a change in income. A high-income elasticity of demand means that the demand for a good increases by a large amount when income increases. However, for inferior goods, the income elasticity of demand is actually negative. This means that the demand for an inferior good decreases when income increases.

234. Which of the following is the correct sequence in the ascending order of the magnitude? *(DECEMBER 2019)*

(a) Repo rate, Reverse Repo rate, Statutory Liquidity rate (SLR) and Marginal Standing Facility Rate (MSFR)

(b) SLR, MSFR, Repo rate, Reverse Repo rate

(c) Repo rate, SLR, MSFR, Reverse Repo rate

(d) Reverse Repo rate, Repo rate, MSFR, SLR

Answer = (d)

Solution: The reverse repo rate is the rate at which the central bank borrows money from commercial banks. The repo rate is the rate at which the central bank lends money to commercial banks. The MSFR is the rate at which the central bank provides liquidity to banks in an emergency. The SLR is the minimum amount of liquid assets that banks must hold.

The reverse repo rate is the lowest of these rates, followed by the repo rate, the MSFR, and the SLR. This is because the central bank is more willing to lend money to banks than it is to borrow money from them. The MSFR is higher than the repo rate because it is a more expensive form of liquidity for banks. The SLR is the highest of these rates because it is the minimum amount of liquid assets that banks must hold.

235. Match the following *(DECEMBER 2019)*

List I

(A) Forward exchange

(B) Hedging

(C) Arbitrage

(D) Specie Point

List II

(i) A device of covering exchange risk against the price rise of foreign currency

(ii) A contract to buy and sell foreign exchange against another currency at some fixed rate in the future at a price agreed upon now.

(iii) The movement of exchange rate between two limits set by the cost of moving gold from one country to another

(iv) A mechanism which makes two markets that are physically separate, a single market in economic sénse

Choose the correct option

(a) (A) –ii, (B) – i, (C) – iv, (D) – iii

(b) (A) – ii, (B) – iii, (C) – iv, (D) – I

(c) (A) – iv, (B) – i, (C) – ii, (D) – iii

(d) (A) – iv, (B) – iii, (C) – ii, (D) – I

Answer - (a)

236. The 'Compensation Criterion' which says that state A is socially preferable to state B, if those who gain from the change can compensate the losers and yet end up with surplus welfare gain is attributed to : *(DECEMBER 2019)*

(a) W Pareto (b) N Kaldor

(c) T Scitovsky (d) Bergson

Answer = (b)

Solution: The compensation criterion that you mentioned is attributed to N. Kaldor. It is also known as the Kaldor-Hicks criterion.

The Kaldor-Hicks criterion states that a change in economic policy is considered to be an improvement if the gainers from the change could compensate the losers and still be better off. This means that the change must increase overall economic welfare, even if it makes some people worse off.

The Kaldor-Hicks criterion is not without its critics. Some argue that it is not fair to make some people worse off, even if it makes others better off. Others argue that the criterion is not always practical, as it may be difficult to measure the gains and losses from a change in economic policy.

Despite its critics, the Kaldor-Hicks criterion is a widely used tool in welfare economics. It is a simple and intuitive way to assess the impact of economic policy changes.

237. Which amongst the following market forms leads to most efficient allocation of resources? *(DECEMBER 2019)*

(a) Monopolistic Competition (b) Monopoly

(c) Oligopoly (d) Perfect Competition

Answer - (d)

Solution: Perfect competition is a market structure in which there are many firms, each producing a homogeneous product. There is no entry or exit barriers, and firms have perfect information about the market. This means that firms are price takers, and they cannot influence the price of the product.

In perfect competition, firms are allocatively efficient. This means that they produce the output level where marginal cost equals marginal revenue. This is the output level that maximizes social welfare.

The other market forms are not as efficient as perfect competition. Monopolistic competition is inefficient because firms have some market power, and they can charge a price above marginal cost. Monopoly is the least efficient market form, because there is only one firm in the market. This firm has a lot of market power, and it can charge a high price and produce a low output level.

238. For oil importing countries, the increase in oil prices in 1970's and mid 2000 contributed to which of the following: *(DECEMBER 2019)*

(A) Improving terms of trade

(B) Balance of trade deficits

(C) Price inflation

(D) Constrained economic growth

Choose the correct option

(a) (A) (B) and (C) only
(b) (B) (C) and (D) only
(c) (C) (D) and (A) only
(d) (A) and (D) only

Answer - (b)

Solution: Oil importing countries have to pay more for oil when the price of oil increases. This can lead to balance of trade deficits, as the country imports more oil than it exports. It can also lead to price inflation, as the cost of oil is passed on to consumers. Finally, it can lead to constrained economic growth, as businesses may have to cut back on investment and production due to higher costs.

239. Match the following *(DECEMBER 2019)*

List I

(A) Head count ratio

(B) Poverty Gap

(C) Square of poverty gap

(D) Multi-dimensional poverty index

List II

(i) **Extent of poverty**

(ii) **Depth of poverty**

(iii) **Poverty as deprivation**

(iv) **Severity of poverty Choose the correct answer:**

(a) (A) – ii, (B) – i, (C) – iv, (D) – iii
(b) (A) – iii, (B) – ii, (C) – i, (D) – iv
(c) (A) – i, (B) – iii, (C) – ii, (D) – iv
(d) (A) – i, (B) – ii, (C) – iv, (D) – iii

Answer - (d)

Solution: The correct answer is 4. (a) – i, (b) – ii, (c) – iv, (d) – iii.

The head count ratio is a measure of the extent of poverty. It is the proportion of the population that is below the poverty line.

The poverty gap is a measure of the depth of poverty. It is the average shortfall from the poverty line for the poor.

The square of poverty gap is a measure of the severity of poverty. It is the average squared shortfall from the poverty line for the poor.

The multidimensional poverty index is a measure of multidimensional poverty. It takes into account multiple dimensions of poverty, such as income, education, and health.

240. The phenomenon of 'Demographic Dividend' is related to which of the following? *(DECEMBER 2019)*

(a) An increase in sex rate

(b) An increase in the share of female population

(c) A decline in TFR

(d) An increase in the share of working age population

Answer - (d)

Solution: The demographic dividend is a period of economic growth that can occur when a country's population structure changes from one with a high proportion of young dependents to one with a high proportion of working-age adults. This change can occur when fertility rates decline and life expectancy increases.

The increase in the share of working-age population means that there are more people who are able to work and contribute to the economy. This can lead to increased economic growth and prosperity.

The other options are not related to the demographic dividend. An increase in the sex rate or the share of female population would not necessarily lead to an increase in the share of working-age population. A decline in TFR (total fertility rate) is a necessary condition for the demographic dividend, but it is not sufficient.

241. Heckscher - Ohlin trade model maintains that: *(DECEMBER 2019)*

(a) Comparative advantage determines the distribution of gains from trade

(b) A country exports goods for which its resource endowments are most suited

(c) Absolute Advantage Theory determines the distribution of the gains from trade

(d) The division of labour is limited by the size of the world market

Answer = (b)

Solution:

Modern theory of trade (factor proportion theory/ factor endowment theory) Heckscher ohlin

"Countries which are rich in labour will export labour intensive growth and countries which are rich in capital will export capital intensive goods. The basis of trade is difference in availability of resources.

Assumptions:-

1) 2×2×2 model
2) Perfect competition
3) Full employment
4) Constant returns to scale
5) Perfectly mobility with the nation and perfect in mobility between Nations.

The countries should export the good which makes intensive use of abundant factor and import the good which makes intensive use of cheap factor.

Leontief Paradox (1953) :-Leontief criticised H-O trade theory. He empirically proved it using the example of US economy saying that US being a capital intensive nation imported capital intensive goods and export labour intensive goods.

Factor intensity reversal:-In a model of 2 factors, factor intensity refers to the proportion at which capital and Labour are combined, i.e capital- labour ratio (K/L). In H-O theorem, one good is capital intensive with higher capital-labor ratio and other good is labour intensive with lower capital-labor ratio. But the capital intensive good must remain capital intensive in both countries and labor intensive good must be labor intensive in both countries. Here, there is no factor intensity reversal.

On the contrary, factor intensity reversal will take place in a case when a good is capital intensive in one country but Labor intensive in other country. In that case H-O theorem will be invalid.

242. Which among the following is not associated with the Optimum Theory of Population? *(DECEMBER 2019)*

(a) T R Malthus
(b) H Dalton
(c) E Cannon
(d) Carr – Saunders

Answer - (a)

Solution: Optimum theory of Population: Optimum population is the ideal population which combined with the other available resources of the country will yield maximum returns.

Concept of optimum population has been defined by Robbins, Carr Saunders and Dalton. Any change in the size of population above or below the optimum level will diminish income for head.

243. Arrange the following events in chronological order *(DECEMBER 2019)*

(A) First phase of nationalization of commercial banks

(B) Establishment of Narashiman committee on banking system

(C) Enactment of FEMA act

(D) Establishment of EXIM bank of India

Choose the correct option:

(A) A C D B

(b) A D B C

(c) A C B D

(d) A D C B

Answer = (b)

Solution:

- The first phase of nationalization of commercial banks took place in 1969, when the government of India nationalized 14 major banks.
- The EXIM bank of India was established in 1981 to provide export credit and other financial services to exporters.
- The Narasimhan committee on banking system was established in 1991 to recommend reforms in the banking sector.
- The FEMA act was enacted in 1999 to regulate foreign exchange transactions in India.

244. On which date and year GST become effective in India? *(DECEMBER 2019)*

(a) 1st April 2017

(b) 1st January 2017

(c) 1st July 2017

(d) 1st March 2018

Answer = (c)

Solution: The Goods and Services Tax (GST) is a value-added tax (VAT) on goods and services, introduced in India on 1 July 2017. The goal of the GST is to create a single market for goods and services in India, and to reduce the cascading effect of taxes.

The GST replaced a number of existing indirect taxes, including:

- Central Value Added Tax (CENVAT)
- State Value Added Tax (VAT)
- Service Tax
- Central Sales Tax (CST)

- Luxury Tax
- Entertainment Tax

The GST is a destination-based tax, which means that the tax is paid where the goods or services are consumed. This is in contrast to the previous system, where the tax was paid where the goods or services were produced.

The GST is levied at different rates on different goods and services. The standard rate of GST is 18%, but there are also lower rates of 5% and 0%.

The GST has been a major reform in the Indian tax system, and it is expected to have a positive impact on the economy. The GST is expected to reduce the cost of doing business in India, and to boost economic growth.

245. For Cobb - Douglas production function Q = 100 $L^{0.7} K^{0.3}$. Which of the following is not true? *(DECEMBER 2019)*

(a) It is a linear homogenous function
(b) It is characterized by constant returns to scale
(c) It is having zero elasticity of factor substitution
(d) It is characterized by unit elasticity of substitution

Answer = (c)

Solution:

Cobb Douglas Production Function: - 1928

1. Linearly Homogenous Production Function.
2. Constant Returns to Scale.
3. $E_S = 1$

$$Q = AL^{\propto}K^{\beta}$$

Q = Output
A = Technology
L = Labour
K = Capital

∝ = tells output elasticity of labour. ∝ = Share of labour in production

β = tells output elasticity of capital.

Some properties of Cobb Douglas production function: -

1. Linear homogeneous production function with constant returns to scale.
2. Diminishing returns to each factor.
3. Coefficients of it represent output elasticity of input.
4. Elasticity of output in relation to labour is '∝' and in relation to capital is 'β'.

5. Share of labour in National Income = $\propto$, share of capital in National Income= β
6. E_S is unity
7. Linear homogeneous production function passes through origin.

$\propto + \beta = 1$	CRS
$\propto + \beta > 1$	IRS
$\propto + \beta < 1$	DRS

Euler Theorem/Product Exhaustion Theorem : - If the factors are paid according to their Marginal productivity, then total output will be exhausted. It holds true in linearly homogenous production function.

$$MP_L * L + MP_K * K = Q$$

246. Choose the correct option for which the allocation of inputs is technically efficient?

(DECEMBER 2019)

(A) Output of one good cannot be decreased without increasing the output of another good

(B) Consumption of one good cannot be increased without decreasing the consumption of another good

(C) Consumer attains maximum satisfaction

Choose the correct option:

(a) (B) only
(b) (A) only
(c) Both (A) and (C)
(d) Both (B) and (C)

Answer = (b)

Solution: Technical efficiency is a state in which a firm is producing the maximum output from a given set of inputs. This means that the firm is using its inputs in the most efficient way possible, and that it cannot produce more output without increasing the amount of inputs used.

The statement in option (a) captures this idea of technical efficiency. If a firm is technically efficient, then it cannot produce more output of one good without decreasing the output of another good. This is because the firm is already using its inputs in the most efficient way possible, and it cannot produce more output of one good without using more inputs.

247. Which among the following are the main pillars of the BASEL III norms?

(DECEMBER 2019)

(A) Minimal capital requirements

(B) Supervisory review process

(C) Market discipline

(D) Maximizing return on capital

Choose the correct option:

(a) a, b and c only

(b) a and d only

(c) b and c only

(d) b c and d only

Answer - (a)

Solution: Basel III is an international regulatory framework for banks that was developed in response to the financial crisis of 2007-08. The framework aims to strengthen the regulation, supervision and risk management of banks.

The main pillars of Basel III are:

- **Capital requirements:** This pillar sets out the minimum capital requirements for banks. The capital requirements are divided into two tiers: Tier 1 capital and Tier 2 capital. Tier 1 capital is the most important type of capital, and it is made up of common equity and retained earnings. Tier 2 capital is less important than Tier 1 capital, and it is made up of subordinated debt and other instruments.
- **Supervisory review process:** This pillar sets out the responsibilities of supervisors in ensuring that banks comply with the Basel III requirements. The supervisors are responsible for assessing the capital adequacy of banks, and they can take action if they believe that a bank is not adequately capitalized.
- **Market discipline:** This pillar encourages market participants to assess the riskiness of banks and to demand higher returns from banks that are perceived to be riskier. This is done through disclosure requirements, which require banks to disclose information about their capital levels and risk exposures.

Other key features of Basel III include:

- **Liquidity requirements:** This pillar sets out requirements for banks to hold liquid assets to meet their short-term funding needs.
- **Counterparty credit risk:** This pillar sets out requirements for banks to measure and manage their exposure to counterparty credit risk.
- **Stress testing:** This pillar requires banks to conduct stress tests to assess their ability to withstand shocks to their balance sheets.

248. The elements given below are some of the parts of the M4 money supply of Indian economy *(DECEMBER 2019)*

(A) Broad money (M3)

(B) All deposits with the post office savings bank

(C) National savings certificate

Choose the correct option which constitute M4

(a) Only A and B
(b) Only B and C
(c) Only A and C
(d) A, B, and C

Answer - (a)

Solution: Money supply [Amount of money in circulation] Measures of money supply :-

M1 = C + DD + other deposits [Narrow def.]

M2 = M1 + Demand Deposits with the post office

M3 = M1 + Time deposits [Broader def.]

M4 = M3 + All deposits with post office [Excluding NSC]

249. Which trade policy results in the government levying both a specific tariff and an ad-valorem tariff on imported goods? *(DECEMBER 2019)*

(a) Effective tariff
(b) Revenue tariff
(c) Compound tariff
(d) Nominal tariff

Answer = (c)

Solution: Tarrifs:-

Tarrifs is a tax levied on export and import of goods. These are the restrictions on free trade.

Types of Tarrifs

1) Revenue tariff- Tarrif implemented to raise the revenue capacity of the government is known as revenue tarrif.
2) Protective Tarrif - Tarrif to protect the domestic Industries from foreign competitors.
3) Ad Valorem duty charged on the total value of the imported commodity.
4) Specific duty charged on the weight of the commodity.
5) Compound duty mixture of both ad valorem and specific duty.
6) Retaliatory tariffs:-It is levied by one country on the imports of another country in order to punish them latter for its trade policy.
7) Countervailing duty:-imposed on a commodity whose export price is reduced by the other country through an export subsidy

250. Kaldor's growth model incorporates some of the following assumptions. *(DECEMBER 2019)*

(A) Total savings include savings out wages and savings out of profits

(B) Marginal propensity to save out of wages is equal to the marginal propensity to save

out of profits

(C) Output consists of wages and profits

(D) There is less than full employment

Choose the correct option

(a) a and b (b) b and c

(c) c and d (d) a and c

Answer - (d)

Solution: Kaldor's Model :- It relates technical progress with capital accumulation. He gave importance to non- economic factors also in the development process. He follows the Keynesian's theory and Harrod's analysis.

Assumptions :-

a) Full employment

b) Technical progress depends on the rate of capital accumulation

c) Income= wages + profit

d) Total savings = savings out of wages and property

e) Constant Returns to scale.

251. Assertion (A): Intellectual Property Rights were brought into the Uruguay Round Trade Negotiations

Reason (R): International trade restrictions can be used to discourage the violation of intellectual property rights *(DECEMBER 2019)*

(a) Both (A) and (R) are true and (R) is the correct explanation of (A)

(b) Both (A) and (R) are true, (R) is not the correct explanation of (A)

(c) (A) is true but (R) is false

(d) (A) is false but (R) is true

Answer = (b)

Solution: Assertion (A) is true because the Agreement on Trade-Related Aspects of Intellectual Property Rights (TRIPS), which was negotiated during the Uruguay Round, established international standards for the protection of intellectual property rights.

Reason (R) is also true because international trade restrictions can be used to discourage the violation of intellectual property rights. However, Reason (R) is not the correct explanation of Assertion (A). The reason why intellectual property rights were brought into the Uruguay Round Trade Negotiations is more complex than simply the fact that international trade restrictions can be used to discourage their violation.

252. Incidence of tax refers to *(DECEMBER 2019)*

(a) Whether a tax is progressive, proportional or regressive

(b) An authority which collects the tax

(c) The person or group who ultimately pays the tax

(d) How a tax is collected

Answer = (c)

Solution: Tax incidence refers to who bears the burden of a tax. It can be the legal payer or the actual economic burden on individuals or groups. It depends on factors like price elasticity and ability to shift the burden. Understanding tax incidence helps policymakers assess the distributional impact and fairness of tax policies.

253. Which is correct chronological order of Economists contributing to input - output analysis? *(DECEMBER 2019)*

(a) Hawkins – Simon, Leontief, Karl Marx, Quesnay

(b) Karl Marx, Quesnay, Leontief, Hawkins - Simon

(c) Quesnay, Karl Marx, Leontief , Hawkins - Simon

(d) Leontief, Hawkins-Simon, Karl Marx, Quesnay

Answer = (c)

254. Consider the following statements *(DECEMBER 2019)*

(I) Preferring to a certain income to a risky income with the same level of expected value lead to a risk averse behavior

(II) Being indifferent between a certain income and uncertain income with the same level of expected value leads to risk averse behaviour

Which of the statements is/are true?

(a) Both I and II

(b) Neither I nor II

(c) Only I is true

(d) Only II is true

Answer = (c)

Solution: Risk aversion is the tendency to prefer outcomes with low uncertainty to those outcomes with high uncertainty, even if the average outcome of the latter is equal to or higher in monetary value than the more certain outcome.

Statement I describes a situation where an individual prefers a certain income to a risky income with the same level of expected value. This is a classic example of risk aversion. The individual is willing to accept a lower expected value in order to avoid the uncertainty of the risky income.

Statement II describes a situation where an individual is indifferent between a certain income and uncertain income with the same level of expected value. This is not a sign of risk aversion.

A risk-neutral individual would be indifferent between the two options. However, a risk-averse individual would prefer the certain income, even though they are indifferent between the two options in terms of expected value. This is because the risk-averse individual would prefer to avoid the uncertainty of the risky income.

255. Arrange in chronological order of the following contributions of economists in theory of consumer. Choose the correct answer *(DECEMBER 2019)*

(a) Linear expenditure system, Revealed preference theory, cardinal theory, ordinal theory

(b) Cardinal theory, ordinal theory, revealed preference theory, linear expenditure system

(c) Cardinal theory, revealed preference theory, ordinal theory, Linear expenditure system

(d) Revealed preference theory, cardinal theory, linear expenditure theory, ordinal theory

Answer = (b)

256. The whole burden of tax will be borne by the consumer if *(DECEMBER 2019)*

(a) The demand for commodity is perfectly elastic and supply is perfectly inelastic

(b) The elasticity of demand for a commodity is same as the elasticity of supply of the commodity

(c) The demand for a commodity is inelastic and supply is perfectly elastic

(d) The elasticity of demand for a commodity is less than the elasticity of supply of that commodity

Answer = (c)

Solution: The burden of a tax, or tax incidence, refers to how a tax affects the distribution of economic welfare between buyers and sellers. It can only be shifted through changes in prices during sales and purchase transactions. The extent of price changes depends on the relative elasticities of demand and supply for the taxed commodity.

According to the theory of tax shifting, the burden of tax is shared between buyers and sellers based on the ratio of the elasticity of supply to the elasticity of demand. If the demand for a commodity is inelastic and the supply is perfectly elastic, the entire burden of tax will be borne by the consumer and vice versa.

In summary, the burden of a tax is determined by the elasticity of demand and supply, and the consumer bears more of the burden when demand is inelastic and supply is elastic.

Theories of shifting of tax:-

Modern theory :-Given by Marshall

Case 1:- When $E_d = E_S$

tax burden equally distributed amongst consumers and producers.

Case 2:- When $E_d < E_S$

tax burdens is more on the buyer as compared to seller

Case 3 :- When $E_d > E_S$

tax burdens are more on the seller as compared to buyer.

Case 4:- When $E_d = \infty$ (perfectly elastic) E_S is inelastic

Burden of tax falls wholly on producer.

Case 5:- When $E_d = 0$ (perfectly inelastic) E_S is elastic

Burden of tax falls wholly on buyer.

Case 6:- When $E_S = \infty$ (perfectly elastic) and E_d is inelastic

Burden of tax wholly on buyer.

Case 7:- When $E_S = 0$ (perfectly inelastic), E_d is elastic

Burden of tax falls wholly on seller.

257. Given the saving function S= -20 + 0.2Y and autonomous investment (I) = Rs. 100 million, the equilibrium of level of consumption would be *(DECEMBER 2019)*

(a) 500 (b) 600

(c) 400 (d) 700

Answer - (a)

Solution:

S = -20 + 0.2Y

I = 100

S = I

-20 +0.2Y = 100

0.2Y=120

Y= 120/0.2

Y=600

S=-20+0.2x600 (or we can directly write S=100 as S=I and I is 100)

S=-20+120

S=100

C=Y-S

C=600-100

C=500.

258. Arrange the following books in correct chronological order *(DECEMBER 2019)*

(A) Das Capital

(B) Value and Capital

(C) Capital and Growth

(D) Accumulation of capital

Choose the correct option:

(a) D B C A
(b) A B D C
(c) A B C D
(d) B A D C

Answer = (c)

Solution:

- Das Kapital was written by Karl Marx and published in three volumes between 1867 and 1894. It is considered to be one of the most important works of political economy ever written.
- Value and Capital was written by Piero Sraffa and written in 1939. It is a critical analysis of Marx's theory of value.
- Capital and Growth was written by Robert Solow and published in 1956. It is a mathematical model of economic growth.
- Accumulation of Capita was written by Michal Kalecki and published in 1971. It is a study of the process of capital accumulation in a capitalist economy.

259. Match the following *(DECEMBER 2019)*

List – I	List – II
(A) E Cannon	**(i) Optimum population**
(B) Frank Netstein	**(ii) Transaction costs**
(C) Brundtland	**(iii) Demographic transition**
(D) Ronald Coase	**(iv) Sustainable development**

Choose the correct option

(a) (A) – i, (B) – ii, (C) – iii, (D) – iv
(b) (A) – ii, (B) – i, (C) – iv, (D) – iii
(c) (A) – i, (B) – iii, (C) – iv, (D) – ii
(d) (A) – iii, (B) – iv, (C) – ii, (D) – i

Answer = (c)

Solution:

Optimum population:

- Edwin Cannan proposed the theory of optimum population.

- It follows the Malthusian theory of population.
- The theory states that an ideal population size, when combined with other resources, maximizes returns or income.
- It explores the relationship between population changes and per capita income.
- The theory aims to determine the population size at which per capita income reaches its maximum.

Demographic transition:

- Frank Notestein introduced the theory of demographic transition in 1945.
- It illustrates the changing patterns of mortality, fertility, and population growth rates.
- The theory explores the relationship between economic development and population growth.

Sustainable development:

- The concept of sustainable development was introduced in the Brundtland Report in 1987.
- It emphasizes meeting the needs of the present generation without compromising the ability of future generations to meet their own needs.
- Sustainable development encompasses economic development, social progress, and environmental considerations.
- The goal is to achieve a balance between economic growth, social well-being, and environmental protection to ensure long-term sustainability.

Transaction cost:

- Transaction costs are incurred during economic exchanges when purchasing goods and services.
- These costs are often hidden or not easily visible.
- Ronald Coase emphasized the importance of transaction costs in exchanges.
- Coase's theorem suggests that if transaction costs are low and property rights are well-defined, the market can function effectively even in the presence of externalities.

260. The solution of the following game is given by *(September 2020)*

Player B

$$\text{Player A}\quad \begin{array}{c} \\ A_1 \\ A_2 \\ A_3 \end{array} \begin{array}{c} \begin{array}{ccc} B_1 & B_2 & B_3 \end{array} \\ \begin{bmatrix} 2 & 4 & 2 \\ 1 & -5 & -4 \\ 2 & 6 & -2 \end{bmatrix} \end{array}$$

(a) Value of the game = 2. Best strategy for player A and B are (A1, B1)respectively

(b) Value of the game = 2. Best strategy for player A and B are (A, B) or (A3, B1) or (A1, B3) respectively

(c) Value of the game = 2. Best strategy for player A and B are (A3, B1) respectively

(d) Value of the game = 2. Best strategy for player A and B are (A1, B3) respectively

Answer = (b)

261. Presence of asymmetric information in the market causes which of the following?

(A) Adverse selection

(B) Marginal benefits of an additional unit of resources diminish with an increasing number of unit of resources

(C) Efficiency wages

(D) Principal-agent problem

(September 2020)

Choose the correct answer

(a) A, B and D

(b) B, C and D

(c) A and D

(d) A and C

Answer = (c)

Solution: The presence of asymmetric information in the market causes the following:

(a) Adverse selection: Asymmetric information can lead to adverse selection, where one party has more information than the other and uses that information to their advantage. This can result in the selection of undesirable or lower-quality goods, services, or contracts.

(d) Principal-agent problem: Asymmetric information can also lead to the principal-agent problem, where the interests of the principal (such as a company or shareholder) and the agent (such as a manager or employee) may not align due to differences in information. This can result in conflicts of interest and suboptimal decision-making.

262. Statement I: Learning curve effect is related to a firm's long run average cost curve
Statement II: A swapped allocation is one that is Pareto efficient as well as an equitable allocation

(September 2020)

Choose the correct answers

(a) Both are true

(b) Both are false

(c) I is correct, Il is false

(d) I is false, Il is true

Answer - (a)

Solution: The learning curve depicts the connection between labor costs and the production of an additional unit. It is a vital factor in analyzing costs and can be defined as the correlation between unit cost and the total output achieved.

The diagram shows that an individual firm can improve its production and its production techniques through experience, which will reduce the cost as well as the number of hours. It helps the firm become more efficient. It looks like the the modern average cost, which also tells us that due to external economies, an individual firm can reduce its costs and improve its product techniques.

Hence, statement 1 is correct.

Pareto efficient: It refers to a situation where no improvement in welfare can be made without making somebody worse off.

Equitable allocation: An allocation is considered equitable if and only if it is fair/unbiased.

Swapped allocation" is the contract between two parties such that they can both exchange or trade with each other. It is related to the allocation of resources. In welfare economics, the exchange can be Pareto efficient as well as an equitable allocation.

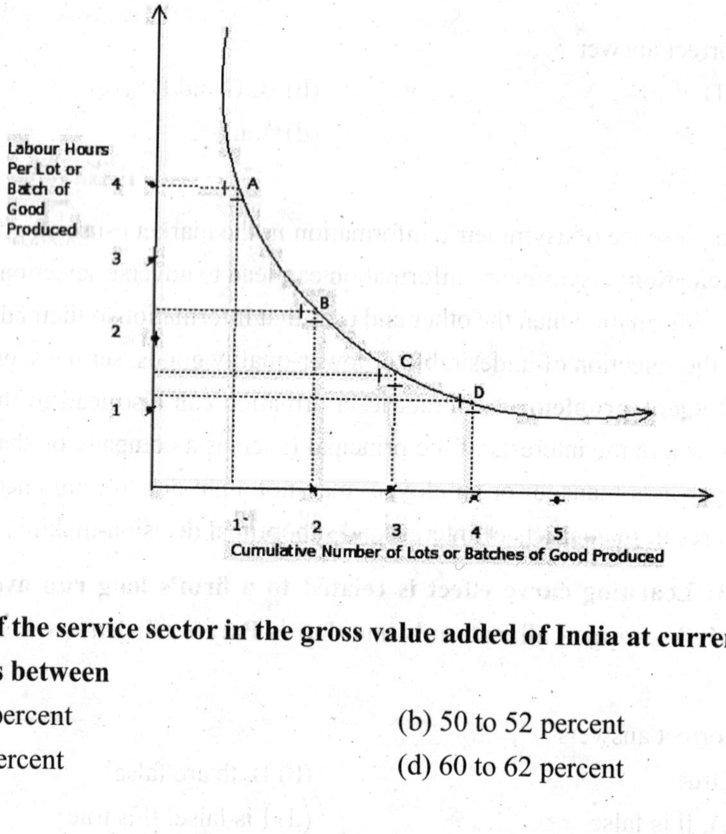

263. The share of the service sector in the gross value added of India at current prices during 2018-2019 is between

(a) 45 to 47 percent
(b) 50 to 52 percent
(c) 53 to 55 percent
(d) 60 to 62 percent

Answer = (c)

Solution: According to the World Bank, the share of the service sector in the gross value added of India at current prices during 2018-2019 was 53.89%. This means that the service sector accounted for more than half of India's GDP. The service sector is the largest sector in India's economy, and it has been growing at a rapid pace in recent years.

264. According to economic survey 2019, the top 5 trading partners of India continue to be USA, China and UAE and *(September 2020)*

(A) Saudi Arabia **(B) Hong Kong**

(B) Singapore **(D) Sri Lanka**

Choose the correct answer

(a) C and D only (b) B and C only

(c) A and D only (d) A and B only

Answer - (d)

265. Which of the situations represents an economic investment in the national income calculation? *(September 2020)*

(A) Buying a newly constructed house for self-occupation

(B) Buying of new shares

(C) Buying a new car by a publishing house for delivering books

(D) Buying a new car by a household

Choose the correct answer

(a) A, B and C (b) A, B, C and D

(c) A, C and D (d) A and D

Answer - (d)

Solution: Economic investment is the purchase of goods or assets that are expected to generate future income or returns. In the national income calculation, economic investment includes the following:

The purchase of new capital goods, such as machinery and equipment. The construction of new buildings and infrastructure.

The purchase of new inventories.

266. Inadequacy or absence of KYC (know your customer) standards can subject a bank to serious and counter party risks as follows *(September 2020)*

(A) Reputation risk

(B) Compliance risk

(C) Legal risk

(D) Bankruptcy risk

Choose the correct answer

(a) A, B and D (b) A, B and C

(c) B, C and D (d) A, C and D

Answer = (b)

Solution: The risks of inadequate or absent KYC standards include reputational risk, compliance risk, and legal risk. Bankruptcy risk is not typically associated with inadequate KYC standards.

- **Reputational risk:** If a bank fails to adequately identify and assess its customers, it may be exposed to reputational risk. This is because the bank may be seen as being complicit in financial crime, such as money laundering or terrorist financing. This could lead to a loss of customers, investors, and partners.
- **Compliance risk:** If a bank fails to comply with KYC regulations, it may be exposed to compliance risk. This is because the bank may be fined or even prosecuted for failing to meet its regulatory obligations. This could lead to financial penalties, legal fees, and damage to the bank's reputation.
- **Legal risk:** If a bank fails to adequately identify and assess its customers, it may be exposed to legal risk. This is because the bank may be sued by its customers or by other parties if it is found to have been negligent in its due diligence. This could lead to financial losses, legal fees, and damage to the bank's reputation.

267. Assertion (A): High powered money is the source of all other forms of money that impact money supply

Reason (R): Credit is created by commercial banks *(September 2020)*

(a) Both A are R are correct, R is the correct explanation of A

(b) Both A are R are correct, R is not the correct explanation of A

(c) A is correct but R is not correct

(d) A is not correct but R is correct

Answer = (b)

Solution: Assertion (A) is correct because high-powered money is the foundation on which all other forms of money are created. The central bank controls the amount of high-powered money in circulation, and this in turn affects the amount of credit that commercial banks can create.

Reason (R) is also correct because commercial banks create credit by lending money to businesses and consumers. When a bank lends money, it creates a new deposit in the borrower's account. This deposit can then be used to make payments, which increases the money supply.

Reason (R) is correct, but it does not explain why high-powered money is the source of all other forms of money. The creation of credit by commercial banks is a separate process that is enabled by the existence of high-powered money.

268. For any two equally likely, exhaustive and events A and B, P(AB) will be equal to *(September 2020)*

(a) 0 (b) 0.25 (c) 0.50 (d) 1

Answer = (b)

Solution: According to the question, P(AUB) = 1

= P(A n B) =P(A). P(B)

= P(A n B) 0.5 x 0.5=0.25

269. A growth model which there are diminishing returns on each factor of production but constant returns to scale and exogenous technological changes that generate long term economic growth is the *(September 2020)*

(a) Leibenstein model

(b) AK Sen model

(c) Kalecki Model

(d) Solow model

Answer - (d)

Solution: Given by solow "A contribution to the theory of economic growth". Also known as exogenous growth model or Neoclassical Growth Model.

Technical progress and population growth rate are treated to be exogenous in nature.

Difference from H-D model

1) H-D model states fixed technical Coefficient and Solow model assumes variable technical Coefficient [In HD model, substitution of labour capital is not possible, but in Solow model it is possible].
2) Under HD model, there is tendency of divergence from equilibrium, while in case of Solow; there is tendency of convergence towards equilibrium.

Assumptions :-

a) Substitution of capital for labour is possible

b) Constant Returns to scale.

c) Full employment

d) Perfect competition

Convergence in solow model: poor countries are poor because they have a less capital but if they save at same rate as rich countries and have access to same technology, they will eventually catch up.

270. Time series under the condition (E_{xt}) = μ and cov (Xt,X_{t+k}) = Y(K) is said to be *(September 2020)*

(a) Strictly stationery

(b) Non stationery

(c) Weakly stationery

(d) Can't be defined

Answer = (c)

Solution: A weakly stationary time series is a time series whose mean and autocovariances are constant over time. In other words, the mean of the time series does not change over time, and the covariance between the time series at two different points in time is the same regardless of the time difference between the two points.

The condition $(E_{xt}) = \mu$ means that the mean of the time series is constant over time. The condition cov $(X_t, X_{t+k}) = Y(K)$ means that the covariance between the time series at two different points in time is constant, regardless of the time difference between the two points.

Therefore, the time series is said to be weakly stationary.

271. Which of the following are the three states, which secured the highest percentage state-wise share of tax revenue among states, as per recommendations of the finance commission? *(September 2020)*

(A) Uttar Pradesh **(B) Bihar**

(C) Madhya Pradesh **(D) Andhra Pradesh**

Choose most appropriate answer

(a) A, B and D only (b) A, C and D only

(c) A, B and C only (d) B, C and D only

Answer = (c)

272. Assertion (A): The main cause of commercial bank failure is because of providing inappropriate loans to bank insiders

Reason (R): Bank employees are provided loans at lower interest rates *(September 2020)*

Choose the appropriate answer

(a) Both A are R are correct, R is the correct explanation of A

(b) Both A are R are correct, R is not the correct explanation of A

(c) A is correct but R is not correct

(d) A is not correct but R is correct

Answer = (b)

Solution

Assertion (A) states that the main cause of commercial bank failure is providing inappropriate loans to bank insiders. This can be one of the causes of bank failure, as loans granted based on personal relationships rather than sound lending criteria can result in higher default rates and financial losses for the bank.

Reason (R) states that bank employees are provided loans at lower interest rates. While it is true that bank employees may have access to certain benefits or loan programs, it is not the main cause of commercial bank failure. Bank failures are typically caused by a combination of factors, including inadequate risk management, poor lending practices, economic downturns, and external shocks to the financial system.

Therefore, both the assertion and reason are correct, but the reason does not provide a complete or accurate explanation of the assertion.

273. Arrange the following in chronological order *(September 2020)*

(A) Rational expectation Doctrine

(B) Keynesian economics

(C) Monetarism

(D) Classical economics

Choose the correct answer

(a) B,D,C,A (b) A,D,C,B

(c) A,B,C,D (d) D,B,C,A

Answer - (d)

274. Match List-I with List-II *(September 2020)*

List-I

(A) Absolute advantage theory of international trade

(B) Factor proportion theory of trade

(C) Offer curve

(D) Opportunity cost

List-II

I. **Heckscher - Ohlin**

II. **Marshall**

III. **Adam Smith**

IV. **Haberler**

Choose the correct option

(a) A-I, B-III, C-II, D-IV (b) A-III, B-I, C-II, D-IV

(c) A-I, B-III, C-IV, D-II (d) A-III, B-I, C-IV, D-II

Answer = (b)

Solution:

(A) Absolute advantage theory of international trade is associated with Adam Smith (III).

(B) Factor proportion theory of trade is associated with Heckscher-Ohlin (I).

(C) Offer curve is associated with Marshall (II).

(D) Opportunity cost is associated with Haberler (IV).

275. Statement I: The endogenous growth theorists suggest, investment in human capital, innovation and knowledge leads to economic growth

Statement II: Investment in human capital, innovation and knowledge reduces the diminishing returns on investment *(September 2020)*

Choose the most appropriate answer

(a) Both are true

(b) Both are false

(c) I is correct, II is false.

(d) I is false, II is true

Answer - (a) Solution:

Statement I correctly reflects the view of endogenous growth theorists, who argue that investment in human capital, innovation, and knowledge plays a crucial role in driving economic growth. These factors contribute to increasing productivity and improving technological advancements, leading to sustained economic expansion.

Statement II is also true as investment in human capital, innovation, and knowledge can help reduce the diminishing returns on investment. By continuously improving skills, fostering innovation, and acquiring new knowledge, individuals and firms can enhance their productivity and generate higher returns from their investments.

Therefore, both statements I and II are true.

276. Given the total cost TC = $Q^3 - 10Q^2 + 60Q$, what will be the minimum average cost? At what level of output will the minimum cost occur? (Q is the level of output) *(September 2020)*

(a) Minimum average cost is AC min = 35 at Q=5

(b) Minimum average cost is AC min = 175 at Q=5

(c) Minimum average cost is AC min = 170 at Q=1

(d) Minimum average cost is AC min = 45 at Q=1

Answer = (a)

Solution:

$$AC = \frac{TC}{Q}$$

For minima put AC' (Furst derivative = 0)
and AC'' (Second derivative)
Should be positive

$\pi = Q^3 - 10Q^2 + 60Q$

$AC = Q^2 - 10Q + 60$

$AC' = 2Q - 10 = 0$

$Q = 5$

For minima $AC'' > 0$

Now $AC = (5)^2 - 10\,(5) + 60$

$= 25 - 50 + 60$

$= 25 + 10$

$=35$

277. Statement I: Mrs. Ursula K Hicks stated that, "Private finance whether of firms of individuals, starts with a given income plan as a framework within which expenditure must be planned: public finance, on the contrary, starts with a given expenditure plan and the authorities adjust their income by means of taxes and resources to match the expenditure"

Statement II: Prof. Shiras pointed Out that "public authorities differ from private expenditure in that the former should balance income and should not necessarily seek a profit in the manner that an individual would" *(September 2020)*

Choose the correct answer

(a) Both are true

(b) Both are false

(c) I is correct, Il is false

(d) I is false, Il is true

Answer - (a)

Solution: Statement I is a summary of Ursula K. Hicks's theory of public finance. She argued that private finance starts with a given income plan, and then expenditure is planned within that framework. Public finance, on the other hand, starts with a given expenditure plan, and then income is adjusted by means of taxes and resources to match the expenditure.

Statement II is a summary of Prof. Shiras's point about the difference between public and private expenditure. He argued that public authorities have a different objective than private individuals. Public authorities are not trying to make a profit, but rather to provide public goods and services. Therefore, they do not necessarily need to balance their income and expenditure in the same way that private individuals do.

Both statements are supported by economic theory and evidence. Therefore, the correct answer is 1.

278. Assertion (A): According to Walt W Rostow, the principle strategy of development necessary for take-off was the mobilization of domestic and foreign savings

Reason (R): mobilization of domestic and foreign savings is necessary to generate sufficient investment to accelerate economic growth *(September 2020)*

Choose the correct answer

(a) Both A are R are correct, R is the correct explanation of A

(b) Both A are R are correct, R is not the correct explanation of A

(c) A is correct but R is not correct

(d) A is not correct but R is correct

Answer - (a)

Solution : Assertion (A) states that according to Walt W Rostow, the principle strategy of development necessary for take-off was the mobilization of domestic and foreign savings. This means that Rostow believed that mobilizing savings, both from within the country and from foreign sources, is crucial to drive investment and economic growth during the take-off stage of development.

Reason (R) states that the mobilization of domestic and foreign savings is necessary to generate sufficient investment to accelerate economic growth. This aligns with the assertion and provides a logical explanation for why mobilizing savings is important for development. By mobilizing savings, countries can accumulate capital and invest it in various sectors, fostering economic growth.

Therefore, both the assertion and the reason are correct, and the reason correctly explains the assertion.

279. Given the sample size 400 with the sample mean 99, the population mean 100 and computed value of z statistic at 2.5, the value of population standard deviation will be *(September 2020)*

(a) 59.17

(b) 123.46

(c) 8

(d) Cannot be determined

Answer = (c)

Solution:

$$z = \frac{\bar{x}-\mu}{\frac{\sigma}{\sqrt{n}}}$$

$$2.5 = \frac{|99-100|}{\frac{\sigma}{\sqrt{400}}}$$

$2.5 = 1 \times 20 / \sigma$

$\sigma\, 2.5 = 20\,,\ \sigma = \dfrac{200}{25}$

$\sigma = 8$

280. Based on the following Blacker's stages of population growth diagram, the portion between A, B and C implies *(September 2020)*

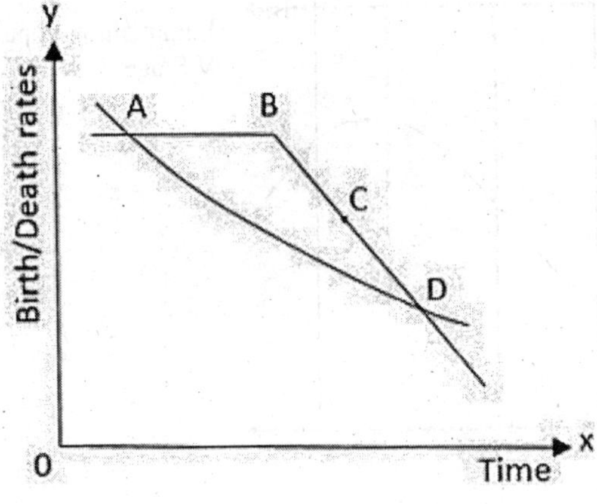

(a) Stages of low stationary

(b) Population declining

(c) Early expanding

(d) Late expanding

Answer = (c)

Solution:

Theory of Demographic Transition : - It explains the effect of changes in birth rate and death rate. on the growth rate of population.

First Stage :- Country is backward. It is characterized by high birth and death rates with the result that the growth rate of population is low.

Second stage :- Country enters in the phase of economic growth. Decline in death rate but no change in birth rate leads to population explosion.

Third Stage :- Birth rate states declining accompanied by death rates .

Fourth Stage :- Fertility rate declines and tends to equal the death rate so that the growth rate of population is stationary. Growth gains momentum and people's level of income increases. Their standard of living rises.

Fifth Stage :- Death rate exceeds birth rates and population growth declines. France appears to approach this stage

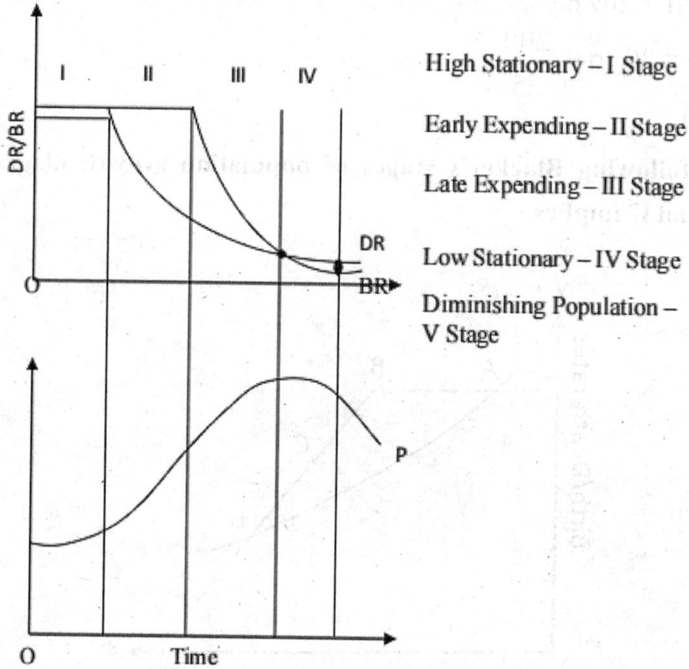

281. According to the last census (2011), which State has the minimum sex ratio?

(September 2020)

(a) Punjab
(b) Delhi
(c) Bihar
(d) Haryana

Answer - (d)

282. For the given income consumption curve in the diagram, which one of the following is correct

(September 2020)

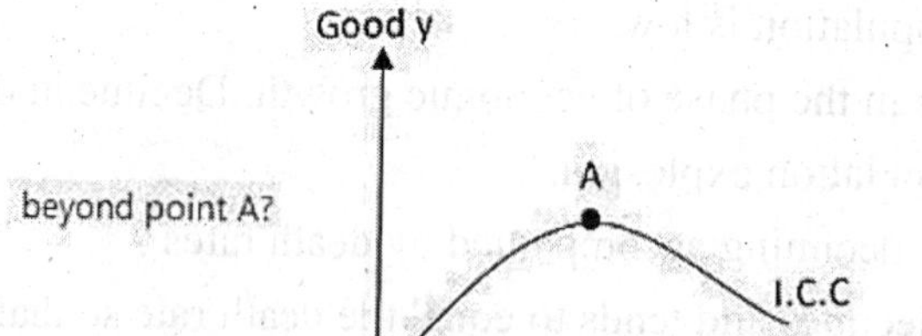

(a) Good x is inferior and good y is normal
(b) Good y is inferior and good x is normal
(c) Good x and good y are normal
(d) Good x and good y are inferior

Answer: (b)

Solution: Income Consumption Curve(ICC) shows the changes in consumer equilibrium with changes in income.

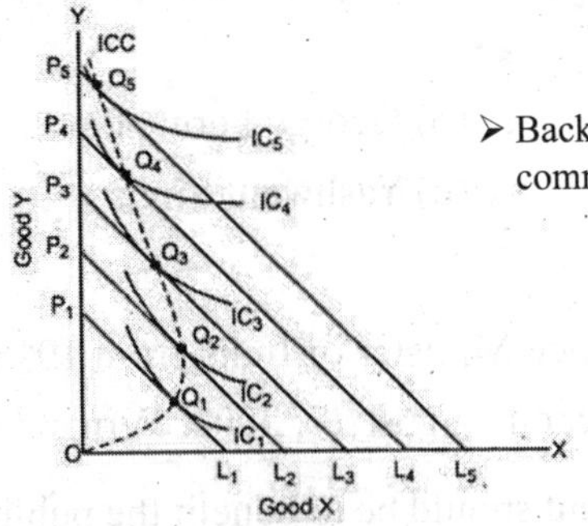

➤ Backward bending ICC, in case of 'x' commodity is inferior.

But in above question as curve is moving away from good Y hence good Y is inferior.

283. A decision free framework to identify a country's most binding constraints on economic growth is termed as *(September 2020)*

(a) Growth paradigm
(b) Growth diagnostics
(c) Growth stimulus
(d) Growth paradox

Answer = (b)

Solution: Growth diagnostics is a decision-free framework to identify a country's most binding constraints on economic growth. It was developed by Dani Rodrik, Harvard University economist, and his colleagues in 2005.

Growth diagnostics is based on the following principles:

- **Country-specific:** The framework is designed to be used in a specific country context, taking into account the country's history, institutions, and economic structure.
- **Problem-oriented:** The framework focuses on identifying the most binding constraints on growth, rather than trying to address all of the problems that a country faces.
- **Decision-free:** The framework does not prescribe specific policy solutions. Instead, it provides a framework for identifying the most binding constraints on growth, so that policymakers can then design the most appropriate policies to address those constraints.

Growth diagnostics has been used in a number of countries, including India, China, and Brazil. It has been found to be a useful tool for identifying the most binding constraints on growth and for designing the most effective policies to address those constraints.

The other options are incorrect.

- Growth paradigm is a broad term that refers to the different theories about how economic growth occurs.
- Growth stimulus is a policy intervention that is designed to increase economic growth.
- Growth paradox is a term that refers to the fact that economic growth has not been as high in recent decades as it was in previous decades.

284. Who said, "I believe that the objective for disinvestment should be to benefit the public, the consumer and the investor at the same time to improve competitiveness and eliminates monopoly?

(September 2020)

(a) Manmohan singh

(b) George Fernandes

(c) Chidambaram

(d) Yashwant Sinha

Answer = (b)

Solution: George Fernandes was the Defence Minister of India from 1998 to 2004. In a letter to the Prime Minister, Atal Bihari Vajpayee, on August 27, 2002, Fernandes wrote:

"I believe that the objective for disinvestment should be to benefit the public, the consumer and the investor at the same time to improve competitiveness and eliminates monopoly."

Fernandes was a strong critic of the government's disinvestment policy, which he argued was benefiting the rich at the expense of the poor. He argued that the government should sell public sector companies to the public at large, rather than to private investors.

285. Match List-I with List-II

(September 2020)

List-I

(A) Kerala

(B) Punjab

(C) Himachal Pradesh

(D) Madhya Pradesh

List-II

I. **Least Urbanized**

II. **Highest percentage of S.C's in their population**

III. **Highest percentage of S.T's in their population**

IV. **Highest sex ratio**

Options

(a) A-IV, B-II, C-I, D-III

(b) A-I, B-III, C-II, D-IV

(c) A-II, B-I, C-III, D-IV

(d) A-IV, B-I, C-III, D-II

Answer - (a)

286. Which one of the following price index numbers satisfies the factor reversal test?

(September 2020)

(a) Lapspeyres price index

(b) Paasche's price index

(c) Walsh's price index

(d) Fisher's price

Answer - (d)

Solution: The factor reversal test is a test of the consistency of a price index. It states that if the price index is multiplied by the quantity index, the product should be equal to the proportionate change in the current values.

The Fisher price index is the only price index that satisfies the factor reversal test. This is because the Fisher price index is a geometric mean of the Laspeyres and Paasche price indices.

The Laspeyres price index is a price index that uses the prices of the base period to weight the quantities of the current period. The Paasche price index is a price index that uses the prices of the current period to weight the quantities of the base period.

The Walsh price index is a price index that is a weighted average of the Laspeyres and Paasche price indices. The weights are chosen so that the Walsh price index satisfies the factor reversal test.

287. Assertion(A): If A is any Matrix given by A

Then det A = 0, since all elements in column II are zero

Reason (R): Laplace expansion permits evaluation of a determinant along any row or column *(September 2020)*

(a) Both A are R are correct, R is the correct explanation of A

(b) Both A are R are correct, R is not the correct explanation of A

(c) A is correct but R is not correct

(d) A is not correct but R is correct

Answer = (a)

Solution:

Matrix: It is a set number arranged in the form of a rectangular array of m rows and n columns. For example, in the question, we have given 3 rows and a 3-column matrix which means we have given a 3 x 3 matrix.

Determinant: It is associated with a square matrix. We can expand it with any row or | column and find a finite value of a determinant.

Laplace expansion: Laplace expansion help to solve the determinant with the expansion method. It helps to solve determinants with cofactors and minors.

Minors: Let us have a matrix of order 3, then minor of an element a11 (the element which belongs to the first row and 1st column). So minor is the determinant of the submatrix obtained from the given matrix by deleting the 1st and 1st column containing the element a11.

Cofactors: It can be written as $C_{11} = (-1)^{1+1}M1$. Here M is the minor.

288. Forward exchange rates are useful for those who wish is

(A) Protect themselves from the risk that the exchange rate will change before a transaction is completed

(B) Gamble that a currency will rise in value

(C) Gamble that a currency will fall in value

(D) Exchange currencies at a point in time in the future

(September 2020)

Choose the correct answer

(a) A, B and C only (b) A and B only

(c) A and C only (d) A, B, C, D

Answer - (d)

Solution: Forward exchange rates are useful for those who wish to:

Protect themselves from the risk that the exchange rate will change before a transaction is completed. This is known as hedging. For example, an importer who knows they will need to pay for goods in euros in 3 months can lock in the exchange rate today by entering into a forward contract.

Gamble that a currency will rise in value. This is known as speculation. For example, if an investor believes that the euro will rise in value against the dollar, they can buy euros forward.

Gamble that a currency will fall in value. This is also known as speculation. For example, if an investor believes that the euro will fall in value against the dollar, they can sell euros forward.

Exchange currencies at a point in time in the future. This is known as forward trading. For example, a company that needs to pay for goods in euros in 3 months can enter into a forward contract to exchange their currency at a predetermined exchange rate.

Therefore, the correct answer is 4. A, B, C, and D.

289. Which are the following correct features of matrices? *(Year 2021)*

(A) An identity matrix is a square matrix

(B) An identity matrix when gets transposed remains an identity matrix

(C) (A.B)T = AT.BT Where A and B are matrices

(D) (A-1)T = (AT)-1 where A is a matrix

Choose the current answer from the options given below :

(a) A and B only (b) A and C only

(c) B and C only (d) C and D only

Answer – a

Solution: An identity matrix has same number of rows and columns. i.e $\begin{bmatrix} 1 & 0 \\ 0 & 1 \end{bmatrix}$, $\begin{bmatrix} 1 & 0 & 0 \\ 0 & 1 & 0 \\ 0 & 0 & 1 \end{bmatrix}$
Transpose means changing rows into columns and vice-versa.

Identity matrix remains same after transpose.

290. Which of the following functions will result in an investment multiplier of value 4? *(Year 2021)*

(a) C = 50 + .25 Y

(b) C = 50 + .75 Y

(c) S = -50 + .75 Y

(d) I = 50 + .75 Y

Choose the correct answer from the options given below:

Answer – (b) **Solution:**

MPC = $\frac{\Delta C}{\Delta Y}$ = 0.75

So, when MPC = 0.75, K will be 4

If K = $\frac{1}{1-MPC}$

4 = $\frac{1}{1-MPC}$

1-MPC = ¼

1-MPC = 0.25

0.75 = MPC

291. The total population of city 'X' in 2011 was 28 lakhs and the total number of live births was 50 thousand. Find out crude birth rate per 1000 population *(Year 2021)*

(a) 0.17857

(b) 1.7857

(c) 17.857

(d) 178.57

Answer – c

Solution: To calculate the crude birth rate (CBR), we need to divide the total number of live births by the total population and multiply by 1,000.

CBR = (Number of live births / Total population) * 1,000

Given:

Total population = 28 lakhs (28,00,000)

Number of live births = 50 thousand (50,000)

CBR = (50,000 / 28,00,000) * 1,000

CBR = (0.01785714) * 1,000

CBR = 17.86 (rounded to two decimal places)

Therefore, the crude birth rate per 1000 population in city 'X' in 2011 was 17.86.

292. Match List I with List II *(Year 2021)*

List I	List II
A. Conserving the Environment for benefit of the future generation	I. Indirect use value
B. Search of Alternative fuels is necessary because traditional sources are non-renewable	II. Option Value
C. Wood from the forest is useful as timber	III. Bequest Value
D. Insects are important as they help inpollination	IV. Use Value

Choose the correct answer from the options given below

(a) A - I, B - II, C - III, D - IV,

(a) A - II, B - IV, C - I, D - III,

(a) A - III, B - II, C - IV, D - I,

(a) A - III, B - IV, C - II, D - I,

Answer: (C)

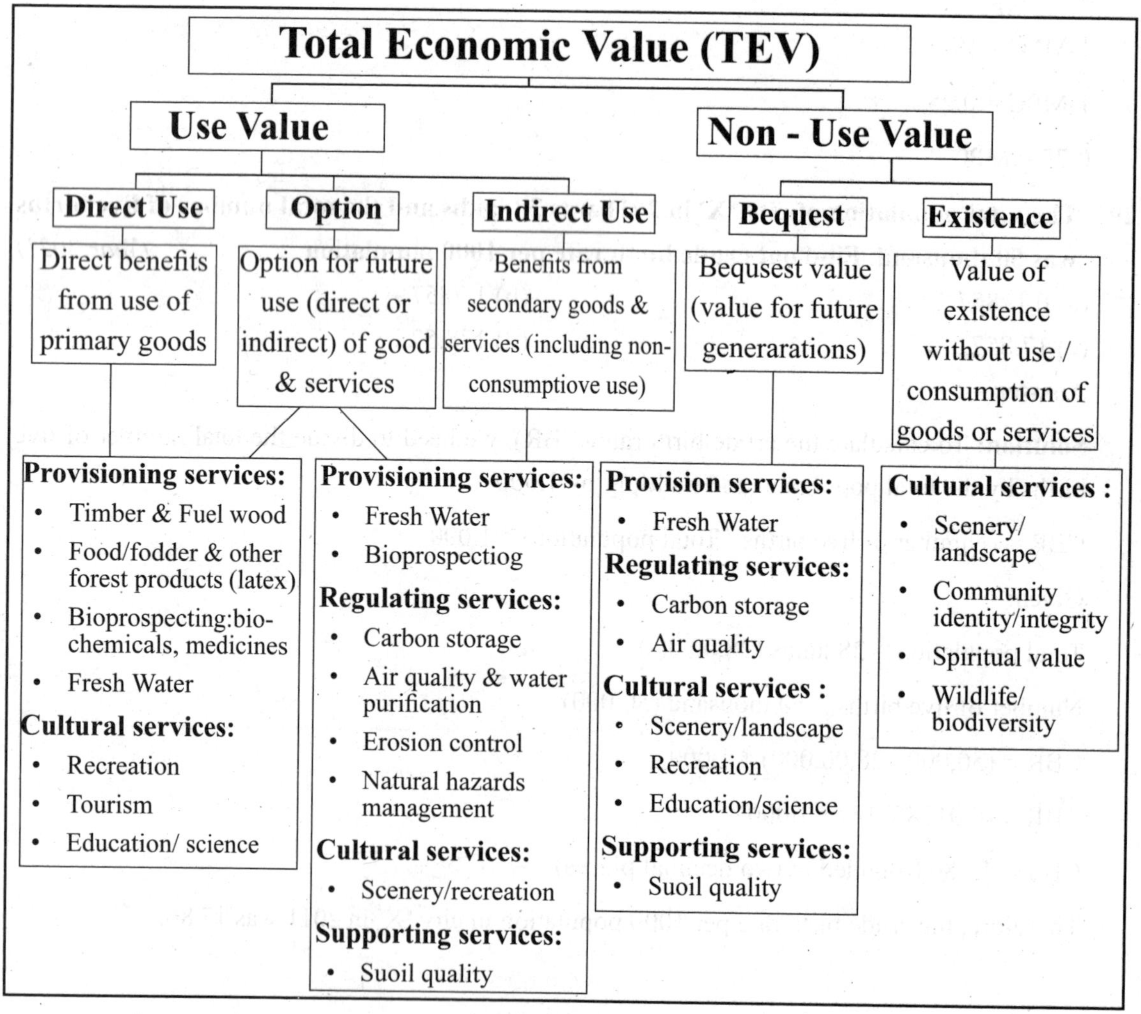

293. Match List I with List II *(Year 2021)*

List I	List II
(A) Carl Friedrich Gauss	I. Central Tendency
(B) Multicollinearity	II. OLS
(C) Mode	III. Karl Pearson
(D) Correlation coefficient	IV. Relationship among explanatory variables

Choose the correct answer from the options given below:

(a) A - II, B - IV, C - I, D - III,
(b) A - II, B - IV, C - III, D - I,
(c) A - III, B - IV, C - I, D - II,
(d) A - IV, B - I, C - II, D - III,

Answer – (a)

294. Match List I with List II

List I	List II
(A) Convex Function	I. Basic Variable
(B) Input-Output Analysis	II. Use of Derivative
(C) Linear Programming	III. Hawkins–Simon condition
(D) Marginal Propensity to Consume	IV. Demand Curve

Choose the correct answer from the options given below:

(a) A - II, B - III, C - I, D - IV,
(b) A - III, B - IV, C - I, D - II,
(c) A - IV, B - I, C - III, D - II,
(d) A - IV, B - III, C - I, D - II,

Answer – (d)

295. Match List I with List II *(Year 2021)*

List I	List II
(A) Perfect competition	I. Many real or perceived differences in products
(B) Monopoly	II. Little or no difference in products
(C) Monopolistic competition	III. Identical products
(D) Oligopoly	IV. Product without close substitutes

Choose the correct answer from the options given below:

(a) A - II, B - IV, C -I, D - III,
(b) A - III, B - I, C - II, D - IV,
(c) A - III, B - IV, C - I, D -II,
(d) A - III, B - IV, C - II, D - I,

Answer – (c)

296. Match List I with List II *(Year 2021)*

List I	List II
(A) Adam Smith	I. Theory of Big Push
(B) R. Rodan	II. Traditional Society

(C) W. W. Rostow	**III. Reserve army of labour**
(D) Karl Marx	**IV. Division of labour**

Choose the correct answer from the options given below

(a) A - I, B - IV, C - III, D - II, (b) A - II, B - III, C - I, D - IV,

(c) A - III, B - II, C - IV, D - I, (d) A - IV, B - I, C - II, D - III,

Answer – (d)

297. Given below are two statements: *(Year 2021)*

Statement l: One of the assumptions under OLS method states that the regression model is linear in the parameters, though it may or may not be linear in the variables.

Statement ll: The variance of the error, or disturbance, term is not the same regardless of the value of the explanatory variable under OLS.

In light of the above statements, choose the most appropriate answer from the options given below

(a) Both statement l and statement ll are correct

(b) Both statement l and statement ll are incorrect

(c) Statement l is correct but statement ll is incorrect

(d) Statement l is incorrect but statement ll is correct

Answer – (c)

Solution: Statement I is true. The OLS method assumes that the regression model is linear in the parameters, but it may or may not be linear in the variables. This means that the relationship between the dependent variable and the independent variables can be linear, but the independent variables themselves can be nonlinear.

Statement II is false. The OLS method assumes that the variance of the error term is the same regardless of the value of the explanatory variable. This is known as the homoscedasticity assumption. If the variance of the error term is not the same, then the OLS estimators will be biased.

298. Match List I with List II

List I	List II
(A) Security Exchange Board of India (SEBI)	**I. 1991**
(B) National Securities Depository Ltd (NSDL)	**II. 1992**
(C) Credit Rating Information Service of India Ltd (CRISIL)	**III. 1988**
(D) Investment Information and Credit Rating Agency of India (ICRA)	**IV. 1996**

Choose the correct answer from the options given below: *(Year 2021)*

(a) A - I, B - II, C - III, D - IV,
(b) A - II, B - IV, C - III, D - I,
(c) A - III, B - II, C - IV, D - I,
(d) A - IV, B - III, C - II, D - I,

Answer – (b)

Credit Rating Agencies

It is a company that assigns credit ratings, that is rating of a debtor's ability to pay back the debt by making timely interest payments and of the likelihood of default.

→ CRISIL (credit rating information services of India Limited) →1988

→ ICRA (Investment information and credit rating Agencies) → 1991

→ CARE (credit analysis and Research Limited) → 1993

National Stock Exchange - 1992 ,Index - Nifty

Bombay Stock Exchange – 1875, Index SENSEX

SEBI - Securities and Exchange Board of India →1988 - formed

→ 1992 - Statutory status

Functions :-

i) Promote interest of investors

ii) Promote development and to regulate securities market

iii) To prevent insider trading and of unfair practices

iv) Investor's education and training

299. Match List I with List II

List I	List II
(A) Menu cost	**I. Monetary Policy**
(B) Quantitative Easing	**II. Inflation**
(C) Pump Priming	**III. Phillips curve**
(D) Trade-off between inflation and unemployment	**IV. Fiscal policy**

Choose the correct answer from the options given below (Year 2021)

(a) A - I, B - II, C - III, D - IV;
(b) A - II, B - I, C - IV, D - III,
(c) A - III, B - IV, C - I, D - II,
(d) A - IV, B - III, C - II, D - I,

Answer – (b)

300. Arrange the following in chronological order in which they were introduced: *(Year 2021)*

(A) SDGs **(B) MPI** **(C) PQLI** **(D) HDI**

Choose the correct answer from the options given below

(a) C, B, A, D,
(b) C, D, B, A,
(c) D, C, A, B,
(d) D, C, B, A,

Answer – (b)

Solution:

- PQLI (Physical Quality of Life Index): 1979
- HDI (Human Development Index): 1990
- MPI (Multidimensional Poverty Index): 2010
- SDGs (Sustainable Development Goals): 2015

The PQLI was developed by the Overseas Development Council (ODC) in 1979. It is a composite index that measures the quality of life in a country based on three indicators: life expectancy, literacy, and infant mortality.

The HDI was developed by the United Nations Development Programme (UNDP) in 1990. It is a composite index that measures the average achievement of a country in three basic dimensions of human development: health, education, and standard of living.

The MPI was developed by the Oxford Poverty & Human Development Initiative (OPHI) and the UNDP in 2010. It is a composite index that measures the multidimensional poverty experienced by a population.

The SDGs were adopted by the United Nations General Assembly in 2015. They are a set of 17 goals that aim to end poverty, protect the planet, and ensure prosperity for all.

301. Match List I with List II *(Year 2021)*

List I	List II
(A) Canons of Taxation	**I. U. K. Hicks**
(B) Canons of Public Expenditure	**II. Adam Smith**
(C) Effective Incidence of Tax	**III. Findlay Shirras**
(D) Benefit received approach of Public Expenditure	**IV. Erik Lindahl**

Choose the correct answer from the options given below:

(a) A - I, B - II, C - III, D - IV,
(b) A - II, B - III, C - I, D - IV,
(c) A - II, B - III, C - IV, D - I,
(d) A - IV, B - I, C - II, D - III,

Answer – (b)

302. Human Development Index (HDI) currently, as published by the UNDP is calculated by using which of the following? *(Year 2021)*

(a) Arithmetic Mean
(b) Geometric Mean
(c) Harmonic Mean
(d) Quadratic Mean

Answer – (b)

Solution: The HDI is calculated as the geometric mean (equally-weighted) of life expectancy, education, and gross national income (GNI) per capita. It incorporates three key dimensions of human development: a long and healthy life, access to knowledge, and a decent standard of living. The specific metrics used for each dimension are:

(a) **Life expectancy at birth:** This metric assesses the health dimension of human development and reflects the average number of years a newborn is expected to live.

(b) **Expected years of schooling:** This metric evaluates access to knowledge for the younger generation and represents the number of years of education a child is anticipated to receive.

(c) **Average years of schooling:** This metric assesses access to knowledge for the older generation and represents the mean number of years of education among the adult population.

(d) **Gross national income (GNI) per capita:** This metric measures the standard of living dimension and reflects the average income per person in a country.

By calculating the geometric mean of these metrics, the HDI provides a comprehensive measure of human development by considering multiple dimensions of well-being.

303. Liquidity Adjustment Facility (LAF) was recommended by *(Year 2021)*

(a) Bimal Jalan Committee (b) Rangarajan Committee

(c) Narasimham Committee - 11 (d) Raghuram Rajan Committee

Answer – (c)

Solution: The Narasimham Committee was appointed by the Reserve Bank of India (RBI) and had two phases, with the second phase report being released in 1998. The committee, chaired by M. Narasimham, made several recommendations for reforms in the Indian banking sector, including the introduction of the LAF. The LAF is a monetary policy tool used by the RBI to manage short-term liquidity in the banking system. It consists of repo and reverse repo operations through which banks can borrow or lend funds for a specified period, allowing the RBI to control money supply and interest rates.

304. Which of the following are NOT properties of Cobb-Douglas production function? *(Year 2021)*

(A) Cobb-Douglas production function is a homogeneous production function

(B) Curves representing average and marginal productivity of inputs are not downward sloping

(C) Marginal productivity of labour and capital in Cobb-Douglas production function are functions of the capital-labour ratio

(D) Iso-quants of Cobb-Douglas production functions are positively sloped

Choose the correct answer from the options given below:

(a) A and B only (b) B and C only/

(c) B and D only/, (d) C and D only/

Answer – (c)

Solution: In case of Cobb Douglas, AP and MP are downward sloping and isoquants are negatively sloped (convex shaped).

Cobb Douglas Production Function: - 1928

1. Linearly Homogenous Production Function.
2. Constant Returns to Scale.
3. $E_S = 1$

Q = Output

A = Technology

L = Labour

K = Capital

$$Q = AL^{\alpha}K^{\beta}$$

α = tells output elasticity of labour. α = Share of labour in production

β = tells output elasticity of capital.

Some properties of Cobb Douglas production function: -

1. Linear homogeneous production function with constant returns to scale.
2. Diminishing returns to each factor.
3. Coefficients of it represent output elasticity of input.
4. Elasticity of output in relation to labour is 'α' and in relation to capital is 'β'.
5. Share of labour in National Income = α, share of capital in National Income= β
6. E_S is unity
7. Linear homogeneous production function passes through origin.

$\alpha + \beta = 1$	CRS
$\alpha + \beta > 1$	IRS
$\alpha + \beta < 1$	DRS

Euler Theorem/Product Exhaustion Theorem : - If the factors are paid according to their Marginal productivity, then total output will be exhausted. It holds true in linearly homogenous production function.

$$MP_L * L + MP_K * K = Q$$

305. Which of the following statements are relevant for Gender Budgeting? *(Year 2021)*

(A) Preparing a separate budget for women

(B) Gender budget is not practised by the Government of India

(C) Evaluating budgetary provisions with a gender perspective

(D) Gender budgeting is a tool for Gender Empowerment

Choose the correct answer from the options given below:

(a) A and D only
(c) A only,
(d) A, B, C and D
(e) C and D only

Answer – (d)

Solution: Gender budgeting is a strategy used to ensure that government budgets address gender disparities and promote gender equality. It involves evaluating budgetary provisions with a gender perspective and incorporating gender considerations into budgetary decision-making.

(A) Preparing a separate budget for women: While it is common to allocate specific funds for programs and initiatives targeting women, gender budgeting goes beyond simply creating a separate budget for women. It aims to analyze and address gender disparities in all aspects of the budget.

(B) Gender budget is not practiced by the Government of India: This statement is incorrect. The Government of India has implemented gender budgeting as a tool to promote gender equality and women's empowerment. It involves integrating gender considerations into budgetary processes and evaluating budget allocations and expenditures based on their impact on gender equality.

(C) Evaluating budgetary provisions with a gender perspective : Gender budgeting involves analyzing budgetary provisions to understand their differential impact on women and men and making adjustments to address gender disparities.

(D) Gender budgeting is a tool for gender empowerment : One of the objectives of gender budgeting is to promote gender equality and empower women by ensuring that budgetary decisions and resource allocations address gender disparities and promote women's empowerment.

306. Identify the proper sequence in the traditional econometric methodology of conducting research *(Year 2021)*

(A) Data collection

(B) Policy prescription

(C) Testing of hypothesis

(D) Formulation of hypothesis

Choose the correct answer from the options given below

(a) A, B, C, D,
(b) A, D, B, C,
(c) D, A, B, C,
(d) D, A, C, B,

Answer – (d)

Solution:

Formulation of hypothesis (D): The first step in conducting research is to formulate a hypothesis or a research question that will guide the study.

Data collection (A): After formulating the hypothesis, researchers gather the necessary data through various methods, such as surveys, experiments, or secondary data sources.

Testing of hypothesis (C): Once the data is collected, researchers apply statistical techniques and econometric models to analyze the data and test the formulated hypothesis.

Policy prescription (B): Based on the results obtained from testing the hypothesis, researchers can make policy recommendations or draw conclusions about the relationships between variables.

Therefore, the correct answer is option (d) D, A, C, B.

307. Improvement in the balance of payments deficit may be effected through: *(Year 2021)*

(A) Import controls

(B) Export promotion

(C) Foreign exchange control

(D) Devaluation

Choose the correct answer from the options given below:

(a) A and B only
(b) A, B and C only
(c) A, B, C and D
(d) C and D only

Answer – (c)

Solution: Improvement in the balance of payments deficit can be achieved through various measures, and all options listed can contribute to addressing the deficit:

(A) Import controls: Implementing measures to restrict imports can help reduce the outflow of foreign currency, which can improve the balance of payments deficit.

(B) Export promotion: Encouraging and supporting exports can increase the inflow of foreign currency, leading to an improvement in the balance of payments.

(C) Foreign exchange control: Implementing controls on foreign exchange transactions can help manage the outflow and inflow of foreign currency, which can contribute to improving the balance of payments.

(D) Devaluation: Devaluing the domestic currency can make exports more competitive and imports relatively more expensive, which can lead to an improvement in the balance of payments.

Therefore, all options A, B, C, and D can be effective measures to improve the balance of payments deficit.

308. The independence of real variables from changes in money supply and nominal variables is called : *(Year 2021)*

(a) Classical dichotomy
(b) Keynesian dichotomy
(c) Money illusion
(d) Money multiplier

Answer – (a)

Solution: Classical Dichotomy

By the term classical dichotomy we mean that there exists two independent sectors in the economy- real sector and monetary sector. There is a complete independence of real variables from nominal variables. This implies that the money is neutral in nature. It acts as a medium of exchange only. Money impacts prices and hence only affects the nominal variables, keeping the real variables unchanged. Real factors are determined by variables totally different from nominal variables

309. Consider the following statements about the rational expectations model : *(Year 2021)*

(A) Monetary policy cannot affect output and employment

(B) Unanticipated changes will not affect real variables in the very short run

(C) There is equilibrium in the markets

(D) Economic agents use all relevant available information to form their expectations

Choose the correct answer from the options given below:

(a) A, B and C only
(b) A, B, C and D
(c) A, C and D only
(d) B, C and D only

Answer – (c)

Solution: Rational Expectations Model:

According to the rational expectations' hypothesis, people make decisions based on the rational nature, the facts at hand, and their prior experiences.

The rational expectations' theory is a concept and theory used in macroeconomics.

The rational expectations' theory is used by economists to explain anticipated economic phenomena like interest rates and inflation rates.

Rational Expectations:- The theory was given by John Muth in 1961. It is a forward looking approach and people are considered to be rational. Any errors in forecasting is random in nature.

310. The concept of 'money illusion' was first given by whom? *(Year 2021)*

(a) Irving Fishe (b) J. M. Keynes

(c) Milton Friedman (d) Robertson

Answer – (a)

Solution: Money illusion is the tendency of people to focus on the nominal value of money, rather than its real value. This means that people may be fooled into thinking that a nominal increase in their income is a real increase, even if prices have also increased.

The concept of money illusion was first introduced by Irving Fisher in his 1928 book, *The Money Illusion*. Fisher argued that money illusion could have a significant impact on economic behavior, and he proposed a number of policies to mitigate its effects.

311. Which of the following statements are CORRECT for correlation analysis? *(Year 2021)*

(A) Degree of linear association is measured between two variables

(B) Predictability is not part of correlation analysis

(C) Spearman has no contribution to correlation analysis

(D) Cause and effect relationship is established through correlation analysis

Choose the correct answer from the options given below:

(a) A and C only (b) A and B only,

(c) A and D only (d) B and C only

Answer – (b)

Solution: Correlation analysis is a statistical method that measures the degree of linear association between two variables. It does not measure the predictability of one variable from the other, nor does it establish a cause-and-effect relationship between the two variables.

The two most common types of correlation analysis are Pearson's correlation coefficient and Spearman's rank correlation coefficient. Pearson's correlation coefficient is used when the two variables are measured on a continuous scale, while Spearman's rank correlation coefficient is used when the two variables are measured on an ordinal scale.

The correlation coefficient is a number between -1 and 1. A correlation coefficient of 1 indicates a perfect positive correlation, a correlation coefficient of -1 indicates a perfect negative correlation, and a correlation coefficient of 0 indicates no correlation.

Therefore, the correct statements about correlation analysis are:

(A) Degree of linear association is measured between two variables

(B) Predictability is not part of correlation analysis

The other statements are incorrect. Option (C) is incorrect because Spearman did contribute to correlation analysis by developing the Spearman's rank correlation coefficient. Option (D) is incorrect because correlation analysis does not establish a cause-and-effect relationship between two variables.

312. In the short-run production function, which one of the following is CORRECT?

(Year 2021)

(a) Technology is assumed to be constant for a given production function relationship

(b) Technology is assumed to change as capital stock changes

(c) Technology is assumed to change as labour input changes

(d) Technology is assumed to change positively until diminishing returns set in

Answer – (a)

Solution: Production Theory

Production function is technical relationship between the inputs and the outputs.

$$Q = f(L, K)$$

$$AP = \frac{TP}{L} \qquad MP = \frac{\Delta TP}{\Delta L}$$

Production Function

Law of Variable Proportion	Law of Returns to scale
[Short Run Law]	[Long Run Law]
[1 factor Variable, others fixed]	[All factors Variable]

Law of variable proportions/ Returns to a factor:-

It is short run theory in which there is at least one factor which is fixed. Beyond a certain point, the MP of the factor would diminish.

Assumptions

1) Technology is fixed.

2) One factor is variable others are fixed.

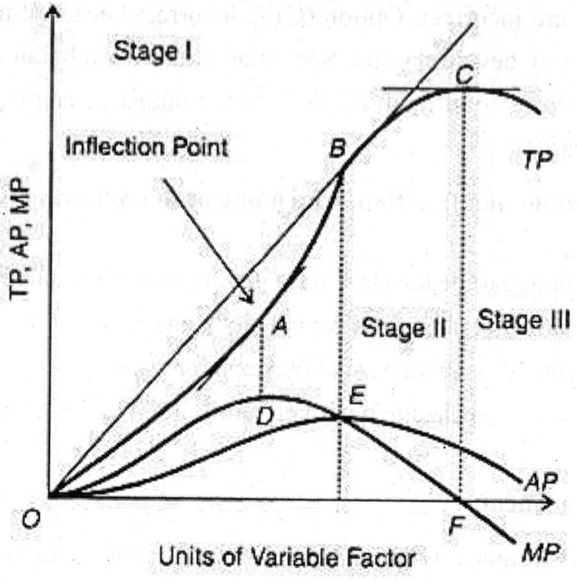

313. Match List I with List II

List I	List II
(A) NIRVIK	I. A project directed to provide piped cooking gas to millions of households
(B) Ayushman Bharat	II. A scheme to enhance energy efficiency
(C) Pradhan Mantri Urja Ganga (PMUG)	III. Export credit insurance scheme
(D) Perform, Achieve and Trade (PAT)	IV. Programme related to health issues in the primary, secondary and tertiary Sectors

Choose the correct answer from the options given below: (Year 2021)

(a) A - II, B - III, C - I, D - IV,
(b) A - II, B - IV, C - III, D - I,
(c) A - III, B - IV, C - I, D - II,
(d) A - III, B - IV, C - II, D - I,

Answer – (c)

314. If a production function admits both Harrod and Hicks neutral technical progress, the elasticity of substitution should be *(Year 2021)*

(a) equal to infinite
(b) to one divided by two
(c) equal to one
(d) equal to zero

Answer – (c)

Solution: Harrod-neutral technical progress is a type of technical progress in which the efficiency of labor increases, but the efficiency of capital remains the same. This means that the production function shifts upwards, but the capital-output ratio remains the same.

Hicks-neutral technical progress is a type of technical progress in which the marginal rate of substitution between labor and capital remains the same. This means that the production function shifts upwards, but the slope of the production function remains the same.

For a production function to admit both Harrod-neutral and Hicks-neutral technical progress, the elasticity of substitution between labor and capital must be equal to one. This is because the elasticity of substitution measures the responsiveness of the marginal rate of substitution to changes in the factor proportions. If the elasticity of substitution is equal to one, then the marginal rate of substitution will remain the same, even if the factor proportions change.

Therefore, the elasticity of substitution should be equal to one if a production function admits both Harrod and Hicks neutral technical progress.

315. Assuming the probability of a male birth as 0.5, find the chances that a family of 3 children will have two boys and one girl *(Year 2021)*

(a) 1/8 (b) 2/8 (c) 3/8 (d) 4/8

Answer – (c)

Solution:

BBG+BGB+GBB

$\left(\frac{1}{2} \times \frac{1}{2} \times \frac{1}{2}\right) + \left(\frac{1}{2} \times \frac{1}{2} \times \frac{1}{2}\right) + \left(\frac{1}{2} \times \frac{1}{2} \times \frac{1}{2}\right)$

1/8 + 1/8 + 1/8

= 3/8

316. Which of the following are a source of market failure?

(A) The existence of public goods

(B) The presence of externalities

(C) The fact that some goods are rivals in consumption

(D) The existence of monopolies

Choose the correct answer from the options given below: *(Year 2021)*

(a) A, B and C only (b) A, B and D only

(c) A, C and D only (d) B, C and D only

Answer – (b)

Solution:

Market failure occurs when the allocation of goods and services by the free market is inefficient and leads to suboptimal outcomes. The sources of market failure include:

(A) The existence of public goods: Public goods are non-excludable and non-rivalrous, meaning that once provided, they are available to everyone and one person's consumption does not diminish the availability to others. Public goods may lead to market failure because private firms have no incentive to produce them efficiently since they cannot exclude non-payers from benefiting.

(B) The presence of externalities: Externalities occur when the actions of one party impose costs or benefits on others who are not directly involved in the transaction. Externalities can lead to market failure because the market does not account for these external costs or benefits, resulting in an inefficient allocation of resources.

(C) The fact that some goods are rivals in consumption: This statement is incorrect as rivalrous goods do not necessarily lead to market failure. Rivalrous goods are goods where one person's consumption reduces the amount available for others. While rivalrous goods may have implications for resource allocation, they do not inherently result in market failure.

(D) The existence of monopolies: Monopolies occur when a single firm has control over a particular market, limiting competition and potentially leading to market failure. Monopolies can result in higher prices, reduced output, and inefficiency compared to a competitive market.

Therefore, options A, B, and D are the correct sources of market failure.

317. In the classical linear regression model, Xi and Ui are assumed to be: *(Year 2021)*

(a) highly correlated
(b) negatively correlated
(c) not correlated
(d) positively correlated

Answer – (c)

Solution: In the classical linear regression model, Xi and Ui are assumed to be not correlated. This assumption is known as the assumption of exogeneity. It means that the explanatory variables (Xi) are assumed to be unrelated to the error term (Ui). In other words, the errors are not systematically related to the values of the explanatory variables. This assumption allows for unbiased and consistent estimation of the regression coefficients using ordinary least squares (OLS) estimation.

318. Given below are two statements, one is labelled as Assertion A and the other is labelled as Reason R *(Year 2021)*

Assertion A: New capital accumulation is the vehicle of technical progress

Reason R: Technical progress is embodied in new machines

In light of the above statements, choose the correct answer from the options given below

(a) A is false but R is true

(b) A is true but R is false

(c) Both A and R are true and R is the correct explanation of A

(d) Both A and R are true but R is NOT the correct explanation of A

Answer – (c)

Solution: Assertion A states that new capital accumulation is the vehicle of technical progress. This means that new machines that embody new technologies are the main way that technical progress is introduced into the economy.

Reason R states that technical progress is embodied in new machines. This means that new technologies are not just ideas, but they are also embodied in the physical form of new machines.

Both assertions are true, and reason R is the correct explanation of assertion A. This is because new machines are the main way that new technologies are introduced into the economy. When new machines are introduced, they embody new technologies that increase the productivity of labor and capital. This leads to economic growth.

319. What is the CORRECT sequence of the following? *(Year 2021)*

(A) Uruguay Round

(B) Kennedy Round

(C) Doha Round

(D) Geneva Round

Choose the correct answer from the options given below

(a) A, B, C, D, (b) B, D, C, A,

(c) C, A, B, D, (d) D, B, A, C,

Answer = (d)

Solution: GATT [General Agreement on Tariffs and Trade]

Formed in 1947

Headquarters in Geneva (Switzerland).

Principles of GATT:-Non Discrimination

Objective -promotes free trade.

Uruguay round replaced GATT with WTO.

WTO- World Trade Organisation-(1995)-

Geneva Round 1947

Annecy round 1949

Torquay round 1951

Geneva round 1955-56

Dillon round 1960-62

Kennedy round 1962-67

Tokyo round 1973-79

Uruguay round 1986-94

Doha round 2001

Bali 2013

320. In which of the following ways have there been structural changes in agricultural and rural areas in India? *(Year 2021)*

(A) Crop diversification within agriculture sector

(B) Diversification from livestock to crop husbandry

(C) Diversification from non-commercial crops to commercial crops

(D) Diversification from traditional inputs to modern inputs

Choose the correct answer from the options given below:

(a) A, B and C only

(b) A, B and D only

(c) A, C and D only

(d) B, C and D only

Answer - (c)

Solution: There have been a number of structural changes in agricultural and rural areas in India in recent years. These changes include:

Crop diversification within the agriculture sector. This means that farmers are growing a wider variety of crops, rather than just a few traditional crops. This is being driven by a number of factors, including the demand for new crops in the market, the need to reduce risk, and the availability of new technologies.

Diversification from non-commercial crops to commercial crops. This means that farmers are shifting from growing crops that are not traded in the market to crops that are traded in the market. This is being driven by the higher prices that commercial crops fetch.

Diversification from traditional inputs to modern inputs. This means that farmers are using more modern inputs, such as fertilizers and pesticides, in their farming practices. This is being driven by the need to increase yields and improve the quality of crops.

The other options, diversification from livestock to crop husbandry, is not a structural change in agricultural and rural areas in India. Livestock husbandry is still an important part of the rural economy, and it is not being replaced by crop husbandry.

321. Given below are two statements: *(Year 2021)*

Statement l: Social Welfare Function (SWF) is a sort of social indifference map consisting of the Social Indifference Curves (SICs) which shows the various combination of utilities that gives the same level of social welfare (SW).

Statement ll: Social Indifference Curves (SICs) may not be convex or concave to the origin.

In light of the above statements, choose the most appropriate answer from the options given below

(a) Both Statement I and Statement II are correct

(b) Both Statement II and Statement II are incorrect,

(c) Statement I is correct but Statement II is incorrect/कथन I

(d) Statement I is incorrect but Statement II is correct

Answer - (a)

Solution: Statement I is correct because a social indifference curve (SIC) shows the various combinations of utilities that give the same level of social welfare (SW). The SICs are analogous to the indifference curves in individual utility theory.

Statement II is also correct because there is no rule that says that SICs must be convex or concave to the origin. In fact, SICs can be any shape, as long as they satisfy the condition that they represent combinations of utilities that give the same level of social welfare.

Therefore, both statements are correct.

Here is a diagram that shows a social indifference curve:

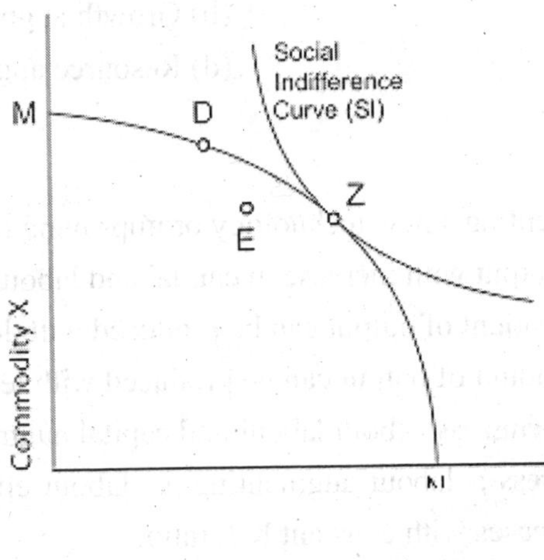

Social indifference curve

The social indifference curve in the diagram shows the various combinations of utilities for two individuals that give the same level of social welfare.

322. The incidence of which of the following will entirely be on the monopolist? *(Year 2021)*

(a) Lump-sum tax
(b) None of these
(c) Regulated monopoly pricing
(d) Specific tax

Answer - (a)

Solution: A lump-sum tax is a fixed amount of money that is paid by a taxpayer, regardless of their income or output. This means that a lump-sum tax cannot be passed on to consumers in the form of higher prices.

Therefore, the incidence of a lump-sum tax will entirely be on the monopolist. The monopolist will have to bear the full burden of the tax, and it will not be able to pass it on to consumers.

The other options are incorrect. Regulated monopoly pricing is a type of price control that limits the amount of profit that a monopolist can make. Specific tax is a tax that is levied on a specific good or service. Both of these types of taxes can be passed on to consumers in the form of higher prices.

Table that shows the incidence of different types of taxes on a monopolist:

Type of tax	**Incidence**
Lump-sum tax	Entirely on the monopolist
Regulated monopoly pricing	Partially on the monopolist and partially on consumers
Specific tax	Partially on the monopolist and partially on consumers

323. Harrod-neutral technical progress is necessarily: *(Year 2021)*

(a) Capital augmenting
(b) Growth augmenting
(c) Labour augmenting
(d) Resource augmenting

Answer - (c)

Solution:

Technical progress :- inventing a new technology or improving existing through innovations.
Neutral :-Produce more output with increase in capital and labour in same proportion.
Capital savings :- same amount of output can be produced with lesser amount of capital.
Labour saving :- same amount of output can be produced with lesser amount of labour.
Hicks neutral technical progress :- both labour and capital augmenting.
Harrod's technical progress :- labour augmenting, i.e labour efficiency improves. Marginal productivity of labour increases with constant K/L ratio.

Hicks vs Harrod neutral technical progress :- Technical progress, in the per-worker production function, is said to be Harrod-neutral if, at any constant value of the capital-output ratio, the marginal product of capital remains unchanged. Harrod's classification compares points at which the capital output ratio is constant as opposed to the Hicks procedure which compares points at which the capital-labour ratio is constant

Solow's :- Capital augmenting. Marginal product of capital increases with constant K/L ratio.

324. Arrange the introduction of the following taxes in India in chronological order.

(Year 2021)

(A) Service Tax

(B) Income Tax

(C) Banking Transaction Tax

(D) Gift Tax

(E) Goods and Services Tax

Choose the correct answer from the options given below

(a) B, A, C, E, D, (b) B, C, A, D, E,

(c) B, D, A, C, E, (d) D, B, A, C, E,

Answer - (c)

Solution: The correct chronological order of the introduction of the following taxes in India is:

- Income Tax (1860)
- Gift Tax (1958)
- Service Tax (1994)
- Banking Transaction Tax (2005)

Goods and Services Tax (2017)

Income Tax was introduced in India in 1860 by Sir James Wilson, the then Finance Minister of India. The tax was initially levied on incomes above a certain threshold. However, the tax has been revised several times since then, and the current tax regime is quite complex.

Gift Tax was introduced in India in 1958. The tax is levied on the transfer of property by way of gift. The tax is payable by the recipient of the gift, and the rate of tax depends on the value of the gift.

Service Tax was introduced in India in 1994. The tax is levied on the provision of services by businesses. The tax is payable by the service provider, and the rate of tax depends on the type of service.

Banking Transaction Tax was introduced in India in 2005. The tax is levied on the transfer of money through banks. The tax is payable by the bank, and the rate of tax depends on the amount of money transferred.

Goods and Services Tax was introduced in India in 2017. The tax is levied on the supply of goods and services. The tax is payable by the supplier of goods and services, and the rate of tax depends on the type of goods or services supplied.

325. Consider some of the schemes/programs introduced by the Government of India to enhance agriculture productivity and farmer's income. Arrange them in chronological order of their appearance. *(Year 2021)*

(A) Soil Health Card Scheme

(B) Kisan Credit Card Scheme

(C) Pradhan Mantri Fasal Bima Yojana

(D) Doubling Farmers' income program

Choose the correct answer from the options given below

(a) A, B, C, D, (b) B, A, C, D,

(c) B, A, D, C, (d) B, C, A, D,

Answer - (b)

Solution:

A. Kisan Credit Card Scheme (1998)

B. Soil Health Card Scheme (2015)

C. Pradhan Mantri Fasal Bima Yojana (2016)

D. Doubling Farmers' Income program (2018)

Therefore, the correct answer is option (2) B, A, C, D.

- Kisan Credit Card Scheme was launched in 1998 by the National Bank for Agriculture and Rural Development (NABARD). The scheme provides easy access to credit for farmers to meet their short-term agricultural needs.
- Soil Health Card Scheme was launched in 2015 by the Ministry of Agriculture and Farmers' Welfare. The scheme provides farmers with a soil health card that contains information about the nutrient content of their soil. This information can help farmers to improve their crop yields by using the right fertilizers and pesticides.
- Pradhan Mantri Fasal Bima Yojana was launched in 2016 by the Ministry of Agriculture and Farmers' Welfare. The scheme provides crop insurance to farmers against crop losses due to natural calamities.
- Doubling Farmers' Income program was launched in 2018 by the Ministry of Agriculture and Farmers' Welfare. The program aims to double the income of farmers by 2022. The program focuses on increasing agricultural productivity, improving access to markets, and providing financial support to farmers.

326. Which among the following is NOT part of the neoclassical theory of growth? *(Year 2021)*

(a) Meade's Model
(b) Pasinetti Model
(c) Solow Model
(d) Swan Model

Answer - (b)

Solution: Neoclassical growth theory is an economic theory that outlines how a steady economic growth rate results from a combination of three driving forces—labour, capital, and technology. Swan Model, Meade's Model, Solow Model are a part of neoclassical theory of growth model.

In the Pasinetti Model, which is a Cambridge Model, two classes of agents, workers and capitalists, save constant proportions of their income. On a balanced growth path in this model, the rate of profit remains constant regardless of the workers' savings propensity. This means that changes in the savings behavior of workers do not impact the rate of profit in the long run.

327. If we have objective function involving a variables :

$U = f\{X_1.X_2.X_3......X_n)$ subject to $Ø\{X_1.X_2.X_3 \quad X_n) = 0$. The second order condition for extremum to be *(December 2021 and June 2022)*

(A) For maximum $|\bar{H}_2| < 0, |\bar{H}_3| < 0,....$
(B) For maximum $|\bar{H}_2| > 0, |\bar{H}_3| < 0,....$
(C) For maximum $|\bar{H}_2| < 0, |\bar{H}_3| > 0,....$
(D) For minimum $|\bar{H}_2| < 0, |\bar{H}_3| < 0,....$
(E) For minimum $|\bar{H}_2| > 0, |\bar{H}_3| > 0,....$

Choose the correct answer from the options given below:

(a) (A) and (D) only
(b) (B) and (D) only
(c) (C) and (E) only
(d) (B) and (E) only

Answer - (2)

Solution: In constrained extremum case, we shall encounter bordered hessian. These are the conditions for extremum in case of bordered hessian matrix.

For maximum $|\bar{H}_2| > 0, |\bar{H}_3| < 0,....$

For minimum $|\bar{H}_2| < 0, |\bar{H}_3| < 0,....$

328. Which of the followings are correct in case of normal distribution? *(December 2021 and June 2022)*

(A) $Q1 + Q_2 = 2Md$
(B) Q.D. = 1/3 σ
(C) Q.D. = 2/3 σ
(D) All moments of odd order about mean are zero
(E) $Q_1 + Q_2 = Md$

Choose the correct answer from the options given below:

(a) (B), (D) and (E) only (b) (A), (B) and (D) only

(c) (A), (C) and (D) only (d) (C), (D) and (E) only

Answer - (c)

Solution:

4SD = 5MD = 6QD

Or

4SD = 6QD

4/6 SD = QD

QD = 2/3 SD

1. Central moments or moments about Actual Mean (u).

$$u_r = \frac{\Sigma(x-\bar{x})^r}{N}$$

$$u_1 = \frac{\Sigma(x-\bar{x})^1}{N} = 0$$

$$u_2 = \frac{\Sigma(x-\bar{x})^2}{N} = \text{Variance}$$

Odd order moments i.e. $u1, u_3$ are zero.

329. Match List-I with List-II : *(December 2021 and June 2022)*

List-I	List-II
(A) Absolute Income Concept	**(I) Milton Friedman**
(B) Relative Income Concept	**(II) J. M. Keynes**
(C) Fixed Income Concept	**(III) James Dussenberry**
(D) Life Cycle Concept	**(IV) Franco Modigalani**

Select the correct answer from the options given below

(a) (A)-(II), (B)-(I), (C) (IV), (D)-(III)

(b) (A)-(II), (B)-(III), (C)-(I), (D)-(IV)

(c) (A)-(IV), (B)-(III), (C)-(II), (D)-(I)

(d) (A)-(III), (B)-(II), (C)-(I), (D)-(IV)

Answer - (b)

Solution:

(A) Absolute Income Concept - (II) J. M. Keynes: The absolute income concept refers to the measurement of income based on its absolute value, regardless of its purchasing power or relative value. It focuses on the actual amount of income earned by individuals or a nation.

J. M. Keynes, a renowned economist, developed various theories related to income and employment, emphasizing the importance of aggregate demand in driving economic growth and stability.

(B) Relative Income Concept - (III) James Deusenberry: The relative income concept emphasizes the comparison of income levels relative to others in society. It considers the distribution of income and the relative position of individuals or groups in terms of their income compared to others.

(C) Fixed Income Concept - (I) Milton Friedman: The fixed income concept refers to a stable and predetermined income that does not vary with changing economic conditions. It often applies to specific financial instruments, such as fixed-income securities, which provide a fixed return to investors.

(D) Life Cycle Concept - (IV) Franco Modigliani: The life cycle concept of income relates to the changes in income that occur over an individual's or household's lifetime. It recognizes that income patterns tend to vary at different stages of life, such as during education, career advancement, and retirement. Franco Modigliani, an Italian-American economist and Nobel laureate, developed the life cycle hypothesis, which suggests that individuals aim to maintain a relatively stable standard of living throughout their lifetime by balancing their saving and borrowing.

330. Suppose the following equations are given for IS and LM curves:

IS curve: Y = 350 - 1000r

LM curve: Y= 200 + 500r

where Y = income and r = rate of interest. What will be the equilibrium values of Y and r?

(A) Y 200, r = 0.04

(B) Y= 250, r = 0.1

(C) Y = 300, r = 0.15

(D) Y = 350, r = 0.2

Answer: (b)

Solution:

$Y = 350 - 1000r = 200 + 500r$

$= 350-200 = 500r + 1000r$

$=150 = 1500r$

$=150/1500 =r$

$1/10 = r$

$0.1 = r$

Y = 350 – 1000*0.1

=350 – 100

= 250

331. In confidence interval estimation, a = 5%, this means that this interval includes the true ß with probability of :

(a) 5% (b) 50% (c) 95% (d) 45%

Answer: (c)

Solution: If level of significance(a) is 5%, than the confidence interval estimation will be 95%.

332. If input-output coefficient matrix is called A, then technology matrix is:

(a) I – A (b) A – 1

(c) (I – A)-1 (d) A2

Answer: (a)

Solution: Technology Matrix is I-A, and I is the identity matrix.

333. In a multiple regression model given by Yi = $\beta_1 + \beta_2 x_{2i} + \beta_3 x_{3i} + u_i$, the partial regression coefficients are given by :

(a) Both β_1 and β_2 (b) Both β_2 and β_3

(c) Both β_1 and β_3 (d) Both β_1 and u

Answer: (b)

334. Formula for coefficient of variation is:

(a) $\bar{X}/\sigma \times 100$ (b) $\bar{X}.\sigma.100$

(c) $\sigma/\bar{X} \times 100$ (d) $1/\sigma\bar{X} \times 100$

Answer: (c)

335. The fitted regression equation is given by $\hat{Y}_I$ = - 12 + 0.5x. What is the value of the residual at the point x = 50, y = 70?

(a) -57 (b) 57 (c) 0 (d) 33

Answer: (b)

Solution:

$\hat{Y}$, = 12 + 0.5x + u

70 = -12 + 0.5(50) + u

70 + 12 + 25 + u

82 - 25 = u

57 = u

336. If AR = 15, MR = 5 the price elasticity of demand is *(June 2019)*

(a) 2.3 (b) 1.5 (c) 1.75 (d) 1

Answer: (b)

$$2d = \frac{AR}{AR - MR}$$

$$= \frac{15}{15-5}$$

$$= \frac{15}{10}$$

$$\boxed{= 1.5}$$

337. The cost function of a monopolist if C = 40 + 12x and demand function as P = 60 – 3x. What is his profit maximizing output level. *(June 2019)*

(a) 12 (b) 11 (c) 8 (d) 9

Answer: (c)

Solution:

Profit maximisation

MR = MC

TR = PX

= (60 - 3x)x

$= 60x - 3x^2$

MR = 6 - 6x

TC = 40 + 12x

. MC + 12

60 - 6x = 12

-6x = 48/,

$$\boxed{x = 8}$$

338. Suppose that for a particular economy for some time period investment = 200 Government expenditure was =75. Net taxes were fixed at 100 and consumption was given by the consumption function C = 25 + 0.8 Yd. Where Yd is disposable income and Y is GDP. What is the value of tax multiplier (ΔY/ΔT) *(June 2019)*

(a) -3 (b) 2 (c) -5 (d) -4

Answer: (d)

Solution:

Yd = Y – Taxes

Tax Multiplier = $\frac{-MPC}{1-MPC}$

C = 25 + 0.8 Yd

= 25 + 0.8 (Y - 100)

=25 + 0.8Y – 80

MPC = 0.8

Tax Multiplier = $\frac{-0.8}{1-0.8}$

= $\frac{-0.8}{0.2}$

= -4

339. The demand and supply functions are given as : P_a = 30-5x and P_s = 3x - 10 respectively (x = quantity). The consumer surplus is

(a) 125

(b) - 62.5

(c) 62.5

(d) -125

Answer: (c)

$$CS = \int_{0}^{x} f(x) - Px$$

Pa = Ps

30 - 5x = 3x - 10

30 + 10 = 3x + 5x

40 = 8x

5 = x

pa = 30 - 5(5) = 5

$$CS = \int_{0}^{x} (30 - 5x)\,dx - 25$$

$$= 30x - \frac{5x^2}{2} - 25$$

$$= 150 - \frac{125}{2} - 25$$

= + 62.5

340. Given that LM function is Y=100+ 10i and the IS function is Y 160-20i, find the correct

value of equilibrium level of income and rate of interest from the given options.

(a) 120 and 2
(b) 90 and 3
(c) 150 and 2
(d) 120 and 3

Answer: (a)

Solution:

100+10i = 160-20i

10i + 20i = 160-100

30i = 60

i = 60/30

= 2

Y = 100 + 10i

Y = 100+10*2

Y = 120

341. The total revenue (R) and total cost (C) functions of a firm are given by :

$R = 30Q - Q^2$, C = 20 + 4Q

What would be the equilibrium output of the firm?

(December 2021 and June 2022)

(a) 9
(b) 13
(c) 17
(d) 11

Answer : (b)

Solution :

$TR = 30Q - Q^2$

TC + 20 + 4Q

MR = 30 - 2Q

MC = 4

MR = MC

30 - 2Q = 4

30 - 4 = 2Q

26/2 = Q

13 = Q

342. Non-negativity constraints in a Linear Programming problem is represented as:

(a) $X \geq 0$ and $Y \leq 0$
(b) $X \leq 0$ and $Y \geq 0$
(c) $X \leq 0$ and $Y \leq 0$
(d) $X \geq 0$ and $Y \geq 0$

Answer: (c)

Solution: Non-negativity constraints in a Linear Programming problem state that the decision variables (X and Y in this case) must be non-negative, meaning that they cannot be negative. This is typically represented by the inequalities $X \leq 0$ and $Y \leq 0$.

343. Which of the following is not true in case of Indifference curves?

(December 2022 - shift 1)

(a) The Indifference curves are usually convex or bowed inward.

(b) Indifference curve for two goods that are perfect compliments is shaped as right angles.

(c) Indifference curve for two goods that are perfect substitutes is a downward sloping straight line.

(d) Indifference curve for two normal goods is a downward sloping straight line.

Answer: (d)

Solution: Indifference curves are usually downward sloping, but they are not always straight lines. In fact, indifference curves can be bowed inward or outward. The shape of an indifference curve depends on the relationship between the two goods. For example, indifference curves for perfect substitutes are downward sloping straight lines, while indifference curves for perfect complements are right angles.

Here is a table summarizing the characteristics of indifference curves:

Characteristics	Perfect Substitutes	PerfectComplements	Normal Goods
Shape	Downward sloping straight line	Right angle	Convex
Slope	Constant	Zero	Diminishing

344. Which one of the following is not true in case of producer's equilibrium?

(December 2022 - shift 1)

(a) $MP_L / MP_K = w / r$

(b) $MRTS_{LK} = MP_L / MP_K = w / r$

(c) $MP_L / w = MP_K / r$

(d) $MRTS_{LK} = r / w$

Answer: (d)

Solution: The marginal rate of technical substitution of labor for capital (MRTSLK) is the amount of capital that a producer is willing to give up to get one more unit of labor, while keeping output constant. The wage rate (w) is the price of labor, and the rental rate of capital (r) is the price of capital.

In producer equilibrium, the $MRTS_{LK}$ is equal to the ratio of the prices of labor and capital.

This is because the producer will only be willing to give up capital for labor if the marginal benefit of doing so (in terms of increased output) is equal to the marginal cost of doing so (in terms of the foregone use of capital).

The equation for producer equilibrium is:

$MRTS_{LK} = w/r$

$MP_L / MP_K = w / r$ represents the condition for profit maximization in terms of input prices. It means that the marginal product of labor (MP_L) divided by the marginal product of capital (MP_K) is equal to the ratio of the wage rate (w) to the rental rate of capital (r).

$MRTS_{LK} = MP_L / MP_K = w / r$ is another way of expressing the condition for producer's equilibrium.

$MP_L / w = MP_L / r$ is a restatement of the first condition (1). It means that the marginal product of labor (MP_L) divided by the wage rate (w) is equal to the marginal product of capital (MP_K) divided by the rental rate of capital (r).

345. A game in which the gains or losses of one player or firm do not come at the expenses of or provide equal benefit to the other player or firm, is known as

(December 2022 - shift 1)

(a) Zero-5um game
(b) Non-Zero Sum game
(c) Mixed game
(d) Balanced game

Answer: (b)

Solution: In a non-zero sum game, the gains and losses of one player or firm do not necessarily come at the expense of or provide equal benefit to the other player or firm. This means that the total utility or payoff for all players involved in the game is not constant. In other words, the sum of the payoffs for each player is not zero.

In contrast, a zero-sum game is a special case where the total utility or payoff is constant, and any gain by one player is exactly balanced by an equal loss by another player, resulting in a total payoff of zero.

Zero Sum Game :-when the gain of one competitor is the loss of the other, then it is a zero-sum game.

Minimax: - Minimum loss out of maximum losses.

Maximin: - Maximum out of Minimum profits.

Fair Game :-It is the point where minmax and maximin are equal to zero.

Nash Equilibrium :-Each player believes that it is doing the best it is given the strategy of the Other player.

346. The condition of preferring a risky income to a certain income with the same expected value is referred as : *(December 2022 - shift 1)*

(a) Risk averse
(b) Risk loving
(c) Risk neutral
(d) Risk premium

Answer: (b)

Solution:

For a Risk Averse: -, Marginal utility of Money diminishes as he has more money.

For a Risk seeker, MU_M increases as money increases with him.

For a risk neutral, MU_M remains constant as money increases.

347. arises when the firm can produce any combination of the two outputs more cheaply than could two independent firms that each produced a single output. *(December 2022 - shift 1)*

(a) Learner's curve
(b) Economies of scale
(c) Dis-economies of scale
(d) Economies of scope

Answer: (d)

Solution: Economies of scope occur when a firm can produce a wider range of goods or services at a lower cost than if it produced each good or service separately. This is because the firm can share some of its fixed costs, such as the cost of machinery and equipment, across the different goods or services it produces. For example, a company that produces both cars and trucks can share the cost of its assembly line. This can lead to lower costs for both the cars and the trucks. Economies of scope are different from economies of scale. Economies of scale occur when the average cost of production falls as the quantity produced increases. This is because the firm can spread its fixed costs over a larger number of units. Economies of scope can exist even when a firm is producing a small quantity of each good or service. This is because the firm can still share some of its fixed costs.

Here are some examples of economies of scope:

- A company that produces both cars and trucks can share the cost of its assembly line.
- A company that produces both software and hardware can share the cost of its research and development.
- A company that produces both food and drinks can share the cost of its distribution network.

Economies of scope can give firms a competitive advantage. This is because they can produce a wider range of goods or services at a lower cost than their competitors.

Economies of Scope: - Joint production of a good is more efficient than the separate production.

Diseconomies of Scope: -Joint production is less efficient than the individual production.

348. In which oligopoly model, firms produce homogenous goods and each firm treats the price of its competitors as fixed and all firms decide simultaneously, what price to change?

(December 2022 - shift 1)

(a) Betrand model

(b) Cournot model

(c) Stackelberg model

(d) Sweezy model

Answer: (a)

Solution:

Bertrand Model:-1883

- ✧ Other firm will keep the price constant.
- ✧ Unlimited productive capacity.
- ✧ By undercutting the price, the firm can capture the entire output.
- ✧ Concluding result Price= AC
- ✧ Total output produced by two firms is perfectly competitive output.

349. Who wrote that "every man thus lives by exchanging or becomes in some measure a merchant, and the society itself grows to be what is properly a commercial society.'

(December 2022 - shift 1)

(a) Milton Friedman

(b) Keynes

(c) Benjamin Olken

(d) Adam Smith

Answer: (d)

Solution: The quote **"every man thus lives by exchanging or becomes in some measure a merchant, and the society itself grows to be what is properly a commercial society" is from Adam Smith's** book *The Wealth of Nations.*

In this quote, Smith is arguing that the division of labor and specialization are essential for economic growth. He argues that when people specialize in producing goods and services, they can produce more of those goods and services than they could if they tried to produce everything themselves. This increased productivity leads to lower prices, which in turn leads to more trade and economic growth.

Smith's quote is still relevant today. The division of labor and specialization are still essential for economic growth. In fact, these forces have only become more important in recent years as the world has become more globalized.

350. The Sticky-Price Model is *(December 2022 - shift 1)*

(a) The upward sloping short run aggregate supply curve

(b) The upward sloping long run aggregate supply curve

(c) The downward sloping short run Aggregate Demand curve

(d) The downward sloping long run Aggregate Demand curve

Answer: (a)

Solution: The sticky-price model is the upward sloping short run aggregate supply curve. It is called the sticky-price model because it assumes that prices are sticky, or slow to adjust, in the short run. This means that when there is a change in aggregate demand, prices do not adjust immediately to bring supply and demand back into equilibrium. Instead, firms adjust output and employment in response to the change in demand.

The upward sloping short run aggregate supply curve shows that there is a positive relationship between the price level and output in the short run.

Aggregate Demand and Aggregate Supply

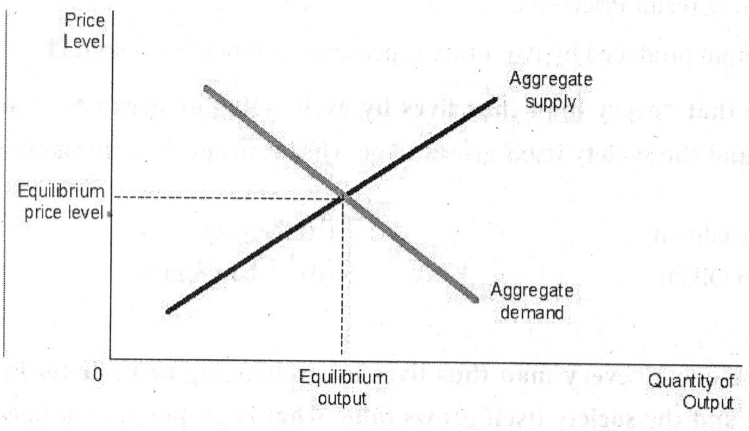

The short run aggregate supply curve is upward sloping because of the following factors:

- **Sticky prices:** As mentioned above, prices are sticky, or slow to adjust, in the short run. This means that when there is a change in aggregate demand, prices do not adjust immediately to bring supply and demand back into equilibrium. Instead, firms adjust output and employment in response to the change in demand.
- **Fixed contracts:** Many prices are set in long-term contracts, which cannot be easily changed in the short run. This also contributes to the upward sloping short run aggregate supply curve.
- **Menu costs:** Changing prices can be costly for firms. This is because they have to print new menus, catalogs, and other materials. These costs are known as menu costs. Menu costs discourage firms from changing prices frequently, even when it would be in their best interest to do so.

The sticky-price model is a key part of Keynesian economics. Keynesian economists believe that the economy is often in a state of disequilibrium, meaning that there is not full employment. They argue that this is because prices are sticky in the short run, which prevents the economy from adjusting to shocks quickly.

351. If the demand for labour increases, then *(December 2022 - shift 1)*

(a) Real wage rises

(b) The amount of labour employed increases

(c) Both 1 and 2 happen

(d) None of the above

Answer: (c)

Solution: When the demand for labor increases, firms are willing to pay higher wages to attract more workers. This increases the real wage, which is the wage that workers are paid in terms of goods and services. The higher real wage encourages more people to enter the labor force, which increases the amount of labor employed.

In the short run, the increase in demand for labor can lead to a shortage of labor. This is because it takes time for firms to adjust their production levels to the higher demand. As a result, firms may have to pay even higher wages to attract the workers they need.

In the long run, firms will be able to adjust their production levels to the higher demand. This will increase the supply of labor, which will eventually lead to a decrease in wages. However, the real wage will still be higher than it was before the increase in demand for labor.

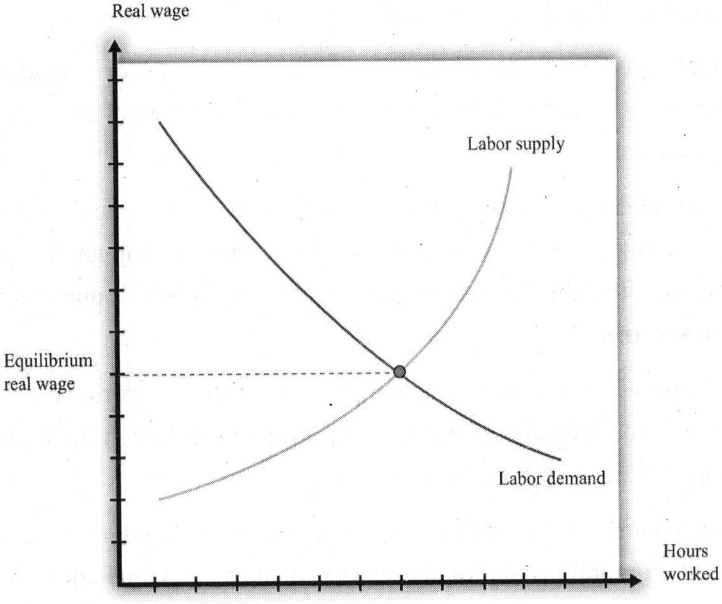

In the diagram, the demand for labor curve is D. The real wage is W. As the demand for labor increases, the demand curve shifts to the right. This means that firms are willing to pay higher wages to attract more workers. As a result, the real wage rises. In addition, the amount of labor employed increases, as shown by the movement along the labor supply curve S.

It is important to note that the relationship between the demand for labor and the real wage is not always a straight line. In some cases, the demand for labor may increase without leading to a rise in the real wage. This can happen if the supply of labor also increases at the same time. For example, if more people enter the workforce, the supply of labor will increase. This can offset the increase in demand for labor, leading to a stable real wage.

Overall, the relationship between the demand for labor and the real wage is complex. However, in general, an increase in the demand for labor will lead to an increase in the real wage and an increase in the amount of labor employed.

352. Macroeconomics distinguishes between real economy and *(December 2022 - shift 1)*

(a) Virtual economy (b) Monetary economy

(c) Normative economy (d) Underground economy

Answer: (b)

Solution: Macroeconomics is the study of the economy as a whole, focusing on aggregate variables such as GDP, inflation, and unemployment. It distinguishes between the real economy and the monetary economy.

- The real economy is the physical production of goods and services. It is the economy that produces real goods and services, such as cars, food, and houses.
- The monetary economy is the system of money and finance that supports the real economy. It is the economy that provides the means of exchange, store of value, and unit of account for the real economy.

Macroeconomics studies the interaction between the real economy and the monetary economy. It looks at how changes in the monetary economy, such as changes in interest rates or the money supply, can affect the real economy, such as GDP growth or unemployment.

The other options are:

- Virtual economy is the economy that exists in the digital world. It is the economy that involves the production and exchange of goods and services in the digital world, such as online shopping and social media advertising.
- Normative economy is the economy that is based on what ought to be. It is the economy that is based on moral principles and values, such as economic equity and environmental sustainability.

Solution:

X no. of heads
0(T T)
1(H T)
1(T H)
2(H H)
4

$$E(x) = \frac{\sum x}{n} = \frac{4}{4} = 1$$

$$x^2 = 0+1+1+4 = 6$$

$$E(x)^2 = \frac{\sum x^2}{n} = \frac{6}{4} = \frac{3}{2}$$

$$V(x) = E(x)^2 - [E(x)]^2$$

$$= \frac{3}{2} - (1)^2$$

$$= \frac{3}{2} - 1$$

$$= \frac{1}{2}$$

356. If the demand and supply functions are given P_d = 20 - 5x and P_s = 4x +8; obtain Producer's surplus *(December 2022 - shift 1)*

(a) 31/9 (b) 32/9 (c) 129/9 (d) 29/9

Answer: (b)

Solution:

$P_d = P_s$

$20 - 5\chi = 4\chi + 8$

$12 = 9\chi$

$4/3 = \chi$

$P = 20 - 5\chi$

$= 20 - 5\,(4/3)$

$= 20 - \dfrac{20}{3}$

$= \dfrac{60-20}{3} = \dfrac{40}{3}$

$$Ps = Px - \int_d^x f(x)\,dx$$

$$= \frac{40}{3} \times \frac{4}{3} - \int_d^x (4x+8)\,dx$$

$$= \frac{160}{9} - \frac{4x^2}{2} + 8x$$

$$\Rightarrow \frac{160}{9} \quad \frac{-4\left(\frac{16}{9}\right)}{2} - 8\left(\frac{4}{3}\right)$$

$$\Rightarrow \frac{160}{9} - \frac{64}{18} - \frac{32}{3}$$

$$\Rightarrow \frac{320-64-192}{18}$$

$$\Rightarrow \frac{64}{18} \Rightarrow \boxed{\frac{32}{9}}$$

357. The demand function for Good A is given by Q_A = 100 - 2 P_A + 0.2Y + 0.3 P_B, Find the cross - price elasticities of demand at P_A = 6, Y=500, P_B = 10.

(December 2022 - shift 1)

(a) 0.06 (b) 0.016 (c) 0.52 (d) -0.06

Answer: (b)

Solution:

$$\varepsilon = \frac{\Delta QA}{\Delta P_B} \cdot \frac{P_B}{QA}$$

$QA = 100 - 2P_A + 0.2Y + 0.3P_B$

$$\frac{\Delta QA}{\Delta P_B} = 0.3$$

Now put values of P_A, Y, P_B

$$Q_A = 100 - 2(6) + 0.2(500) + 0.3(10)$$

$$= 100 - 12 + 100 + 3$$

$$= 191$$

$$\text{Now } \xi = 0.3 \times \frac{10}{191}$$

$$\boxed{= 0.016}$$

Cross elasticity of demand : measures the degree of responsiveness of change in the demand for one good in response to the change in price of another good.

$$Ec = \frac{\Delta Q_X}{\Delta P_Y} \times \frac{P_Y}{Q_X}$$

For substitute goods, Ec is positive

For complements, Ec is negative

For unrelated goods, Ec is zero

358. Test statistics used to test stationary of a time series in the presence of correlated error term is *(December 2022 - shift 1)*

(a) Dickey - Fuller test

(b) Engle- Granger test

(c) Error - Correction mechanism

(d) Augmented Dickey-Fuller test

Answer: (d)

Solution:

The Augmented Dickey Fuller test (ADF test) is a statistical test used to test the null hypothesis that a time series is non-stationary (has a unit root). The test is based on the idea that if a time series is non-stationary, its first difference will be stationary. The ADF test calculates a test statistic and compares it to critical values to determine whether to reject the null hypothesis.

The Engle Granger test is used to test for cointegration between two or more time series. Cointegration means that two or more time series move together in the long run, even if they are not perfectly correlated. The Engle-Granger test is based on the idea that if two or more time series are cointegrated, then their first differences will be stationary.

The error correction mechanism is a statistical model that is used to account for the effects of cointegration on the relationship between two or more time series. The error-correction mechanism allows for the possibility that the relationship between two time series may not be perfectly linear, and that there may be some lag in the adjustment process.

Therefore, the Augmented Dickey Fuller test is the only test that is specifically designed to test for stationarity in the presence of correlated error terms. The Engle-Granger test and the error-correction mechanism are not designed to test for stationarity, but they can be used to test for cointegration, which is a necessary condition for stationarity in the presence of correlated error terms.

359. In logit model as P; goes from 0 to 1, logit L varies from *(December 2022 - shift 1)*

(a) 0 to + ∞ (b) - ∞ to + ∞

(c) 0 to 1 (d) - ∞ to 0

Answer: (b)

Solution: Logit follows logistic distribution

$$L_i = \ln\left(\frac{P_i}{1-P_i}\right)$$

Pi is probability of happening an event i.e. adoption of technology.

(1-pi) is probability of not happening an event.

P goes from 0 to 1, L from - ∞ to ∞

Logit assumptions:

1. No need of linear relation between dependent and independent variables.
2. No need of homoscedasticity of independent variables
3. The error terms need to be independent.
4. Absence of perfect multicollinearity.

360. Find the Elasticity of Substitution (σ) of Constant elasticity of substitution (CES) Production function. When the substitution parameter(p) lies between 0 < p < ∞ *(December 2022 - shift 1)*

(a) $\sigma > 1$ (b) $\sigma < 1$ (c) $\sigma = \infty$ (d) $\sigma = 1$

Answer: (b)

Solution:

CES Production Function: - 1961

Arrow, Minhas,Chenery, Solow

$$Q = \gamma\left[\alpha L^{-\beta} + (1-\alpha)K^{-\beta}\right]^{-\frac{1}{\beta}}$$

γ = Coeff. Of Technical Efficiency.

α = Distribution Parameter.

β = Substitution Parameter.

$$E_S = \frac{1}{1+\beta}$$

When p = 1, then σ = 1. This means that the factors of production are perfect substitutes, meaning that they can be used interchangeably. For example, if you are making a cake, you can use either flour or cornstarch as a binding agent.

When p > 1, then σ > 1. This means that the factors of production are substitutes, meaning that they can be used in different proportions. For example, if you are making a pizza, you can use more or less cheese, depending on your preferences.

Therefore, when the substitution parameter (p) lies between 0 < p < 1, then the elasticity of substitution (σ) is less than 1.

E_s= 1/1+(p)

=1/1+(6)

=1/7

$= \sigma < 1$

361. The regression model Yt = $\alpha 1 + \alpha 2\ Dt + \beta 1$Xt + $\beta 2(YtDt)$ + Ut is used to

(December 2022 - shift 1)

(a) Deseasonalize a time series data
(b) Analyze the seasonal trend in data
(c) Analyse structural break in data
(d) Analyse piecewise linear relationship in data

Answer: (c)

362. A box of nine golf gloves contains two left handed and seven right-handed gloves. If two gloves are randomly selected from the box without replacement, what is the probability that one is left-handed and the other is a right-handed glove?

(December 2022 - shift 1)

(a) 7/12 (b) 2/9 (c) 7/18 (d) 1/9

Answer: (c) **Solution:**

L L

R R R R R R R

P (1 left hand , other right hand with replacement)

$$= LR + RL$$

$$= \frac{2}{9} \times \frac{7}{8} + \frac{7}{9} \times \frac{2}{8}$$

$$= \frac{14}{72} + \frac{14}{72}$$

$$= \frac{28}{72}$$

$$= \frac{7}{18}$$

363. Which institution has published the Human Development Report annually since 1990

(December 2022 - shift 1)

(a) International Monetary Fund

(b) World Bank

(c) Asian Development Bank

(d) United National Development Programme

Answer: (d)

Solution: The institution that has published the Human Development Report annually since 1990 is the United Nations Development Programme (UNDP). The Human Development Report is an annual report that assesses the progress of countries in terms of human development. It is based on the Human Development Index (HDI), which is a composite measure of life expectancy, education, and income.

The first Human Development Report was published in 1990 by Mahbub ul Haq, a Pakistani economist, and Amartya Sen, an Indian economist and Nobel laureate. The report was commissioned by the UNDP to provide a new way of measuring development that went beyond traditional economic measures such as GDP.

The Human Development Report has been published annually since 1990, and it has become an influential tool for measuring and promoting human development. The report has been used by policymakers, academics, and civil society organizations to track progress on human development and to advocate for policies that promote human well-being.

364. Which Five year plan proposed to make India, "Self-reliant and Self generating economy"? *(December 2022 - shift 1)*

(a) IInd Five year plan
(b) IIIrd Five year plan
(c) IVth Five year plan
(d) Vth Five year plan

Answer: (b)

Solution:

First Five Year Plan (1951-1956): The first five-year plan was launched in 1951 with the objective of laying the foundation for a self-reliant economy. (Harrod Domer Model)

Second Five Year Plan (1956-1961): The plan focused on developing infrastructure, such as roads, railways, and power generation.(Mahanlobis)

Third Five Year Plan (1961-1966): The third five-year plan was focused on making India a "self-reliant and self-generating economy".

Fourth Five Year Plan (1969-1974): The plan focused on stabilizing the economy and reducing poverty.(Growth with Stability, Garibi Hatao)

Fifth Five Year Plan (1974-1979): (Minimum needs programme) Sixth Five Year Plan (1980-1985):

Seventh Five Year Plan (1985-1990):

Eighth Five Year Plan (1992-1997): (Human Resource Development)

Ninth Five Year Plan (1997-2002) : The plan focused on growth with social justice and equity.

Tenth Five Year Plan (2002-2007) :

Eleventh Five Year Plan (2007-2012) : The plan focused on faster and more inclusive growth.

Twelfth Five Year Plan (2012-2017): The plan focused on faster, sustainable and more inclusive growth.

365. The birth of World Trade Organisation emerged from which round? *(December 2022 - shift 1)*

(a) Geneva
(b) HongKong
(c) Uruguay
(d) Tokyo

Answer: (c)

Solution:

GATT [General Agreement on Tariffs and Trade]

Formed in 1947

Headquarters in Geneva (Switzerland).

Principles of GATT:-Non Discrimination

Objective -promotes free trade.

Uruguay round replaced GATT with WTO.

WTO- World Trade Organisation-(1995)-

- ✧ Geneva Round 1947
- ✧ Annecy round 1949
- ✧ Torquay round 1951
- ✧ Geneva round 1955-56
- ✧ Dillon round 1960-62
- ✧ Kennedy round 1962-67
- ✧ Tokyo round 1973-79
- ✧ Uruguay round 1986-94
- ✧ Doha round 2001
- ✧ Bali 2013

366. Total Budget Allocation in year 2022-23. For "Har Ghar, Nal Se Jal" in rupees is:

(December 2022 - shift 1)

(a) 50,000/- crore (b) 80,000/- crore

(c) 60,000/- crore (d) 70,000/- crore

Answer: (c)

Solution: The total budget allocation for "Har Ghar, Nal Se Jal" in the financial year 2022-23 is Rs. 60,000 crore. This was announced by the Finance Minister, Nirmala Sitharaman, in her Budget speech on February 1, 2022.

The "Har Ghar, Nal Se Jal" scheme is a flagship program of the Government of India to provide piped water to every household in rural India by 2024. The scheme was launched in 2019, and it has already covered over 100 million households.

The allocation of Rs. 60,000 crore for the "Har Ghar, Nal Se Jal" scheme in the financial year 2022-23 is a significant increase from the allocation of Rs. 30,000 crore in the previous financial year. This increase is in line with the government's commitment to provide piped water to every household in rural India by 2024.

The "Har Ghar, Nal Se Jal" scheme is a major step towards achieving the Sustainable Development Goal (SDG) of ensuring access to clean water and sanitation for all by 2030. The scheme is expected to have a positive impact on the health, education, and productivity of rural households.

367. A toll is a tax on those citizens who use toll roads. This policy can be viewed as an application of

(December 2022 - shift 1)

(a) The benefit principle
(b) Horizontal equity
(c) Vertical equity
(d) Tax progressivity

Answer: (a)

Solution:

The benefits principle of taxation states that people should be taxed according to the benefits they receive from government services. In the case of toll roads, the people who use the roads receive the benefits of the roads, so they should be the ones who pay for them.

The other principles of taxation mentioned in the options are:

- ✧ Horizontal equity states that people who are in similar circumstances should be taxed in a similar way. This means that people with the same income should pay the same amount of tax.
- ✧ Vertical equity states that people who are in different circumstances should be taxed in different ways, with those who are better off paying more taxes than those who are worse off. This means that people with higher incomes should pay a higher percentage of their income in taxes.
- ✧ Tax progressivity refers to the degree to which the tax system takes into account a taxpayer's ability to pay. A progressive tax system is one in which the tax rate increases as the taxpayer's income increases.

The benefits principle is the most relevant principle in the case of toll roads, as it ensures that people who use the roads pay for them. The other principles are also important, but they are not as relevant in this case.

368. Which of the following formulae is used to measure the tax mutiplier:

(December 2022 - shift 1)

(a) –MPC / 1 - MPC
(b) 1 / 1 – MPC
(c) 1 – MPC / MPC
(d) 2 – MPC / MPC

Answer: (a)

Solution:

Investment = 200

Govt Expenditure =75

Net Taxes = 100

C=25+0.8yd

find tax multiplier

Sol $\frac{-MPC}{1-MPC}$

$$C = 25 + 0.8(y - 100)$$

$$= 25 + 0.8y - 80.$$

$$MPC = 0.8$$

$$\text{TAX MULTIPLIER} = \frac{-0.8}{1-0.8} = \frac{-0.8}{0.2} = -4$$

369. The Free-rider problem arises: *(December 2022 - shift 1)*

(a) when goods are congestible.

(b) when goods are of a rival nature.

(c) when number of beneficiaries is large and exclusion of any one of them is impossible.

(d) when goods are available freely but on a first cum first serve basis till stocks last.

Answer: (c)

Solution: The free-rider problem arises when number of beneficiaries is large and exclusion of any one of them is impossible.

Some examples of goods that suffer from the free-rider problem:

- **Public goods:** Public goods are goods that are non-excludable and non-rivalrous. This means that it is impossible to prevent people from consuming the good, and one person's consumption of the good does not reduce the amount that is available for others to consume. Examples of public goods include national defense, lighthouses, and public parks.
- **Common-pool resources:** Common-pool resources are goods that are rivalrous and non-excludable. This means that it is possible to prevent people from consuming the good, but it is difficult and costly to do so. Examples of common-pool resources include fish stocks, grazing land, and forests.
- The free-rider problem can lead to underprovision of public goods and common-pool resources. This is because people have an incentive to free-ride, meaning that they will consume the good without paying for it. This can lead to a situation where the good is not provided at all, or it is provided at a lower level than is optimal.
- There are a number of ways to address the free-rider problem. One way is to make the good excludable. This can be done by charging a fee for the good, or by making it difficult for people to access the good. Another way to address the free-rider problem is to provide the good in a way that makes it difficult for people to free-ride. For example, a public park could be designed so that it is difficult for people to enter without paying.
- The free-rider problem is a complex problem, and there is no easy solution. However, by understanding the problem, we can develop ways to address it and ensure that public goods and common-pool resources are provided at an optimal level.

370. The money supply in the IS-LM model is assumed to be *(December 2022 - shift 1)*

(a) Real narrow money
(b) Nominal money supply
(c) Nominal Broad money
(d) Real money supply

Answer: (d)

Solution:

The LM curve shows the combinations of interest rates and levels of real income for which the money market is in equilibrium. It shows where money demand equals money supply. For the LM curve, the independent variable is income and the dependent variable is the interest rate.

Money supply is determined by central bank decisions and willingness of commercial banks to loan money. Money supply in effect is perfectly inelastic with respect to nominal interest rates. Thus, the money supply function is represented as a vertical line – money supply is a constant, independent of the interest rate, GDP, and other factors. Mathematically, the LM curve is defined by the equation M/P = L(I,Y), where the supply of money is represented as the real amount M/P (as opposed to the nominal amount M), with P representing the price level and L being the real demand for money, which is some function of the interest rate and the level of real income.

An increase in GDP shifts demand for money curve rightward and hence increases the interest rate. Thus, the LM function is positively sloped.

Derivation of the LM-Curve

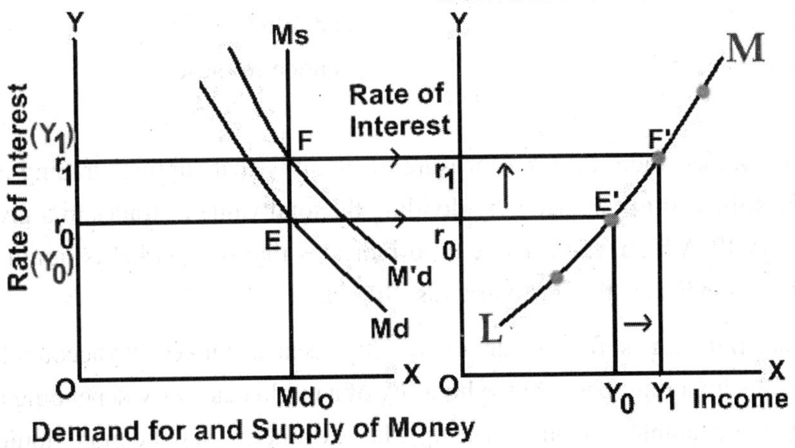

371. Which of the following two economists are associated with the problem of time inconsistency? *(December 2022 - shift 1)*

(a) J. M. Keynes and Joan Robinson
(b) Kydland and Prescott
(c) Baumol and Tobin
(d) Friedman and Scwartz

Answer: (b)

Solution:

The answer is 2. Kydland and Prescott.

Finn Kydland and Edward C. Prescott are the economists who are associated with the problem of time inconsistency. They introduced the concept in their 1977 paper, "Rules Rather than Discretion: The Inconsistency of Optimal Plans."

The time inconsistency problem arises when a policymaker announces a policy rule that is optimal at the time of the announcement, but then has an incentive to deviate from the rule later on. This is because the policymaker's preferences may change over time, or because the environment may change.

Kydland and Prescott showed that the time inconsistency problem can lead to suboptimal economic outcomes. For example, a central bank that announces a policy of low inflation may have an incentive to deviate from that rule if inflation starts to fall too low. This is because the central bank may worry that low inflation will lead to a recession.

The time inconsistency problem is a major challenge for policymakers. There are a number of ways to try to address the problem, such as making the policy rule more credible or giving the policymaker less discretion.

372. The Value-Trade ratio captures trading relative to the size of the

(December 2022 - shift 1)

(a) economy
(b) market
(c) market and economy
(d) none of these

Answer: (a)

Solution: The Value-Trade ratio is a measure of liquidity that captures trading relative to the size of the **economy**. It is calculated by dividing the total value of trades in a given period by the country's GDP. A high Value-Trade ratio indicates that the market is liquid, while a low Value-Trade ratio indicates that the market is illiquid.

The Value trade ratio is a useful measure of liquidity because it takes into account the size of the economy. This is important because the liquidity of a market can vary depending on the size of the economy. For example, a small market in a large economy may be more liquid than a large market in a small economy.

The Value trade ratio is not a perfect measure of liquidity, but it is a useful indicator. Other factors that can affect liquidity include the number of traders in the market, the depth of the market, and the volatility of the market.

373. "Under-developed countries are the slums of the world economy", is a statement given by *(December 2022 - shift 1)*

(a) Keynes
(b) G. Myrdal
(c) Adam Smith
(d) Cairncross

Answer: (d)

Solution: The statement "Under-developed countries are the slums of the world economy" was made by Alexander Cairncross, a Scottish economist who was a leading figure in the development of Keynesian economics. Cairncross made this statement in his 1953 book, "The Economics of Growth."

374. The greater the divergence between the shadow price and the market price: *(December 2022 - shift 1)*

(a) the greater the need for social cost-benefit analysis in public investment decisions.
(b) the lesser the need for social cost-benefit analysis in public investment decisions.
(c) then there will be no social benefit in public investments.
(d) then the social cost will be minimum.

Answer: (a)

Solution: Shadow prices are the economic values of goods and services that are not traded in the market. They are often used in social cost-benefit analysis (SCBA) to account for the social benefits and costs of public investments.

When the shadow price of a good or service is significantly different from the market price, it means that there is a market failure. This could be due to a number of factors, such as monopoly power, externalities, or information asymmetry.

In these cases, SCBA can be used to estimate the true social benefits and costs of the public investment. This information can then be used to make more informed decisions about whether or not to invest.

Therefore, the greater the divergence between the shadow price and the market price, the greater the need for SCBA in public investment decisions.

375. Which one of the following pairs is NOT correctly matched? *(December 2022 - shift 1)*

	Author	Book
(A)	**Simon Kuznets**	**Asian Drama**
(B)	**J. Robinson**	**Essays on the Theory of Economic growth**
(C)	**Karl Marx**	**Das Capital**
(D)	**Arthur W. Lewis**	**Theory of Economic Growth**

(a) 1
(b) 2
(c) 3
(d) 4

Answer: (a)

Solution: Simon Kuznets was an American economist who is best known for his work on economic growth and development. His most famous book is National Income and Its Composition, 1919-1938. He did not write a book called Asian Drama.

The other pairs are correctly matched. J. Robinson wrote Essays on the Theory of Economic Growth, Karl Marx wrote Das Capital, and Arthur W. Lewis wrote Theory of Economic Growth.

376. Which of the following is not true about the basic postulates of the Malthusian Perspective on population? *(December 2022 - shift 1)*

(a) The human population will invariably grow where the means of subsistence increase

(b) The total amount of land available for agriculture is immutably fixed

(c) Factor substitutions and technological advances can alleviate resource scarcities

(d) The growth of population is limited by the amount of food available for subsistence

Answer: (c)

Solution: The Malthusian Perspective, named after Thomas Malthus, is based on his theory outlined in his 1798 work "An Essay on the Principle of Population." According to this perspective, the growth of population tends to outstrip the growth of the means of subsistence, leading to a natural check on population growth in the form of positive checks (e.g., famine, disease) and preventive checks (e.g., moral restraint, delayed marriages).

The correct explanation for the other statements is as follows:

1. The human population will invariably grow where the means of subsistence increase.
   According to Malthus, an increase in the means of subsistence, such as food production, would lead to population growth as more people can be supported with the available resources.
2. The total amount of land available for agriculture is immutably fixed.
   Malthus believed that land, as a resource for agriculture, is ultimately limited and cannot be expanded indefinitely.
3. The growth of the population is limited by the amount of food available for subsistence.
   Malthus argued that population growth would be constrained by the availability of food. When population growth exceeds the capacity of food production, positive checks like famine and disease would naturally reduce the population to a sustainable level.

Malthus mainly examined the relation between population size and the measures of subsistence, in particular the production of food. He postulated that any increase in living standards would result in an increase in population size. But, food production could not be increased at the same rate due to the operation of the Law of Diminishing Returns.

377. Which of the following criterion is used to judge the performance of instruments for environmental policy? *(December 2022 - shift 1)*

(a) Ensuring that for each firm, the marginal abatement cost is equal to the marginal damage from pollution

(b) Achieving equality of marginal abatement costs across polluters

(c) Minimising the total cost of the externality to the society

(d) All of the above

Answer: (d)

Solution: The performance of instruments for environmental policy can be judged by a number of criteria, including:

- ✧ **Efficiency:** The instrument should achieve the desired environmental outcome at the least cost to society.
- ✧ **Equity:** The instrument should distribute the costs of pollution control fairly across polluters.
- ✧ **Political feasibility:** The instrument should be politically acceptable to the relevant stakeholders.

The three criteria that are mentioned are all important considerations when judging the performance of environmental policy instruments.

- Ensuring that for each firm, the marginal abatement cost is equal to the marginal damage from pollution ensures that polluters are only paying for the costs of their pollution. This is the most efficient way to achieve environmental goals.
- Achieving equality of marginal abatement costs across polluters ensures that polluters are not bearing a disproportionate share of the costs of pollution control. This is important for fairness reasons.
- Minimising the total cost of the externality to the society is the overall goal of environmental policy. All of the other criteria are important, but they are all subordinate to this goal.

In practice, it is often difficult to achieve all of these criteria simultaneously. However, it is important to consider all of them when designing environmental policy instruments.

- marginal cost of abatement refers to the marginal loss in company profits from avoiding the last unit of pollution

378. Which of the following is true in the case of externaility? *(December 2022 - shift 1)*

(a) It is not related to human interactions

(b) It is not tied to consumer sovereignty

(c) It is based on higher order judgements of right and wrong

(d) It is an amoral concept

Answer: (d)

Solution:

An externality is a cost or benefit that is not reflected in the market price of a good or service. It is a consequence of human interactions and tied to consumer sovereignty. Externalities can be either positive or negative, and they can be caused by either production or consumption.

Externalities are not based on higher order judgements of right and wrong. They are simply a consequence of the way that markets work. In some cases, externalities can be considered to be moral or immoral, but this is not always the case.

For example, the pollution caused by a factory is an externality. The factory is not paying for the full cost of its pollution, so the cost is borne by society as a whole. This can be considered to be immoral, but it is also a consequence of the way that markets work.

In other cases, externalities can be considered to be neutral. For example, the benefits of a beautiful park are an externality. The people who enjoy the park are not paying for it, but this is not necessarily considered to be immoral.

379. What does the case of 'Immiserising growth' state? *(December 2022 - shift 1)*

(a) Growth in richer nations would actually be self defeating

(b) Growth in poorer nations would actually be self defeating

(c) Growth in poorer nations would actually be self promoting

(d) Growth in richer nations would actually be self promoting

Answer: (b)

Solution: Immiserizing growth is a theoretical situation first proposed by ***Jagdish Bhagwati, in 1958***, where economic growth could result in a country being worse off than before the growth. If growth is heavily export based, it might lead to a fall in the terms of trade of the exporting country. In rare circumstances, this fall in the terms of trade may be so large as to outweigh the gains from growth. If so, this situation would cause a country to be worse off after growth than before. This result is only valid if the growing country is able to influence world prices.

Example of how immiserizing growth could occur. Suppose a poor country starts to export a lot of agricultural products. As the country exports more, the world price of agricultural products will start to fall. This will reduce the income of the country from its exports, and it will also make it more expensive for the country to import manufactured goods. The net effect of this could be that the country is worse off than it was before it started to export agricultural products. Immiserizing growth is a rare phenomenon, but it is a possibility that should be considered when designing economic policies for poorer nations.

380. In which stage of the product cycle model, the imitating country starts under selling the innovating country in third markets? *(December 2022 - shift 1)*

(a) Stage - V
(b) Stage - II
(c) Stage - Ill
(d) Stage - IV

Answer: c

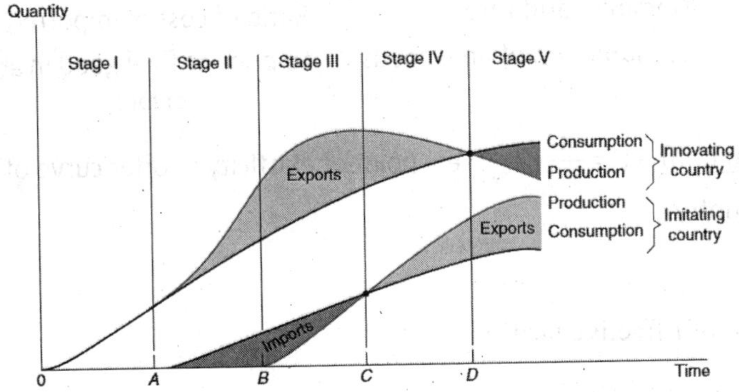

In stage I (time OA), the product is produced and consumed only in the innovating country. In stage II (AB), production is perfected in the innovating country and increases rapidly to accommodate rising demand at home and abroad. In stage III (BC), the product becomes standardized and the imitating country starts producing the product for domestic consumption. In stage IV (CD), the imitating country starts underselling the innovating country in third markets, and in stage V (past point D) in the latter's market as well.

381. If the nominal tariff rate (t) on consumers of the final commodity is 10 percent; the ratio of the cost of the imported input to the price of the final commodity in the absence of tariffs a_i = 0.8; and the nominal tariff rate on the imported input t_i = 20%, then find the rate of effective protection. *(December 2022 - shift 1)*

(a) 10%
(b) 8%
(c) 3%
(d) -30%

Answer: (d)

Solution:

Nominal rate of protection :-By how much price of commodity increase as a result of tariff

[Important for consumers]

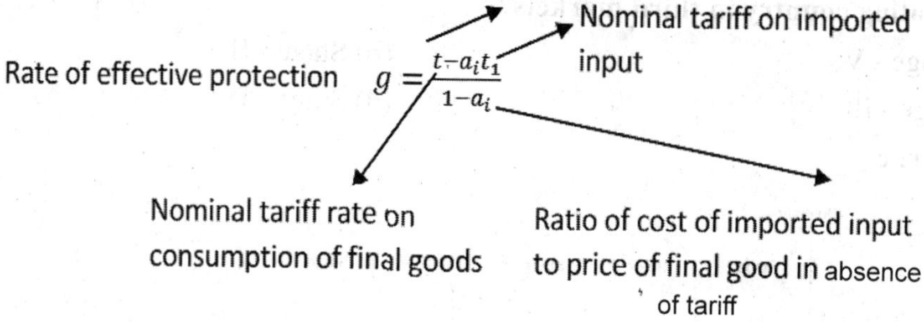

<u>Optimum tariff</u> – $t^* = \frac{1}{e-1}$ e = point of elasticity of offer curve of other country.

= Rate of Effective tariff :

$= \frac{10/100 - (0.8*20/100)}{1-0.8}$

$= \frac{0.1 - (0.8*0.2)}{0.2}$

= - 0.3

= - 30%

382. The level of intra-industry index (T) can be measured as: *(December 2022 - shift 1)*

1. $T = 1 - \frac{|X-M|}{X+M}$
2. $T = 1 + \frac{|X-M|}{X+M}$
3. $T = 1 - \frac{X-M}{|X+M|}$
4. $T = 1 - \frac{|X-M|}{|X+M|}$

Answer: (a)

Solution:

✧ Intra-industry trade is the trade that occurs between countries but within the same industry. The products that are traded are of a similar type such as oil or cars.

✧ Value of T ranges from 0 to 1. If T=0, there is no intra industry trade. If T=1, exports and imports of a good are equal. Intra industry trade is maximum.

383. Nash equilibrium represents *(December 2022 - shift 1)*

(A) The outcome each time the game is played

(B) Long-run equilibrium

(C) A situation in which one player will not deviate, given the strategy of other player

(D) Best response of the first mover

(E) The pair of dominated strategies

Choose the correct answer from the options given below:

(a) A, B and C only (b) B and D only

(c) B and C only (d) A, C and D only

Answer: (c)

Solution: Nash equilibrium is a central concept in game theory, named after the mathematician and economist John Nash. It represents a stable strategic situation in a game where each player's chosen strategy is the best response to the strategies chosen by all other players. In other words, at a Nash equilibrium, no player has an incentive to unilaterally change their strategy, given the strategies of the other players.

Nash equilibrium represents:

B. Long-run equilibrium

C. A situation in which one player will not deviate, given the strategy of the other player

Explanation:

- Option A (The outcome each time the game is played) is not correct because Nash equilibrium represents a stable strategic situation, not just a one-time outcome.
- Option D (Best response of the first mover) is not correct because Nash equilibrium considers the best response of all players, not just the first mover.
- Option E (The pair of dominated strategies) is not correct because Nash equilibrium involves strategies that are not dominated, meaning no player can unilaterally improve their payoff by choosing a different strategy.

384. Which of the following are correct about loanable fund theory?

(December 2022 - shift 1)

(A) Dishoarding is a only major source of supply of loanable funds.

(B) Demand for hoarding is inversely related to the interest rate.

(C) Equality between demand and supply of loanable funds is the only condition required for a stable equilibrium.

(D) Wicksell was one of the propounders of the theory.

(E) It introduced monetary factors into the theory of interest.

Choose the correct answer from the options given below:

(a) A, B and D only
(b) C, D and E only
(c) B, D and E only
(d) A, D and E only

Answer: (c)

Solution: The loanable funds theory is a theory of interest that explains the determination of the interest rate by the interaction of the supply and demand for loanable funds. The supply of loanable funds comes from savings and dishoarding, while the demand for loanable funds comes from investment and hoarding. The interest rate is determined at the point where the supply and demand for loanable funds are equal.

The loanable funds theory was developed by Swedish economist Knut Wicksell in the early 20th century. Wicksell argued that the interest rate is determined by the real forces of saving and investment, and not by the monetary policy of the central bank.

Here is a summary of the key points of the loanable funds theory:

- ✧ The supply of loanable funds comes from savings and dishoarding.
- ✧ The demand for loanable funds comes from investment and hoarding.
- ✧ The interest rate is determined at the point where the supply and demand for loanable funds are equal.
- ✧ The loanable funds theory was developed by Knut Wicksell.
- ✧ The loanable funds theory introduces monetary factors into the theory of interest.

The supply of loanable funds is the amount of money that savers are willing to lend to borrowers. The supply of loanable funds is determined by a number of factors, including:

- ✧ The level of income. As income rises, people have more money to save, and the supply of loanable funds increases.
- ✧ The interest rate. A higher interest rate makes it more attractive to save money, and the supply of loanable funds increases.
- ✧ Risk. The risk of default on a loan makes it less attractive to lend money, and the supply of loanable funds decreases.

The demand for loanable funds is the amount of money that borrowers are willing to borrow to invest. The demand for loanable funds is determined by a number of factors, including:

- ✧ The level of investment opportunities. The more investment opportunities there are, the greater the demand for loanable funds.
- ✧ The interest rate. A lower interest rate makes it less expensive to borrow money, and the demand for loanable funds increases.

✧ Risk. The risk of default on a loan makes it more expensive to borrow money, and the demand for loanable funds decreases.

The interest rate is determined by the interaction of the supply and demand for loanable funds. When the supply of loanable funds is greater than the demand, the interest rate will fall. When the demand for loanable funds is greater than the supply, the interest rate will rise. The interest rate will eventually reach an equilibrium point where the supply of loanable funds is equal to the demand..

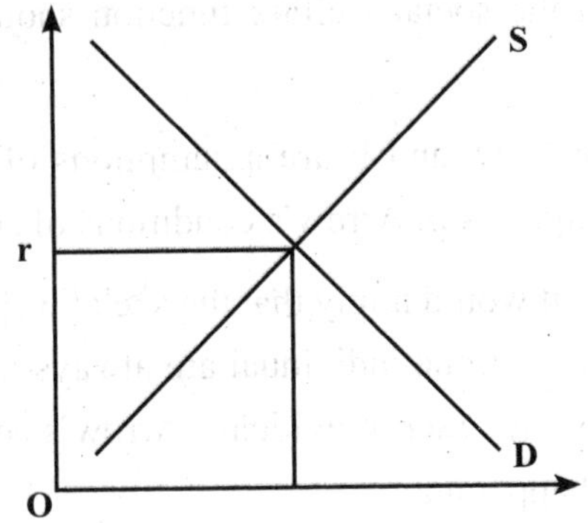

S is suppuly & D is demand of lonable funds

385. Which of the following are correct assumptions of Arrow's conditions of Social Welfare?
(December 2022 - shift 1)

(A) Responsiveness to individual preferences
(B) Impositions
(C) Dictatorship
(D) Transitivity or consistency
(E) Independent of irrelevant alternatives

Choose the correct answer from the options given below:

(a) A, B and D only
(b) B, D and E only
(c) B, C and D only
(d) A, D and E only

Answer: (d)

Solution: The correct answer is 4. A, D and E only.

Arrow's conditions of social welfare are a set of five conditions that any social welfare function must satisfy in order to be considered fair and democratic. The five conditions are:

1. **Non-dictatorship:** No single individual's preferences should always be imposed on the rest of society.
2. **Pareto efficiency:** If everyone prefers one alternative to another, then the social welfare function should also prefer the first alternative to the second.

3. **Independence of irrelevant alternatives:** The social welfare function should not change its ranking of alternatives if the ranking of those alternatives is not affected by the addition or removal of other alternatives.
4. **Unrestricted domain:** The social welfare function should be able to rank any set of alternatives, regardless of the number of alternatives or the complexity of the preferences of the individuals.
5. **Responsiveness to individual preferences:** If one individual's preference for an alternative changes, then the social welfare function should change its ranking of that alternative accordingly.

Of the above conditions, only A, D, and E are assumptions of Arrow's conditions of social welfare. B and C are not assumptions of Arrow's conditions of social welfare.

B is not an assumption because it would imply that the social welfare function is a dictatorship. In a dictatorship, the preferences of one individual are always imposed on the rest of society, regardless of the preferences of the other individuals. Arrow's conditions of social welfare are designed to prevent this from happening.

C is not an assumption because it would imply that the social welfare function is not responsive to individual preferences. In a social welfare function that is not responsive to individual preferences, the ranking of alternatives would not change if the preferences of the individuals changed. Arrow's conditions of social welfare are designed to ensure that the social welfare function is responsive to individual preferences.

386. The consequences of a country having a persistent current account surplus include

(December 2022 - shift 1)

A. **Employment generation**
B. **Higher standard of living**
C. **Low inflation pressure**
D. **Currency appreciates in value**
E. **More pressure on public debt**

Choose the correct answer from the options given below:

(a) A, B, C and D only
(b) A, B and D only
(c) A and E only
(d) A, D and E only

Answer: (b)

Solution:

A. **Employment generation :** A persistent current account surplus can lead to increased export revenues and economic growth, which can, in turn, lead to job creation and lower unemployment rates.

B. **Higher standard of living :** A current account surplus reflects that a country is exporting more than it imports. This can lead to increased income and resources for the country, potentially resulting in a higher standard of living for its citizens.

C. **Low inflation pressure :** This statement is incorrect. While a current account surplus may contribute to lower inflation pressure in some cases, it is not a universal outcome. Inflation is influenced by a wide range of factors, including domestic monetary policy, fiscal policy, supply and demand dynamics, and global economic conditions. A country can have a current account surplus and still experience inflation due to other internal factors.

D. **Currency appreciates in value :** A current account surplus can lead to an increase in demand for the country's currency, driving up its value in the foreign exchange market. This appreciation can make imports cheaper and exports relatively more expensive, potentially impacting the trade balance over time.

E. **More pressure on public debt :** This statement is not correct. A current account surplus is typically associated with reduced reliance on foreign borrowing, which can actually alleviate pressure on public debt. However, a persistent surplus might also result in an accumulation of foreign exchange reserves, and how these reserves are managed can influence public debt dynamics. In general, a current account surplus does not directly lead to more pressure on public debt.

387. For the computation of National income by the product method, which of the following sectors are considered: *(December 2022 - shift 1)*

A. Registered manufacturing

B. Agricultural and allied activities

C. Mining and quarrying

D. Unregistered manufacturing

E. Non-monetised activities

Choose the correct answer from the options given below:

(a) A, B and Conly (b) B and C only

(c) A, B, C and D only (d) B, C and D only

Answer: (c)

Solution: The product method is one of the three methods used to calculate national income. The product method involves adding up the value of all goods and services produced in an economy during a given period of time.

Here's the formula for calculating national income using the product method:

Gross domestic product (GDP) = C + I + G + NX

- **Consumption (C):** This refers to the spending of households on goods and services.

- **Investment (I):** This refers to the spending of businesses on new capital goods, such as machinery and equipment.
- **Government spending (G):** This refers to the spending of the government on goods and services, such as education, healthcare, and defense.
- **Net exports (NX):** This refers to the difference between the value of exports and the value of imports.

The product method of calculating national income is one of the three main methods used by economists. This method calculates national income by adding up the value of all final goods and services produced in an economy over a specific period of time.

The sectors considered for the computation of national income by the product method are:

- ✧ Registered manufacturing: This includes the production of goods by firms that are registered with the government.
- ✧ Agricultural and allied activities: These include the production of crops, livestock, and other agricultural products.
- ✧ Mining and quarrying: This includes the extraction of minerals from the earth.
- ✧ Unregistered manufacturing: This includes the production of goods by firms that are not registered with the government.

Non-monetized activities are not considered for the computation of national income by the product method. Non-monetized activities are activities that are not exchanged for money. This includes activities such as subsistence farming, household production, and volunteer work.

The reason why non-monetized activities are not considered for the computation of national income by the product method is because it is difficult to measure the value of these activities. Non-monetized activities are difficult to measure because they are often done in informal settings and are not recorded in any official records.

388. Which of the following statements are correct? *(December 2022 - shift 1)*

(A) According to the accelerator model, investment demand is proportional to the change in GDP.

(B) The real rate of interest is the nominal rate of interest plus the inflation rate.

(C) The higher the real interest rate, the higher is the rental cost of capital.

(D) Investment is a stock concept.

(E) Residential investment is low when mortgage interest rates are high. Choose the correct answer from the options given below:

(a) B, C and D only (b) A, C and E only (c) A, B and E only (d) C, D and E only

Answer: (b)

389. The properties of Mathematical Expectation are *(December 2022 - shift 1)*

A. **E(C) = 0, where C is constant**

B. **If X and Y are random variables, then E(X+Y) = E(X) + E(Y)**

C. **Var(X ± C) = Var(X), where C is constant**

D. **If X and Y are independent random variables, then E(X Y) = E(X).E(Y)**

E. **Var(aX) = a.Var(X), where a is constant**

Choose the correct answer from the options given below:

(a) A, B and D only (b) B, D and E only

(c) B, C and D only (d) B, C and E only

Answer: (c)

Solution:

Mathematical expectation

Mathematical expectation of a particular random variable means the average value of the random variable i.e. E(x) where x is a random variable and E(x) means mean(avg) of 'x'.

$Var(x) = E(x^2) - [E(x)]^2$

Random variable is a variable whose value is unknown.

Properties of Mathematical Expectations:

E (a) = a ; 'a' is constant

E (x + a) = E (x) + a

E (x + y) = E (x) + E (y)

E (x, y) = E (x) . E (y) [x and y are independent r.v's]

$V (a x) = a^2 V(x)$

E (a x) = a E (x)

Var (x + a) = V (x)

390. Which of the following are correct are OLS estimation in the presence of autocorrelation? *(December 2022 - shift 1)*

A. The estimated coefficients are linear

B. The estimated coefficients are unbiased

C. The estimated coefficients are biased

D. The estimated coefficients are consistent

E. The estimated coefficients are efficient

Choose the correct answer from the options given below:

(a) A, C and D only
(b) A, B and D only
(c) A, C and E only
(d) C, D and E only

Solution:

Autocorrelation

Correlation between successive values of same variable. In other words, correlation between different values of disturbance term is zero.i.e. E(uiuj) = 0. If this assumption is violated then there is Autocorrelation.

Consequences: Variance of OLS estimates becomes large but remain unbiased. Invalid test of significance and misleading confidence internals.

Tests :

1. Durbin - watson Test (for small samples) d = 2[1 -ê]

d = d - w statistic

ê = coeff. Of Autocorrelation

d lies between 0 to 4

2. Non - Neuman Ratio Test (for large samples).

391. Which of the following are correct in case of area under the standard normal probability curve. *(December 2022 - shift 1)*

A. Distance from the mean ordinates in terms of $\pm\sigma$ at Z = ± 0.6745 is 0.55

B. Distance from the mean ordinates in terms of $\pm\sigma$ at Z = ± 1.96 is 0.95

C. Distance from the mean ordinates in terms of $\pm\sigma$ at Z = ± 2.0 is 0.9544

D. Distance from the mean ordinates in terms of $\pm\sigma$ at Z = ± 2.58 is 0.98

E. Distance from the mean ordinates in terms of $\pm\sigma$ at Z = ± 3.0 is 0.9973

Choose the correct answer from the options given below:

(a) A, C and E only
(b) B, C and E only
(c) B, C and D only
(d) A, B and E only

Answer: (b)

Solution:

Normal Dist. = Given by AD Moivre, Karl gauss in 1733.

Poissin Distribution is Limiting case of Normal Distribution.

Properties: The distribution is symmetrical., hence it resembles a bell- shaped curve.

✧ The two tails do not touch the axis.

✧ Total area under normal

Curve is 1. Belong to mesokurtic distribution

✧ MEAN= MEDIAN= MODE

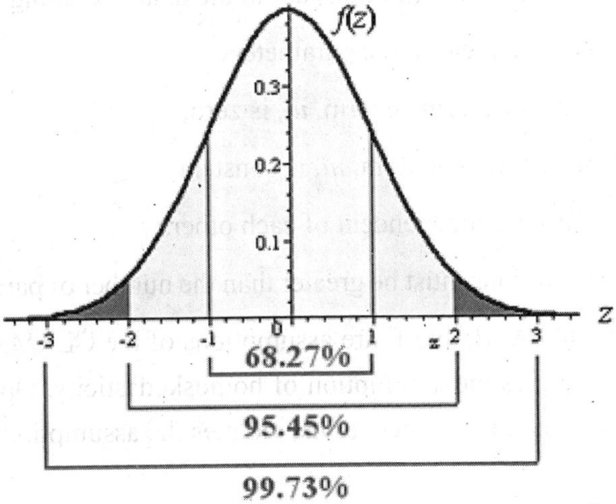

Mean = 0 SD =1 Variance = 1 Skewness measure = 0	Measure of Kurtosis = Three

For each significance level, the z test has single critical value

At 5% significance level for two tailed test, z value is 1.96

At 1% significance level for two tailed test , it is 2.58

At 5% significance level, for one tailed test, it is 1.645

At 1% significance level for one tailed test, it is 2.33

392. Which of the following satisfy the assumptions of the classical linear regression model? *(December 2022 - shift 1)*

A. The regression model is linear in the parameters

B. Zero mean value of disturbance Ui

C. The variance of Ui is not constant

D. There is a serial autocorrelation between the disturbance terms

E. The number of observations must be greater than the number of parameters to be estimated

Choose the correct answer from the options given below:

(a) B, C and E only

(b) A, B and E only

(c) B, D and E only

(d) A, C and D only

Solution: The classical linear regression model (CLRM) is a statistical model that is used to estimate the relationship between a dependent variable and one or more independent variables. The CLRM makes a number of assumptions about the data, including:

- The regression model is linear in the parameters.
- The mean value of the disturbance term, *ui*, is zero.
- The variance of the disturbance term, *ui*, is constant.
- The disturbance terms are independent of each other.
- The number of observations must be greater than the number of parameters to be estimated.

Of the options listed, only A, B, and E are assumptions of the CLRM. Option C, the variance of *ui* is not constant, violates the assumption of homoskedasticity. Option D, there is a serial autocorrelation between the disturbance terms, violates the assumption of independence of the disturbance terms.

393. If A, B and C are three different non-empty sets, then find which of the following are correct in laws of the set operation. *(December 2022 - shift 1)*

A. $A \cap \emptyset = \emptyset$

B. $A \cap (B \cup C) = (A \cap B) \cup (A \cap C)$

C. $A \cap A' = \emptyset$

D. $B - A = B' \cap A'$

E. $(A \cup B)' = A' \cup B'$

Choose the correct answer from the options given below:

(a) A, B, C and E only
(b) A, C and E only
(c) A, C and D only
(d) A, B and C only

Answer: (d)

Solution:

Here A' is A complement, $\emptyset$ *is a empty set*.

You can take any example of A, B, C and prove it whether LHS = RHS or not.

Commutative laws for union and Intersection of two sets.

$A \cup B = B \cup A$

$A \cap B = B \cap A$

Associative laws for union and intersection for two sets.

$A \cup (B \cup C) = (A \cup B) \cup C$

$A \cap (B \cap C) = (A \cap B) \cap C$

Distributive law

$$A \cap (B \cup C) = (A \cap B) \cup (A \cap C)$$

$$A \cup (B \cap C) = (A \cup B) \cap (A \cup C)$$

Identity Property

$$A \cup \Phi = A \qquad A \cap U = A$$

394. Which among the following are main components of PM e-Vidya:

(December 2022 - shift 1)

A. One Nation, One Digital Education.

B. Infrastructure and Electronic Governance.

C. One Class, One T.V. Channel.

D. Extensive use of radio, Community radio and Podcasts.

E. Information and Communication Technology.

Choose the correct answer from the options given below:

(a) A, C, D and E only
(b) A, B, C and E only
(c) B, C, D and E only
(d) A, B, D and E only

Answer: (a)

Solution: Pradhan Mantri e-Vidya (PMEV) is a national initiative to provide digital education to students across India. The program was launched in 2020 in response to the COVID-19 pandemic, which forced many schools to close. PMEV aims to provide students with access to high-quality educational content and resources, regardless of their location or socio-economic background.

PMEV is a comprehensive program that includes a number of components, including:

- **Online classes:** PMEV provides online classes for students from class 1 to 12. These classes are taught by qualified teachers and are available 24/7.
- **Digital textbooks:** PMEV provides digital textbooks for students from class 1 to 12. These textbooks are interactive and can be customized to meet the needs of individual students.
- **Assessments:** PMEV provides assessments for students from class 1 to 12. These assessments are used to track student progress and to provide feedback to teachers.
- **Parental involvement:** PMEV encourages parental involvement in their children's education. Parents can access information about PMEV, including online classes, digital textbooks, and assessments.

PMEV is a valuable resource for students across India. The program provides access to high-quality educational content and resources, regardless of location or socio-economic background.

PMEV is helping to ensure that all students have the opportunity to succeed in school and in life.

395. Which of the followings are the alternative estimates of poverty in India?

(December 2022 - shift 1)

A. Dandekar and Rath Estimate

B. O.P Chopra Estimate

C. P. D. Ojha Estimate

D. B. 5. Minhas Estimate

E. D. K. Rangnekar Estimate

Choose the correct answer from the options given below:

(a) A, B and C only
(b) B, C and E only
(c) A, C and D only
(d) C, D and E only

Answer: (c)

Solution: The alternative estimates of poverty in India include:

- **Dandekar and Rath Estimate:** This estimate was developed by Dandekar and Rath in 1971. It is based on the concept of minimum level of living, which is defined as the amount of money required to meet the basic needs of a household.
- **Ojha Estimate:** This estimate was developed by P.D. Ojha in 1976. It is based on the concept of calorie intake, which is defined as the amount of calories required to maintain a healthy body weight.
- **Minhas Estimate:** This estimate was developed by B.S. Minhas in 1974. It is based on the concept of consumer expenditure, which is defined as the amount of money spent on goods and services by a household.

396. Which of the following objectives are correct for the Public Sector?

(December 2022 - shift 1)

A. To create employment opportunities

B. To promote balanced regional growth

C. To promote agriculture growth

D. To promote rapid economic development

E. To promote the banking sector of the economy

Choose the correct answer from the option given below:

(a) A, B and D only
(b) B, C and E only
(c) C, D and E only
(d) A, B, C, D and E

Answer: (d)

Solution: The public sector has a number of objectives, including:

- ✧ **To create employment opportunities:** The public sector can create employment opportunities by providing jobs in government agencies, public enterprises, and public-private partnerships.
- ✧ **To promote balanced regional growth:** The public sector can promote balanced regional growth by investing in infrastructure and development projects in different parts of the country.
- ✧ **To promote agriculture growth:** The public sector can promote agriculture growth by providing subsidies, loans, and other support to farmers.
- ✧ **To promote rapid economic development:** The public sector can promote rapid economic development by investing in infrastructure, education, and healthcare.
- ✧ **To promote the banking sector of the economy:** The public sector can promote the banking sector of the economy by providing loans to businesses and individuals, and by regulating the banking system.

These are just some of the objectives of the public sector. The specific objectives of the public sector may vary from country to country, depending on the country's specific needs and priorities.

397. Which of the following are required for a good tax system? *(December 2022 - shift 1)*

A. Revenue yield should be adequate.

B. Tax system should be so that different income groups of people pay tax equally.

C. Administrative and compliance cost of tax should be as minimum as possible.

D. Tax system should not permit scope for tax leakage and tax evasion.

E. Tax should be chosen to maximise interference with market efficiency.

Choose the correct answer from the options given below:

(a) A and C only
(b) A, C and E only
(c) A, C and D only
(d) A, B, C and D only

Answer: (c)

Solution: A good tax system is one that is fair, efficient, and simple. It should be fair in the sense that it should not place an undue burden on any one group of taxpayers. It should be efficient in the sense that it should minimize the administrative costs of collecting taxes. And it should be simple in the sense that it should be easy for taxpayers to understand and comply with.

Here are some of the characteristics of a good tax system:

- ✧ **Fairness:** The tax system should be fair in the sense that it should not place an undue burden on any one group of taxpayers. This means that the tax system should be progressive, meaning that taxpayers with higher incomes should pay a higher percentage of their income in taxes.

- ✧ **Efficiency:** The tax system should be efficient in the sense that it should minimize the administrative costs of collecting taxes. This means that the tax system should be simple to administer and that there should be a minimum of loopholes and exemptions.
- ✧ **Simplicity:** The tax system should be simple in the sense that it should be easy for taxpayers to understand and comply with. This means that the tax system should be easy to read and understand, and that there should be a minimum of jargon and technical terms.
- ✧ **Certainty:** The tax system should be certain in the sense that taxpayers should know what their tax liability is. This means that the tax laws should be clear and unambiguous, and that there should be a minimum of uncertainty about how the tax laws will be applied.
- ✧ **Transparency:** The tax system should be transparent in the sense that taxpayers should be able to see how their taxes are being used. This means that the government should publish detailed information about how tax revenue is collected and spent.

These are just some of the characteristics of a good tax system. The specific characteristics of a good tax system may vary from country to country, depending on the country's specific needs and priorities.

398. Federal transfers to states are required mainly: *(December 2022 - shift 1)*

A. to offset unequal assignment of resources and responsibilities between Federal Government and State Government.

B. to correct spillovers of benefits of public goods between jurisdictions.

C. to address horizontal fiscal imbalances.

D. to augment resources of local bodies.

E. for overall efficiency of tax system.

Choose the correct answer from the options given below:

(a) A, B and C only
(b) A, C and D only
(c) A, B, C and D only
(d) A, B,C, D and E

Answer: (d)

Solution: Federal transfers to states are required for a number of reasons, including:

- **To offset unequal assignment of resources and responsibilities between Federal Government and State Government:** In a federal system, the central government and the state governments have different responsibilities. However, the resources available to the two levels of government may not be equal. This can lead to horizontal fiscal imbalances, where some states are richer than others. Federal transfers can be used to offset these imbalances and to ensure that all states have the resources they need to provide essential services.
- **To correct spillovers of benefits of public goods between jurisdictions:** Public goods

are goods that are non-excludable and non-rivalrous. This means that it is difficult to prevent people from consuming public goods, even if they do not pay for them. As a result, public goods can generate spillovers, where the benefits of the good spill over into neighboring jurisdictions. Federal transfers can be used to correct these spillovers and to ensure that all jurisdictions share in the benefits of public goods.

- **To augment resources of local bodies:** Local bodies are responsible for providing a range of essential services, such as education, healthcare, and sanitation. However, local bodies often do not have the resources they need to provide these services. Federal transfers can be used to augment the resources of local bodies and to ensure that they have the resources they need to provide essential services.
- **For overall efficiency of tax system:** The tax system can be made more efficient by transferring resources from richer states to poorer states. This is because poorer states often have a lower tax base than richer states. As a result, they are unable to raise enough revenue to provide essential services. Federal transfers can help to equalize the tax base and to make the tax system more efficient.

These are just some of the reasons why federal transfers to states are required. The specific reasons for federal transfers may vary from country to country, depending on the country's specific needs and priorities.

399. Which of the following are expansionary monetary policy measures to cure deflation?
(December 2022 - shift 1)

A. The Central bank buys government securities from commercial banks and public.

B. The Central bank may hike the bank rate.

C. The Central bank may increase the cash reserve ratio.

D. The Central bank may reduce the cash reserve ratio.

E. The Central bank may lower the bank rate.

Choose the correct answer from the options given below:

(a) A, B and D only | (b) A, Cand E only

(c) B and C only | (d) A, D and E only

Answer: (d)

Solution: Deflation is a situation where the prices of goods and services are falling. This can lead to a number of problems, including:

✧ **Reduced economic growth:** Deflation can lead to reduced economic growth, as businesses are less likely to invest and hire workers in a deflationary environment.

✧ **Increased unemployment:** Deflation can lead to increased unemployment, as businesses are less likely to hire workers when prices are falling.

✧ **Increased debt burden:** Deflation can increase the debt burden of households and businesses, as the real value of their debt increases.

Expansionary monetary policy is a policy that is used to increase the money supply and stimulate economic growth. The following are expansionary monetary policy measures that can be used to cure deflation:

✧ The Central bank buys government securities from commercial banks and public: This increases the money supply in the economy.

✧ The Central bank may lower the bank rate: This makes it cheaper for banks to borrow money from the central bank, which can lead to them lending more money to businesses and consumers.

✧ The Central bank may reduce the cash reserve ratio: This frees up more money for banks to lend to businesses and consumers.

The other two options, hiking the bank rate and increasing the cash reserve ratio, are contractionary monetary policy measures. These measures would make it more expensive for banks to borrow money from the central bank, which would lead to them lending less money to businesses and consumers. This would have the opposite effect of curing deflation and would actually make deflation worse.

400. The main features of Treasury bills are that: *(December 2022 - shift 1)*

A. they are issued at a discount and are repaid at par on maturity.

B. they have low liquidity on account of their short tenure.

C. there is no default risk.

D. they offer an assured yield.

E. they have a high transaction cost.

Choose the correct answer from the options given below:

(a) A, B and C only
(b) A, C and D only
(c) A, D and E only
(d) A, C and E only

Answer: (b)

Solution: A Treasury bill (T-bill) is a short-term debt obligation issued by the Treasury Department with a maturity of one year or less. T-bills are sold at a discount to their face value, and investors earn their return by the difference between the purchase price and the face value when the T-bill matures.

A. They are issued at a discount and are repaid at par on maturity. This means that investors purchase Treasury bills at a price below their face value and receive the full face value upon maturity, effectively earning interest.

B. There is no default risk. Treasury bills are backed by the government, so they are considered to have no default risk. They are considered one of the safest forms of investment.

C. They offer an assured yield. Since Treasury bills are issued at a discount and repaid at par, the difference between the purchase price and the face value represents the yield, providing investors with an assured return.

The incorrect features are:

D. They have low liquidity on account of their short tenure. Treasury bills are actually considered highly liquid because they have a short maturity period, typically ranging from a few days to one year. Investors can easily buy or sell Treasury bills in the secondary market.

E. They have a high transaction cost. Treasury bills are typically traded with low transaction costs because they are highly liquid and widely traded in the financial markets.

401. Which of the following are correct in case of probability of two independent events A and B ? *(December 2022 - shift 1)*

A. $P(A/B) = P(A)$

B. $P(A/B) = P(B)$

C. $P(A \cap B) = P(A)\,P(B)$

D. $P(\bar{A} \cap \bar{B}) = P(\bar{A}).P(\bar{B})$

E. $P(A \cap \bar{B}) = P(\bar{A}).P(B)$

Choose the correct answer from the options given below:

(a) B, C and E only
(b) A, C and D only
(c) B, C and D only
(d) A, C and E only

Answer: (b)

Solution:

Independent Events [Happening of one event does not affect happening of other event]

$P(A \cap B) = P(A) . P(B)$

$P(A/B) = P(A)$

$P(B/A) = P(B)$

Dependent Events [Happening of one event effect happening of other event]

$P(A \cap B) = P(A) . P(B/A)$

402. Harrod-Domar classification of growth includes, which of the following? *(December 2022 - shift 1)*

A. **Natural growth rate**

B. **Desired growth rate**

C. Warranted growth rate

D. Possible growth rate

E. Population growth rate

Choose the correct answer from the options given below:

(a) A and B only
(b) A and C only
(c) A, B, C and E only
(d) B, C and D only

Answer: (b)

Solution:

Type of growth	Definition	Determined by
Natural growthrate	The rate of growth that is necessary tomaintain full employment	Growth of the labor force and productivity of labor
Warranted growth rate	The rate of growth that is consistent with the economy's productive capacity	Level of savings and investment
Actualgrowth rate	The rate of growth that the economy isactually achieving	Variety of factors, including government policies, business cycle, and externalshocks

Models of Growth :-

Harrod - Domar model

The main variables in theory are investment and saving. They explored dual nature of investment. Investment will create income and has generated demand .On the other hand investment will also generate productive capacity and hence create supply.

Assumptions :-

1) Full employment
2) No government interference
3) Closed economy
4) No lags in adjustment
5) Capital/ Income and Labour/ Income ratio constant
6) No substitution of factors
7) Constant returns to scale

Three concepts of growth :-

1) **Actual growth rate** :- $G = \frac{S}{C}$

G is growth rate of output

S is saving

C is capital

2) **Warranted growth rate** full capacity or potential-growth rate which tells us the entrepreneurial equilibrium.

$G_w C_r = S$

G_W Required capital to maintain warranted growth rate.

3) **Natural growth rate :-** It is the maximum growth rate or full employment that can be achieved.

Knife-edge equilibrium:- If $G = G_w = G_n$

There can be deviations from the st

Case 1 $\rightarrow G < G_w$ - depression

$C > C_r$ - depression

Case 2 $\rightarrow G > G_w$ - Inflation

$C < C_r$ - Inflation

If $G_n > G_w \rightarrow$ Inflation/Boom

If $G_w > G_n \rightarrow$ depression

Domar's Model → Domar equations

i) Demand side→$Y_d = \frac{1}{\alpha} I$

$\alpha \rightarrow$ MPS I=Net Investment

2) Supply side →$Y_S = OK$

O = Productivity of Capital

K =Real Capital

→Condition for achieving steady growth.

$\Delta Y_d = \Delta Y_S$

$\frac{1}{\alpha}\Delta I = \sigma \Delta K$ $\Delta K = I$

$\frac{1}{\alpha}\Delta I = \sigma I$

$\Delta I/I = \sigma.\alpha$

Razor - edge equilibrium and the condition to maintain steady growth.

$\Delta I/I > \sigma.\alpha$→ Inflation

$\Delta I/I < \sigma.\alpha$→ Depression

403. Which of the following are true for an oligopolistic market? *(December 2022 - shift 1)*

A. The demand curve of oligopolistic market is indeterminate.

B. There is a possibility of only two sellers.

C. The product may be homogenous or differentiated.

D. There is free entry into and free exit out of the market.

E. There is an importance of advertisement cost.

Choose the correct answer from the options given below:

(a) A, B, C and D only
(b) B, C and D only
(c) A, B, C and E only
(d) B, C, D and E only

Answer: (c)

Solution: An oligopolistic market is a market structure where there are a few sellers who control a large share of the market. The demand curve for an oligopolistic market is indeterminate, meaning that it is not possible to know for sure what the demand curve will be. This is because the demand curve depends on the actions of the other sellers in the market.

There is a possibility of only two sellers in an oligopolistic market, but there could also be more than two sellers. The product in an oligopolistic market can be homogenous or differentiated. If the product is homogenous, then the sellers will compete on price. If the product is differentiated, then the sellers will compete on product features, quality, and advertising. The barriers to entry are often high, so it is difficult for new firms to enter the market.

Advertisement is important in an oligopolistic market because it can help a seller to differentiate its product from the products of its competitors. Advertisement can also help to increase the demand for a seller's product.

404. Which of the following trends conform to the population projections for India based on the Census of India 2011, as carried out by the Technical Group on Population Projections under the aegis of National Commission on Population.

(December 2022 - shift 1)

A. The infant mortality rate is expected to decline in all states during 2011-2035.

B. The average age of Indians is expected to be higher in 2036 compared to 2011.

C. The crude birth rate is expected to increase due to increasing level of total fertility.

D. The crude death rate is expected to decrease owing to the changing age structure of the population.

E. As per the projected sex ratio, the population in 2036 is expected to be more feminine compared to the population in 2011.

Choose the correct answer from the options given below:

(a) A, B and C only (b) A, B and E only

(c) A, D and E only (d) B, C and E only

Answer: (b)

Solution:

A. The infant mortality rate is expected to decline in all states during 2011-2035. This is a reasonable projection given the advancements in healthcare and the general trend of improving infant mortality rates over time.

B. The average age of Indians is expected to be higher in 2036 compared to 2011. This is likely to be true as a result of declining fertility rates and increased life expectancy, leading to an aging population.

E. As per the projected sex ratio, the population in 2036 is expected to be more feminine compared to the population in 2011. This could be a valid projection based on historical trends of higher life expectancy for females.

The incorrect options are:

C. The crude birth rate is expected to increase due to the increasing level of total fertility. This is unlikely to be true as most projections suggest a decline in the crude birth rate due to factors such as urbanization and improvements in family planning.

D. The crude death rate is expected to decrease owing to the changing age structure of the population. While the crude death rate might decrease due to advancements in healthcare and an aging population, it is not necessarily tied to changes in the age structure alone. It could be affected by various other factors as well.

405. Consider a competitive polluting industry with identical firms and free entry. If the regulator sets an emission cap for each firm equal to the socially optimal long run level per firm, which of the following will characterize the long run impact of such an environmental policy on this competitive industry? *(December 2022 - shift 1)*

A. The industry size will be larger than the social optimum.

B. The output produced by each firm will be less than socially optimal.

C. The industry size will be smaller than the social optimum.

D. The output produced by each firm will be larger than socially optimal.

E. Total output and total pollution are greater than the social optimum.

Choose the correct answer from the options given below:

(a) A, D and E only (b) B, C and E only

(c) C, D and E only (d) A, B and E only

Answer: (d)

406. Which of the following are the members of SAARC countries?

(December 2022 - shift 1)

A. India
B. Pakistan
C. Sri Lanka
D. Afghanistan
E. China

Choose the correct answer from the options given below:

(a) A, C and E only
(b) B, C and E only
(c) A, D and E only
(d) A, B, C and D only

Answer: (d)

Solution: The South Asian Association for Regional Cooperation (SAARC) is an intergovernmental organization of eight countries in South Asia. Its member states are:

- Afghanistan
- Bangladesh
- Bhutan
- India
- Maldives
- Nepal
- Pakistan
- Sri Lanka

SAARC was established in 1985 with the goal of promoting economic cooperation, social progress, and cultural development in South Asia. The organization has its headquarters in Kathmandu, Nepal.

In addition to the eight member states, SAARC also has nine observer states:

- Australia
- China
- European Union (EU)
- Iran
- Japan
- Mauritius
- South Korea

- ✧ United States of America (USA)
- ✧ Myanmar

The observer states are not members of SAARC, but they can participate in the organization's activities.

407. Which of the following forms the credit side of the Balance of Payments?

(December 2022 - shift 1)

A. Unilateral transfer received

B. Capital transfer received

C. Income Payments (Import of factor services)

D. Exports of factor services

E. Merchandise imports

Choose the correct answer from the options given below:

(a) A, B and E only (b) B, C and D only

(c) A, C and D only (d) A, B and D only

Answer: (d)

Solution: The credit side of the balance of payments records the flows of money into the country. This includes:

- ✧ **Unilateral transfers received:** These are payments made by one country to another without any quid pro quo. For example, foreign aid or remittances from migrant workers.
- ✧ **Capital transfers received:** These are transfers of capital assets between countries, such as gifts or inheritances.
- ✧ **Exports of goods and services:** This includes the sale of goods and services to other countries. Income receipts (export of factor services): This includes payments to residents of the country for the use of their factors of production, such as labor and capital.

The debit side of the balance of payments records the flows of money out of the country. This includes:

- ✧ **Unilateral transfers made:** These are payments made by one country to another in return for goods or services. For example, foreign aid or remittances from migrant workers.
- ✧ **Capital transfers made:** These are transfers of capital assets between countries, such as investments or loans.
- ✧ **Imports of goods and services:** This includes the purchase of goods and services from other countries.
- ✧ **Income payments (import of factor services):** This includes payments made to non-residents of the country for the use of their factors of production, such as labor and capital.

408. Match List I with List Il *(December 2022 - shift 1)*

Choose the correct answer from the options given below:

List I	List II
A. Extra risk that an investor must incur to enjoy a higher exected return	I Risky Asset
B. Tendency of individuals to value an item more when they own it than when they do not.	II Moral Hazard
C. Provides an uncertain flow of money or services to its owner	III. Price of Risk
D. When a party whose actions are unobserved can affect the probability of payment associated with an event	IV Endowment effect

(a) A-I, B-IV, C-III, D-II
(b) A-III, B-IV, C-I, D-II
(c) A-III, B-IV, C-II, D-I
(d) A-I, B-II, C-III, D-IV

Answer: (b)

Solution:

List I	List II
Price of risk	Extra risk that an investor must incur to enjoy a higher expected return.
Risky Asset	Provides an uncertain flow of money or services to its owner.
Endowment effect	Tendency of individuals to value an item more when they own it thanwhen they do not.
Moral Hazard	When a party whose actions are unobserved can affect the probability of payment associated with an event.

Price of risk: The extra risk that an investor must incur to enjoy a higher expected return. For example, if an investor buys a stock, they are taking on the risk that the stock price could go down. In return for taking on this risk, the investor expects to earn a higher return on their investment than they would if they invested in a safe asset, such as a government bond.

Risky Asset: An asset that provides an uncertain flow of money or services to its owner. For example, a stock is a risky asset because the future price of the stock is uncertain. This means that the return on an investment in a stock is also uncertain.

Endowment effect: The tendency of individuals to value an item more when they own it than when they do not.

Moral hazard: When a party whose actions are unobserved can affect the probability of payment associated with an event. For example, Insured consumers are likely to take greater risk, knowing that a claim will be paid by their cover.

409. Match List I with List II *(December 2022 - shift 1)*

List I	List II
A. A.W. Phillips	I. Trade off between wage and unemployment
B. Findley Shiraz	II. Money illusion
C. Modigliani	III. Life cycle hypothesis
D. Pigou	IV. Taxable capacity

Choose the correct answer from the options given below:

(a) A-II, B-I, C-III, D-IV
(b) A-I, B-IV, C-III, D-II
(c) A-I, B-II, C-III, D-IV
(d) A-III, B-IV, C-I, D-II

Answer: (b)

Solution:

Tradeoff between wage and unemployment: This theory, proposed by A. W. Phillips, states that there is an inverse relationship between wage inflation and unemployment. This means that when wage inflation is high, unemployment is low, and vice versa.

Money illusion: This theory states that people tend to focus on the nominal value of money, rather than its real value. This means that they may not be aware of the true cost of goods and services, which can lead to inflation.

Life cycle hypothesis: This theory, proposed by Modigliani, states that people's spending patterns change over their lifetimes. In their younger years, people tend to save money for retirement. In their later years, they tend to spend down their savings.

Taxable capacity: This theory states that the amount of tax that a person can pay is limited by their income. This means that if taxes are too high, people will have less incentive to work, which can lead to economic growth.

List I	List II
A. W. Phillips	Trade off between wage and unemployment
Pigou	Money illusion
Modigliani	Life cycle hypothesis
Findley Shiraz	Taxable capacity

410. Match List I with List II *(December 2022 - shift 1)*

List I	List II
A. Censored regression Model	I. Probit Model
B. Normit Model	II. Marc Nerlove
C. Distributed - lags Model	III. Tobit Model
D. Partial adjustment Model	IV. L. M. Koyck

Choose the correct answer from the options given below:

(a) A-I, B-III, C-II, D-IV (b) A-III, B-I, C-IV, D-II

(c) A-III, B-IV, C-I, D-II (d) A-IV, B-III, C-I, D-II

Answer: (b)

Two types :

1) Binary Logit Model
2) Binary Probit Model

Logit, Probit and Tobit models

These are dummy dependent variable models.

Logit follows logistic distribution

$$L_i = \ln(\frac{P_i}{1-P_i})$$

Pi is probability of happening an event i.e. adoption of technology.

(1-pi) is probability of not happening an event.

P goes from 0 to 1, L from -∞ to ∞

Logit assumptions:

1. No need of linear relation between dependent and independent variables.
2. No need of homoscedasticity of independent variables
3. The error terms need to be independent.
4. Absence of perfect multicollinearity.

Probit: follows lognormal distribution. It is also called normit model. Dependent variable can take only two values i.e. married or not married. Its purpose is to estimate probability.

Tobit model is extension of probit model. It is used when a sample in which information on the regressand is available only for some observations. Such samples are called censored samples. Therefore, Tobit model is also called censored model or limited dependent variable regression model.

i.e. suppose we have a set of consumers and we are interested in finding amount of money a person spends on a house in relation to other socio economic variables. If consumer do not purchase house, we have no data for housing expenditure for such consumer.

411. Match List I with List II *(December 2022 - shift 1)*

List I	List II

Two - Variable Linear Regression Model	Elasticity
A. $Y = \beta_1 + \beta_2 X$	I. $\beta_2 X$
B. In $Y = \beta_1 + \beta_2 X$	II. β_2
C. $Y = \beta_1 + \beta_2$ InX	III. β_2 (X/Y)
D. In $Y = \beta_1 + \beta$ InX	IV. β_2 (1/Y)

Choose the correct answer from the options given below:

(a) A-III, B-IV, C-I, D-II
(b) A-III, B-I, C-IV, D-II
(c) A-II, B-I, C-III, D-IV
(d) A-II, B-III, C-IV, D-I

Answer: (b)

Solution L:

$$Y = \beta_1 + \beta_2 X$$

$$\frac{\Delta Y}{\Delta X} = \beta 2$$

$$\varepsilon = \frac{\Delta Y}{\Delta X} \times \frac{X}{Y} = \beta 2\left(\frac{X}{Y}\right)$$

412. Match List I with List II *(December 2022 - shift 1)*

List I	List II
A. GATS Mode -1	I. Cross - border trade
B. GATS Mode -2	II. Commercial presence
C. GATS Mode -3	III. Temporary movement of natural persons
D. GATS Mode -4	IV. Consumption abroad

Choose the correct answer from the options given below:

(a) A-I, B-IV, C-III, D-II
(b) A-I, B-IV, C-II, D-III
(c) A-I, B-II, C-IV, D-III
(d) A-I, B-II, C-III, D-IV

Answer: (b)

413. Match List I with List II *(December 2022 - shift 1)*

List I	List II
A. Functional Finance	I. Peacock and Wiseman
B. Displacement effect	II. Keynes and Learner
C. Law of increasing state activity	III. Wagner
D. Allocative, stabilization and distributive function of state	IV. Musgrave

Choose the correct answer from the options given below:

(a) A-II, B-I, C-III, D-IV
(b) A-IV, B-I, C-III, D-II
(c) A-II, B-III, C-I, D-IV
(d) A-I, B-II, C-IV, D-III

Answer: (a)

414. Match List I with List II *(December 2022 - shift 1)*

List I	List II
A. The establishment of a clearing house for settlement of transactions in BSE.	I. 1994
B. Serial bomb blasts in BSE.	II. 1997
C. Screen - based trading commenced in BSE.	III. 1921
D. BSE launched the first stock index with 30 scrips.	IV. 1986

Choose the correct answer from the options given below:

(a) A-I, B-III, C-II, D-IV
(b) A-III, B-II, C-IV, D-I
(c) A-III, B-I, C-II, D-IV
(d) A-II, B-I, C-III, D-IV

Answer: (c)

415. Match List I with List II *(December 2022 - shift 1)*

List I	List II
A. SCP approach	I. James Buchanan
B. Transaction cost theory	II. New classical theory
C. Public choice theory	III. H.H. Index
D. Industrial connection	IV. Williamson

Choose the correct answer from the options given below:

(a) A-II, B-IV, C-I, D-III
(b) A-III, B-IV, C-II, D-I
(c) A-I, B-III, C-IV, D-II
(d) A-IV, B-II, C-I, D-III

Answer: (a)

416. Match List I with List II *(December 2022 - shift 1)*

List I	List II
Conference of the Parties (COP) - UNFCCC	Location
A. COP - 15	I. Bali, Indonesia
B. COP - 21	II. Sharm el - Sheikh, Egypt
C. COP - 13	III. Copenhagen, Denmark
D. COP - 27	IV. Paris, France

Choose the correct answer from the options given below:

(a) A-IV, B-I, C-II, D-III
(b) A-III, B-IV, C-I, D-II
(c) A-III, B-I, C-II, D-IV
(d) A-IV, B-III, C-I, D-II

Answer: (b)

COPs: The Conference of the Parties (COP) is the decision-making body of the United Nations Framework Convention on Climate Change (UNFCCC).

- » COPs bring together representatives from countries worldwide to address climate change and make decisions on global climate policy.
- » COP meetings are held annually and serve as a platform for countries to discuss and negotiate actions related to climate change mitigation, adaptation, and finance.
- » COPs have resulted in significant international agreements that shape global climate action.

Important COPs:

1. **COP 1 (Berlin, 1995):** Established the UNFCCC and laid the foundation for future climate negotiations.
2. **COP 3 (Kyoto, 1997):** Led to the adoption of the Kyoto Protocol, which set binding emission reduction targets for developed countries.
3. **COP 7 (Marrakech, 2001):** Finalized the operational details of the Kyoto Protocol.
4. **COP 13 (Bali, 2007):** Launched negotiations for a post-2012 climate regime, leading to the adoption of the Paris Agreement.
5. **COP 15 (Copenhagen, 2009):** Aimed to achieve a legally binding global climate agreement but resulted in a political declaration known as the Copenhagen Accord.
6. **COP 17 (Durban, 2011):** Led to the Durban Platform, initiating negotiations for a new legally binding climate agreement applicable to all countries.
7. **COP 21 (Paris, 2015):** Marked a historic moment with the adoption of the Paris Agreement, aiming to limit global warming well below 2 degrees Celsius.
8. **COP 24 (Katowice, 2018):** Finalized the implementation guidelines for the Paris Agreement, addressing issues such as transparency, finance, and carbon markets.
9. **COP 26 (Glasgow, 2021):** Focused on enhancing countries' climate commitments under the Paris Agreement and mobilizing finance for climate action.
10. **COP 27:** The conference is scheduled to be held in Sharm el-Sheikh, Egypt in November 2022.

417. Match List I with List II *(December 2022 - shift 1)*

List I	List II
A. Santa Cruz	I. West Bengal
B. Kandla	II. Andhra Pradesh
C. Falta	III. Gujarat
D. Vushakhapatnam	IV. Maharashtra

Choose the correct answer from the options given below:

(a) A-I, B-II, C-IV, D-III (b) A-IV, B-III, C-I, D-II

(c) A-II, B-IV, C-III, D-I (d) A-III, B-I, C-II, D-IV

Answer: (b)

418. Arrange the percentage share of nominal GVA(RE), 2019-20 for the following sectors in descending order *(December 2022 - shift 1)*

A. Agriculture and Allied

B. Manufacturing

C. Construction

D. Finance, Real estate and Professional services

E. Mining and Quarrying

Choose the correct answer from the options given below:

(a) D, A, B, C, E (b) A, D, B, C, E (c) D, B, A, C, E (d) B, A, D, E, C

Answer: (a)

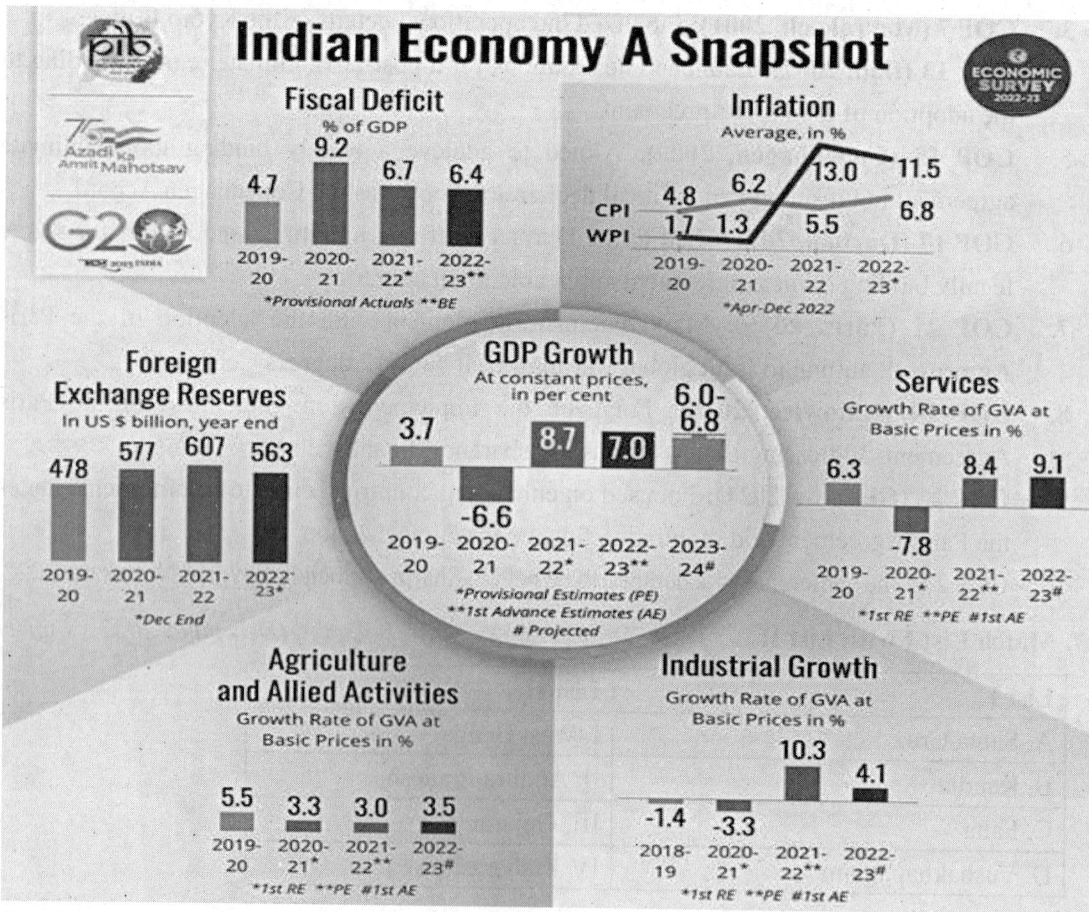

419. Arrange the books in ascending order based on their year of publication

(December 2022 - shift 1)

A. **An Inquiry Into the Nature and Causes of Wealth of Nations**
B. **The Theory of Moral Sentiments**
C. **Capitalism, Socialism and Democracy**
D. **The Great Transformation: The Political and Economic Origin of Our Time**
E. **The Affluent Society**

Choose the correct answer from the options given below:

(a) B C D E A (b) B A C D E
(c) D E A B C (d) A C E B D

Answer: (b)

Solution:

1. **The Theory of Moral Sentiments (1759)** - Explores human morality and ethics.
2. **An Inquiry Into the Nature and Causes of Wealth of Nations (1776)** - Foundational work in economics, discussing market principles.
3. **The Great Transformation (1944)** - Focuses on the shift to modern market economies.
4. **The Affluent Society (1958)** - Examines post-WWII consumer-driven economies and social inequalities.
5. **Capitalism, Socialism and Democracy (1942)** - Discusses capitalism, challenges, and potential transformations.

Books and Authors :-

General theory of employment, interest and money 1936→ Keynes

Affluent society 1958 →Kenneth

Asian drama →Myrdal

Development as freedom (1999) → Amartya Sen

Capitalism and freedom →Friedman

Rise and fall of nations →Ruchir Sharma

Capital in 21st century →Thomas Piketty

Principles of Economics (1890) → Alfred Marshall

An enquiry into nature and cause of wealth of nations (1776) → Adam Smith

The Economics of welfare (1920) → AL Pigou

Value and capital (1939)

A revision of demand theory (1956)→JR Hicks

Principles of political economy and taxation (1817) →Ricardo

Nature and significance of economic science →Robbins

Principles of political economy →Mill

Behavioral Theory of firm→ Cyert and Mark

420. Arrange the following in descending order on the basis of the year of WTO Ministerial Conferences held. *(December 2022 - shift 1)*

A. Cancun, Mexico Conference.

B. Nairobi, Kenya Conference.

C. Bali, Indonesia Conference.

D. Buenos Aires, Argentina Conference.

E. Seattle, United States Conference.

Choose the correct answer from the options given below:

(a) A C D B E
(b) D B C A E
(c) B C A E D
(d) E A C E D

Answer: (b)

Solution:

1. **Buenos Aires, Argentina Conference** - Held in 2017.
2. **Nairobi, Kenya Conference** - Held in 2015.
3. **Bali, Indonesia Conference** - Held in 2013.
4. **Cancun, Mexico Conference** - Held in 2003.
5. **Seattle, United States Conference** - Held in 1999.

421. Arrange the following stages of the Budget in the correct sequence. *(December 2022 - shift 1)*

A. Appropriation Bill.

B. General Discussion.

C. Finance Bill.

D. Presentation to the Legislative Assembly.

E. Voting on the Demand for Grants.

Choose the correct answer from the options given below:

(a) B C E A D
(b) A B E C D
(c) D A C B E
(d) D B A C E

Answer: (d)

Solution:

1. **Presentation of the Budget :** The Finance Minister presents the Budget to the Lok Sabha (Lower House of Parliament) in February or March every year.
2. **General Discussion :** The Budget is then discussed in the Lok Sabha for a period of three to four days.
3. **Voting on the Demand for Grants :** After the general discussion, the Lok Sabha votes on the Demand for Grants, which is a detailed statement of the government's proposed expenditure for the coming financial year.
4. **Passing of the Finance Bill :** The Finance Bill is then introduced in the Lok Sabha to authorize the government to raise revenue through taxes and other means. The Finance Bill is usually passed by the Lok Sabha without much debate.
5. **Appropriation Bill :** The Appropriation Bill is then introduced in the Lok Sabha to authorize the government to spend money from the Consolidated Fund of India. The Appropriation Bill is usually passed by the Lok Sabha without much debate.

422. Indicate the chronological sequence of the following in terms of their implementation in India. *(December 2022 - shift 1)*

A. Service Tax

B. Expenditure Tax

C. State VAT

D. Income Tax

E. Goods and Services Tax (GST)

Choose the correct answer from the options given below:

(a) B D C A E (b) D B C A E

(c) D B A C E (d) B A D C E

Answer: (c)

Solution:

The chronological sequence of the implementation of the following taxes in India is:

1. **Income Tax:** The Income Tax Act was enacted in 1961 and came into effect on April 1, 1962.
2. **Service Tax:** Service Tax was introduced in India on July 1, 1994.
3. **State VAT:** State VAT was introduced in India in April 2005.
4. **Expenditures Tax:** Expenditure Tax was introduced in India in 1987 and abolished in 1997.
5. **Goods and Services Tax (GST):** GST was introduced in India on July 1, 2017.

423. According to the CMIE data (September, 2022) arrange the states in ascending order based on their unemployment rate. *(December 2022 - shift 1)*

A. Madhya Pradesh

B. Gujarat

C. Chhattisgarh

D. Assam

E. Uttarakhand

Choose the correct answer from the options given below:

(a) D B A C E (b) C D E A B

(c) C B D E A (d) A B C D E

Answer: (b)

424. Arrange the rates in descending order based on 'Reserve Bank of India' data, December 2022. *(December 2022 - shift 1)*

A. Cash Reserve Ratio

B. Repo rate

C. Bank rate

D. Reverse Repo rate

E. Standing Deposit Facility rate

Choose the correct answer from the options given below:

(a) A B C D E (b) E C D B A

(c) C B E A D (d) A B D E C

Answer: (c)

Solution:

- » Reverse Repo Rate (RRR): 3.35%
- » Repo Rate: 6.50%
- » Bank Rate: 6.50%
- » Standing Deposit Facility Rate (SDF): 6.00%
- » Cash Reserve Ratio (CRR): 4.50%

Note: These rates frequently change, keep yourself updated from RBI 's official website.

425. Arrange the followings chronologically in order of their introduction. *(December 2022 - shift 1)*

A. Ad hoc Treasury bills (T-bills)

B. 28 Days T-bills

C. 14 Days T-bills

D. 364 Days T-bills

E. 182 Days T - bills

Choose the correct answer from the options given below:

(a) A D E B C (b) A E D C B

(c) D E A B C (d) E A C D B

Answer: (b)

426. Arrange the following in chronological order starting from the oldest relating to the theory of money. *(December 2022 - shift 1)*

A. Patinkin

B. Fisher

C. Friedman

D. Marshall

E. Keynes

Choose the correct answer from the options given below:

(a) E B C A D (b) B D E A C

(c) A B C D E (d) D B A C E

Answer: (b)

Solution:

Economist	**Contribution**
Alfred Marshall	Cambridge Cash Balance Theory of Money (1911)
Irving Fisher	Quantity Theory of Money (1911)
John Maynard Keynes	Liquidity Preference Theory of Money (1936)
Don Patinkin	General Theory of Money and Prices (1956)
Milton Friedman	Modern Quantity Theory of Money (1956)

427. Arrange the trading groups as per their year of establishment starting from the oldest *(December 2022 - shift 1)*

A. European Free Trade Association

B. North American Free Trade Agreement

C. Asia Pacific Economic Cooperation

D. Andean Community

E. Association of South-East Asian Nations

Choose the correct answer from the options given below:

(a) A E D B C (b) A D E B C

(c) A E D C B (d) B C D E A

Answer: (c)

Solution:

1. European Free Trade Association (EFTA): Established in 1960.
2. Andean Community: Established in 1969.
3. Association of Southeast Asian Nations (ASEAN): Established in 1967.
4. Asia Pacific Economic Cooperation (APEC): Established in 1989.
5. North American Free Trade Agreement (NAFTA): Established in 1994.

428. Given below are two statements: *(December 2022 - shift 1)*

Statement I: Every point on the Contract curve is Pareto efficient because one person could not be made better off without making someone else worse off.

Statement II: Every point on the Contract curve necessarily indicates equal level of economic welfare for the society.

In light of the above statements, choose the most appropriate answer from the options given below:

(a) Both Statement I and Statement Il are correct.

(b) Both Statement I and Statement Il are incorrect.

(c) Statement I is correct but Statement Il is incorrect.

(d) Statement I is incorrect but Statement Il is correct

Answer: (c)

Solution:

- ✧ Statement I is correct. The concept of Pareto efficiency suggests that a situation is Pareto efficient if it is impossible to make one person better off without making someone else worse off. This idea is captured by the concept of the Contract curve in economics, where any point on the Contract curve represents a Pareto efficient allocation.
- ✧ Statement II is incorrect. While the Contract curve represents Pareto efficient allocations, it does not necessarily indicate an equal level of economic welfare for the society. Pareto efficiency only ensures that no individual can be made better off without making someone else worse off, but it doesn't address the distribution of welfare among individuals. Therefore, the Contract curve may include allocations where the economic welfare is not equal among all individuals.

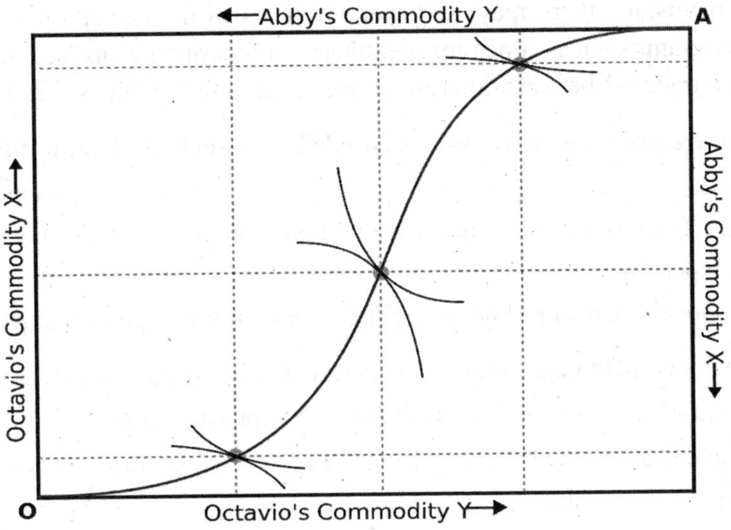

The contract curve is the curve that connects all the Pareto efficient allocations of goods and services between two individuals. The points inside the contract curve are not Pareto efficient, and the points outside the contract curve are not attainable.

429. Given below are two statements: *(December 2022 - shift 1)*

Statement I: A rising ratio of interest payments to GNP imposes a burden because taxation is needed to finance the interest payment and imposes a dead weight loss.

Statement II: A rising rate of interest payment in the budget tends to crowd out other public programs.

In light of the above statements, choose the correct answer from the options given below:

(a) Both Statement I and Statement II are true.

(b) Both Statement I and Statement II are false.

(c) Statement I is true but Statement II is false.

(d) Statement I is false but Statement II is true.

Answer: (a)

Solution:

- Statement I is true. A rising ratio of interest payments to GNP (Gross National Product) does impose a burden because the government needs to allocate funds for interest payments, which could have been used for other productive purposes. Additionally, financing interest payments through taxation can lead to deadweight losses due to the distortionary effects of taxes on economic activities.
- Statement II is also true. A rising rate of interest payment in the budget can indeed crowd out other public programs. When a significant portion of the budget is allocated to servicing

interest payments, there may be fewer resources available for funding other essential public programs such as education, healthcare, infrastructure, and social welfare. This can result in a trade-off between interest payments and other public spending priorities.

430. Given below are two statements, one is labelled as Assertion (A) and the other is labelled as Reason (R). *(December 2022 - shift 1)*

Assertion (A) : The low income countries are far more likely to borrow money to finance their public sector expenditure.

Reason (R) : Governments need not repay their loans, along with interest payment.

In light of the above statements, choose the correct answer from the options given below:

(a) Both (A) and (R) are true and (R) is the correct explanation of (A).

(b) Both (A) and (R) are true but (R) is NOT the correct explanation of (A).

(c) (A) is true but (R) is false.

(d) (A) is false but (R) is true.

Answer: (c)

Solution:

- ✧ Assertion (A) is true. Low-income countries are more likely to borrow money to finance their public sector expenditure because their domestic revenue may not be sufficient to cover their expenses, and they may lack the necessary infrastructure and resources for economic development.
- ✧ Reason (R) is false. Governments do need to repay their loans along with interest payments. Loans obtained by governments, like any other loans, have to be repaid according to the terms and conditions agreed upon with the lenders. Failure to repay loans can lead to financial and economic consequences, including default and loss of credibility in international financial markets. The statement in Reason (R) is not accurate and does not correctly explain Assertion (A).

431. Given below are two statements, one is labelled as Assertion (A) and the other is labelled as Reason (R). *(December 2022 - shift 1)*

Assertion (A) : Partisan theory views macroeconomic policy outcomes as the result of ideologically motivated decisions by leaders of different political parties.

Reason (R) : The parties represent constituencies with different preferences concerning macroeconomic variables.

In light of the above statements, choose the correct answer from the options given below:

(a) Both (A) and (R) are true and (R) is the correct explanation of (A).

(b) Both (A) and (R) are true but (R) is NOT the correct explanation of (A).

(c) (A) is true but (R) is false.

(d) (A) is false but (R) is true.

Answer: (a)

Solution:

Assertion (A) is true because partisan theory argues that political parties have different ideological preferences about macroeconomic variables, such as inflation and unemployment. These ideological preferences lead to different policy choices by the parties when they are in power. For example, left-wing parties are more likely to pursue expansionary policies that lead to higher inflation, while right-wing parties are more likely to pursue contractionary policies that lead to lower inflation.

Reason (R) is also true because political parties represent different constituencies with different preferences concerning macroeconomic variables. For example, labor unions tend to support left-wing parties because they believe that these parties will pursue policies that will lead to higher wages and lower unemployment. Business groups, on the other hand, tend to support right-wing parties because they believe that these parties will pursue policies that will lead to lower taxes and less regulation.

The fact that political parties represent different constituencies with different preferences concerning macroeconomic variables is the reason why partisan theory believes that macroeconomic policy outcomes are the result of ideologically motivated decisions by leaders of different political parties. In other words, the policies that are chosen by the government are not simply the result of economic conditions, but also the result of the ideological preferences of the ruling party.

432. Given below are two statements: *(December 2022 - shift 1)*

Statement I: Supply side policies are long term measures to increase the productive capacity of the economy leading to an outward shift in the production possibility curve.

Statement II: Privatization is the act of selling state owned assets in order to increase competition, productivity and efficiency.

In light of the above statements, choose the correct answer from the options given below:

(a) Both Statement I and Statement II are true.

(b) Both Statement I and Statement II are false.

(c) Statement I is true but Statement II is false.

(d) Statement I is false but Statement II is true.

Answer: (a)

Solution:

Statement I is true because supply side policies are long-term measures that aim to increase the productive capacity of the economy. This can be done by reducing taxes, deregulation, and privatization. All of these measures can lead to an outward shift in the production possibility curve, which means that the economy can produce more goods and services.

Statement II is also true because privatization is the act of selling state-owned assets to the private sector. This can lead to increased competition, productivity, and efficiency in the economy. When state-owned assets are privatized, they are usually subject to market forces, which can lead to more efficient use of resources. Additionally, private owners are usually more motivated to improve efficiency and productivity than government owners.

433. In case of two goods for which the MRS is zero or infinite, then the nature of goods is : *(December 2022 - shift 2)*

(a) Perfect substitutes
(b) Normal goods
(c) Perfect compliments
(d) Close substitutes

Answer = (c)

Solution:

- **Perfect substitutes:** In the case of perfect substitutes, the marginal rate of substitution (MRS) remains constant, indicating that consumers are willing to substitute one good for the other at a fixed ratio. For example, if a consumer is indifferent between consuming one unit of good A and one unit of good B, and is equally willing to exchange one unit of A for one unit of B, then the MRS is constant.
- **Normal goods:** Normal goods do not necessarily have a fixed MRS of zero or infinite. The MRS depends on consumer preferences and utility.
- **Perfect compliments:** When goods are perfect compliments, the MRS is either zero or infinite. This means that the consumer must consume both goods in fixed proportions. For example, a left shoe and a right shoe are perfect compliments, as one without the other is of no use.
- **Close substitutes:** Close substitutes imply that the MRS is not necessarily fixed at zero or infinite. Consumers may be willing to substitute one good for another, but not necessarily at a constant rate.

434. Which of the following is not true? *(December 2022 - shift 2)*

(a) Total effect of price change on consumption of a good is a combination of income effect and substitution effect
(b) For inferior goods, income effect is always larger than substitution effect, in absolute terms.
(c) For corner solution $MRS_{xy} \neq P_x/P_y$
(d) For a normal good both the income and substitution effect hold

Answer = (b)

Solution:

- ✧ **Total effect of price change:** True. The total effect of a price change on the consumption of a good is indeed a combination of the income effect and the substitution effect. The direction and magnitude of the total effect depend on the specific characteristics of the good and the consumer's preferences.
- ✧ **For inferior goods:** Not always true. In the case of inferior goods, the income effect and substitution effect work in opposite directions. If the income effect dominates, the consumption of an inferior good may decrease as income increases despite the price reduction. However, it is not always the case that the income effect is larger than the substitution effect in absolute terms.
- ✧ **For corner solution MRSxy Px/Py:** True. In economics, a "corner solution" refers to a situation where a consumer chooses to consume only one of two goods due to budget constraints or preferences. In such cases, the marginal rate of substitution (MRS) between the two goods is indeed equal to the ratio of their prices (Px/Py).
- ✧ **For a normal good both the income and substitution effect hold:** True. For a normal good, both the income effect and substitution effect generally hold. When the price of a normal good decreases, the consumer may consume more due to the combined effect of being able to afford more (income effect) and finding the good relatively more attractive compared to other goods (substitution effect).

435. The negative network externality in which a consumer wishes to own an exclusive or unique good such as specially designed sports car is: *(December 2022 - shift 2)*

(a) Bandwagon effect (b) Tequila effect

(c) Snob effect (d) Pigou effect

Answer = (c)

Solution:

- ✧ **Bandwagon effect:** The bandwagon effect occurs when the demand for a good increases as more people buy it, leading to a desire to conform to popular trends.
- ✧ **Tequila effect:** The tequila effect refers to the contagion of financial crises from one country to another due to investor panic and loss of confidence in emerging markets.
- ✧ **Snob effect:** The snob effect occurs when a consumer desires to own a unique or exclusive good that is not widely possessed by others. The consumer values the exclusivity and prestige associated with owning such a good.
- ✧ **Pigou effect:** The Pigou effect is an economic concept where lower prices during deflation increase real wealth and stimulate consumer spending, potentially aiding in economic recovery.

In this case, the negative network externality described, where a consumer desires an exclusive or unique good like a specially designed sports car, is known as the snob effect.

436. When each player has chosen his or her optimal strategy given the strategy chosen by other player, the situation is referred to as: *(December 2022 - shift 2)*

(a) Nash Equilibrium
(b) Wicksel's Equilibrium
(c) Prisoner's dilemma
(d) Co-operative Game

Answer = (a)

Solution:

- **Nash Equilibrium:** In game theory, a Nash equilibrium is a situation in which each player's strategy is optimal given the strategies chosen by the other players. No player has an incentive to unilaterally deviate from their chosen strategy, as doing so would not improve their payoff.
- **Wicksell's Equilibrium:** There is no widely known concept in game theory referred to as "Wicksell's Equilibrium."
- **Prisoner's Dilemma:** The prisoner's dilemma is a specific type of game where two players each have the option to cooperate or betray the other, and the outcome depends on the combined choices. It often results in a suboptimal outcome due to conflicting interests.
- **Co-operative Game:** A cooperative game involves players working together to achieve a common goal. The focus is on how players can collaborate to distribute the total gains among themselves.

437. A firm has the following total cost and demand functions: *(December 2022 - shift 2)*

C =1/3 Q^3 -7Q^2+ 111Q+50 , Q = 100 - P. then find the profit maximizing level of output (Q*) and maximum profit of the firm.

(a) 50 and 100 (b) 111 and 2150 (c) 11 and 111*1/3 (d) 7 and 84

Answer = (c)

$$\mathbf{C = \frac{1}{3} Q^3 - 7Q^2 + 111Q + 50}$$

$$\mathbf{MC = \frac{3}{3} Q^2 - 14Q + 111}$$

Now, TR = PQ

Q = 100-P or P = 100-Q

TR = 100Q - Q^2

MR = 100-2Q

Now, MR = MC

$\frac{3}{3}Q^2 - 14Q + 111 = 100 - 2Q$

$Q^2 - 14Q + 111 - 100 + 2Q = 0$

$Q^2 - 12Q + 11 = 0$

$Q2 - 11Q - Q + 11 = 0$

$Q(Q-11) - 1(Q-11)$

$(Q-1)(Q-11)$

Q =11

For profit maximisation slope of MR < MC

So,

$-2 < 2Q - 14$

$-2 < 22 - 14$

$-2 < 8$

So 11 is the profit maximising output

If you have to find maximum profit, you can do this question by making profit equation and put Q in profit equation.

Profit = Revenue – Cost.

438. The condition of preferring a certain income to a risky income with same expected value is referred to as: *(December 2022 - shift 2)*

(a) Risk neutral (b) Risk loving (c) Risk averse (d) Risk Premium

Answer = (c)

Solution:

- **Risk neutral:** Risk-neutral individuals are indifferent between a certain income and a risky income with the same expected value. They are willing to accept any fair gamble, regardless of risk.
- **Risk loving:** Risk-loving individuals prefer a risky income over a certain income, even if the risky income has the same expected value. They are willing to take on additional risk for the possibility of higher returns.
- **Risk averse:** Risk-averse individuals prefer a certain income over a risky income with the same expected value. They require a risk premium to compensate for taking on uncertainty or risk.
- **Risk Premium:** The risk premium is the additional return that an investor demands for holding a risky asset compared to a risk-free asset.

439. Which one of the following is not a component of M1 ? *(December 2022 - shift 2)*

(a) Currency (b) Traveler's cheque

(c) Commercial paper (d) Demand deposits

Answer = (c)

Solution: M1 money supply consists of highly liquid assets that can be quickly converted into cash. The main components of M1 typically include:

1. **Currency in Circulation:** This includes physical money in the form of coins and banknotes that is actively used for transactions in the economy.
2. **Demand Deposits:** Demand deposits are funds held in checking accounts that account holders can withdraw on demand. They are also known as current or checking account balances.
3. **Traveler's Checks:** Traveler's checks are a form of prepaid payment instruments that can be used for transactions while traveling. They are considered part of the M1 money supply due to their high liquidity.
4. **Other Checkable Deposits:** These are deposits in financial institutions that can be withdrawn by writing checks. They include some types of savings accounts that offer check- writing privileges.

440. The Keynes's animal spirits are closely associated with *(December 2022 - shift 2)*

(a) Past investment (b) Current investment

(c) Aggregate income (d) Aggregate expenditure

Answer = (b)

Animal spirits is a term used by John Maynard Keynes to describe the unpredictable and unquantifiable factors that influence investment decisions. Keynes argued that animal spirits are important because they can lead to fluctuations in investment, which can in turn lead to fluctuations in aggregate demand and output.

Current investment is the most closely associated with animal spirits because it is the most uncertain. Businesses make investment decisions based on their expectations about the future, and these expectations can be volatile. For example, businesses may be more likely to invest if they are optimistic about the future, but they may be less likely to invest if they are pessimistic about the future.

Past investment and aggregate income are also associated with animal spirits, but they are not as closely associated as current investment. Past investment can influence current investment decisions because it can provide businesses with information about the future. For example, if a business has a history of making successful investments, it is more likely to make new investments in the future.

Aggregate income can also influence current investment decisions because it can affect the demand for goods and services. For example, if aggregate income is high, businesses may be more likely to invest in order to meet the demand for goods and services.

However, past investment and aggregate income are not as volatile as current investment, so they are not as closely associated with animal spirits.

441. In the Mundell-Fleming model, the monetary policy will be more effective when there is

(December 2022 - shift 2)

(a) Perfect capital mobility and flexible exchange rate

(b) Perfect capital mobility and fixed exchange rate

(c) Imperfect capital mobility and flexible exchange rate

(d) Imperfect capital mobility and fixed exchange rate

Answer = (a)

Solution:

Mundell Fleming model -IS-LM-BP model

→In case of fixed exchange rate, expansionary fiscal policy more effective.

→In case of fixed exchange rate, monetary policy is not effective.

→In case of flexible exchange rate, fiscal policy ineffective.

→In case of flexible exchange rate, monetary policy is effective

442. If the two events A and B are not independent then which of the following is correct?

(December 2022 - shift 2)

1. $P(A \cap B) = P(A).P(B)$
2. $P(A \cap B) = P(A) .P(B/A)$
3. $P(A \cap B) = P(A) .P(A/B)$
4. $P(A \cap B) = 1 - P(A \cup B)$

Answer = (b)

Solution:

Independent Events : [Happening of one event does not affect happening of other event]

$P(A \cap B) = P(A) . P(B)$ $P(A/B) = P(A)$

$P(B/A) = P(B)$

Dependent Events : [Happening of one event effect happening of other event]

$P(A \cap B) = P(A) . P(B/A)$

443. The chain-weighted index is *(December 2022 - shift 2)*

(a) The total market value of goods and services produced in each year

(b) The percentage growth in real GDP

(c) A method for calculating changes in prices that used an average of base year from neighbouring years

(d) An Index that measures how the prices of goods and services included in GDP change.

Answer = (c)

Solution: A chain-weighted index is a method for calculating changes in prices that uses an average of base year from neighbouring years. This is in contrast to a simple index, which uses the prices in the base year as the weights.

The chain-weighted index is more accurate than a simple index because it takes into account changes in the composition of GDP over time. For example, if the production of a particular good increases in one year, but the price of that good decreases, the chain-weighted index will show a smaller increase in prices than a simple index.

444. If the consumption function passes through the origin and APC = MPC then it must be: *(December 2022 - shift 2)*

(a) Linear without any intercept

(b) Non-linear without any intercept

(c) Linear with a negative intercept on the income axis

(d) Linear with a positive intercept on the consumption axis

Answer = (a)

Solution: The consumption function is a relationship between consumption and income. It shows how much people consume at different levels of income. If the consumption function passes through the origin and APC = MPC, then it must be a linear function without any intercept.

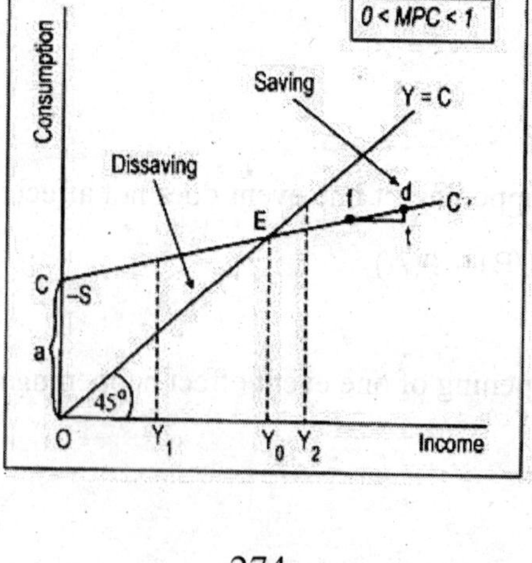

The consumption function is represented by the line C. The income axis is on the x-axis and the consumption axis is on the y-axis.

The consumption function passes through the origin is long run consumption function given by Kuznets, which means that consumption is zero when income is zero.

Long run consumption function is C=bY

Here APC = b and MPC also b.

445. Find the producer's surplus when *(December 2022 - shift 2)*

Pd = $3x^2$ - 20x+5

Ps = 15 + 9x (x is the quantity)

(a) 400 (b) 350 (c) 450 (d) 500

Answer = (c)

Solution:

Pd = Ps

$3x^2 - 20x + 5 = 15 + 9x$

$3x^2 - 20x + 9x + 5 - 15 = 0$

$3x^2 - 29x - 10 = 0$

$\because ax^2 + bx + C = 0$

$$x = \frac{-b \pm \sqrt{b^2 - 4ac}}{2a}$$

$$= \frac{(-29) \pm \sqrt{29^2 - 4 \times 3 \times (-10)}}{2 \times 3}$$

$$= \frac{-29 \pm \sqrt{841 + 120}}{6}$$

$$= \frac{29+31}{6}, \frac{29-31}{6}$$

$$= \frac{60}{6}, \frac{2}{6}$$

$x = 10$

P = 15 + 9 (10)

=15 + 90

= 105

$$Ps = Px - \int_0^x f(x)\,dx$$

$$= 105 \times 10 - \int_0^x 15 + 9(x)dx$$

$$= 1050 - 15x - \frac{9x^2}{2}$$

$$= 1050 - 150 - \frac{900}{2}$$

= 1050 - 150 - 450

=1050 - 600

=450

446. The demand function for good A is given by QA = 100 - 2PA + 0.2Y + 0.3 PB. Find the income elasticities of demand PA = 6,Y=500,PB=10 *(December 2022 - shift 2)*

(a) 0.06 (b) 0.02 (c) 0.52 (d) -0.06

Answer = (c)

Solution:

Income Elasticity of Demand:- It is the responsiveness of change in quantity demanded due to change in income levels.

$$\text{Income elasticity} = \frac{\Delta Q}{Q} \times \frac{Y}{\Delta Y}$$

$$E_I = \frac{\Delta Q}{Q} \times \frac{Y}{\Delta Y}$$

$$\frac{\Delta Q}{\Delta Y} = 0.2$$

Put value of Y, PA,& PB

QA = 100 - 2PA + 0.2Y+0.3 PB

= 100 - 2(6) + 0.2(500) + 0.3 (10)

= 100 - 12 + 100 + 03

= 191

$$Ec = 0.2 \times \frac{500}{191}$$

$$= \frac{100}{191}$$

$$\boxed{= 0.52}$$

447. Find the substitution parameter p(rho) of constant elasticity of substitution (CES) production function when the elasticity of substitution () is greater than one

(December 2022 - shift 2)

(a) p = 0 (b) p = 1 (c) -1 < p < ∞ (d) 0 < p < ∞

Answer = (c)

Solution:

E_s= 1/1+(p)

Let us take Es = 2(greater than 1)

2=1/1+(p)

2(1+p)=1

= 1+p = ½

P = ½ - 1

P = -½

So, -1 < p < ∞

448. In logit model, as the odds ratio decreases from 1 to 0, the logit becomes

(December 2022 - shift 2)

(a) Negative (b) Equal to 0 (c) Positive (d) Fraction

Answer = (a)

Solution:

Two types :

1) Binary Logit Model
2) Binary Probit Model

Logit, Probit and Tobit models

These are dummy dependent variable models.

Logit follows logistic distribution

$$L_i = \ln\left(\frac{P_i}{1 - P_i}\right)$$

Pi is probability of happening an event i.e. adoption of technology.

(1-pi) is probability of not happening an event.

P goes from 0 to 1, L from -∞ to ∞

Probit : follows lognormal distribution. It is also called normit model. Dependent variable can take only two values i.e. married or not married. Its purpose is to estimate probability.

Tobit model : is extension of probit model. It is used when a sample in which information on the regressand is available only for some observations. Such

The logit model is a statistical model that is used to predict the probability of an event occurring. The odds ratio is a measure of the relative likelihood of an event occurring. The logit is the logarithm of the odds ratio.

As the odds ratio decreases from 1 to 0, the logit becomes negative. This is because the logarithm of 0 is negative infinity.

The logit model is a powerful tool for predicting the probability of an event occurring. It is often used in economics, marketing, and political science.

449. Given regression model as $Yi = \alpha_1 + \beta_1 Xi + \beta_2 (X_i - X^*) D_i + U_i$ such a model is used to:

(December 2022 - shift 2)

(a) Deseasonalise a quarterly time series data

(b) Seasonally adjust a monthly time series data

(c) To conduct chow test for structural break in time series data

(d) Test piecewise linear relationship in the data

Answer = (d)

450. A player tosses two fair coins. He wins Rs. 5 if 2 heads occur, Rs 2 if 1 head occurs and Rs. | if no head occurs. Find his expected gain. *(December 2022 - shift 2)*

(a) Rs. 2

(b) Rs. 2.25

(c) Rs. 2.75

(d) Rs. 2.50

Answer = (d)

Solution:

Saple space = (HH) (HT) (TH) (TT)

X	P	Px
5	1/4	5/4
2	2/4	1
1	1/4	1/4

$$\frac{1}{4}+\frac{2}{4}+\frac{1}{4}=1$$

$$\frac{5}{4}+1+\frac{1}{4}=\frac{5+4+1}{4}=\frac{10}{4}$$

$$\Sigma(x)=\frac{\Sigma Px}{\Sigma P}$$

$$=\frac{10/4}{1}$$

$$\boxed{=2.50}$$

451. A card is thrown from a well shuffled pack of playing cards. Find the probability that it is either a diamond or a king. *(December 2022 - shift 2)*

(a) 17/52
(b) 16/52
(c) 18/52
(d) 15/52

Answer = (b)

Solution

Types of Cards in a Deck

Suits (Clubs, Hearts, Spades, Diamonds)

The simplest way to break down the types of cards in a deck is by suit.

There are four suits in a standard deck of cards:

- Clubs
- Hearts
- Spades
- Diamonds
  - Because there are four suits in a deck, there are four of each individual card value in a deck.
  - For example, there are four Kings, four Jacks, four Queens, etc. in every standard deck of cards… One of each suit.
  - Accounting for all 52 cards and four suits, there are 13 cards of each suit in a deck

There are 26 red cards and 26 black cards in a deck — Hearts and Diamonds are red, Clubs and Spades are black.

A card is thrown from a well shuffled pack of playing cards. Find the probability that it is either a diamond or a king.

1. 17/52
2. 16/52
3. 18/52
4. 15/52

» P(A)=13/52 (A denotes diamond and B king)

» P(B)=4/52

» P(A∩B)=1/52

» P(AUB)=P(A)+P(B)-P(A∩B) = 13/52 + 4/52 - 1/52= 16/52

452. In simultaneous equation models, OLS can be applied directly if

(December 2022 - shift 2)

(a) It is a recursive model
(b) Order condition is satisfied
(c) Rank condition is satisfied
(d) Both order and rank conditions are satisfied

Answer = (a)

Solution:

Recursive Model

✧ First equation includes only predetermined variables (Independent) at the right.

✧ Second equation includes predetermined and endogenous variables at the right.

y1 = f (x1,x2.............xk,u1)

y2 = f (x1,x2.............xk, y1, u2)

y3 = f (x1,x2.............xk, y1, y2, u3)

✧ System is recursive and triangular.

✧ OLS can be applied directly on each equation.

✧ Independent variables are correlated with error term.

✧ OLS are unbiased and consistent.

✧ Endogenous variable in one equation may appear as explanatory variable in another.

453. The Rural Landless Employment guarantee Programme (RLEGP) was launched on :

(December 2022 - shift 2)

(a) 15th August 1947
(b) 15th August 1950
(c) 15th August 1983
(d) 15th August 2000

Answer = (c) **Solution:**

The Rural Landless Employment Guarantee Programme (RLEGP) was introduced in India on August 15, 1983, with the goal of offering employment opportunities to rural households without land. The program aimed to address unemployment and poverty in rural areas by focusing on labor-intensive projects and wage payments. It later merged with the Jawahar Rozgar Yojana in 1989, contributing to the evolution of subsequent rural employment guarantee initiatives like the Mahatma Gandhi National Rural Employment Guarantee Act (MGNREGA).

454. The Foreign Trade Policy (2015-2020) was announced on which date ?

(December 2022 - shift 2)

(a) 1 August 2015 | (b) 1 April 2015

(c) 30 August 2015 | (d) 30 April 2015

Answer = (b)

Solution: The Foreign Trade Policy (2015-2020) was announced by the Government of India on April 1, 2015. This policy aimed to promote exports and boost the country's trade performance by implementing various measures and incentives to support Indian businesses in the global market.

455. Who was the chairman of 14th Finance Commission in India ?

(December 2022 - shift 2)

(a) Dr. Vijay Kelkar | (b) Dr Y.V. Reddy

(c) Dr. C. Rangarajan | (d) Dr. N.K. Singh

Answer = (b)

Solution:

The 14th Finance Commission of India was chaired by Mr. Y. V. Reddy. He served as the Chairman of the 14th Finance Commission, which was constituted to make recommendations regarding the distribution of financial resources between the central government and the states for the five-year period from 2015 to 2020.

The 15th Finance Commission of India was chaired by Shri N. K. Singh. He served as the Chairman of the 15th Finance Commission, which was constituted to make recommendations regarding the distribution of financial resources between the central government and the states for the five-year period from 2021 to 2026.

456. Zamindari Tenure was introduced by : *(December 2022 - shift 2)*

(a) Thomas Munro | (b) Lord Cornwallis

(c) H. Venkatasubbiah | (d) G. Myrdal

Answer = (b)

Solution:

Zamindari tenure was introduced by Lord Cornwallis during his tenure as Governor-General of India. This tenure system, also known as the Permanent Settlement of Bengal, was implemented in 1793 and aimed to stabilize revenue collection by fixing the land revenue to be paid by the zamindars (landlords) to the British East India Company. This system led to significant changes in land ownership and had a lasting impact on agrarian relations in India.

457. Which of the following is true in case of the non-marketed environmental resources?

(December 2022 - shift 2)

(a) Non excludable and non-rival in consumption

(b) Excludable but not rival in consumption

(c) Excludable and rival in consumption

(d) Non-excludable but rival in consumption

Answer = (d)

Solution:

Non-marketed environmental resources are those that are not traded in the market. They are often characterized by being non-excludable and rival in consumption.

- Non-excludable means that it is difficult or impossible to prevent people from consuming the resource. For example, it is difficult to prevent people from breathing the air or drinking the water.
- Rival in consumption means that one person's consumption of the resource reduces the amount of the resource that is available for others to consume. For example, if one person pollutes the air, it makes it harder for others to breathe clean air.

458. Suppose 'X' places Rs. 8 value on one bread packet and 'Y" places Rs. 6 value on it. If there is no tax on bread, then price of bread packet is Rs. 5. so both X and Y choose to buy one packet each. Now suppose government levies a tax of Rs.. 2 per unit, the price of bread rises to Rs. 7. Then the deadweight loss and tax revenue collected respectively are:

(December 2022 - shift 2)

(a) Rs. 1 and Rs. 2 (b) Rs. 2 and Rs. 4

(c) Rs. 2 and Rs. 2 (d) Rs. 1 and Rs. 4

Answer = (a)

459. The component which distinguishes primary deficit from fiscal deficit is :

(December 2022 - shift 2)

(a) Non-debt component of capital receipt (b) Interest payment

(c) Debt component of capital receipt (d) Revenue deficit

Answer = (b)

Solution:

The primary deficit is the difference between the government's total revenue and its total expenditure, excluding interest payments. The fiscal deficit is the difference between the government's total revenue and its total expenditure, including interest payments.

460. Which of the following is not an assumption or conclusion of the inflation targeting approach ? *(December 2022 - shift 2)*

(a) Interest rate is the major instrument of monetary policy

(b) Higher interest rate controls aggregate demand

(c) Inflation is a supply side phenomenon

(d) Quantity of money supply is not very effective in controlling inflation

Answer = (c)

Solution:

Inflation targeting is a monetary policy framework in which the central bank sets a target for inflation and then uses monetary policy tools to achieve that target. The three main assumptions of inflation targeting are:

1. Interest rate is the major instrument of monetary policy.
2. Higher interest rate controls aggregate demand.
3. Quantity of money supply is not very effective in controlling inflation.

Inflation targeting does not assume that inflation is a supply side phenomenon. In fact, inflation targeting recognizes that inflation can be caused by both demand and supply factors. However, inflation targeting focuses on controlling aggregate demand because it is the most effective way to control inflation in the long run.

The other three assumptions of inflation targeting are more consistent with the framework. Interest rate is the major instrument of monetary policy because it is the most direct way to control aggregate demand. Higher interest rates make it more expensive for businesses to borrow money, which reduces investment and spending. This, in turn, reduces aggregate demand and puts downward pressure on prices.

The quantity of money supply is not very effective in controlling inflation in the long run because it can be easily offset by changes in velocity. Velocity is the rate at which money changes hands. If velocity increases, then a given amount of money can support a higher level of prices. This is why inflation targeting focuses on controlling aggregate demand rather than the quantity of money supply.

461. In context of monetary policy the sacrifice ratio refers to the *(December 2022 - shift 2)*

(a) Interest cost arising because of crowding out effect

(b) Loss of real value of money at the face of increasing inflation

(c) Output cost of reducing inflation

(d) Labour cost raising minimum wage

Answer = (c)

Solution:

In the context of monetary policy, the sacrifice ratio refers to the amount of output that is lost in order to reduce inflation by a certain amount. The sacrifice ratio is calculated as the percentage decrease in GDP that is necessary to reduce inflation by 1 percentage point.

The sacrifice ratio is an important concept in monetary policy because it shows the trade-off between inflation and output. In order to reduce inflation, the central bank must raise interest rates. This can lead to a decrease in investment and spending, which can cause a recession.

462. Which of the following formula is used to calculate the yield of treasury bills (T-bills) where *(December 2022 - shift 2)*

Y = Discounted yield

P= Price

D = Days to maturity

(a) Y = P x 365 x 100 / P x D

(b) Y = D x 365 x 100 / P x D

(c) Y = (100 – P) x 365 x 100 / P x D

(d) Y = (100 – D) x 365 x 100 / P x D

Answer = (c)

463. The faster growth and more equal distribution of income can be examined simultaneously by *(December 2022 - shift 2)*

(a) Gini ratio

(b) Poverty-weighted growth rate

(c) Kuznet curve

(d) None of the above

Answer = (b)

Solution: The poverty-weighted growth rate is a measure of economic growth that takes into account the distribution of income. It is calculated by multiplying the growth rate by the inverse of the Gini coefficient. The Gini coefficient is a measure of income inequality, with a value of 0 indicating perfect equality and a value of 1 indicating perfect inequality.

A poverty-weighted growth rate of 0 indicates that there is no growth, while a poverty-weighted growth rate of 1 indicates that all of the growth is going to the poorest people in society. A poverty-weighted growth rate of 0.5 indicates that half of the growth is going to the poorest people in society and half of the growth is going to the richest people in society.

The Kuznet curve is a hypothesis that argues that there is an inverse relationship between economic growth and income inequality. The hypothesis argues that in the early stages of economic development, income inequality will increase as the economy grows. However, as the economy develops further, income inequality will start to decrease.

The Kuznet curve is not a universally accepted hypothesis. Some economists argue that the Kuznet curve is not supported by the data. Other economists argue that the Kuznet curve is valid, but that it only applies to certain countries or regions.

Overall, the poverty-weighted growth rate is a better tool for examining the relationship between faster growth and more equal distribution of income than the Kuznet curve.

464. Marx refers to the concept of organic composition of capital. Which one of the following ratios is used for this (where C is constant capital, V is variable capital and S is surplus value)? *(December 2022 - shift 2)*

(a) C / V + S

(b) C / V

(c) C / (C + V)

(d) (C + V) / V

Answer = (b)

Solution:

The organic composition of capital is a concept in Marxian economics that measures the ratio of constant capital to variable capital. Constant capital is the value of the machinery, equipment, and other inputs that are used in production but do not change in value over the course of production. Variable capital is the value of the labor power that is used in production and which changes in value over the course of production.

- C is constant capital
- V is variable capital

A high organic composition of capital means that a large proportion of the value of production is accounted for by constant capital. This can happen if there is a lot of machinery and equipment used in production, or if the workers are highly skilled and therefore earn a high wage.

A high organic composition of capital can lead to a fall in the rate of profit. This is because the value of the output is divided between a large amount of constant capital and a small amount of variable capital. This means that the profit per unit of output will be low.

Marx argued that the organic composition of capital would tend to rise over time as technological progress led to the use of more machinery and equipment in production. This would lead to a fall in the rate of profit and a crisis in capitalism.

465. 'Which of the following is not true in the case of externality?

(December 2022 - shift 2)

(a) It is related to human interactions

(b) It 1s tied to consumer sovereignty

(c) It is based on higher order judgements of right and wrong

(d) It is an amoral concept

Answer = (c)

Solution:

An externality is a cost or benefit that is not reflected in the market price of a good or service. It is related to human interactions because it is caused by the actions of one person or group of people that affects the well-being of another person or group of people.

Externalities can be either positive or negative. Positive externalities are benefits that are not reflected in the market price of a good or service. For example, the benefits of education are not fully reflected in the market price of education. This is because the benefits of education go beyond the individual who receives the education. Education can benefit society as a whole by reducing crime, increasing productivity, and improving public health.

Negative externalities are costs that are not reflected in the market price of a good or service. For example, the pollution caused by a factory is a negative externality. The factory owners do not have to pay for the pollution they cause, which means that the cost of the pollution is borne by the people who live near the factory and by society as a whole.

Externalities are not based on higher order judgements of right and wrong. They are simply the unintended consequences of human interactions. The fact that an externality exists does not mean that it is good or bad. It simply means that the market price of a good or service does not reflect all of the costs and benefits of production and consumption.

466. Compensating variation for a price decrease of a good can be interpreted as :

(December 2022 - shift 2)

(a) Willingness to pay

(b) Willingness to accept

(c) Both 1 and 2

(d) None

Answer = (a)

Solution:

Compensating variation refers to the amount of money a consumer would need to be given (compensated) to maintain the same level of utility or satisfaction after a price decrease for a good. It measures the consumer's willingness to pay to avoid the price decrease and still achieve the same level of satisfaction.

In other words, when the price of a good decreases, the compensating variation indicates how much money the consumer would need to receive in compensation to be indifferent between the new price and the original price. It reflects the consumer's willingness to pay to avoid the price reduction.

467. Equivalent variation for a price increase of a good can be interpreted as:

(December 2022 - shift 2)

(a) Willingness to pay
(b) Willingness to accept
(c) Both 1 and 2
(d) None

Answer = (a)

Solution: Price increase reduces the real income of consumer. So, he has the willingness to pay.

468. According to the specific factors model, which of the following is correct?

(December 2022 - shift 2)

(a) Trade benefits the factor specific to the export sector of each country but hurts the factor specific to the import competing sectors with ambiguous effects on mobile factors
(b) Trade hurts the factor specific to the export sector of each country and also hurts the factor specific to the import competing sectors, with ambiguous effects on mobile factors
(c) Trade benefits the factor specific to the import sector of each country but hurts the factor specific to the export competing sectors, with ambiguous effects on mobile factors
(d) Trade benefits the factor specific to the export sector as well as import-competing sector of each country, with ambiguous effects on mobile factors.

Answer = (a)

Solution: In specific factor model, trade will have an ambigious/uncertain(gain or loss) effect on the nation's mobile factors, benefits the immobile factors specific to the nation's export commodities and harm the immobile factor specific to the nation's import competing commodities.

The model's name refers to its distinguishing feature—that one factor of production is assumed to be "specific" to a particular industry. A specific factor is one that is stuck in an industry or is immobile between industries in response to changes in market conditions. A factor may be immobile between industries for a number of reasons. Some factors may be specifically designed (in the case of capital) or specifically trained (in the case of labor) for use in a particular production process. In these cases, it may be impossible, or at least difficult or costly, to move these factors across industries.

469. 'What does 'immiserising growth' argued? *(December 2022 - shift 2)*

(a) Export-biased growth by poor nations would worsen their terms of trade so much that they would be worse off than if they had not grown at all

(b) Export-biased growth by rich nations would worsen their terms of trade so much that they would be worse off than if they had not grown at all

(c) Import-biased growth by poor nations would worsen their terms of trade so much that they would be worse off than if they had not grown at all

(d) Import-biased growth by Rich nations would worsen their terms of trade so much that they would be worsen off than if had not grown at all.

Answer = (a)

Solution: "Immiserizing growth" is an economic concept that suggests that a country's growth strategy, particularly one that heavily relies on exporting specific goods, could lead to a situation where the country becomes worse off despite economic growth. This can occur if the growth leads to such a significant decrease in the country's terms of trade that the negative effects on welfare outweigh the benefits of increased output and income.

In the context of the options provided:

- **Option 1:** This is the correct interpretation of "immiserizing growth." It argues that export-biased growth by poor nations could lead to a substantial deterioration in their terms of trade, resulting in a situation where they are worse off than if they had not pursued such growth.
- **Option 2:** This does not accurately represent the concept of "immiserizing growth." It focuses on rich nations, whereas the concept primarily relates to poor nations.
- **Option 3:** This is not the standard interpretation of "immiserizing growth." The concept is more related to export-biased growth, not import-biased growth.
- **Option 4:** Similar to Option 2, this option focuses on rich nations rather than the core concept of "immiserizing growth."

470. 'Which of the following postulates the Gravity Model correctly ?

(December 2022 - shift 2)

(a) The smaller and the closer the two countries are, the smaller the volume of trade between them is expected to be

(b) The larger and the closer the two countries are, the larger the volume of trade between them is expected to be

(c) The larger and the closer the two countries are, the smaller the volume of trade between them is expected to be

(d) The smaller and farther the two countries are, the larger the volume of trade between them is expected to be.

Answer = (b)

Solution: The Gravity Model is a widely used economic theory that predicts the volume of trade between two countries based on their economic sizes (usually measured by GDP) and their geographical distance from each other. According to the Gravity Model:

- Larger economies have more goods and services to trade, leading to higher trade volumes.
- Closer geographical distance reduces transportation costs and trade barriers, leading to higher trade volumes.
- The gravity model of international trade in international economics is a model that, in its traditional form, predicts bilateral trade flows based on the economic sizes and distance between two units. Research shows that there is "overwhelming evidence that trade tends to fall with distance."

471. If the nominal tariff rate (t) on consumers of the final commodity is 10 per cent, the ratio of the cost of the imported input to the price of the final commodity in the absence of tariffs (ai) is = 0.8, and the nominal tariff rate on the imported input (ti) = 0, then find the rate of effective protection. *(December 2022 - shift 2)*

(a) 5% (b) 8% (c) 50% (d) 10%

Answer = (c)

Solution:

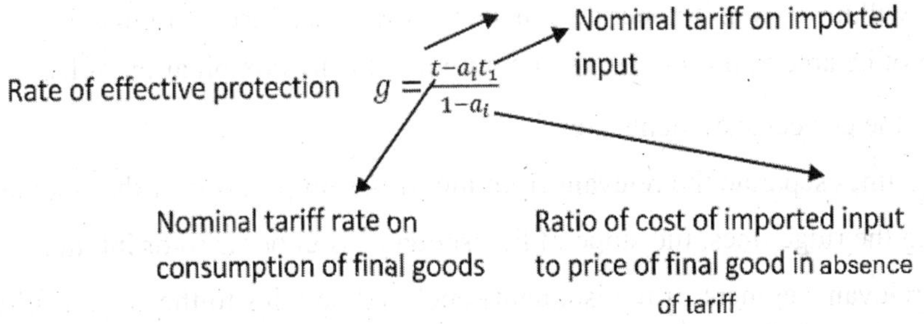

Optimum tariff – $t^* = \frac{1}{e-1}$ e = point of elasticity of offer curve of other country.

472. Which of the followings are true for ridge lines? *(December 2022 - shift 2)*

A. they separate the relevant from the irrelevant portions of the isoquants

B. along the ridge lines, the slope of the isoquants is either zero or infinite

C. The relevant segment of the isoquants enclosed pertains to the stage II of production for labour and capital

D. Producers will never want to operate outside the region enclosed within the ridge lines.

E. The marginal product of both inputs-labour and capital is positive but declines for the portion of the isoquants within the ridge lines.

Choose the correct answer from the options given below:

(a) A, C and D only
(b) B, C and E only
(c) A, C, D and E only
(d) A, B, C, D and E only

Answer = (d)

Solution: Ridge lines are the portions of the isoquants where the marginal rate of technical substitution (MRTS) is zero. The MRTS is the ratio of the marginal product of labor to the marginal product of capital. It measures how much labor a firm is willing to give up in order to get one more unit of capital.

Along the ridge lines, the MRTS is zero, which means that the firm is indifferent to the mix of labor and capital it uses. The firm can produce the same output with any combination of labor and capital along the ridge lines.

The relevant segment of the isoquants enclosed pertains to the stage II of production for labor and capital. This is because in stage II, the marginal product of both inputs is positive but declining. The firm will want to operate in the stage II of production because it is the most efficient stage of production.

Producers will never want to operate outside the region enclosed within the ridge lines because they will not be able to produce the same output with any combination of labor and capital.

Therefore, the correct statements are:

- ✧ Ridge lines separate the relevant from the irrelevant portions of the isoquants.
- ✧ Along the ridge lines, the slope of the isoquants is either zero or infinite.
- ✧ The relevant segment of the isoquants enclosed pertains to the stage II of production for labor and capital.
- ✧ Producers will never want to operate outside the region enclosed within the ridge lines.
- ✧ The marginal product of both inputs-labor and capital is positive but declines for the portion of the isoquants within the ridge lines.

Ridge Lines : - Are the locus of points where Marginal productivity of at least one factor is zero.

The optimum stage of production is the region between the two ridge lines and hence is called the region of economic production.

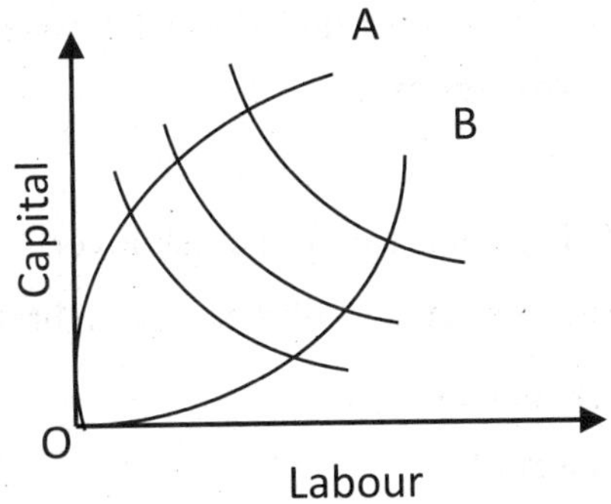

473. 'Which of the followings are true about a fair game or fair bet ?

(December 2022 - shift 2)

A. The entry of a fair bet is zero

B. The person who accepts fair bet is said to be risk lover

C. expected value of income from the bet is equal to the same amount of income with certainty

D. The person who refuses a fair bet is said to be risk neutral

E. The person who refuses a fair bet is said to be risk averse.

Choose the correct answer from the options given below:

(a) A and C only
(b) B and E only
(c) C and D only
(d) C and E only

Answer = (d)

Solution:

A fair game or fair bet is a game or bet in which the expected value of the outcome is zero. This means that the player is neither likely to gain nor lose money in the long run.

The entry of a fair bet is zero. This means that the player does not have to pay anything to enter the game or bet.

The expected value of income from the bet is equal to the same amount of income with certainty.

This means that the player is indifferent to whether they play the game or bet or not.

The person who refuses a fair bet is said to be risk averse. This means that the player would rather have a certain amount of money than a risky bet, even if the expected value of the bet is positive.

Therefore, the correct statements are:

- The expected value of income from the bet is equal to the same amount of income with certainty.

✧ The person who refuses a fair bet is said to be risk averse.

The statements that are not correct are:

✧ The entry of a fair bet is zero.

✧ The person who accepts fair bet is said to be risk lover.

✧ The person who refuses a fair bet is said to be risk neutral.

474. According to the modern theory of rent *(December 2022 - shift 2)*

A. All the factors may earn rent

B. Rent can only be earned in long-run

C. Transfer earning of an unused factor is zero

D. Only land can earn rent

E. Entire earning of an unused factor is economic rent.

Choose the correct answer from the options given below:

(a) A, B and C only (b) A, C and E only

(c) B, C and E only (d) A, C and D only

Answer = (b)

Solution:

The modern theory of rent states that all factors of production can earn rent, not just land. Rent is the payment to a factor of production in excess of its transfer earnings. Transfer earnings are the earnings that a factor of production could earn in its best alternative use.

The correct statements are:

✧ All the factors may earn rent.

✧ Transfer earning of an unused factor is zero.

✧ Entire earning of an unused factor is economic rent.

The traditional theory of rent states that only land can earn rent. This is because land is a fixed factor of production. The supply of land cannot change in response to changes in prices.

However, the modern theory of rent argues that all factors of production can earn rent, including land. This is because the supply of factors of production can change in response to changes in prices. For example, if the price of land increases, then farmers may be willing to invest in irrigation or other land improvements in order to increase the productivity of their land. This will increase the supply of land and lower the price of land.

475. Rational expectations views include ; *(December 2022 - shift 2)*

A. The market clearing rational expectations do not approach to the Phillips curve

B. Rational expectation as a theory of expectations

C. An emphasis on the credibility of policy makers

D. A preference for policy making rules rather than discretion

E. Generally insists that markets do not clear rapidly.

Choose the most appropriate answer from the options given below:

(a) B, C and D only (b) A and E only

(c) A, B, C,D and E (d) A, D and E only

Answer = (a)

Solution:

Rational Expectations:- The theory was given by John Muth in 1961. It is a forward looking approach and people are considered to be rational. Any errors in forecasting is random in nature.

476. In the budget at glance, which of the following items are included ?

(December 2022 - shift 2)

A. budget estimate of the current year

B. Revised estimate of the current year

C. Actuals of the current year

D. Actuals for the preceding year

E. Budget estimate for the forthcoming year.

Choose the most appropriate answer from the options given below:

(a) A and D only (b) A, B, D and E only

(c) A, B and C only (d) C and D only

Answer = (b)

477. How do adverse technology shocks affect labour demand and supply?

(December 2022 - shift 2)

A. Decrease the demand for labour

B. Both real wage and employment fall

C. Real wage increases and employment falls

D. Real wage falls and employment increases

E. Adverse effect on market equilibrium.

Choose the correct answer from the options given below:

(a) A, C and D only (b) B, D and E only

(c) A, B, C and D only (d) A, B and E only

Answer = (d)

Solution:

Adverse technology shocks can affect labour demand and supply in the following ways:

- Decrease the demand for labour: Adverse technology shocks can lead to a decrease in the demand for labour. This is because the new technology may make some workers obsolete. For example, the introduction of computers led to a decrease in the demand for typists.
- Both real wage and employment fall: Adverse technology shocks can lead to both a decrease in real wage and employment. This is because the decrease in demand for labour will lead to a decrease in the price of labour, which is the real wage. The decrease in demand for labour will also lead to a decrease in the number of jobs, which is employment.
- Adverse effect on market equilibrium: Adverse technology shocks can have an adverse effect on market equilibrium. This is because the decrease in demand for labour will lead to a surplus of labour. The surplus of labour will put downward pressure on the price of labour, which will further decrease the demand for labour. This can lead to a spiral of falling wages and employment.

Therefore, the correct statements are:

- Decrease the demand for labour.
- Both real wage and employment fall.
- Adverse effect on market equilibrium.

478. 'Which of the followings are correct in case of Poisson distribution ?

(December 2022 - shift 2)

A. 'n' the number of trials is indefinitely large i.e. n – ∞

B. 'p', the constant probability of success for each trial is indefinitely large

C. np = m is finite

D. $\mu 3 = m + 2$

E. $\mu 4 = m + 3m^2$

Choose the correct answer from the options given below:

(a) A, C and D only
(b) A, C and E only
(c) B, C and E only
(d) B, C and D only

Answer = (b) **Solution:**

Poisson Distributions : it was given by Denies Poisson in 1937. It is used when the no. of trails is infinite but probability of success is very small. It is used in case of finding no. of defects, no. of accidents etc. It is discrete prob. Distribution.

$$\frac{e^{-m} m^r}{r!}$$

m= mean of prob. Distribution.

M (mean) = np
SD = √np
Variance = np

Mean = Variance

479. Which of the followings are correct conclusions without error in case of testing of Hypothesis? *(December 2022 - shift 2)*

A. Reject null hypothesis (Ho), when it is true

B. Accept Ho, when it is true

C. Accept Ho, when Alternate hypothesis (H1) is true.

C. Reject Ho when H1 is true.

E. Accept Ho when H1 is false.

Choose the correct answer from the options given below:

(a) A, B and D only

(b) B, D and E only

(c) B, C and E only

(d) A, C and E only

Answer = (b)

Solution:

Types of Errors

Type I – Hypothesis is true, but our test reject it.

Type II – Hypothesis is false, but our test accept it.

Possible Hypothesis Test Outcomes		
	Actual Situation	
Decision	H0 True	H0 False
Accept H0	No error	Type II error
	Probability = 1 - α	Probability = β
Reject H0	Type I error	No error
	Probability = α	Probability = 1 - β

480. 'Which of the followings are correct for OLS estimation in the presence of Heteroscedasticity ? *(December 2022 - shift 2)*

A. The estimated coefficients are linear

B. The estimated coefficients are unbiased

C. The estimated coefficients are biased

D. The estimated coefficients are consistent

E. The estimated coefficients are efficient.

Choose the correct answer from the options given below:

(a) A, C and D only
(b) A, B and D only
(c) A, C and E only
(d) A, C and D only

Answer = (b)

Solution :

Heteroscadasticity

A regression model in which disturbance variance change from observation to observation is known as Heteroscadasticity.

Regression Model

i.e. Var (ui) = σ^2 u (Homoscedasticity)

Var (ui) = σ^2 ui (Heteroscadisticity)

Consequences : OLS estimates have large variance but remain unbiased and linear.

Tests : Spearman Rank Correlation Test

Gold Fed Quandt Test

Glejer Test

Park Test

481. Which of the followings satisfy the assumptions of the classical linear regression model ? *(December 2022 - shift 2)*

A. Zero mean value of disturbance Ui

B. The explanatory variables and the error terms are not independent

C. Homoscedasticity or constant variance of Ui

D. No auto correlation between the disturbances

E. There is more than one exact linear relationship between explanatory variables.

Choose the most appropriate answer from the options given below:

(a) A, B, C and D only
(b) A, C, D and E only
(c) A, C and D only
(d) C, D and E only

Answer = (c)

Solution :

Assumptions

1. $E(u_i) = 0$ (Mean is Zero)
2. $E(u_i^2) = \sigma^2$ u (variance is constant)
3. Error terms are random.

4. X's are non - random i.e. 1,2,3,.........
5. ui has normal distribution.
6. Errors are non - auto correlated. E(uiuj) = 0
7. u is independent of the explanatory variables.
8. X's are assumed to be fixed.
9. X's are uncorrelated.

482. If A. B and C are three different non-empty sets, then find which of the following are correct in laws of set operations ? *(December 2022 - shift 2)*

A. $(A')' = A$
B. $(A \cup B) = 1 - (A \cap B)$
C. $A \cup (B \cup C) = (A \cup B) \cup C$
D. $A \cup (B \cap C) = (A \cap B) \cup (A \cap C)$
E. $A - B = A \cap B'$

Choose the correct answer from the options given below:

(a) A, C and D only
(b) A, C and E only
(c) A, B and C only
(d) C, D and E only

Answer = (b)

Solution : A' is complement of set. we can take any random set and can prove whether RHS Equals LHS

Commutative laws for union and Intersection of two sets.

$$A \cup B = B \cup A$$

$$A \cap B = B \cap A$$

Associative laws for union and intersection for two sets.

$$A \cup (B \cup C) = (A \cup B) \cup C$$

$$A \cap (B \cap C) = (A \cap B) \cap C$$

Distributive law

$$A \cap (B \cup C) = (A \cap B) \cup (A \cap C)$$

$$A \cup (B \cap C) = (A \cup B) \cap (A \cup C)$$

Complement of a set:-

Let U be the universal set and A be its sub – set, the set of all those elements of U which do not

Belong to A, is called complements of A and is written as A^C

i.e. U = { x : x is a natural number < 12 }

A = {1, 2, 5, 6, 10, 11}

A^C = {3, 4, 7, 8, 9}

De Morgan's Law

$(A \cup B)^C = A^C \cap B^C$

$(A \cap B)^C = A^C \cup B^C$

Cartesian product of two sets

If A = {1, 2, 3}, B = {2, 4} find A x B

A x B = { (1,2) , (1,4), (2,2), (2,4), (3,2) (3,4) }

Difference of sets

If A = {5, 6, 9, 10, x, y} B = {9, x, 15, 12}

A – B = {5, 6, 10, y}

Symmetric difference of two sets

If A = {1, 2, 3, 4, 5, 6}

B = {3, 5, 7, 9, 11}(A – B) ∪ (B – A)= {1, 2, 4, 6, 7, 9, 11}

Unit set or singleton set → It contains only one element: -

A = {0} is aunit set.

Universal set → it is the total of elements under consideration.

i.e. U = {1, 2, 3, 4, 5, 6} is a universal set obtained by throwing a dice.

Idempotent Property:

A ∪ A = A b) A ∩ A = A

Identity Property

A ∪ Φ = A A ∩ U = A

483. In multiple regression model, a hypothesis such as $H_0 : \beta_2 = \beta_3 = 0$ can be tested using

(December 2022 - shift 2)

(a) t-test
(b) Chi-square test
(c) ANOVA test
(d) F-test

Answer = (d)

Solution :

Variance Ratio Test :

1. F -Test : Given by Fisher.
2. F -Test is used to the test two independent estimation of population variance.
3. Small sample test (Two sample $S_1{}^2$ and $S_2{}^2$ have same variance).
4. Variance Ratio $= \frac{S_1{}^2}{S_2{}^2}$

Degree of freedom for larger population variance is V1 and smaller isV_2.

V_1=n1-1 V_2= n2-1

F-test are design to test if two population variance are equal.

F-test never be -ve as upper value is greater than lower.

Testing of overall significance of regression by F-test.

Test for the significance of the adjusted coefficient of multiple deter mination is F-test. Value of F-test lies between 0 to ∞.

484. Which of the followings are the indicators of Human Development Index?

(December 2022 - shift 2)

A. Real GDP per capita
B. Adult literacy rate combined with enrolment ratio
C. Life expectancy at birth
D. Malnutrition under five
E. IMR under five.

Choose the correct answer from the options given below:

(a) A, B and E only
(b) B, Cand D only
(c) A, B and C only
(d) C, D and E only

Answer = (c)

Solution:

The Human Development Index (HDI) is a composite index that measures and compares the overall development and well-being of countries based on three key dimensions:

A. **Real GDP per capita:** This represents the economic aspect of human development, reflecting the average income and living standards in a country.

B. **Adult literacy rate combined with enrolment ratio:** This reflects the educational attainment of the population, including both literacy and access to education.

C. **Life expectancy at birth:** This measures the health aspect of human development by indicating the average number of years a newborn can expect to live.

D. **Malnutrition under five:** This is not a direct indicator of the Human Development Index. HDI focuses more on broader dimensions like income, education, and health.

E. **IMR under five :** Infant mortality rate (IMR) is related to health and child mortality, but it is not one of the direct indicators used in the calculation of the Human Development Index.

485. Which of the following are correct for the Finance Commission ?

(December 2022 - shift 2)

A. **It is constituted under Article 380 of the Constitution**

B. **It is a statutory body**

C. **It is constituted under Article 280 of the Constitution**

D. **Prof. K C Pant was Chairman of 10th Finance Commission**

E. **Dr. Vijay Kelkar was Chairman of 14th Finance Commission.**

Choose the most appropriate answer from the options given below.

(a) B, C and D only (b) A, B and D only

(c) C, D and E only (d) A, C and E only

Answer = (a)

Solution: The Finance Commission is constituted under Article 280 of the constitution. It is a statutory body. Dr. Y.V. Reddy was the Chairman of 14th Finance Commission.

486. Which of the following are true ? *(December 2022 - shift 2)*

A. **Product taxes will raise prices less under monopoly than under competition**

B. **A tax on capital income tends to be progressive, whereas tax on wage income tends to be regressive**

C. **The burden of tax will be distributed between sellers and buyers in the ratio of elasticity of demand to that of supply.**

D. **A unit tax enters through a parallel downward shift in the supply schedule**

E. **Imposition of tax raises price and quantity.**

Choose the most appropriate answer from the options given below:

(a) A and B only (b) A, B and C only

(c) A, B, C and D only (d) A, B, C and E only

Answer = (b)

487. Which of the following are correct ? *(December 2022 - shift 2)*

A. A competitive market can secure efficient resource use in the provision of private goods, but market failure occurs in that of social goods

B. Efficient provision of social goods involves horizontal rather than vertical addition of Individual pseudo-demand schedules

C. To seek efficient provision of social goods, a political process of budget determination is needed

D. Corrective action may be needed when consumer choice is based on false advertising

E. There are mixed cases between the extremes of purely private and purely social goods.

Choose the most appropriate answer from the options given below:

(a) A, B and C only (b) A, B and E only

(c) A, B, C and D only (d) A, C, D and E only

Answer = (d)

Solution:

1. Competitive markets tend to allocate resources efficiently for private goods, but they can face difficulties in providing public or social goods due to issues like free-rider problem and lack of incentives.
2. The efficient provision of social goods often involves vertical addition of individual demand schedules to determine the overall demand for the good. This is because social goods are non-rivalrous and non-excludable, unlike private goods.
3. Efficient provision of social goods often requires a political or collective decision-making process to allocate resources and determine budgets.
4. False advertising can mislead consumers and lead to inefficient allocation of resources. Corrective actions, such as regulations or consumer protection measures, may be necessary.
5. There are goods that possess characteristics of both private and social goods, leading to mixed cases. For example, quasi-public goods like education and healthcare may have elements of both private and public provisioning.

Private goods are characterized by two key characteristics: excludability and rivalry.

(a) Excludability: A good is considered excludable if it is possible to prevent someone from using or consuming it. In other words, access to the good can be restricted and limited to those who have paid for it. Examples of excludable private goods include clothing, food, electronics, and other consumer products.

(b) Rivalry: A good is considered rivalrous if consumption by one person reduces its availability for others. In other words, one person's use of the good diminishes its availability for others. For instance, if you eat a piece of cake, no one else can eat that same piece of cake. Most physical goods, such as a car or a sandwich, are rivalrous.

Public goods are characterized by two key characteristics : non-excludability and non-rivalry.

(a) Non-excludability: A good is considered non-excludable if it is difficult or impossible to prevent someone from using or benefiting from it, even if they haven't paid for it. This means that individuals cannot be easily excluded from enjoying the benefits of the good. Examples of non-excludable public goods include clean air, street lighting, and national defense.

(b) Non-rivalry: A good is considered non-rivalrous if consumption by one person does not diminish its availability for others. In other words, one person's use of the good does not impact its availability to others. For instance, enjoying a fireworks display or listening to a public radio station doesn't prevent others from doing the same.

488. Which of the following monetary measure is used to control inflation ?

(December 2022 - shift 2)

A. The Central Bank purchases government securities from Commercial Banks

B. The Central Bank sells the government securities to the Commercial Banks

C. The bank rate may be raised

D. The bank rate may be reduced

E. Raising of cash reserve ratio.

Choose the correct answer from the options given below"

(a) A, C and E only (b) B, C and E only

(c) A, D and E only (d) A and D only

Answer = (b)

Solution:

B. The Central Bank sells the government securities to the Commercial Banks: When the central bank sells government securities to commercial banks, it absorbs excess money from the banking system, reducing the money supply and helping to control inflation.

C. The bank rate may be raised: Increasing the bank rate makes borrowing more expensive for commercial banks. This, in turn, reduces lending and spending, helping to control inflation.

E. Raising of cash reserve ratio: When the central bank raises the cash reserve ratio, commercial banks are required to hold a higher percentage of their deposits as reserves. This reduces the amount of money available for lending and spending, which can help control inflation.

489. Which of the followings are correct in case of money market in India?

(December 2022 - shift 2)

A. Commercial bill is a short-term instrument with high risk

B. Treasury bill is an instrument of short-term borrowing by the government with absence of default risk

C. RBI uses refinance to relieve liquidity shortages in the system

D. The RBI has switched over from daily fixed rate repos auction system to discriminatory price auction repos.

E. SLR enables to impose secondary and supplementary reserve requirements on the banking system.

Choose the correct answer from the options given below :

(a) A, B and D only
(b) B, C and D only
(c) B, C and E only
(d) C, D and E only

Answer = (c)

490. The causes and consequences of poverty include: *(December 2022 - shift 2)*

A. Unemployment

B. Low wages

C. Poor health

D. Low Population Growth

E. Low Literacy rates.

Choose the most appropriate answer from the options given below:

(a) A and C only
(b) B, D and E only
(c) B, C, D and E only
(d) A, B, C and E only

Answer = (d)

Solution:

Poverty is a complex issue with many causes and consequences. Some of the common causes of poverty include:

- ✧ **Unemployment** - When people are unemployed, they do not have an income, which makes it difficult to meet their basic needs.
- ✧ **Low wages** - Even if people are employed, they may not earn enough to meet their basic needs. This is especially true in countries with low minimum wages or high levels of inequality.

✧ **Poor health** - People who are poor are more likely to experience poor health. This can be due to a number of factors, including lack of access to healthcare, poor nutrition, and stress.

✧ **Low literacy rates** - People who are illiterate are less likely to be able to find good jobs or participate in society. This can lead to a cycle of poverty that is difficult to break.

✧ **High population growth** - High population growth can put a strain on resources and lead to poverty. This is especially true in countries with low levels of economic development. It is important to note that the causes and consequences of poverty are complex and interrelated. Poverty can be caused by a number of factors, and it can lead to a number of consequences.

491. Measurement of income inequality is done by : *(December 2022 - shift 2)*

A. **Gini coefficient**
B. **Lorenz curve**
C. **Palma Ratio**
D. **Deprivation ratio**
E. **Phillips Curve**

Choose the correct answer from the options given below:

(a) B and E only (b) A and B only
(c) A, B and C only (d) C and A only

Answer = (c)

Solution: The Gini coefficient, Lorenz curve, and Palma ratio are all measures of income inequality. The Gini coefficient is a single number that measures the deviation of the distribution of income from a perfectly equal distribution. The Lorenz curve is a graphical representation of the distribution of income. The Palma ratio is the ratio of the income share of the top 10% of earners to the income share of the bottom 40% of earners.

The deprivation ratio is not a measure of income inequality. It is a measure of the proportion of people who lack basic necessities, such as food, shelter, and healthcare.

The Phillips curve is a relationship between inflation and unemployment. It is not a measure of income inequality.

492. Choose the correct statement for Schumpeter's theory of development. *(December 2022 - shift 2)*

A. **Development is financed by real saving.**
B. **Capitalism keeps its character intact overtime**
C. **Development is evolutionary**
D. **Development creates inflation**

E. Unlimited Supply of labour.

Choose the correct answer from the options given below:

(a) A and B only (b) C and D only

(c) A, B, C and D only (d) None of the above

Answer = (d)

Solution:

Schumpeter theory of development:-

Schumpeter ideas about economic development first appeared in his book "The theory of economic development" in 1911. According to him, Development is a spontaneous and discontinuous change in the flow channels which cause a disturbance in equilibrium and hence to alters and displaces the equilibrium state forever. According to Schumpeter, "development will happen only when circular flow is disturb. The circular flow can only be disturbed through innovation.

Five kinds of innovations :-

a) New product
b) New method of production
c) New source of raw material
d) New industrial organization
e) New market

Qualities of innovator :-

1) He should have a technical know how
2) Must able to manage funds

→Through the process of development, old things are replaced by new things - Primary wave of expansion will be followed by secondary waves.

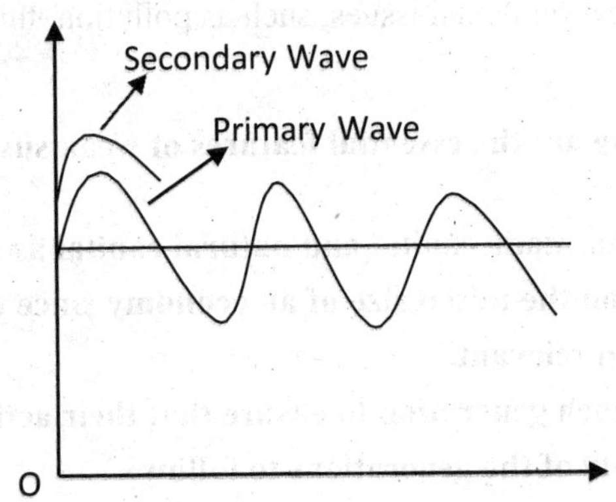

Why downturn of economic starts ;-

when innovation becomes popular, other entrepreneurs follows it. In other words, When the original innovation proves profitable, other competitors follow it in "swarm-like clusters." Innovation in one field induces innovation in other fields. New products replacing old, speculation takes place, old firms vanished. Innovators start repaying loans out of profit.

493. Which of the following are the features of Environmental Economics as a field of study ? *(December 2022 - shift 2)*

A. It has its roots in the theory of externalities and public goods.

B. It is based on neoclassical welfare theory

C. It envisions human economy as a sub-system of the biosphere

D. It engages with the law of transformations of matter and energy

E. It focuses on finding the most efficient ways to reducing environmental damages.

Choose the correct answer from the options given below:

(a) A, B and C only
(b) B, C and D only
(c) A, B and E only
(d) C, D and E only

Answer = (c)

Solution:

A. It has its roots in the theory of externalities and public goods: Environmental economics indeed originated from the study of externalities (environmental impacts not reflected in market prices) and the characteristics of public goods (such as clean air and water).

B. It is based on neoclassical welfare theory: Neoclassical welfare theory is a foundational framework in environmental economics, which seeks to maximize societal welfare while considering environmental factors.

E. It focuses on finding the most efficient ways to reducing environmental damages: One of the key goals of environmental economics is to identify economically efficient ways to address environmental issues, such as pollution, through tools like market-based instruments.

494. Which of the following are the essential features of weak sustainability? *(December 2022 - shift 2)*

A. It considers human-made capital and natural capital as close substitutes.

B. It puts emphasis on the initial size of an economy since the size of the initial capital stock is considered relevant.

C. It requires from each generation to ensure that their actions do not compromise the productive capacity of the generations to follow

D. the composition of the capital stock of an economy does not hold great significance

E. It renders natural capital as an absolute necessity for sustaining net national income over an indefinite period.

Choose the most appropriate answer from the options given below:

(a) A, C and D only
(b) A, B and C only
(c) C, D and E only
(d) A, B and E only

Answer = (a)

Solution:

Weak sustainability is a concept in environmental economics that states that the total capital stock of an economy can be kept constant over time, even if the composition of the capital stock changes. This means that human-made capital and natural capital can be substituted for each other, as long as the total capital stock remains the same.

Weak sustainability is based on the following assumptions:

- ✧ The total capital stock of an economy is relevant, but the composition of the capital stock is not.
- ✧ Each generation must ensure that their actions do not compromise the productive capacity of the generations to follow.
- ✧ Human-made capital and natural capital are close substitutes.

Therefore, the essential features of weak sustainability are A, C, and D. Statement E is incorrect because weak sustainability does not render natural capital as an absolute necessity for sustaining net national income over an indefinite period.

Weak Sustainability	Strong Sustainability
Natural, human and reproducible capital can be substituted for each other.	Cannot always substitute for natural capital with reproducible or human capital.
Natural, human and reproducible capital are an aggregate, homogeneous stock.	Cannot view natural, reproducible and human capital as a homogeneous stock.
Natural capital should be used efficiently over time.	Certain environmental sinks, processes and services are unique and essential, subject to irreversible loss, and there is uncertainty over their future value and importance.
As long as depleted natural capital is replaced with even more valuable reproducible and human capital, then the value of the aggregate stock will increase.	Maintaining and enhancing the value of the value of the aggregate capital stock is necessary but not sufficient.
Maintaining and enhancing the value of this aggregate capital stock is sufficient for sustainability.	Sustainability also requires preserving unique and essential natural capital.

Weak sustainability

- Sustainable development requires that across generations there should be no decline in th possibility of total capital to generate flows of service
- The aim of sustainable development is the increase (at least non-diminution) of total welfare which is comprised of natural, physical and human capital
- Any form of capital can be substituted by the others

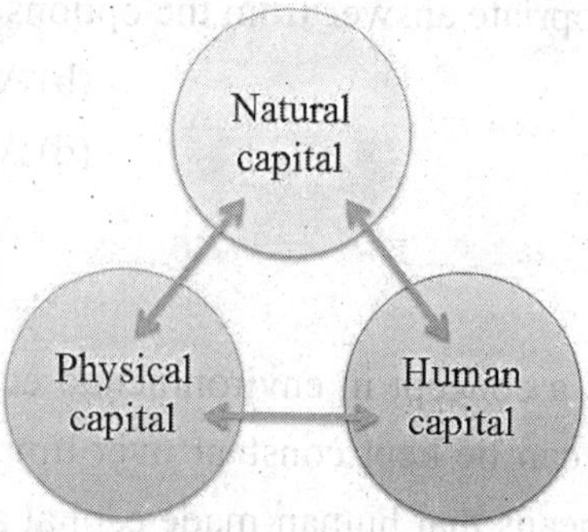

495. Which of the following are part of non-tariff barriers ? *(December 2022 - shift 2)*

A. Import quotas

B. Voluntary export restraint

C. Export subsidy

D. Compound tariff

E. Ad Valorem tariff.

Choose the correct answer from the options given below:

(a) A, B and D only
(b) A, B and E only
(c) A, B and C only
(d) B, C and D only

Answer = (c)

Solution:

Non-tariff barriers (NTBs) are trade barriers that restrict imports or exports of goods or services through mechanisms other than tariffs. Some examples of NTBs include:

- **Import quotas** - A limit on the quantity of goods that can be imported from a particular country.
- **Voluntary export restraints (VERs)** - An agreement between two countries in which one country agrees to limit its exports of a particular good to the other country.
- **Export subsidies** - A government payment to producers of a good that is exported. This can make the good cheaper for foreign buyers and give domestic producers an unfair advantage.
- **Technical barriers to trade (TBTs)** - Standards or regulations that make it difficult or impossible for foreign goods to meet the requirements of the importing country.
- **Sanctions** - Restrictions on trade with a particular country that are imposed as punishment

for a violation of international law or other wrongdoing.

Tariffs and compound tariffs are types of tariffs, which are taxes on imports. Ad valorem tariffs are tariffs that are calculated as a percentage of the value of the imported good. Compound tariffs are tariffs that are calculated as a combination of ad valorem and specific tariffs.

496. Marshall-Lerner condition states that: *(December 2022 - shift 2)*

A. Devaluation will improve the country's balance of payments if the sum of price elasticities of demand for exports and imports in absolute terms is greater than one.

B. Devaluation will increase the balance of payments deficit if the sum of the price elasticities of demand for exports and imports is less than one.

C. Devaluation will have no effect on the balance of payment situation if the sum of the price elasticises of demand for exports and imports is equal to one

D. In no case, devaluation can improve the balance of payment disequilibrium if either the price elasticities of demand for export or that of import is zero.

E. Marshall-Lerner condition has no relation with BOP situation.

Choose the correct answer from the options given below:

(a) A, B and E only (b) B, C and D only

(c) C, D and A only (d) A, B and C only

Answer = (d)

Solution: The Marshall-Lerner condition states that a devaluation will improve the balance of payments of a country if the sum of the absolute values of the price elasticities of demand for exports and imports is greater than one. This is because a devaluation will make exports cheaper and imports more expensive, which will lead to an increase in exports and a decrease in imports. If the sum of the price elasticities is greater than one, then the increase in exports will be greater than the decrease in imports, and the balance of payments will improve.

If the sum of the price elasticities is less than one, then the decrease in imports will be greater than the increase in exports, and the balance of payments will worsen. If the sum of the price elasticities is equal to one, then there will be no change in the balance of payments.

The Marshall-Lerner condition does not apply if either the price elasticity of demand for exports or the price elasticity of demand for imports is zero. This is because if the price elasticity of demand for exports is zero, then a devaluation will not affect the quantity of exports. Similarly, if the price elasticity of demand for imports is zero, then a devaluation will not affect the quantity of imports. In both cases, the devaluation will not have any effect on the balance of payments.

497. Match List I with List II *(December 2022 - shift 2)*

	List I		List
A	One firm sets its output before other firms do	I.	Cournot Model
B	Each firm correctly assumes how much its competitor will produce and sets its own production level	II.	Betrand Model
C	Firms are reluctant to change price even if costs or demand change	III.	Stackelberg Model
D	Each firm treats the price of its competitors as fixed and all firms decide simultaneously what price to change	IV.	Sweezy Model

Choose the correct answer from the options given below :

(a) A - III, B - II, C - IV, D - I (b) A - II, B - III, C - IV, D - I

(c) A - III, B - I, C - IV, D - II (d) A - II, B - IV, C - III, D - I

Answer = (c)

- Cournot output is the 2/3rd of the Maximum output or Perfectly Competitive Output.
- Firms maximized individual profits but not joint profits.

Bertrand Model:-1883

- Each firm assume that Other firm will keep the price constant.
- Unlimited productive capacity.
- By undercutting the price, the firm can capture the entire output.
- Concluding result Price= AC
- Total output produced by two firms is perfectly competitive output.

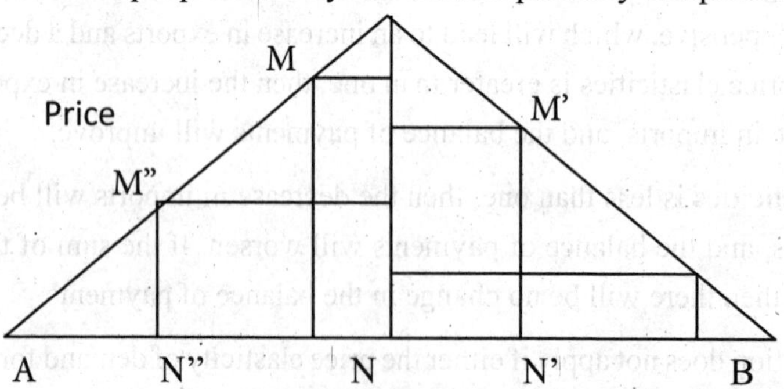

Firm A set price MN. B sets slightly lower from it (M'N') to increase its demand assuming firm A will not change its price. Then A again lowers it to M"N" assuming firm B will not change its price. At the end both will charge perfectly competitive price

Non-Collusive Oligopoly:-firms have not tacit agreement.

Cournot Model:-1838 by Augustine Cournot.

- ✧ Two firms.
- ✧ Firms produce homogeneous goods.
- ✧ Firms assume that other firm will keep its output constant.
- ✧ MC of producing a good is zero.
- ✧ The firms simultaneously take the decision.
- ✧ The output produced by other firm is the 1/2 of the remainder.
- ✧ At the end, both forms produce 1/3rd of the total output.
- ✧ Cournot price is between Monopoly price and Competitive price.
- ✧ Cournot price is the 2/3rd of the most profitable price.

Stackelberg model: - Development over Cournot model

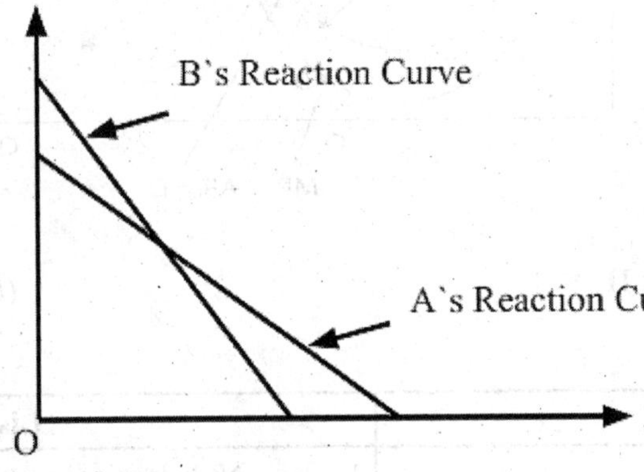

Situation 1 A: Leader B: Follower

Situation 2 A: Follower B: Leader

Situation 3 Both A and B want to be leaders.

Disequilibrium arises.

Outcome is economic warfare.

Situation 4 Both A and B want to be followers.

Situation 4 is indeterminate solution

Kinked Demand Curve:-Sweezy 1939

If a firm raises price, then others will not rise their prices. If a firmreduces price, others will also reduce it.

✧ Prices and quantities are rigid at Kink

✧ Decline in costs; keep the prices stable but the gap in elasticities increase. As a result, the break in MR curve increases.

✧ Decline in demand keep the prices stable.

✧ Due to kink in demand curve, MR is discontinuous.

✧ Discontinuity of MR implies the range within costs may change with out affecting equilibrium price and quantity.

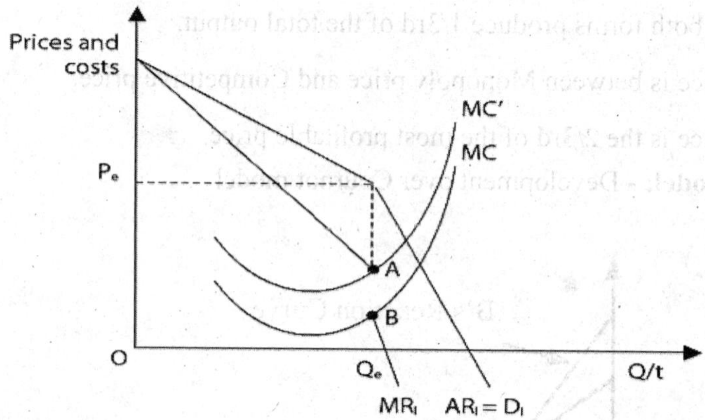

498. Match List I with List II *(December 2022 - shift 2)*

List I		List	
A	Robert Solow	I.	Neoclassical growth theory
B	Paul Romer and Robert Lucas	II.	Unemployment - Output
C	Paul Samuelson	III.	Endogenous growth theory
D	Okun	IV.	Foundation of Economic growth

Choose the correct answer from the options given below :

(a) A - II, B - III, C - I, D - IV
(b) A - I, B - II, C - III, D - IV
(c) A - I, B - III, C - IV, D - II
(d) A - III, B - I, C - II, D - IV

Answer = (c)

Solow Model

Given by solow "A contribution to the theory of economic growth". Also known as exogenous growth model or Neoclassical Growth Model.

Technical progress and population growth rate are treated to be exogenous in nature.

Endogenous growth models :-

1) **Romer's Model :-** learning by investment .Creation of knowledge is a side product of investment [Ideas are important than Natural sources].
2) **Lucas Model :-** focused upon investment in human capital.
3) **Arrow learning by doing :-** A firm over time, learns to produce more efficiently and increases its stock of knowledge. It helps in decreasing the average cost.

- ✧ Okun's law is an observed relationship between a country's GDP (or GNP) and employment levels.
- ✧ Okun's law predicts that a 1% drop in employment tends to be accompanied by a drop in GDP of around 2% Likewise, a 1% increase in employment is associated with a 2% GDP increase.

Samuelson contributed to many areas of economic theory through powerful mathematical techniques that he employed essentially as puzzle- solving devices. His Foundations of Economic Analysis (1947) provides the basic theme of his work, with the universal nature of consumer behaviour seen as the key to economic theory.

499. Match List I with List II *(December 2022 - shift 2)*

	List I		List
A	Detecting Serial Correlation	I.	Goldfeld - Quandt test
B	Detection of Heteroscadasticity	II.	The Run' s test
C	Detection of Multicollinearity	III.	Ramsay' s RESET test
D	Test of specification error	IV.	Condition Index

choose the correct answer from the options given below.

(a) A - III, B - I, C - IV, D - II (b) A - II, B - IV, C - I, D - III

(c) A - II, B - I, C - IV, D - III (d) A - IV, B - I, C - III, D - II

Answer = (c)

Solution

Heteroscadasticity

A regression model in which disturbance variance change from observation to observation is known as Heteroscadasticity.

Regression Model

i.e. Var (ui) = σ^2 u (Homoscedasticity)

Var (ui) = σ^2 ui (Heteroscadisticity)

Consequences : OLS estimates have large variance but remain unbiased and linear.

Tests : Spearman Rank Correlation Test

Gold Fed Quandt Test

Glejer Test

Park Test

Multicollinearity

Correlation among explanatory variables of a regression model is termed as Multicollinearity. i.e. Correlation among x1, x2, x3,… x3in following model.

$Yi = \beta0 + \beta1x1 + \beta2x2 + \ldots + \beta nxn + ui$

Tests to Detect : Farrar Glauber Test

Frisch's confluence or Bunch Map Analysis

VIF (Variance Inflation Factor)

Condition Index

Consequences : If there is perfect multicollinearity ,OLS estimates are indeterminate, Variance and covariance infinitely large, test of significance become invalid

500. Match List I with List II *(December 2022 - shift 2)*

LIST I		LIST II	
A.	Linear function	I.	
B.	Exponential function	II.	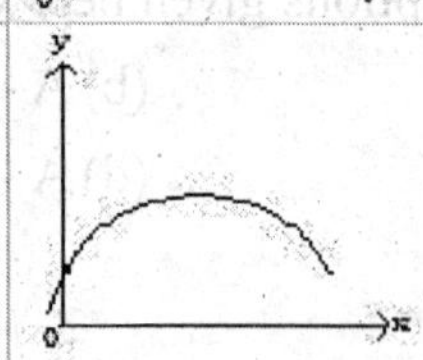
C.	Quadratic function	III.	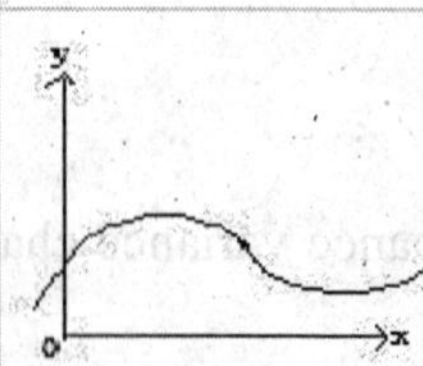
D.	Cubic function	IV.	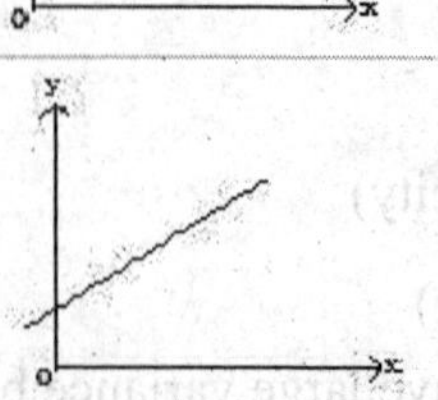

Choose the correct answer from the options given below :

(a) A - IV, B - II, C - I, D - III (b) A - I, B - IV, C - III, D - II

(c) A - IV, B - I, C - II, D - III (d) A - IV, B - III, C - II, D - I

Answer = (c)

Functions

Function shows the relationship between variables. For eg. if Y is dependent variable and X is an independent variable then $Y = 2X^2$ is a function.

Explicit function → It is that function in which a dependent variable Y is a function of an independent variable x.

For e.g. Y =5 x + 3

Implicit function is that function which shows the mutual relationship between variable Y and X.

For e.g. $x^2 + y^2 + 2xy = 0$

Linear function → Highest power unity.

Y = 5x + 3

Quadratic function Highest power of X is 2.

$Y = 2x^2 + 7x + 6$

Exponential function → It is in the form

$f(x) = a^x$

Polynomial function → It is in the form

$f(x) = a_0 x^n + a_1 x^{n-1} + a_2 x^{n-2} + \text{-------} a_n$

i.e. $Y = 5x^4 + 3x^3 + 6x^2 - 7x + 8$

Constant function → degree zero.

i.e. y = a

Rational function → It is in the form.

$Y = \frac{f(x)}{g(x)} \quad g(x) \neq 0$

$Y = \frac{5x^2+6}{6x-1}$

Composite function →function of a function

Y= f (u) and U = g(x)

Y = f [g(x)] is composite function of x.

Inverse function:-

Demand is a function of price i.e. D = f(p)

In some conditions price is also a function of Demand i.e. P = f (D)

Hence, D = f (p) is an inverse function.

Of P = f (D)

Reciprocal function: - It is in the form

$Y = \frac{1}{x}$ where $x \neq 0$

Quadratic function :-

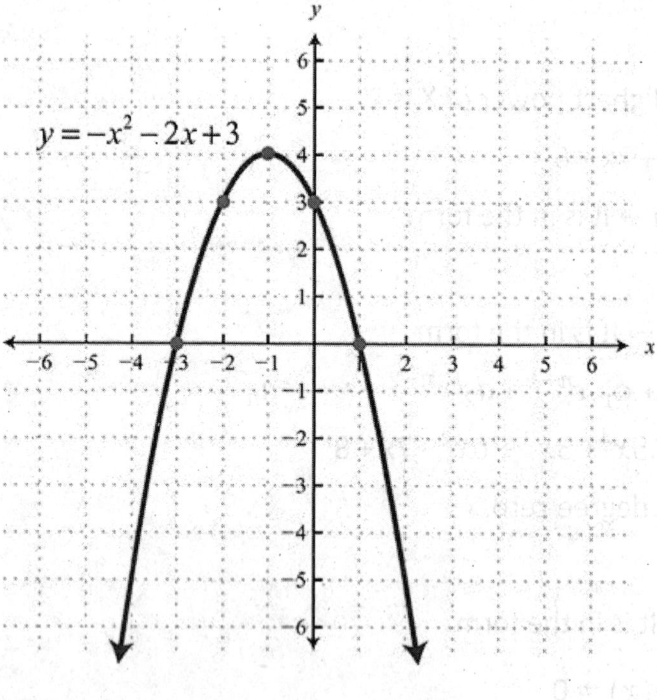

Exponential function :-

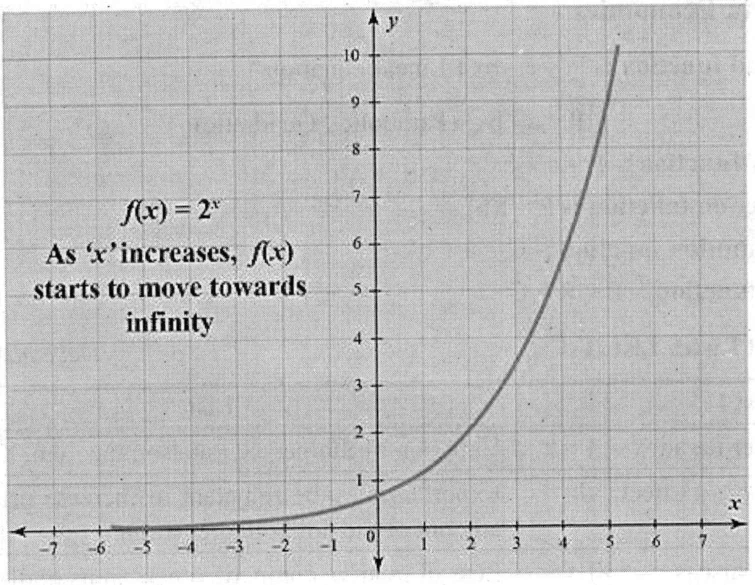

Cubic function :- A cubic function is a polynomial function of degree 3 and is of the form $f(x) = ax^3 + bx^2 + cx + d$

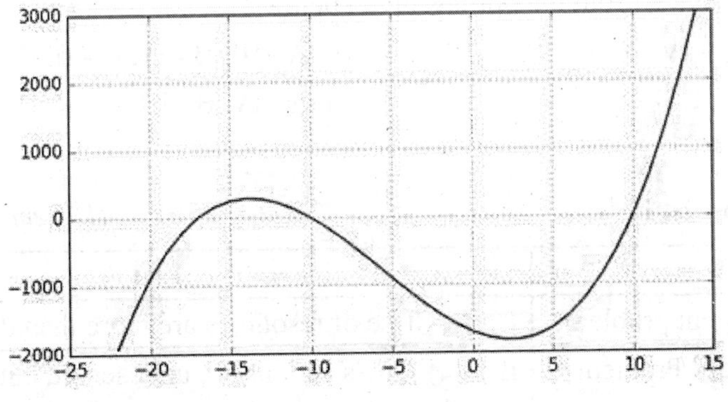

Linear function :

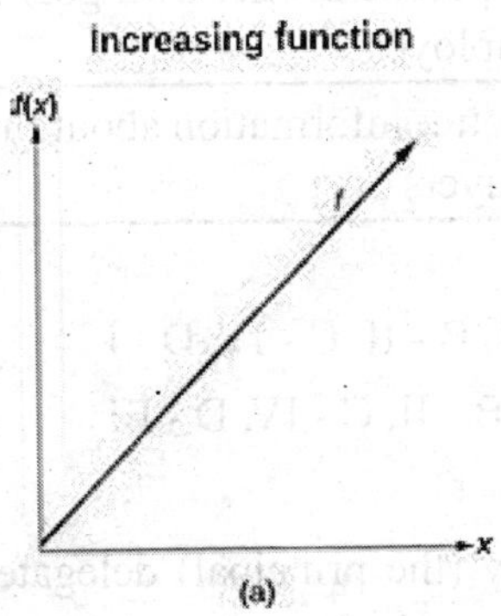

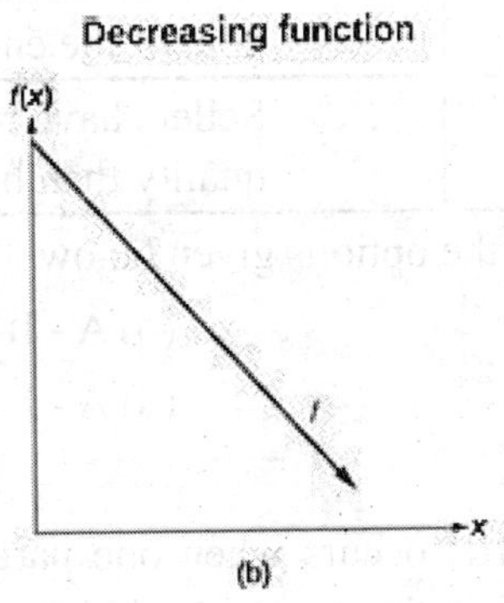

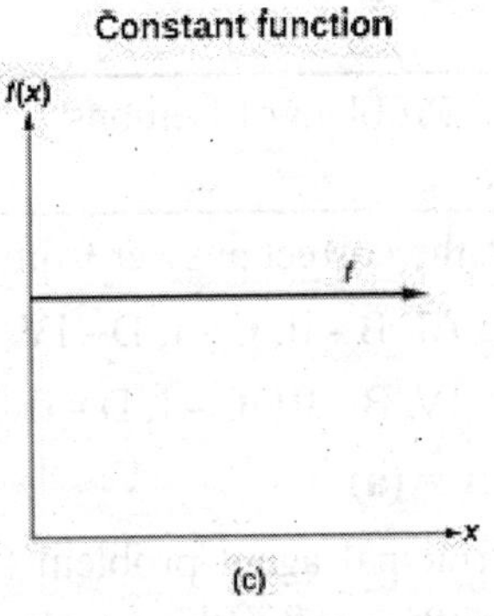

Functions in Economics:-

a) **Demand function :-** P = a – bx (Linear equation)

$P = a - bx^2$ (Parabolic / Quadratic)

b) **Supply function :-** P = a + bx

c) **Production function :-** P = f(b)

d) **Consumption function :-** C = a + bY

e) **Profit function :-** P = R – C

501. Match List I with List II *(December 2022 - shift 2)*

List I		List	
A	Metzler Paradox	I.	Violation of Stolper- Samuelson theorem
B	Beachhead Effect	II.	Exporters may be reluctant to increase prices by the full amount of the dollar depreciation.
C	Dutch disease	III.	Loss of relative competitiveness in its traditional industrial sector
D	J Curve	IV.	Nations,s trade valance may actually worsen soon after decaluation or depreciartion

choose the correct answer from the options given below.

(a) A - II, B - III, C - IV, D - I
(b) A - III, B - IV, C - II, D - I
(c) A - I, B - II, C - III, D - IV
(d) A - IV, B - III, C - II, D - I

Answer = (c)

502. Match List I with List II *(December 2022 - shift 2)*

List I		List	
A	Principal agent problem	I.	Use of resources are more than desirable
B	Moral Hazard Problem	II.	One's actions are unobserved but it can affect the magnitude of payment
C	Tragedy of commons	III.	An individual pursue his/her own goal rather the goal of the employer
D	Problem of Lemons	IV.	Sellers have better information about the product quality than buyers.

choose the correct answer from the options given below.

(a) A - III, B - II, C - I, D - IV
(b) A - III, B - II, C - IV, D - I
(c) A - IV, B - III, C - I, D - II
(d) A - I, B - II, C - IV, D - III

Answer = (a)

✧ Principal agent problem (III) occurs when one party (the principal) delegates work to another party (the agent), but the agent has different goals from the principal. This can lead to the agent acting in their own self-interest, rather than the best interests of the principal. For example, a company may hire a manager to oversee its operations, but the manager may have more incentive to make decisions that benefit themselves, such as taking on more risky projects that could lead to higher bonuses, even if those projects are not in the best interests of the company.

- Moral hazard problem (II) occurs when one party (the insured) takes on more risk because they know that they will be compensated for any losses. For example, a person with car insurance may be more likely to drive recklessly, knowing that they will not have to pay for any damage to their car if they get into an accident.
- Tragedy of the commons (I) occurs when a shared resource is overused because each individual user has an incentive to use as much of the resource as possible, even if it means depleting the resource for everyone else. For example, if a group of farmers all have cows that graze on a common field, each farmer may have an incentive to add more cows to their herd, even if it means overgrazing the field and eventually destroying it.
- Problem of lemons (IV) occurs when buyers have less information about the quality of a product than sellers. This can lead to buyers being tricked into buying a low-quality product, or paying too much for a high-quality product. For example, a used car buyer may have less information about the condition of the car than the seller, which can make it difficult for the buyer to determine whether the car is a good deal or not.

Adverse selection and Moral Hazard Asymmetric Information

Adverse selection [Market of Lemons]	Moral Hazard
sellers want to sell bad cars (lemons) and keep good ones	Insured consumers are likely to take greater risk, knowing that a claim will be paid by their cover.
Adverse selection can drive good cars from the market [Buyer or seller knows that the product value is greater than it's worth]	The consumer knows more about his intended action than the producer

503. Match List I with List II *(December 2022 - shift 2)*

	List I		List
A	Launch of S&P CNX Nifty	I.	July 1995
B	Establishment of Investor Protection Fund in NSE	II.	May 1998
C	Launch of NSE's website: www. nseindia.com	III.	April 1996
D	NSE recognized as a stock exchange	IV.	April 1993

choose the correct answer from the options given below.

(a) A - III, B - II, C - I, D - IV
(b) A - III, B - I, C - II, D - IV
(c) A - II, B - IV, C - III, D - I
(d) A - III, B - II, C - IV, D - I

Answer = (b)

504. Match List I with List II *(December 2022 - shift 2)*

	List I		List
A	Karl Marx	I.	Division of Labour
B	Adam Smith	II.	Big Push Theory
C	R.Rodan	III.	Traditional Society
D	W. W. Rostow	IV.	Reserve army

choose the correct answer from the options given below.

(a) A - III, B - II, C - I, D - IV (b) A - IV, B - I, C - III, D - II

(c) A - I, B - III, C - IV, D - II (d) A - IV, B - I, C - II, D - III

Answer = (d)

- ✧ Karl Marx (A) is associated with the reserve army (IV). The reserve army is a term used by Marx to describe the pool of unemployed workers who are available to be hired by businesses. Marx argued that the reserve army is necessary for capitalism to function, as it keeps wages low and prevents workers from demanding higher wages.
- ✧ Adam Smith (B) is associated with the division of labor (I). The division of labor is a term used by Smith to describe the specialization of workers in different tasks. Smith argued that the division of labor leads to increased productivity, as workers become more efficient at their specialized tasks.
- ✧ R. Rodan (C) is associated with the Big Push Theory (II). The Big Push Theory is a theory of economic development that argues that a country cannot develop without a large-scale investment in infrastructure and industry. Rodan argued that a country needs to make a big push in order to overcome the initial barriers to development.
- ✧ W.W. Rostow (D) is associated with the Traditional Society (III). The Traditional Society is the first stage in Rostow's model of economic development. Rostow argued that Traditional Societies are characterized by low levels of productivity, high levels of poverty, and a lack of technology.

505. Match List I with List II *(December 2022 - shift 2)*

	List I		List
A	Rajasthan	I.	91,276
B	Tamil Nadu	II.	68,548
C	West Bengal	III.	72,627
D	Mdhya Pradesh	IV.	72,147

choose the correct answer from the options given below.

(a) A - II, B - IV, C - I, D - III (b) A - IV, B - II, C - I, D - III

(c) A - II, B - I, C - IV, D - III

(d) A - III, B - I, C - IV, D - II

Answer = (a)

Solution:

State	Population	Rank
Uttar Pradesh	199,812,341	1
Maharashtra	112,374,333	2
Bihar	104,099,452	3
West Bengal	91,276,115	4
Andhra Pradesh	84,665,038	5
Madhya Pradesh	72,627,809	6
Tamil Nadu	72,147,921	7
Rajasthan	68,439,334	8
Gujarat	60,383,638	9

506. Match List I with List II (December 2022 - shift 2)

List I		List	
A	NABARAD	I.	1964
B	IFCI	II.	1955
C	IDBI	III.	1948
D	ICICI	IV.	1982

choose the correct answer from the options given below.

(a) A - I, B - IV, C - III, D - II

(b) A - II, B - I, C - IV, D - III

(c) A - IV, B - III, C - I, D - II

(d) A - III, B - II, C - I, D - IV

Answer = (c)

Solution:

- ✧ NABARD stands for National Bank for Agriculture and Rural Development. It is an apex development bank in India, headquartered in Mumbai. NABARD was established in 1982 by the Government of India with the mandate of facilitating credit flow for promotion and development of agriculture, cottage and village industries.
- ✧ IFCI stands for Industrial Finance Corporation of India. It is a financial institution in India, headquartered in Mumbai. IFCI was established in 1948 by the Government of India with the mandate of providing medium-term and long-term loans to industrial enterprises.
- ✧ IDBI stands for Industrial Development Bank of India. It is a financial institution in India, headquartered in Mumbai. IDBI was established in 1964 by the Government of India with the mandate of providing financial assistance to industrial enterprises.

✧ ICICI stands for Industrial Credit and Investment Corporation of India. It is a private sector bank in India, headquartered in Mumbai. ICICI was established in 1955 as a financial institution and converted into a bank in 1994.

507. According to the IMF's World Economic Outlook report, arrange the estimated real GDP Growth rate (YOY) of the following countries for the year 2021 in descending order.
(December 2022 - shift 2)

A. USA

B. Germany

C. United Kingdom

D. China

E. India

Choose the correct answer from the options given below:

(a) D E C B A
(b) E D C A B
(c) E C D A B
(d) D E B C A

Answer = (b)

508. Arrange the Nobel laureates in Economics as per their year of receiving award in descending order.
(December 2022 - shift 2)

A. Amartya Sen

B. Paul Krugman

C. James Tobin

D. Friedrich Hayek

E. Milton Friedman

Choose the correct answer from the options given below:

(a) A B D C E
(b) E C A B D
(c) A C E D B
(d) B A C E D

Answer = (d)

Solution:

1. Paul Krugman - Received the Nobel Prize in 2008.
2. Amartya Sen - Received the Nobel Prize in 1998.
3. James Tobin - Received the Nobel Prize in 1981.
4. Friedrich Hayek - Received the Nobel Prize in 1974.
5. Milton Friedman - Received the Nobel Prize in 1976.

509. Arrange the following in descending order on the basis of year of starting the scheme

(December 2022 - shift 2)

A. **Jal Jeevan mission**

B. **Swachh Bharat Mission (Gramin)**

C. **Pradhan Mantri Awas Yojana (Gramin)**

D. **Pradhan Mantri Sadak Yojana (Gramin)**

E. **Pradhan Mantri Koushal VikashYojana**

Choose the correct answer from the options given below:

(a) B C E D A (b) C A D B E

(c) B E C A D (d) C D B E A

Answer = (c)

Solution:

A. **Jal Jeevan Mission :** The scheme was launched in August 2019.

B. **Swachh Bharat Mission (Gramin) :** The scheme was launched on October 2, 2014.

C. **Pradhan Mantri Awas Yojana (Gramin) :** The scheme was launched in November 2016.

D. **Pradhan Mantri Sadak Yojana (Gramin) :** The scheme was launched in December 2000.

E. **Pradhan Mantri Kaushal Vikas Yojana :** The scheme was launched in July 2015.

A. **Jal Jeevan Mission:** Launched in August 2019, it aims to provide tap water connections to all rural households in India by 2024, ensuring safe and adequate drinking water supply.

B. **Swachh Bharat Mission (Gramin):** Started on October 2, 2014, this initiative aims to promote sanitation and hygiene practices in rural areas, eliminate open defecation, and construct toilets.

C. **Pradhan Mantri Awas Yojana (Gramin):** Launched in November 2016, it aims to provide affordable and pucca houses to homeless and eligible rural households, as well as upgrade existing kutcha houses.

D. **Pradhan Mantri Sadak Yojana (Gramin):** Launched in December 2000, it focuses on providing all-weather road connectivity to unconnected and remote habitations in rural areas.

E. **Pradhan Mantri Kaushal Vikas Yojana:** Started in July 2015, this skill development initiative aims to provide training to youth across various sectors, enhancing their employability and contributing to economic growth.

510. Arrange the followings in ascending order on the basis of Fund Allocation (Budget 2022-23)

(December 2022 - shift 2)

A. Ministry of Railways

B. Ministry of Defence

C. Ministry of Agriculture and Farmers Welfare

D. Ministry of Road Transport and Highways

E. Ministry of Rural Development.

Choose the correct answer from the options given below:

(a) A C D B E (b) E B C D A (c) C E A D B (d) B C D E A

Answer = (c)

Solution:

The ascending order of the fund allocation for the ministries in Budget 2022-23 is as follows:

1. Ministry of Defence (Rs. 5,25,166 crore)
2. Ministry of Agriculture and Farmers Welfare (Rs. 2,33,053 crore)
3. Ministry of Road Transport and Highways (Rs. 1,25,065 crore)
4. Ministry of Rural Development (Rs. 1,15,000 crore)
5. Ministry of Railways (Rs. 1,12,290 crore)

Therefore, the correct ascending order of the ministries is C E A D B.

511. Arrange the following sources of revenue as per their share of contribution to total revenue in Union Budget 2022-23 in descending order. *(December 2022 - shift 2)*

A. Custom Duty

B. Income Tax

C. GST

D. Union Excise Duty

E. Non debt capital receipts.

Choose the correct answer from the options given below:

(a) E B C D A (b) E C B D A (c) C B D A E (d) C B A D E

Answer = (c)

Solution:

1. GST (28.1%)
2. Income Tax (24.7%)
3. Custom Duty (17.8%)
4. Union Excise Duty (12.5%)
5. Non-debt Capital Receipts (6.9%)

512. According to CMIE data (September 2022), arrange the states in descending order based on unemployment rate *(December 2022 - shift 2)*

A. Haryana
B. Rajasthan
C. Jammu Kashmir
D. Jharkhand
E. Tripura.

Choose the correct answer from the options given below:

(a) A C D E B (b) B C A D E (c) A B C D E (d) B C A E D

Answer = (d)

513. Arrange the states in ascending order based on population who are multidimensionally poor as per NITI Aayog Report 2021. *(December 2022 - shift 2)*

A. Punjab
B. Kerala
C. Sikkim
D. Goa
E. Tamil Nadu.

Choose the correct answer from the options given below:

(a) B D C E A (b) D E B C A (c) A E D B C (d) C B A D E

Answer = (a)

514. Arrange the following policy rate (as on 31-12-2022) of the RBI in the descending order of their magnitude. *(December 2022 - shift 2)*

A. Repo rate
B. Bank rate
C. CRR
D. SLR
E. Reserve repo Rate.

Choose the correct answer from the options given below:

(a) A B D C E (b) D A B C E (c) B D A E C (d) D B A C E

Answer = (d)

Solution:

1. Repo Rate (4.00%)
2. Bank Rate (4.25%)
3. Reserve Repo Rate (3.75%)

4. CRR (4.00%)

5. SLR (18.00%)

✧ **Repo Rate :**This is the rate at which the RBI lends money to commercial banks.

✧ **Bank Rate :** This is the rate at which the RBI discounts commercial bills.

✧ **CRR :** This is the percentage of deposits that commercial banks have to keep with the RBI.

✧ **SLR :** This is the percentage of their net demand and time liabilities that commercial banks have to invest in government securities.

✧ **Reserve Repo Rate :** This is the rate at which the RBI reverse repo operations.

Note: These rates change frequently, visit RBI website for updates.

515. Arrange the following chronologically in order to their year of first occurrence starting from oldest: *(December 2022 - shift 2)*

A. Liquidity Preference Theory

B. Multiplier by R.F. Kahn

C. Division of Labour, Adam Smith

D. Quantity theory of Money, Fisher

E. Great Depression.

Choose the correct answer from the options given below:

(a) C D E B A (b) E D C B A (c) B C D E A (d) B A D C E

Answer = (a)

Solution:

✧ **Division of Labour :** This is the concept that specialization of labor leads to increased productivity. It was first described by Adam Smith in his book The Wealth of Nations in 1776.

✧ **Quantity theory of Money :** This is the theory that the money supply determines the price level. It was first proposed by Irving Fisher in 1911.

✧ **Liquidity Preference Theory :** This is the theory that people hold money for different reasons, such as to make transactions, to save for the future, or to speculate. It was first developed by John Maynard Keynes in 1936.

✧ **Multiplier by R.F. Kahn :** This is the concept that a change in investment can lead to a larger change in output. It was first developed by R.F. Kahn in his article "The Relation of Home Investment to Unemployment" in 1931.

✧ **Great Depression :** This was a severe economic depression that occurred in the 1930s. It began in the United States and spread to other countries around the world.

516. Arrange the following organizations as per their years of establishment starting from the oldest. *(December 2022 - shift 2)*

A. WTO

B. ADB

C. UNCTAD

D. World Bank

E. WIPO.

Choose the correct answer from the options given below:

(a) D C B E A (b) D B C E A

(c) D B C A E (d) D B A C E

Answer = (a)

Solution:

Organization	Year Established
World Trade Organization (WTO)	1995
Asian Development Bank (ADB)	1966
United Nations Conference on Trade and Development (UNCTAD)	1964
World Bank	1944
World Intellectual Property Organization (WIPO)	1967

517. Given below are two statements: One is labelled as Assertion A and the other is labelled as Reason R. *(December 2022 - shift 2)*

Assertion A: A form of market failure results when products of different qualities are sold at a single price.

Reason R : A buyer and a seller possess different information about the product transacted.

In the light of the above statements, choose the most appropriate answer from the options given below:

(a) Both A and R are true and R is the correct explanation of A

(b) Both A and R are true but R is not the correct explanation of A

(c) A is true but R is false

(d) A is false but R is true

Answer = (a)

Solution:

Assertion A is true because when products of different qualities are sold at a single price, the buyers who are willing to pay more for the higher quality product are not able to do so, and the sellers of the higher quality product are not able to charge a higher price. This is a form of market failure because it prevents the buyers and sellers from reaching an efficient outcome.

Reason R is also true because when a buyer and a seller possess different information about the product transacted, the buyer may not be able to tell the difference between the higher quality product and the lower quality product. This means that the buyer will be willing to pay the same price for both products, even though they are not of equal value.

The reason why R is the correct explanation of A is because the asymmetry of information between the buyer and the seller is the reason why the products of different qualities are sold at a single price. If the buyer had perfect information about the quality of the product, they would be willing to pay more for the higher quality product, and the seller would be able to charge a higher price.

Therefore, both A and R are true, and R is the correct explanation of A.

518. Given below are two statements : *(December 2022 - shift 2)*

Statement I : When the level of investment is itself determined within the system then the effectiveness of monetary policy is enhanced by an elastic investment and inelastic liquidity preference schedule, whereas the opposite holds for the effectiveness of fiscal policy.

Statement II : Monetary policy, by accommodating fiscal policy may forestall the crowding out effect.

In the light of the above statements, choose the correct answer from the options given below:

(a) Both Statement I and Statement II are true

(b) Both Statement I and Statement II are false

(c) Statement I is true but Statement II is false

(d) Statement I is false but Statement II is true

Answer = (a)

Solution:

Statement I:

The level of investment is determined by a number of factors, including the interest rate, the level of technology, and the expected rate of return on investment. If the level of investment is itself determined within the system, then the effectiveness of monetary policy will depend on the shape of the investment schedule and the liquidity preference schedule.

An elastic investment schedule means that a small change in interest rates will lead to a large change in investment. This is because businesses are more responsive to changes in interest rates when the level of investment is already high. An inelastic liquidity preference schedule means that people are less willing to hold money, so they will be more responsive to changes in interest rates. This will also amplify the effect of monetary policy.

Therefore, when the level of investment is itself determined within the system, then the effectiveness of monetary policy is enhanced by an elastic investment schedule and an inelastic liquidity preference schedule.

Statement II:

The crowding out effect occurs when government borrowing drives up interest rates and crowds out private investment. This can happen when the government borrows money to finance a budget deficit. When the government borrows money, it increases the demand for loanable funds, which drives up interest rates. This higher interest rate can make it more expensive for businesses to borrow money, which can lead to a decrease in investment.

Monetary policy can be used to offset the crowding out effect by increasing the money supply. When the money supply increases, interest rates will fall, which will make it cheaper for businesses to borrow money and invest. This can help to stimulate economic growth.

Therefore, monetary policy, by accommodating fiscal policy may forestall the crowding out effect.

In conclusion, both Statement I and Statement II are true.

519. Given below are two statements : *(December 2022 - shift 2)*

Statement I : Capital deepening is the process by which capital grows at a faster rate than labour and the capital labour ratio rises.

Statement II : The growth of output per worker is result of technological change which decreases output per worker for a given capital/labour ratio.

In the light of the above statements, choose the most appropriate answer from the options given below:

(a) Both Statement I and Statement II are correct

(b) Both Statement I and Statement II are incorrect

(c) Statement I is correct but Statement II is incorrect

(d) Statement I is incorrect but Statement II is correct

Answer = (c)

Solution:

Statement I: Capital deepening refers to the increase in the amount of capital (machinery, equipment, etc.) per worker in an economy. When capital grows at a faster rate than labor, and the capital-labor ratio rises, it is known as capital deepening. This process is often associated with increased productivity and economic growth.

Statement II: The statement is incorrect. Technological change typically results in an increase in output per worker rather than a decrease. Technological advancements can lead to more efficient production methods, better tools and machinery, and improved processes, all of which can boost output per worker and contribute to economic growth.

So, Statement I is correct as it accurately defines capital deepening, but Statement II is incorrect as it wrongly suggests that technological change decreases output per worker, which is not the case in reality.

520. Given below are two statements : *(December 2022 - shift 2)*

Statement I : Countries always want to have foreign markets open for their exporters. But if a country limits access to its own market, foreign countries may take action to limit access to their own market.

Statement II : Trade agreement can help lower barrier to international commerce, but countries still have to believe that other countries are "playing fair".

In the light of the above statements, choose the correct answer from the options given below:

(a) Both Statement I and Statement II are true

(b) Both Statement I and Statement II are false

(c) Statement I is true but Statement II is false

(d) Statement I is false but Statement II is true

Answer = (a)

Solution:

Statement I: Countries often seek open foreign markets for their exporters to expand their economic opportunities. However, if a country restricts access to its own market, other countries may retaliate by limiting access to their markets. This is known as trade retaliation or protectionism.

Statement II: Trade agreements can indeed help lower barriers to international commerce, promoting smoother trade between countries. However, for such agreements to be successful, countries involved must trust that their trading partners are acting fairly and adhering to the terms of the agreement.

521. Given below are two statements : *((December 2022 - shift 2))*

Statement I : The IS curve is negatively sloped because an increase in the interest rate reduces planned investment spending and therefore reduces the equilibrium level of income.

Statement II : The smaller the multiplier and the less sensitive investment spending is to changes in the interest rate, the steeper is the IS curve.

In the light of the above statements, choose the correct answer from the options given below:

(a) Both Statement I and Statement II are correct

(b) Both Statement I and Statement II are incorrect

(c) Statement I is correct but Statement II is incorrect

(d) Statement I is incorrect but Statement II is correct

Answer = (a)

Solution:

IS - LM Model :-

Given by Hicks and Hansen

Product Market :-

IS curve shows equilibrium in the product market.

↓in rate of interest→ ↑in investment→ ↑in AD→ ↑in income

Slope of IS curve depends on

1) Interest elasticity of investment Demand Higher the elasticity of demand, flatter will be the IS curve and vice versa.
2) Size of the Multiplier More the size of the multiplier, flatter will be the IS curve and vice versa.

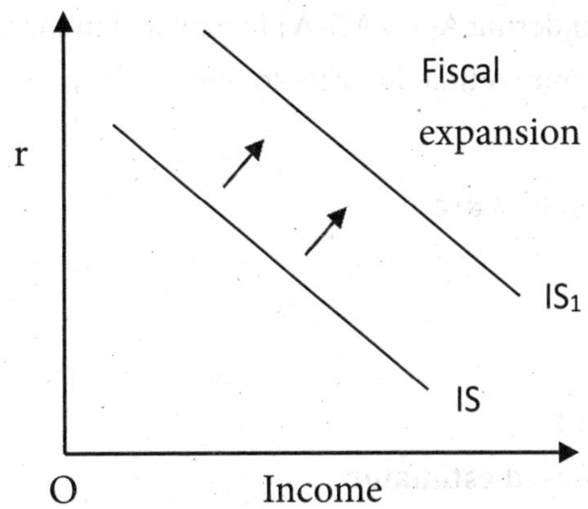

Money market :-Money market equilibrium is represented by LM curve ↑increase in income→MD ↑ →r↑

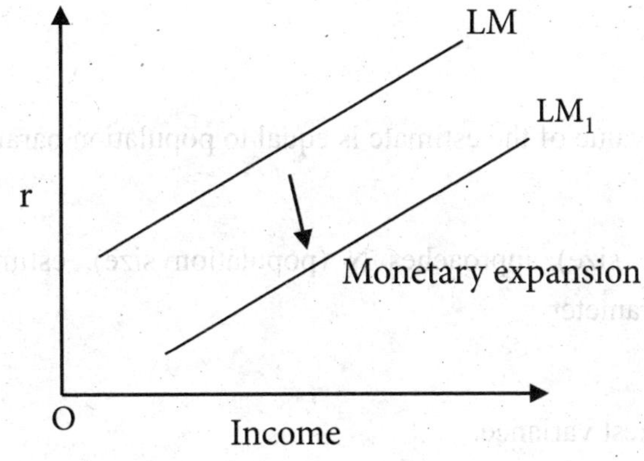

Slope of LM curve depends on

Income elasticity of demand for money :- More the income elasticity of demand for money, steeper will be the LM curve and vice versa.

Interest elasticity of demand for money :-

→Lesser the interest elasticity of demand for money, steeper the LM curve and vice versa.

522. Prevention of Money Laundering Act was enacted in the year? *(JUNE 2023)*

(a) 2001 (b) 2002 (c) 2003 (d) 2004

Answer: (b)

Solution: Money laundering is a heinous crime which not only affects the social and economic fabric of the country but also tends to promote other serious offences like terrorism and drug trafficking which India has been witnessing a lot lately. It's a growing problem that needs to be addressed.

The Prevention Of Money Laundering Act (PMLA) formulated in the year 2002 has undergone various critical changes from time to time in order to give itself more strength to deal with the offence of money laundering.

523. Properties of sufficient estimators are *(JUNE 2023)*

A. It may not be unbiased

B. It may be unbiased

C. It is always consistent

D. It is not always consistent

E. Minimum variance unbiased estimator

Choose the correct answer from the option given below:

(a) A, B and C only **(b)** A, C and E only

(c) A, B, C and D only **(d)** A, B, C and E only

Answer (d)

- ✧ Unbiased
  - » The expected value of the estimate is equal to population parameter
- ✧ Consistent
  - » As n (sample size) approaches N (population size), estimator converges to the population parameter
- ✧ Efficient
  - » With the smallest variance.
- ✧ Minimum Mean-Squared Error
  - » Variance of estimator be as low as possible.

✧ Sufficient

» Contains all information about the parameter through a sample of size n

✧ An *estimator* is *sufficient* if it makes so much use of the information in the sample that no other *estimator* could extract from the sample, additional information about the *population* parameter being estimated.

✧ The sample mean — utilizes all the values included in the sample so it is *sufficient estimator of the population mean*

✧ *Sufficient estimators* are often used to develop the *estimator* that has *minimum variance among all unbiased estimators* (MVUE).

524. Match List I with List II *(JUNE 2023)*

List I		List	
A	Cost - effectiveness	I.	A policy that directly regulates polluters through the use of standards
B	Pollution permit trading system	II.	An incentive based policy that encourages conservation practices or pollution reduction technoligies.
C	Market approach	III.	Requires that the least amount of resources be used to achieve and object.
D	Command - and - control approach	IV.	A market instrument that establishes a market for rights to pollute.

Choose the correct answer from the options given below:

(a) A-I, B-II, C-III, D-IV
(b)A-III, B-IV, C-III, D-I
(c) A-IV, B-III, C-II, D-I
(d) A-III, B-IV, C-I, D-II

Answer (d)

INTERVENTION OPTIONS

Command-and-control measures:

Use of legislative or administrative regulations that prescribe certain outcomes;

Usually target outputs or quantity, e.g. minimum ambient air quality standards, within which business must operate.

Market-based instruments:

✧ Policy instruments that attempt to internalise environmental externalities through the market by altering relative prices that consumers and firms face;

✧ Utilise the price mechanism and complement command- and-control measures. Under certain circumstances MBIs are considered more efficient than command-and- control measures.

525. The Hausman's specification error test is used to test whether *(JUNE 2023)*

(a) An exogenous variable is correlated with the error term.

(b) An endogenous variable is correlated with the error term.

(c) Both and exogenous variable is correlated with the error term and an endogenous variable is correlated with the error term

(d) OLS method is appropriate to estimate the SEM.

Answer (b)

Solution: The Hausman Test (also called the Hausman specification test) detects endogenous regressors (predictor variables) in a regression model. Endogenous variables have values that are determined by other variables in the system. Having endogenous regressors in a model will cause ordinary least squares estimators to fail, as one of the assumptions of OLS is that there is no correlation between an predictor variable and the error term.

526. Suppose good 1 is taken on horizontal axis and good 2 on vertical axis, then what happens to the budget line if the price of good 1 doubles and price of good 2 triples? *(JUNE 2023)*

(a) The budget line becomes steeper.

(b) The budget line becomes flatter

(c) The budget line become vertical

(d) The budget line remains unchanged

Answer (b)

Solution:

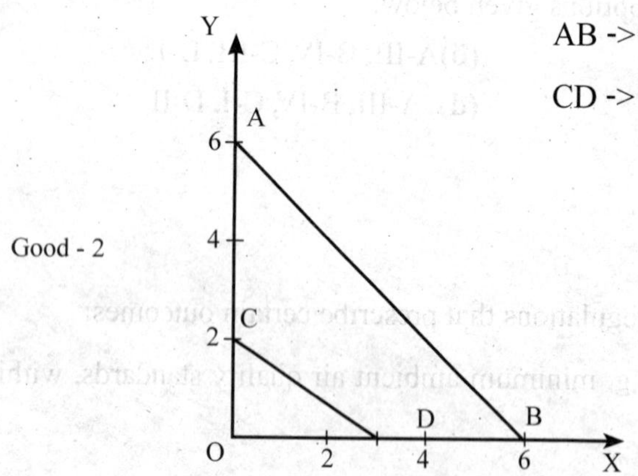

AB -> Price line before price increase

CD -> Price line after price increase (Flatter)

527. Which is not a dimension of Human Development Index (HDI)? *(JUNE 2023)*

(a) Ability to lead a long and healthy life

(b) Ability to achieve knowledge

(c) Ability to achieve decent standard of living

(d) Ability to access clean environment

Answer (d)

Solution:

HDI [Human Development Index] given by Amartya Sen and Mehboob -Ul - Haq in 1990 and published by UNDP

Indicators are :-

1) Income or Standard of living

2) Education

3) Longevity

In Order to remember:-

GM of three indicators

$$3\sqrt{Paida\ Hota \quad . \quad Padta \quad . \quad Paisa\ Kmata}$$

$$3\sqrt{Longenity \quad . \quad Reduction \quad . \quad Income}$$

HDI value ranges b/w 0 and 1, where 0 is considered to be worst while 1is best.

528. With the same monetary base, which of the following will lead to an increase in broad money? *(JUNE 2023)*

(a) High transaction cost of converting deposit into cash.

(b) Higher investment under SLR

(c) Higher use of cash

(d) Increase in financial literacy and banking habit

Answer (d)

Solution:

Increase in financial literacy and banking habit leads to more deposits with bank. Hence it will increase broad money.

529. Which of the following is/are true about paradox of thrift? *(JUNE 2023)*

A. Paradox of thrift was popularized by J.M. Keynes.

B. It states that personal savings can be detrimental to overall economic growth.

C. It shows the relationship between output growth and rate of unemployment.

D. It shows the relationship between inflation and rate of interest.

E. It states that individuals saving during an economic recession leads to fall in aggregate demand.

Choose the correct answer from the option given below:

(a) A,B,C only **(b)** B,C, D only

(c) C,D,E only **(d)** A,B,E only

Answer : (d)

Solution:

The Paradox of Thrift

- The paradox of thrift is important to the keynesian story
- According to the paradox of thrift, an increase in savings can lead to a decrease in expenditures, decreasing output and causing a recession.

530. Find the extremum of u = $x^2+y^2+z^2$ subject to x+y+z =1. *(JUNE 2023)*

1. $(\bar{x},\bar{y},\bar{z})=(\frac{1}{3},\frac{1}{2},\frac{1}{2})$
2. $(\bar{x},\bar{y},\bar{z})=(\frac{1}{2},\frac{1}{2},\frac{1}{3})$
3. $(\bar{x},\bar{y},\bar{z})=(\frac{1}{2},\frac{1}{2},\frac{1}{2})$
4. $(\bar{x},\bar{y},\bar{z})=(\frac{1}{3},\frac{1}{3},\frac{1}{3})$

Answer: 4

Solution :

$$L=(x^2+y^2+z^2)-\lambda(x+y+z-1)\begin{bmatrix}lagrange\\Multiplier\end{bmatrix}$$

$$\Rightarrow \frac{\partial L}{\partial x}=2x-\lambda,\quad \frac{\partial L}{\partial y}=2y-\lambda,\quad \frac{\partial L}{\partial z}=2z-\lambda$$

$$\Rightarrow \frac{\partial L}{\partial \lambda}=-x-y-z+1$$

$\Rightarrow 2x-\lambda=0$	$2y-\lambda=0$	$2z-\lambda=0$
$\lambda=2x$	$\lambda=2y$	$\lambda=2z$
$\frac{\lambda}{2}=x$	$\frac{\lambda}{2}=y$	$\frac{\lambda}{2}=z$

$$\begin{cases} -x-y-z+1=0 \\ -\frac{\lambda}{2}-\frac{\lambda}{2}-\frac{\lambda}{2}+1=0 \\ -\frac{3\lambda}{2}+2=0 \\ \boxed{\lambda=\frac{2}{3}} \end{cases}$$

$$Now\ \frac{2}{3}\times\frac{1}{2}=x$$

$$\frac{2}{3}\times\frac{1}{2}=y$$

$$\frac{2}{3}\times\frac{1}{2}=z$$

$$So\ \ x=y=z=\frac{1}{3}$$

531. Which of the following applies to the physical linkage approach for the valuation of environmental benefits. *(JUNE 2023)*

(a) Methods that assess responses immediately related to environmental changes.

(b) Methods that examine responses not about the environmental good itself but some set of market conditions related to it.

(c) Methods that estimate benefits using observations of behavior in actual markets.

(d) Methods that estimate benefits based on a technical relationship between an environmental resource and the user of that resource.

Answer (d)

532. Allocation of budget for Ministry of Agriculture and Farmers' Welfare in the Union Budget 2023-24 is *(JUNE 2023)*

(a) 2.25 lakh crores

(b) 1.25 lakh crores

(c) 1.78 lakh crores

(d) 1.68 lakh crores

Answer: (b) (1.25 lakh crores)

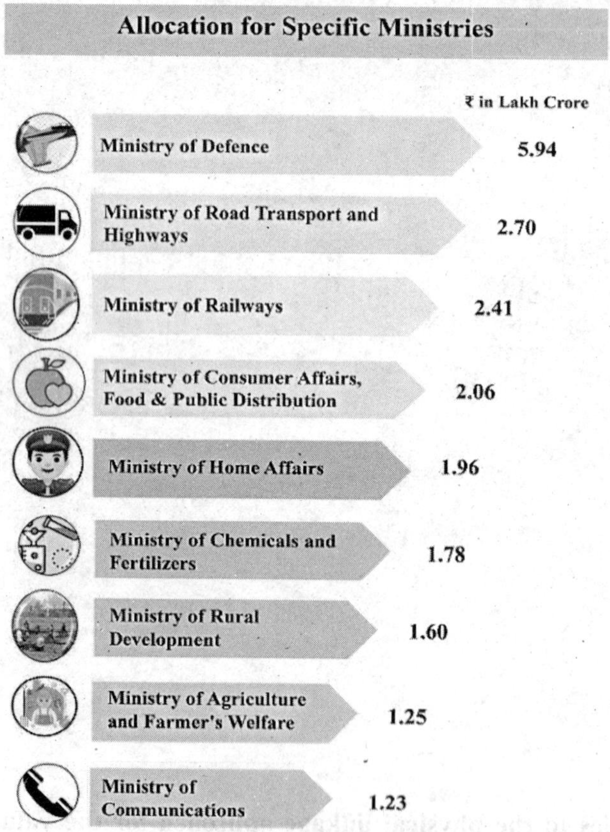

533. Which of the following is not true in case of incidence of tax: *(JUNE 2023)*

(a) Imposition of tax raises price and lower quantity.

(b) The resulting price increase of tax rise will be dampened if tax is imposed in monopolistic market.

(c) One would be in a better position to avoid the tax and leave the seller with a larger part if demand is inelastic while supply is elastic.

(d) A unit tax enters through a parallel upward shift in the supply.

Answer (c)

Solution: A unit tax is the tax imposed on per unit of the output sold. Due to the imposition of unit tax, the cost of production per unit of output increases, which ultimately increases the marginal cost.

Consequently, the (Long run marginal cost)LMC curve will shift leftward upward and as the supply curve is a portion of LMC, so the supply curve will also shift leftward upward.

Case 1:- When $E_d = E_S$

tax burden equally distributed amongst consumers and producers.

Case 2:- When $E_d < E_S$

tax burdens is more on the buyer as compared to seller

Case 3 :- When $E_d > E_S$

tax burdens are more on the seller as compared to buyer.

534. Match List I with List II *(JUNE 2023)*

List I	List
A $f'(Y) > 0$ and $f''(Y) > 0$	I. 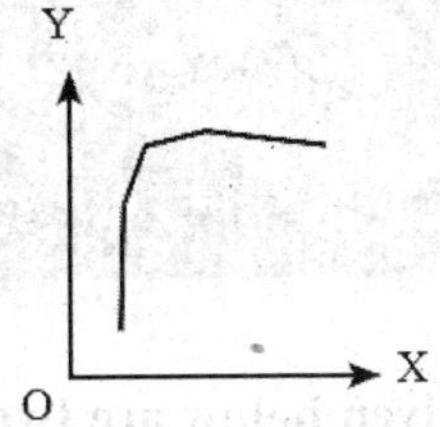
B $f'(Y) > 0$ and $f''(Y) < 0$	II. 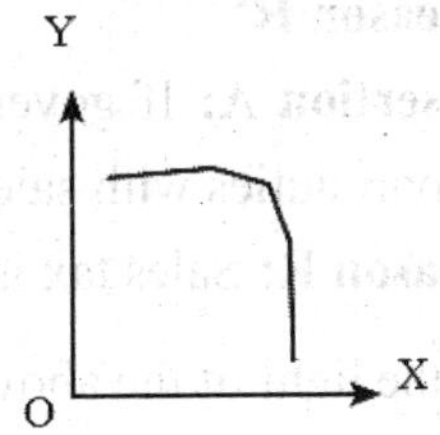
C $f'(Y) < 0$ and $f''(Y) < 0$	III. 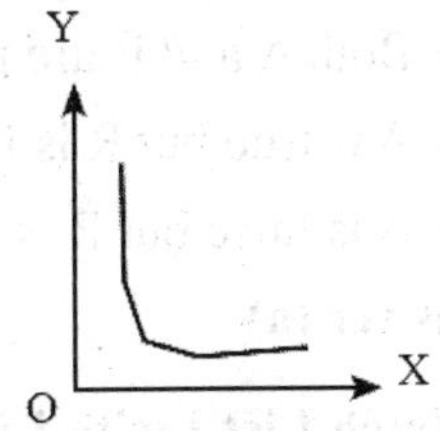
D $f'(Y) < 0$ and $f''(Y) > 0$	IV. 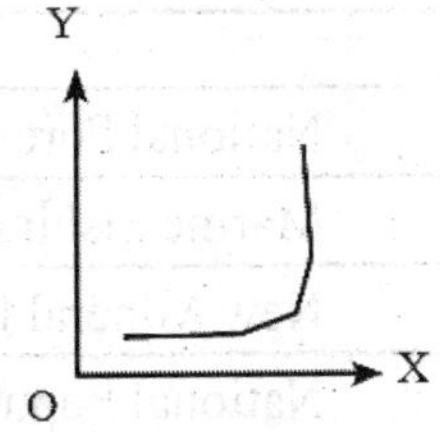

Choose the correct answer from the options given below:

(a) A-I, B-IV, C-III, D-II

(b) A-IV, B-II, C-III, D-I

(c) A-IV, B-I, C-II, D-III

(d) A-I, B-III, C-II, D-IV

Answer: (c)

Solution :

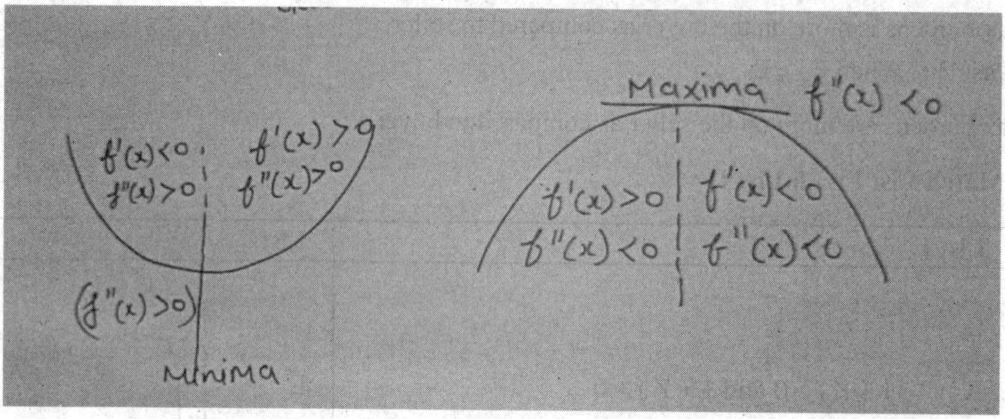

535. Given below are two statements: One is labelled as Assertion A and Other is labelled as Reason R *(JUNE 2023)*

Assertion A: If government do not care about protectionists' rents, they would replace all import duties with sales taxes.

Reason R: Sales tax is more efficient means of raising revenue than import tariff.

In the light of the above statements, choose the correct answer from the options given below:

(a) Both A and R are true and R is the correct explanation of A.

(b) Both A and R are true but R is NOT the correct explanation of A.

(c) A is true but R is false.

(d) A is false but R is true.

Answer (a)

536. Match List I with List II *(JUNE 2023)*

List I (Policy)		List II (Year)	
A	National Forest Policy	I.	2000
B	Marine Fishing Policy	II.	1994
C	New Mineral Policy	III.	2004
D	National Population Policy	IV.	1988

Choose the correct answer from the options given below:

(a) A-IV, B-III, C-II, D-I

(b) A-II, B-III, C-IV, D-I

(c) A-II, B-IV, C-III, D-I

(d) A-IV, B-II, C-III, D-I

Answer (a)

537. Which one of the following is not correct about LM schedule *(JUNE 2023)*

(a) The LM Schedule slopes upward to the right.

(b) The LM schedule will be relatively flat (steep) if the interest elasticity of money demand is relatively high(low).

(c) The LM schedule will shift downward (upward) to the right (left) with an increase (decrease) in the quantity of money.

(d) The LM schedule is the schedule giving the combination of values of investment and interest rate that produce equilibrium in the money market.

Answer (d)

Solution:

Money market :- Money market equilibrium is represented by LM curve

↑increase in income→M_D ↑ →r↑

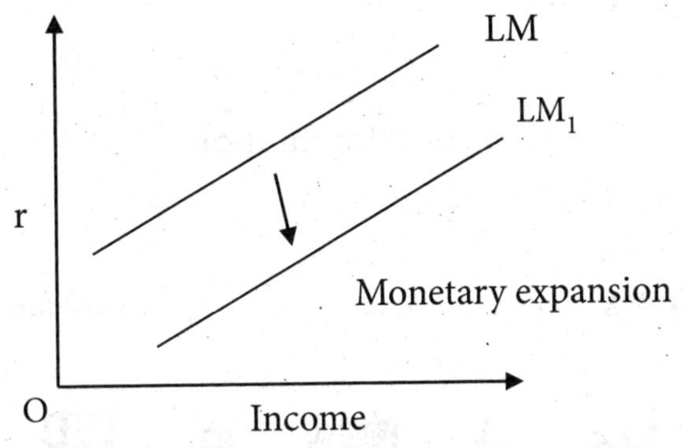

Slope of LM curve depends on

Income elasticity of demand for money :- More the income elasticity of demand for money, steeper will be the LM curve and vice versa.

Interest elasticity of demand for money :-

→Lesser the interest elasticity of demand for money, steeper the LM curve and vice versa.

538. Given below are the two statements: *(JUNE 2023)*

Statement I: The terms of trade of a nation are defines as the ratio of the cost of its export commodity to the price of its important commodity.

Statement II: The terms of trade of the trade partner are equal to the inverse of the terms of trade of the other nation.

In the light of the above statements, choose the correct answer from the options Given below:

(a) Both Statement I and Statement II are true

(b) Both Statement I and Statement II are false

(c) Statement I is true but Statement II is false

(d) Statement I is false but Statement II is true

Answer (d)

Solution:

Terms of Trade

$$= \frac{\text{Index of exports prices}}{\text{Index of imports prices}} \times 100$$

539. Which one of the following is not a characteristic of market structure? *(JUNE 2023)*

(a) Degree of buyers' concentration

(b) Degree of Sellers' concentration

(c) Conditions of entry

(d) Vertical integration

Answer (d)

Solution:

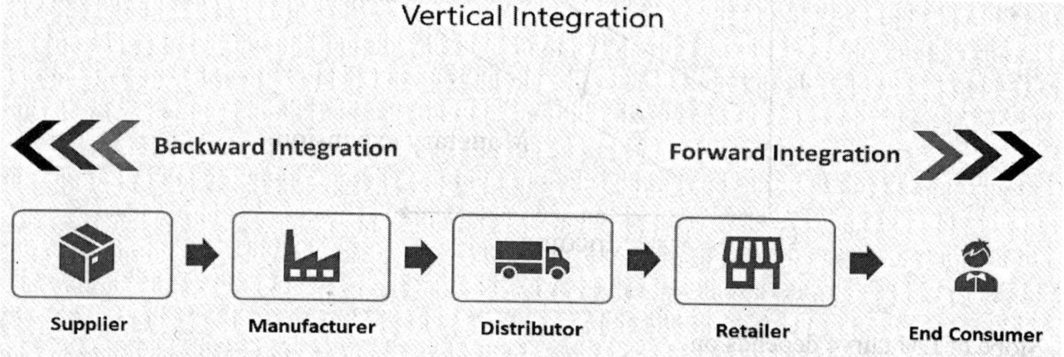

540. Based on NITI Aayog estimate of poverty for the year 2011-12, the states with above 30 percent rural poverty are *(JUNE 2023)*

A. Manipur

B. Bihar

C. Sikkim

D. Uttar Pradesh

E. Nagaland

Choose the answer from the options given below:

(a) A and B only

(b) B and D only

(c) B, C and D only

(d) A, B and D only

Answer (d)

541. As per the total revenue received by the government under the head of GST on the domestic supply of goods and services for 2021-22, arrange the following states in ascending order: *(JUNE 2023)*

A. Odisha

B. Rajasthan

C. Delhi

D. West Bengal

E. Madhya Pradesh

Choose the correct answer from the option given below:

(a) D, C, E, B, A (b) E, B, A, C, D

(c) B, E, C, A, D (d) C, E, A, D, B

Answer (b)

542. The merchant's file of 20 accounts contains 6 delinquent and 14 no-delinquent accounts. An auditor randomly selects 5 of these accounts for examination. What is the probability that the auditor finds exactly 2 delinquent cases? *(JUNE 2023)*

(a) 0.2562 (b) 0.3

(c) 0.3087 (d) 0.4526

Answer (c)

Solution:

$$P(\text{exactly 2 delinquent}) = \frac{{}^{6}C_{2} \cdot {}^{14}C_{3}}{{}^{20}C_{5}}$$

$$\Rightarrow \frac{\frac{{}^{3}\not{6}\times 5}{1\times \not{2}} \times \frac{14\times 13\times 12}{\not{1}\times \not{2}\times \not{3}}}{\frac{{}^{5}\not{20}\times 19\times 18\times 17\times 16}{\not{1}\times \not{2}\times \not{3}\times \not{4}\times \not{5}}}$$

$$\Rightarrow \frac{15\times 14\times 13\times 12}{19\times 18\times 17\times 16}$$

$$\boxed{\Rightarrow 0.35}$$

543. When MPS is 0.25 and initial increase in autonomous spending is Rs. 100, then the expenditure multiplier and resultant increase in GDP respectively are: *(JUNE 2023)*

(a) 1, Rs. 100 (b) 0.75, Rs. 75

(c) 4, Rs. 400 (d) 1.33, Rs. 133

Answer (c)

Solution:

MPS= 0.25

Autonomous Spending = 100

Expenditure Multiplier: Change in income/ Change in expenditure

$K = \frac{1}{MPS}$

$K = \frac{1}{0.25}$

K = 4

Multiplier = 4

$K = \frac{\Delta y}{100}$

400 = Change in Income

Increase in GDP = 400

544. The Intensive Agriculture District Programme (IADP) was launched in the year *(JUNE 2023)*

(a) 1960-61
(b) 1961-62
(c) 1962-63
(d) 1963-64

Answer (a)

Solution: A new programme named as IADP was formulated which was launched gradually from 1960. The third five year plan (1961-1966) incorporated this programme into the planned development process. This programme was popularly known as a "package programme".

545. If S is a sample space and E is an event then the probability axioms can be written as *(JUNE 2023)*

A. $P(A) \geq 0$

B. $P(S) = 1$

C. $P\left(\bigcup_{t=1}^{\infty} At\right) = \sum_{t=1}^{\infty} P(At)$

D. $P(A) \leq 0$

E. $P\left(\bigcup_{i=1}^{\infty} S_j\right) = \sum_{t=1}^{\infty} P(S_i)$

Choose the correct answer from the option given below

(a) A and B only
(b) A, B and D only
(c) A, B and E only
(d) A, B and C only

Answer (d)

Axioms of Probability

There are three axioms of probability that make the foundation of probability theory-

Axiom 1: Probability of Event

The first one is that the probability of an event is always between 0 and 1. 1 indicates definite action of any of the outcome of an event and 0 indicates no outcome of the event is possible.

Axiom 2: Probability of Sample Space

For sample space, the probability of the entire sample space is 1.

Axiom 3: Mutually Exclusive Events

And the third one is- the probability of the event containing any possible outcome of two mutually disjoint is the summation of their individual probability.

Mutually exhaustive events: Exhaustive events that are mutually exclusive are said to be mutually exhaustive events or mutually exclusive collectively exhaustive events (MECE). Such events cannot occur more than one at the same time and one of them will definitely occur whenever the experiment is performed. Some of the common examples of mutually exhaustive events are: When rolling a die, the set of all possible six outcomes {1, 2, 3, 4, 5, 6} is mutually exhaustive as no two numbers can appear at the same time and one of them will definitely appear.

1. Probability of Event

The first axiom of probability is that the probability of any event is between 0 and 1.

$$\text{For any event } E,\ 0 \leq P(E) \leq 1$$

As we know the formula of probability is that we divide the total number of outcomes in the event by the total number of outcomes in sample space.

$$P(event) = \frac{\textit{count of outcomes in Event}}{\textit{count of outcomes in Sample Space}}$$

And the event is a subset of sample space, so the event cannot have more outcome than the sample space. Clearly, this value is going to be between 0 and 1 since the denominator is always greater than the numerator.

2. Probability of Sample Space

The second axiom is that the probability for the entire sample space equals 1.

For Sample Space, P (S) = 1

Let's take an example from the dataset. Suppose we need to find out the probability of churning for the female customers by their occupation type.

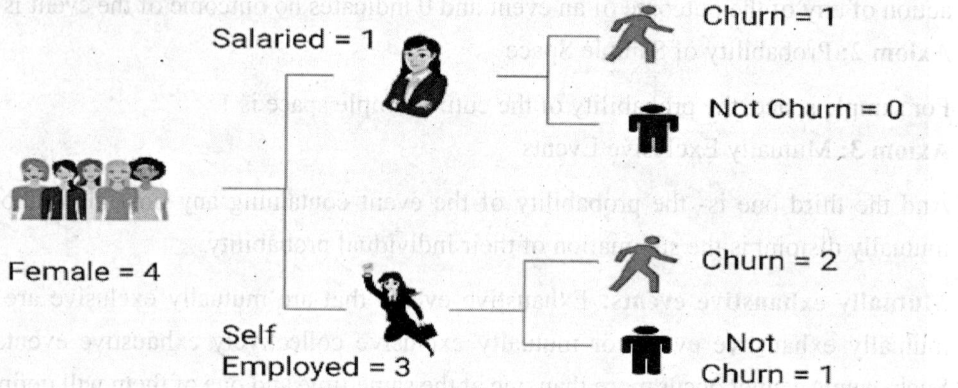

3. Mutually Exclusive Event

$$P(A \cup B) = P(A) + P(B) \text{ for mutually exclusive events}$$

If you remember the union formula you will recall that the intersection term is not here, which means there is nothing common between A and B. Let us understand these particular type of events which is called **Mutually Exclusive Events.**

These Mutually exclusive events mean that such events cannot occur together or in other words, they don't have common values or we can say their intersection is zero/null. We can also represent such events as follows:

$$P(A \cap B) = 0$$

Mutually Exhaustive

One more important concept is **Mutually Exhaustive Event** which is often confused with mutually inclusive events. Mutually exhaustive events mean that such events together make up everything that can possibly happen in a random experiment. That means the union of these events makes the sample space:

$$P(\cup E^{n}_{i=1}) = S$$

Let's understand this with an example-

Event A: Getting a number greater than 2 after a die, possible outcomes would be-

Event B: Getting a number less than 4 after rolling a die. Here the possible outcomes would be:

546. Which of the following are not symptoms of multicollinearity in a regression model. *(JUNE 2023)*

A. High R2 with few significant t ration for coefficients.

B. High pair-wise correlation among regressors.

C. The closer the Tolerance (TOLj) is to zero.

D. Variance Inflation Factor (VIF) of a variable is below 10.

E. The closer the Tolerance (TOLj) is to 1.

Choose the correct answer from the option given below:

(a) C and D only (b) D and E only

(c) A and C only (d) B and D only

Answer:(b)

Detection of Multicollinearity

$$Tol = 1 - R_j^2$$

$$VIF = \frac{1}{Tol}$$

✧ Generally, a VIF above 4 or tolerance below 0.25 indicates that multicollinearity might exist, and further investigation is required. When VIF is higher than 10 or tolerance is lower than 0.1, there is significant multicollinearity that needs to be corrected.

547. Here is given international organisations and their headquarters. Which of the following are correct combinations of institutions and their headquarters. *(JUNE 2023)*

A. GATT : Geneva

B. IMF : Washington DC

C. World Bank : Washington DC

D. International Development Association (IDA) : New York

E. Asian Development Bank : Mandaluyong

Choose the correct answer from the options given below:

(a) A, B and C only (b) A and B only

(c) C and D only (d) A, B, C and E only

Answer:(d)

The IDA is a member of the World Bank Group and is headquartered in Washington, D.C. in the United States.

548. The idea of creative destruction is associated with *(JUNE 2023)*

(a) Marx (b) Adam Smith

(c) Ricardo (d) Schumpeter

Answer: (d)

Definition of creative destruction This refers to the process of how capitalism leads to a constantly changing structure of the economy. Old industries and firms, which are no longer profitable, close down enabling the resources (capital and labour) to move into more productive processes.

- Creative destruction means that the company closures and job losses are good for the long-term well-being of the economy.
- It can be seen from both a negative and positive perspective.
- Joseph Schumpeter popularised the concept of creative destruction in 'Capitalism, Socialism and Democracy' (1942). He used the phrase 'gale of Creative Destruction' and the concept is sometimes known as Schumpeter's Gale. He derived his ideas from a close reading of Marx. However, whilst Marx believed capitalists crisis and destruction would lead to its demise, Schumpeter saw creative destruction as a necessary and natural way to enable new markets and new growth.

549. Given the income multiplier formula $m = 1/ 1-MPC$, lower the marginal propensity to save, *(JUNE 2023)*

(a) Higher will be the multiplier effect

(b) Lower will be the multiplier effect

(c) Multiplier will become infinite

(d) Multiplier will become zero

Answer: (a)

Solution:

$$K = \frac{1}{MPS}$$

550. Given below are two statements: *(JUNE 2023)*

Statement I: Friedman's theory of the demand for money is partly Keynesian and partly non-Keynesian.

Statement II: It is non-Keynesian in that Friedman neglects completely Keynes' clarification of the motives for holding money and the corresponding components of demand for money.

In the light of the above statements, choose the correct answer from the options Given below:

(a) Both Statement I and Statement II are true

(b) Both Statement I and Statement II are false

(c) Statement I is true but Statement II is false

(d) Statement I is false but Statement II is true

Answer:(a)

Solution: Inspite of similarities between Keynes and friedman theories , here is the difference between the two approaches with regard to the motives for holding money balances. Keynes divides money balances into "active" and "idle" categories. The former consist of transactions, precautionary motives, and speculative motive for holding money. On the other hand, Friedman makes no such division of money balances.

551. Which of the following is not true in the case of second theorem of welfare economics? *(JUNE 2023)*

(a) If consumers exhibit convex preference, every pareto efficient allocation is a possible competitive equilibrium in a pure exchange economy.

(b) In an economy involving production, the convexity of production sets ensures that a pareto efficient allocation can be achieved as a market equilibrium.

(c) It holds when there are increasing returns to scale.

(d) It implies that in the market system, the allocative role and the distributive role can be separated from each other.

Answer:(c)

Solution:

First Fundamental Theorem :-

1) General competitive equilibrium is Pareto optimal.

2) Ensures Pareto efficiency but not Social Justice.

Requirements:- Pareto optimality Second order conditions

Externalities in production and consumption do not exist.

Second Fundamental Theorem:-

- For every Pareto-optimal situation, there is a competitive equilibrium, given the initial income distribution.

552. Gunnar Myrdal is author of *(JUNE 2023)*

A. Asian Drama

B. An American Dilemma

C. Theory of economic development

D. Principles of Political Economy

E. Economic Theory and underdeveloped regions

Choose the correct answer from the options given below:

(a) A, B and C only
(b) A, C and D only
(c) A, B and D only
(d) A, B and E only

Answer: (d)

Solution:

Books and Authors :-

General theory of employment, interest and money 1936→ Keynes

Affluent society 1958 →Kenneth

Asian drama →Myrdal

Development as freedom (1999) → Amartya Sen

Capitalism and freedom →Friedman

Rise and fall of nations →Ruchir Sharma

Capital in 21st century →Thomas Piketty

Principles of Economics (1890) → Alfred Marshall

An enquiry into nature and cause of wealth of nations (1776) → Adam Smith

The Economics of welfare (1920) → AL Pigou

Value and capital (1939)

A revision of demand theory (1956)→JR Hicks

Principles of political economy and taxation (1817) → Ricardo

Nature and significance of economic science →Robbins

Principles of political economy →Mill

Behavioral Theory of firm→ Cyert and Mark

Foundation of economic Analysis and

Interaction between multiples and accelerator → Samuelson

✧ Theory of economic development: Schumpeter

553. In which of the following year IMF has set up the extended Fund Facility (EFF) to support member's structural reforms to address balance of payment difficulties of a long term character. *(JUNE 2023)*

(a) 1974 (b) 1997

(c) 1963 (d) 2009

Answer:(a)

The EFF was established in 1974 as a vehicle for longer-term lending to coun- tries in need of structural economic reforms.

554. Sequence of steps followed in the estimation of Indirect Least Square (ILS) starting from the beginning: *(JUNE 2023)*

A) Identification of the structural equations

B) Application of OLS

C) Obtaining structural coefficients

D) Obtaining reduced from equation

E) Use the model for policy

Choose the correct answer from the options given below:

(a) A, D, B, C and E (b) A, B, D, C and E

(c) B, D, A, E and C (d) B, A, c, D and E

Answer:(a)

Step 1: Identification using Rank and Order Conditions

Step 2: Obtain Reduced Form Equations and coefficients:We need to construct the Reduced-Form equations which express the endogenous variables in terms of all the exogenous variables. That is, we need to have endogenous variables on the left side and exogenous variables on the right side of the equation.

Step 3: Apply OLS: we apply OLS to Reduced-Form equations separately and obtain the estimates of Reduced-Form coefficients.

Step 4: Obtain the values of Structural Parameters: Since we have the values of all Reduced-Form coefficients from OLS, we can use these to obtain the structural parameters.

555. In the extreme case of liquidity trap *(JUNE 2023)*

(a) There will be tendency to buy bonds

(b) Most of the investors will show bearish behavior

(c) Cash will be less preferred

(d) Price of the bond will be low.

Answer (b)

Solution: In a liquidity trap, people assume that the prices of the bonds are already too high and the interest rates are extremely low.

Liquidity trap :- Interest rate is so low that the demand for money becomes infinitely elastic.

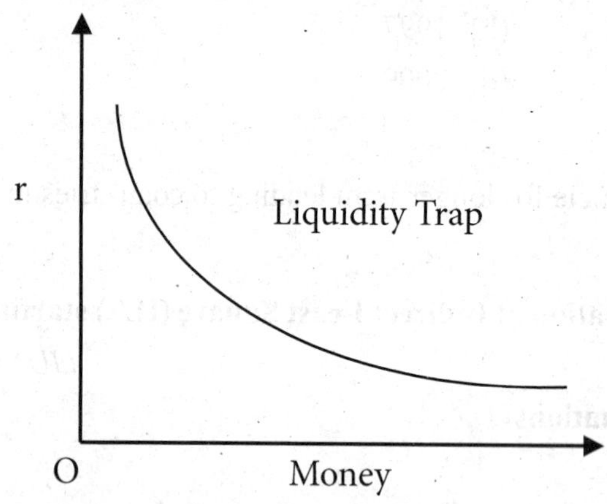

556. The utility function of a consumer is given by U = $f(q_1,q_2) = q_1 \cdot q_2$, suppose the price of q_1 is p q_1 =1 and price of q_2 is $Pq_2 = 2$. The consumer wants to spend amount of k units only what will be his demand for q_1 and q_2 ? *(JUNE 2023)*

(a) $(q_1,q_2)=\left(k,\frac{k}{2}\right)$

(b) $(q_1,q_2)=\left(\frac{k}{4},\frac{k}{6}\right)$

(c) $(q_1,q_2)=\left(\frac{k}{2},\frac{k}{4}\right)$

(d) $(q_1,q_2)=\left(\frac{k}{2},\frac{k}{3}\right)$

Answer (c)

Solution:

$L = (q_1, q_2) - h\,(q_1\,p_1 + q_2\,p_2 - k)$

$L = (q_1, q_2) - h\,(q_1 + 2q_2 - k)$

- $\frac{\partial L}{\partial q_1} = q_2 - h$
- $\frac{\partial L}{\partial q_2} = q_1 - 2h$
- $\frac{\partial L}{\partial h} = -q_1 - 2q_2 + k$

$q_2 - h = 0, h = q_2$ $\qquad$ $q_1 - 2h = 0, 2h = q_1$

$-q_1 - 2q_2 + k = 0$

$-2h - 2h + k = 0$ $\qquad$ $q_2 = k/4$

$-4h = -k$ $\qquad$ $\boxed{q_1 = \frac{2k}{4} = \frac{k}{2}}$

$h = k/4$

557. In the national income identity Y = C+I+G, investment (I) is a function of, *(JUNE 2023)*

a) Real income

b) Nominal income

c) Real interest rate

d) Nominal interest rate

Answer: (c)

Solution:

A real interest rate is an interest rate that has been adjusted to remove the effects of inflation. Once adjusted, it reflects the real cost of funds to a borrower and the real yield to a lender or to an investor. A real interest rate reflects the rate of time preference for current goods over future goods.

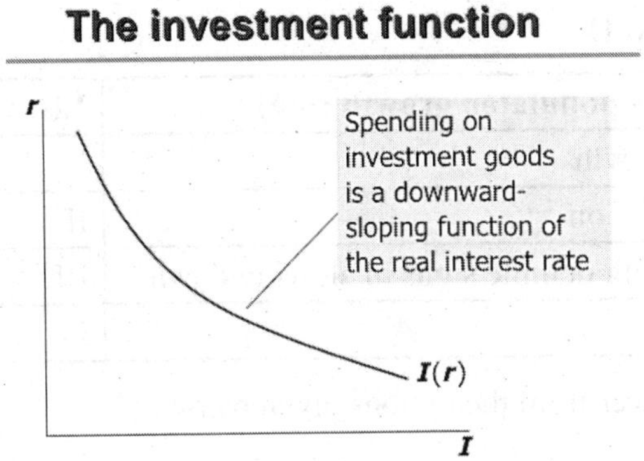

558. Pillar 1 of Basel III norms focus on *(JUNE 2023)*

A. Quality and level and capital

B. Risk coverage

C. Containing leverage

D. Risk management and supervision

E. Market discipline

Choose the correct answer from the options given below:

a) A and B b) B and C

c) C and D d) D and E

Answer: (a) and (b)

Basel III's 3-Pillar Framework		
Pillar 1	Pillar 2	Pillar 3
Minimum Capital Requirements	Supervisory Review Process	Market Discipline

559. Which of the following is true for the Clark-Wicksteed-Walras product exhaustion theorem *(JUNE 2023)*

A. The assumption of homogeneous production function tis necessary.

B. It is an identity that holds for all values of the variable.

C. The assumption of a homogeneous production function is not necessary.

D. It is not identity since it holds only for the values of the variables in the long-run equilibrium.

E. It holds for all types of production functions.

Choose the correct answer from the options given below:

(a) A and B only (b) A and D only

(c) B, C and E only (d) C, D and E only

Answer (d)

560. Match List I with List II *(JUNE 2023)*

List I (Type of India's populaton growth rate)		List II (Period)	
A	Rapid High Crowth	I.	1981-2011
B	Stagnant Population	II.	1921-1951
C	High growth with definite signs of slowing down	III.	1951-1981
D	Steady Growth	IV.	1891-1921

Choose the correct answer from the options given below:

(a) A-IV, B-II, C-III, D-I **(b)** A-III, B-IV, C-I, D-II

(c) A-III, B-IV, C-II, D-I **(d)** A-IV, B-III, C-II, D-I

Answer (b)

561. Which of the following can be an equation representing the money market. *(JUNE 2023)*

(a) $300 = 2Y - 1.5i$ (b) $I = 150 - Y$

(c) $Y = 100 - I$ (d) $i = (150 - 2Y)/2$

Answer (a) **Solution:**

Equation 1 depicts positive relation between Income and rate of interest as shown by LM curve.

Money market :-Money market equilibrium is represented by LM curve

↑increase in income→M_D ↑ →r↑

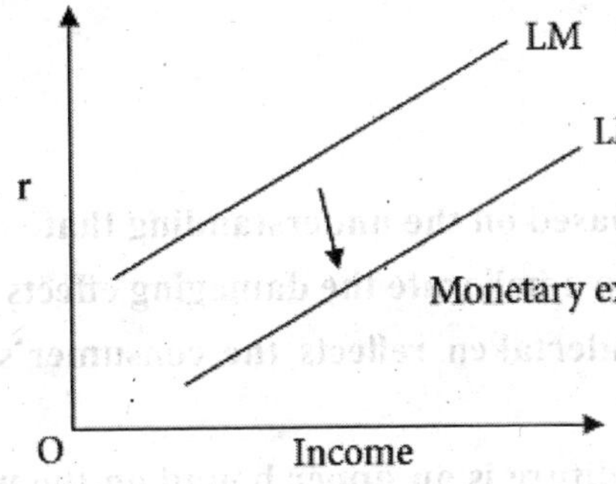

562. According to the Census, 2011 arrange the states in the descending order based on the literacy rate (aged group 7 year and above): *(JUNE 2023)*

A. **Nagaland**
B. **Tripura**
C. **Sikkim**
D. **Manipur**
E. **Meghalaya**

Choose the correct answer from the option given below:

(a) D,C,B,E,A (b) C,B,D,A,E

(c) B,C,A,D,E (d) A,C,B,E,D

Answer (c)

563. Which of the following is a correct measure of gross fiscal deficit of the state government. *(JUNE 2023)*

(a) Revenue Expenditure(RE) + Capital disbursement – Revenue Receipts (RR)

(b) RE + Repayment of loans to the Centre – RR

(c) Revenue Deficit + Capital Outlays + Net lending

(d) RE + Discharge of Internal Debt - RR

Answer (c)

Solution:

Concept of Deficits:-

1) Revenue deficit(RD) :-Revenue expenditure(RE) - Revenue receipts(RR).
2) Capital deficit(CD) :- Capital expenditure(CE) - Capital receipts.
3) Budget deficit :- Capital deficit + Revenue deficit.
4) Primary deficit :- fiscal deficit - net interest payment.
5) Fiscal deficit :- Total expenditure - Total revenue [excluding borrowings] .

OR (RE+CE)-RR

OR RD+CE

564. Defensive expenditure method is based on the understanding that *(JUNE 2023)*

A. The consumer spends money to ameliorate the damaging effects of the bad.

B. The defensive expenditure undertaken reflects the consumer's willingness to pay avoid the bad.

C. The observed defensive expenditure is an upper bound on the willingness to pay to avoid the bad.

D. The defensive expenditure provide no additional services other than provisioning to desired environmental quality.

E. The observed defensive expenditure is a lower bound on the willingness to pay to avoid the bad.

Choose the correct answer from the options given below:

(a) A, B and C only
(b) C, D and E only
(c) A, B, C and D only
(d) A, B, D and E only

Answer (d)

Solution: In environmental accounting, defensive expenditures are expenditures that seek to minimise potential damage to oneself. Examples include defence and insurance.

565. The concept of "excess sensitivity" and "excess smoothness" are explained by following statement(s). *(JUNE 2023)*

A. 'Excess sensitivity' refers to a situation where consumption over responds to temporary income shocks.

B. 'Excess smoothness' refers to a situation where consumption under responds to temporary income changes.

C. With excess sensitivity, anticipated rise in income is associated with relatively small change in consumption.

D. With excess smoothness, changes in aggregate income are associated with relatively small change in consumption.

E. 'Excess sensitivity' and 'Excess smoothness' are related to the empirical evidence of permanent income hypothesis.

Choose the correct answer from the options given below:

(a) A,B,C,D only (b) A, B, C, E only

(c) A, B, D only (d) A, B, E only

Answer (d)

Solution: The excess smoothness puzzle is the empirical regularity that changes in aggregate income are associated with relatively small changes in aggregate consumption.

- ✧ Excess sensitivity: consumption responds too much to. predictable changes in income.
- ✧ The excess smoothness puzzle is the empirical regularity that changes in aggregate income are associated with relatively small changes in aggregate consumption and variations in consumption about trend are smaller than variations in income about trend. This phenomenon implies that consumers are not quick to re-optimize their consumption decisions in response to macroeconomic shocks.
- ✧ The pioneering work of Milton Friedman (1957) resulted in the permanent income hypothesis, which posits that consumers' optimal current consumption choices are not a function of current income but rather a discounted stream of expected future income. This theory offers a rather straightforward solution to the excess smoothness puzzle, as consumers will ignore business-cycle related income shocks and base their consumption decisions on real wealth—long term factors such as equity assets, health, expected retirement age, and education level. Therefore, as time progresses, consumption will be smooth, and only shocks to permanent income will result in changes in consumption spending patterns.

566. Taylor's rule tells, *(JUNE 2023)*

(a) How monetary authority sets interest rate in response to economic activity.

(b) How monetary authority maintains bank rate.

(c) How monetary authority maintains exchange rate.

(d) How government decides the tax rate to increase the tax base.

Answer (a)

Solution: The Taylor Rule suggests that the Federal Reserve should raise rates when inflation is above target or when gross domestic product (GDP) growth is too high and above potential. It also suggests that the Fed should lower rates when inflation is below the target level or when GDP growth is too slow and below potential.

567. Acompany has 140 employees, of which 30 supervisors, 80 of the employees are married and 20% of the married employees are supervisors. If a company employee is randomly selected, what is the probability that the employee is married and is a supervisor?

(JUNE 2023)

(a) 0.1531 (b) 0.1253

(c) 0.0923 (d) 0.1143

Answer (d)

Solution: 20% of married are supervisors

80x 20/100

16 married and supervisor

Probability of married and supervisor = 16/140

= 0.1143

568. Arrange the following events of equity trading in India starting from the oldest:

(JUNE 2023)

A. The BSE introduced screen-based trading.

B. Foreign Institutional Investors (FIIs) are permitted to invest in the Indian Securities Market.

C. NSE commenced operations in wholesale debt market segment.

D. The SEBI banned badla trading on the BSE.

E. The NSE overtook the BSE as the largest stock exchange in terms of volume trading.

Choose the correct answer from the options given below:

(a) A,B,D,E,C

(b) B,D,C,E,A

(c) D,B,E,C,A

(d) C,B,D,E,A

Answer (b)

- ✧ BSE's pivotal and pre-eminent role in the development of the Indian capital market is widely recognized. It migrated from the open outcry system to an online screen-based order driven trading system in 1995.
- ✧ Foreign Institutional Investors (FIIs) have retained their faith in the resilient Indian

economy ever since the markets were opened up to them in 1993

- ✧ The erstwhile Wholesale Debt Market (WDM) segment of the Exchange commenced operations on June 30, 1994.
- ✧ Badla were banned by the Securities and Exchange Board of India (SEBI) in 1993, effective March 1994,
- ✧ NSE was incorporated in 1992. It was recognised as a stock exchange by SEBI in April 1993 and commenced operations in 1994 with the launch of the wholesale debt market

569. What is the motto of G-20 18th meeting? *(JUNE 2023)*

(a) One Earth, One Family, One Future

(b) One Earth, One Nature, One Family

(c) One World, One Family, One Life

(d) One Earth, One Nature, One Future

Answer (a)

Solution: The 18th Heads of State and Government Summit of the Group of 20 (G20) will take place in September 2023 in New Delhi, India. Under the Indian Presidency, the G20 in 2023 will focus on the theme, 'One Earth, One Family, One Future'.

570. Which of the following statements are correct about trilemma in momentary policy *(JUNE 2023)*

A. It is related to closed economy model

B. It involves exchange rate, capital mobility and monetary policy.

C. It arises because perfect capital mobility aligns the domestic interest rate to the world interest rate.

D. Flexible exchange rate is not compatible with independent monetary policy.

E. It is related to capital immobility and flexible exchange rate.

Choose the correct answer from the options given below:

(a) B and C only

(b) C and D only

(c) A and D only

(d) B and E only

Answer: a

Solution: Monetary autonomy means domestic interest rates can be independently determined from world interest rates.

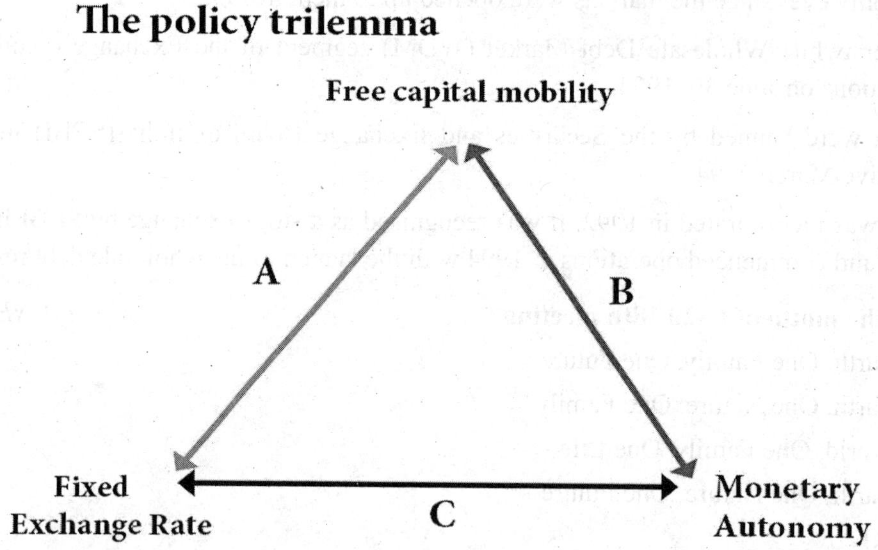

571. Why subsidies are not an effective policy instrument in the long-run for internalizing externalities under competitive output markets? *(JUNE 2023)*

(a) A subsidy that is equal to marginal damages translates to a de facto decrease in firm's fixed costs.

(b) subsidy payments are available to all firms and can induce excessive market entry.

(c) The level of industrial production in the sector would exceed the socially desired level.

(d) All of the above.

Answer (d)

Solution: Marginal damage function is a relationship between quantity of emissions and the damage caused by emissions.

572. Match List I with List II *(JUNE 2023)*

List I (States)		List II (Food grain production (2021-22) Thousand Tonnes	
A	Telangana	I.	11266.0
B	Jharkhand	II.	14984.2
C	Chhattisgarh	III.	8897.0
D	Andhra Pradhesh	IV.	15095.4

Choose the correct answer from the options given below:

(a) A-I, B-II, C-III, D-IV

(b) A-IV, B-III, C-II, D-I

(c) A-I, B-III, C-IV, D-II

(d) A-IV, B-II, C-III, D-I

573. Factor price equalization theorem is given by, *(JUNE 2023)*

(a) David Ricardo
(b) J.S. Mill
(c) Paul Samuelson
(d) Adam Smith

Answer (c)

Solution:

(1948) Samuelson's factor price equalization theorem:-

Heckscher and Ohlin suggested that there is not complete factor price equalization will occur. Samuelsson showed that free commodity trade will, under certain specified conditions, in enviably lead to complete factor price equalization. Prices of factors of production Such as wage rate or rent of capital will be equalised across countries as a result of International Trade.

Assumes: - Two goods, Two factors, same commodity prices, free trade, same technology.

When the prices of the output goods are equalised between countries as they move to free trade, then the prices of the factors will also be equalised between countries.

Before international trade, factor receives lowest price. After international trade, it becomes more expensive. While those with the highest price will tend to become cheaper.

574. Match List I with List II *(JUNE 2023)*

	List I		List II
A	J.M. Keynes	I.	Inventory theoretic approach to transaction demand for money
B	Kydland-Prescott	II.	Liquidity Preference
C	Baumol-Tobin	III.	Time inconsistency Problem
D	Friedman-Schwartz	IV.	Monetary History of United States

Choose the correct answer from the options given below:

(a) A-II, B-III, C-IV, D-I
(b) A-III, B-II, C-I, D-IV
(c) A-III, B-I, C-II, D-IV
(d) A-II, B-III, C-I, D-IV

Answer (d)

575. Arrange the following Acts in chronological order of their year of enactment starting from the oldest: *(JUNE 2023)*

A. Foreign Exchange Regulation Act
B. Competition Act
C. MRTP Act
D. Foreign Regulation Act
E. Foreign Exchange Management Act

Choose the correct answer from the options given below:

(a) C,B,A,D,E (b) C,A,B,E,D

(c) B,A,D,E,C (d) A,B,C,D,E

Dropped

Answer:

Various Acts and dates	
Competition Act	2002 [Replaced MRTP act]
MRTP act [Monopolies Restrictive Trade Practices Act]	1969 [prevent concentration oneconomic power]
FERA [Foreign Exchange Regulation Act]	1973 [Regulating the foreignexchange market]
FEMA[foreign exchangemanagement Act]	1999 [Management of foreignexchange]
first national commission on labor	1966
second National LaborCommission	1999
RBI Nationalized	1949

576. Given below are two statements: *(JUNE 2023)*

Statement I: Under first degree price discrimination, monopolist sells different units of output for different prices and these prices may differ from person to person.

Statement II: Under third degree price discrimination, monopolist sells different units of output for different prices, but every individual who buys the same amount of the good pays the same price.

In the light of the above statements, choose the correct answer from the options Given below:

(a) Both Statement I and Statement II are true

(b) Both Statement I and Statement II are false

(c) Statement I is true but Statement II is false

(d) Statement I is false but Statement II is true

Answer (c)

Solution:

Degrees of Price Discrimination:-

First degree price discrimination: Extracts entire consumer surplus.

Monopoly is able to sell each separate unit of the product at a different price.

Second degree price Discrimination: Monopolist is able to charge separate price for different quantities or blocks of a commodity from buyers.

Some consumer surplus is left with the buyers.

Third degree price Discrimination: Different prices are charged in different markets depending on the elasticities.

Ex.- Dumping [electric company sells electric power at a lower price to the house holds, at higher price to the manufacturers.]

577. According to Sample Registration System, which of the following Indian States has the highest level of life time risk during 2018-2020. *(JUNE 2023)*

(a) Bihar (b) Uttar Pradesh

(c) Madhya Pradesh (d) Chhatisgarh

Answer (c)

578. Given below are two statements: *(JUNE 2023)*

Statement I: Division of labour is the starting point of Smith's theory of economic growth.

Statement II: It is division of labour that results in the greatest improvement in the productive power of labour.

In the light of the above statements, choose the correct answer from the options Given below:

(a) Both Statement I and Statement II are true

(b) Both Statement I and Statement II are false

(c) Statement I is true but Statement II is false

(d) Statement I is false but Statement II is true

Answer (a)

Solution:

Theories of Development:-

1) Classical theory of development :- (Adam Smith)

Adam Smith is father of Political economy and is the founder of classical school of economics.

Smith's work is "An enquiry into the nature and causes of the wealth of nations".

2) His views on development :-

- ✧ Capital accumulation should be encouraged.
- ✧ Promoted the concept of division of labor and specialization.
- ✧ Favored laissez-faire policy.
- ✧ Promoted concept of invisible hand. Here invisible hand means market forces of demand and supply.

According to him, development is not sudden; rather it is cumulative and slow process.

Assumptions :-

- ✧ Laissez-faire
- ✧ Two sectors Agriculture and Industry
- ✧ Agriculture is subject to law of diminishing returns
- ✧ Two inputs - labor, capital
- ✧ Subsistence law of wages
- ✧ say's laws of market
- ✧ Perfect competition

579. Which of the following are corrcct in case of theory of sets. *(JUNE 2023)*

A. $(A\cup B')\cap(A'\cup C)\cap(B\cup C'')=(A\cap B\cap C)\cup(A\cup B\cup C)$

B. $(A\cup B')\cap(A'\cup C)\cap(B\cup C'')=(A\cap B\cap C)\cup(A\cup B\cup C)'$

C. $A\cup(B\cap C)=(A\cup B)\cap(A\cup C)$

D. $A\cap(B\cup C)=(A\cup B)\cap(A\cup C)$

E. $(A\cup B')\cap(A'\cup C)\cap(B\cup C'')=(A\cap B\cap C)\cup(A'\cap B'\cap C')$

Choose the correct answer from the options given below:

(a) A, C, E only
(b) B, D, E only
(c) B, C, E only
(d) A, B, D only

Answer (c)

Solution:

Commutative laws for union and Intersection of two sets.

A ∪ B = B ∪ A

A ∩ B = B ∩ A

Associative laws for union and intersection for two sets.

$A \cup (B \cup C) = (A \cup B) \cup C$

$A \cap (B \cap C) = (A \cap B) \cap C$

Distributive law

$A \cap (B \cup C) = (A \cap B) \cup (A \cap C)$

$A \cup (B \cap C) = (A \cup B) \cap (A \cup C)$

580. Match List I with List II *(JUNE 2023)*

List I		List II	
A	Kleins rule of thumb	I.	Structural break
B	Ljung Box (LB) statistic	II.	Unit Root
C	KPSS	III.	Significance of autocorrelation coefficients
D	Bai-Perron	IV.	Multicollinearity

Choose the correct answer from the options given below:

(a) A-IV, B-III, C-II, D-I
(b) A-IV, B-III, C-I, D-II
(c) A-II, B-IV, C-I, D-III
(d) A-II, B-III, C-IV, D-I

Answer (a)

Solution:

- ✧ Use the Ljung-Box q statistic to test whether a series of observations over time are random and independent. If observations are not independent, one observation can be correlated with a different observation k time units later, a relationship called autocorrelation.
- ✧ The KPSS test, short for, Kwiatkowski-Phillips-Schmidt-Shin (KPSS), is a type of Unit root test that tests for the stationarity of a given series around a deterministic trend. In other words, the test is somewhat similar in spirit to the ADF test.
- ✧ Bai-Perron is an algorithm for efficiently finding the least squares break points in a linear regression model

DETECTION OF MULTICOLLINEARITY

- ✧ High R-square but few significant t-ratio
- ✧ High pair-wise correlation among regressors
- ✧ Examination of partial correlations (Farrar and Glauber)
- ✧ Auxiliary regressions
- ✧ Klein's rule of thumb (R_2 aux; overall R_2)
- ✧ Eigenvalues and condition index
- ✧ Tolerance and variance inflation factor

581. Which of the following are true in case of social goods: *(JUNE 2023)*

A. Public goods are non-rivalry in nature.

B. Efficient provision of social goods needs a political process of budget determination

C. Efficient provision of social goods involve horizontal rather than vertical addition of individual pseudo-demand-lines.

D. Among purely private and purely social goods, there are mixed cases which generate benefit or cost externalities

E. Individual consumers will not bid for social good, but will act as free-riders. Choose the correct answer from the option given below:

(a) A, C, D and E only
(b) A, B, C and E only
(c) A and B only
(d) A, B, D and E only

Answer (d)

Solution:

Public Goods: - A public good is one who has properties of non excludable and non-rivalrous.

Non excludable : if it can be consumed by anyone.

Non-rivalrous : if no one has an exclusive right over its consumption.

582. Match List I with List II *(JUNE 2023)*

	List I (Policy)		List II (Year)
A	Tax Evasion	I.	Bond Financing
B	Effective incidence of tax	II.	Illegal free riding
C	Legal incidence of tax .	III.	Obliged to deliver tax revenue to Government
D	Fiscal Illusion	IV.	Not necessarily correspond to on whom tax is imposed

Choose the correct answer from the options given below:

(a) A-II, B-III, C-IV, D-I
(b) A-IV, B-III, C-II, D-I
(c) A-II, B-IV, C-III, D-I
(d) A-III, B-I, C-II, D-IV

Answer (c)

Solution:

Fiscal illusion occurs to leading taxpayers due to the mistaken perception of living in a context where there was a reduction in the overall level of taxation or even an increase in expenditure on public goods provided without any increase in taxation. Fiscal illusion becomes evident in those contexts in which an increase in provided public services is unperceived by economic agents. They do not get the perception that this increase in services is not made up during the same period of taxation, but rather through the use of public deficit. This implies a simple shift of the increase in taxation to future years, or of an increase in the supply of money, that generates inflationary pressures. Such pressures will cause increases in fiscal pressure and tax revenues, but only in future years.

- ✧ The legal incidence is on the person or company who is legally obliged to pay the tax. Effective, or final, incidence refers to who actually ends up paying the tax;
- ✧ Tax evasion is illegal action in which a individual or company to avoid paying tax liability.

583. Arrange the relative weights in percentage assigned to following criteria by the XIV finance commission in ascending order. *(JUNE 2023)*

A. Income distance

B. Area

C. Population (1971)

D. Demographic change (2011 population)

E. Forest Cover

Choose the correct answer from the options given below:

(a) B,E,D,C,A (b) E,D,B,C,A

(c) A,C,D,B,E (d) E,B,D,C,A

Answer (b)

Solution:

Key Recommendations :-

Devolution of taxes to states :-

The share of taxes to states decreased form 42% to 41 [Vertical Devolution].

→ Horizontal Devaluation→	14th FC	15th FC
Income distance [States with higher average income will get less share]	50	45
Population 1971	17.5	-
Population 2011	10.0	15.0
Area	15.0	15.0
Forest Cover	7.5	-
Forest and Ecology	-	10
[share of dense forest of each state in the aggregate dense forest of all states]		
Demographic Performance	-	12.5
[States with lower fertility ratio will bescored higher]		

Tax effort [Reward States with higher tax collection efficiency	-	2.5
Total	100	100

584. Normalized Poverty Gap (NPG) is measured as a ratio of *(JUNE 2023)*

(a) Average Poverty Gap to poverty line

(b) Total Poverty Gap to poverty line

(c) Total Poverty Gap to total population

(d) Average Poverty Gap to total popultaion

Answer (a)

Solution: The Average poverly gap (APG) is found by dividing the TPG by the total population: TPG/N. Normalized Poverty gap (NPG) = APG/Yp

Average Income shortfall (AIS) = the total poverty gap divided by the headcount of the poor: AIS = TPG/H. It tells us by which amount the income of a poor person falls below the poverty line.

Normalized Income Shortfall, NIS= AIS/Yp.

585. Which of the following holds for Bertrand's Duopoly model. *(JUNE 2023)*

A. the reaction curves are derived from isoprofit maps which are convex to the axis

B. The point of intersection of the two reaction curves reflects a stable equilibriumC. The reaction curves are derived from isoprofit maps which are concave to the axes.

D. The point of intersection of the two reaction curves reflects an unstable equilibrium

E. Firm's behavioral pattern is such that they learn from past experience. Choose the correct answer from the option given below:

(a) A and B only
(b) C and D only
(c) A, D and E only
(d) B, C and E only

Answer (a)

✧ Bertrand developed his duopoly model in 1883. His model differs from Cournot's in that he assumes that each firm expects that the rival will keep its price constant, irrespective of its own decision about pricing.

✧ Thus, each firm is faced by the same market demand, and aims at the maximization of its own profit on the assumption that the price of the competitor will remain constant.

✧ The model may be presented with the analytical tools of the reaction functions of the duopolists.

✧ In Bertrand's model the reaction curves are derived from isoprofit maps which are convex to the axes, on which we now measure the prices of the duopolists. Each isoprofit curve for firm A shows the same level of profit which would accrue to A from various levels of prices charged by this firm and its rival.

- ✧ Talking about the isoprofit curve, an isoprofit curve for a specific level of profit is represented on the basis of the different combinations of prices charged by the rival firm.

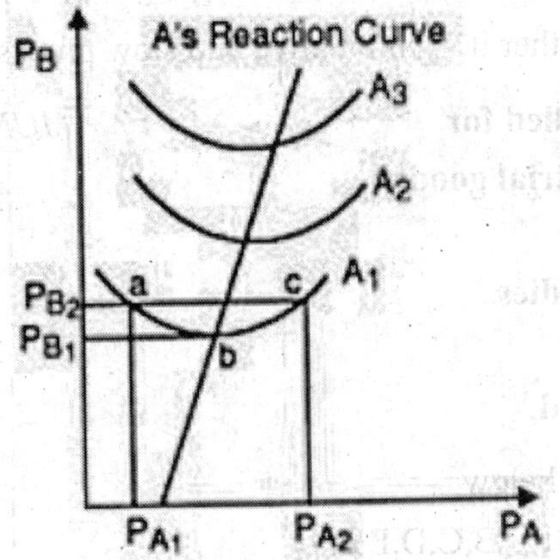

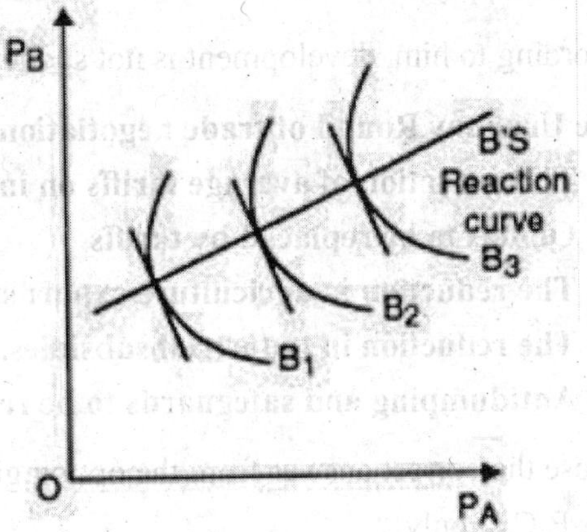

586. Adam Smith contributions are *(JUNE 2023)*

A. Division of labour

B. Notion of increasing returns

C. Notion of diminishing returns

D. Dialectical Materialism

E. Socially necessary abstract labour time

Choose the correct answer from the option given below:

(a) A and B only (b) A and C only

(c) A and D only (d) A and E only

Answer (a)

Solution:

Theories of Development:-

1) Classical theory of development :- (Adam Smith)

Adam Smith is father of Political economy and is the founder of classical school of economics.

Smith's work is "An enquiry into the nature and causes of the wealth of nations".

His views on development :-

1) Capital accumulation should be encouraged.

2) Promoted the concept of division of labor and specialization.

3) Favored laissez-faire policy.

4) Promoted concept of invisible hand. Here invisible hand means market forces of demand and supply.

According to him, development is not sudden; rather it is cumulative and slow process.

587. The Uruguay Round of trade negotiations called for *(JUNE 2023)*

A. The reduction of average tariffs on industrial goods.

B. Quotas to be replaced by tariffs

C. The reduction in agriculture export subsidies.

D. The reduction in industrial subsidies.

E. Antidumping and safeguards to be relaxed.

Choose the correct answer from the option given below:

(a) A,B,C,D only (b) B,C,D,E only

(c) C,D,E,A only (d) D,E,A,B only

Answer (a)

Solution:

GATT[General Agreement on Tariffs and Trade]

Formed in 1947, Headquarters in Geneva (Switzerland).

Principles of GATT:-Non Discrimination

Objective -promotes free trade.

Uruguay round replaced GATT with WTO.

Scope of WTO:-

TRIPS : [Trade related Intellectual Property Rights] Related to patents, copyrights etc.

TRIMS :[Trade related investment measures] Abolition of protection to domestic investment and to allow 100% foreign equity participation in certain cases.

GATS : [General agreement on trade and services] service trade is included in WTO.

AOA : (Agreement on Agriculture)-

Agriculture Subsidies:-

(1) Green box:-No or minimum trade distorting effects.

(2) red box: - All agricultural subsidies which are considered to distort trade and production fall.

(3) Blue box:-red Box subsidies with conditions.

Domestic support:-Reduction of Agricultural subsidies.

Export subsidies:-Abolish

Market access :-Reduction in tariff and non tariff barriers of agriculture products.

Agreement on Textiles and clothing :-Reduction in tariff on textile and clothing.

Agreement on Anti- Dumping :– set rules for allowing countries to take action against dumping in order to defend its domestic industries.

588. Arrange the following in ascending order on the basis of degree of economic integration *(JUNE 2023)*

A. Custom Union
B. Free Trade Area
C. Economic Union
D. Common Market
E. Preferential Trade Arrangements

Choose the correct answer from the option given below:

(a) A,B,C,D,E (b) B,C,D,A,E
(c) E,A,B,C,D (d) E,B,A,D,C

Answer (d)

Economic Integration:- four stages

Free trade area:- Group of nations having no trade restrictions among the members. Example NAFTA (North American Free Trade Association).

Custom Union:- freedom of trade and common tariff policy with non-memvers.

Common Market:- has features of free trade area and custom Union and also there is a free movement of labour and capital.

Economic Union:- Highest level of integration. There is monetary and fiscal unification also.

The fundamental difference between a free trade agreement and a preferential trade agreement is that a preferential trade agreement can be unilateral. In other words, they are relaxations on trade restrictions from one country towards another, without the other country necessarily reciprocating.

589. Match List I with List II *(JUNE 2023)*

	List I		List I
A	Kuznet	I.	Innovation and Entrepreneurship
B	Nurkse	II.	Balanced growth theory
C	Leibenstein	III.	Inverted U- curve hypothesis
D	Schumpeter	IV.	Critical minimum effort thesis

Choose the correct answer from the options given below:

(a) A-I, B-IV, C-III, D-II (b) A-III, B-II, C-IV, D-I

(c) A-IV, B-III, C-II, D-I (d) A-II, B-I, C-IV, D-III

Answer (b)

590. Given below are the alternative formulae for F- test statistics. We are interested in testing the statistical significance of the incremental contribution of X_3 at 5% level of significance to $Y = \beta_0 + \beta_1 X_1 + \beta_2 X_2 + U$. Which of these is not appropriate? Where RSS is residual sum of square and ESS is explained sum of square. *(JUNE 2023)*

$$(a).\ F = \frac{R^2_{UR} - R^2_R / d.f.}{\left(1 - R^2_{UR}\right) / d.f.}$$

$$(b).\ F = \frac{ESS / d.f.}{RSS / d.f.}$$

$$(c).\ F = \frac{ESS_{new} - ESS_{old} / d.f.}{ESS_{new} / d.f.}$$

$$(d)\ F = \frac{R^2 / d.f.}{\left(1 - R^2\right) / d.f.}$$

Answer: (c)

Solution: Show that the test statistic can be calculated as

$$F = \frac{(R^2_{ur} - R^2_r)/q}{(1 - R^2_{ur})/(n-k-1)}$$

where R^2_{ur} and R^2_r are the R-squares from the unrestricted and restricted models, respectively.

$$F = \frac{MSR}{MSE} = \frac{RSS/k}{SSE/(n-k-1)}$$

where:
RSS = regression sum of squares
SSE = sum of squared errors
MSR = mean regression sum of squares
MSE = mean squared error

$$F = \frac{explained\ variation/(k-1)}{unexplained\ variation/(n-k)}$$

$$F = \frac{R^2/(k-1)}{(1-R^2)/(n-k)}$$

591. *(JUNE 2023)*

Integrate : $\int x\sqrt{x^2+1}\,dx \quad x>0$

1. $\frac{1}{2}(x^2+1)^{\frac{3}{2}}+C$
2. $\frac{1}{3}(x^2+1)^{\frac{3}{2}}+C$
3. $\frac{1}{3}(x^3+1)^{\frac{2}{3}}+C$
4. $\frac{1}{2}(x^3+1)^{\frac{2}{3}}+C$

Answer:(b)

$$\int\left(x\sqrt{x^2+1}\right)dx$$

let $x^2+1 = U$

Then $dU = 2x$

But in equation are have anly X, So mulltiply & devide by 2

$$\int\left(\frac{2x\sqrt{x^2+1}}{2}\right)dx$$

$$=\frac{1}{2}\int dU\,(U)^{\frac{1}{2}}$$

$$=\frac{1}{2}\int U^{\frac{1}{2}}\,dx$$

$$=\frac{1}{2}\,\frac{U^{\frac{3}{2}}}{\frac{3}{2}}+C$$

$$=\frac{1}{2}\,U^{\frac{3}{2}}\times\frac{2}{3}+C$$

$$=\frac{1}{3}\,(x^2+1)^{\frac{3}{2}}+C$$

592. According to Tobin's Q theory of investment, when should a firm invest? *(JUNE 2023)*

A. There is increase in the price of output

B. There is an increase in marginal product of capital

C. There is an increase in rate of interest

D. There is a decrease in rate of depreciation

E. Marginal benefit of investment exceeds marginal cost

Choose the correct answer from the option given below:

(a) B,C,D,E only **(b)** A,C,D,E only

(c) A,B,D,E only **(d)** A,B,C,D only

Answer: (c)

Solution: Tobin's q(or the q ratio, and Kaldor's v), is the ratio between a physical asset's market value and its replacement value. It was first introduced by Nicholas Kaldor in 1966. If Tobin's q is greater than 1.0, then the market value is greater than the value of the company's recorded assets.. High Tobin's q values encourage companies to invest more in capital because they are "worth" more than the price they paid for them.

593. Arrange the following chronologically in order of their publication starting from the oldest: *(JUNE 2023)*

A. General Theory of Employment, Interest and Money

B. A treatise on probability

C. Essays in Persuasion

D. The End of Laissez Faire

E. A Tract on Monetary Reform

Choose the correct answer from the option given below:

(a) B,C,D,A,E **(b)** B,E,D,C,A

(c) E,B,D,C,A **(d)** D,E,B,A,C

Answer (b)

594. Arrange the following in order to their year of establishment starting from oldest *(JUNE 2023)*

A. The industrial Credit and Investment Corporation of India (ICICI)

B. National Bank for Agriculture and Rural Development (NABARD)

C. The Industrial Finance Corporation of India (IFCI)

D. The Industrial Reconstruction Bank of India (IRBI)

E. Export-Import Bank of India

Choose the correct answer from the option given below:

(a) A,C,E,B,D (b) C,A,D,E,B

(c) E,C,A,B,D (d) A,D,C,B,E

Answer (b)

SEBI	Setup 1988
IDBI	1964
SIDBI	1989
IFCI	1948
EXIM	1982
UTI	1964
LIC	1956
RRB	1975

ICICI → 1955 (finance small and medium enterprises)

Industrial credit and Investment Corporation of India

Non Banking Financial Intermedaries

Institutions which provide banking services without meeting the legal

definition of bank, that is, one that does not hold a banking license.NBFI's hinder the operation of effective monetary policy. If central bank tries to control lending by commercial banks, it will not be

successful if the lending of NBFI'S are not under its control.

N A B A R D → National bank for Agriculture and Rural Development is an apex development finance institution fully owned by Government of India.

Founded in 1982

Headquarter → Mumbai

Established on the recommendations of Shivaraman committee.

595. Which of the following are recommendations of the Narasumham Committee, 1991. *(JUNE 2023)*

A. Deregulation of the interest rate structure.

B. Need for greater use of informaion technology.

C. Permitting only private sector baanks to access the capital market.

D. Freedom to appoint ehief executive and officers of the banks.

E. Capital adequacy norma were implemented in stages.

Choose the correct answer from the option given below:

(a) A,B and E only (b) A,C and D only

(c) A,D and E only (d) C,D and E only

Answer (c)

Solution:

Banking sector reforms

→ Narsimha committee had brought banking sector reforms

→ Two phases - 1991 and 1998

→ Main aim was to improve the banking sector and change the bank data

Main provisions

1) Reduces SLR and CRR
2) Dual control of banking system by Ministry of Finance and RBI to be abolished
3) liberal view for allowing foreign banks to the country
4) Should have 4 - tier banking system

3 – 4 International Banks

↓

8 – 10 National Banks

↓

Regional Banks

↓

Rural Banks

5) More autonomy to the banks

596. According to Robinson the term 'Golden Age' in the context of HarrodDomar model is used to emphasize *(JUNE 2023)*

(a) Its mythical nature (b) Its superiority

(c) Natural growth rate (d) Warranted growth rate

Answer (a)

Solution: Joan Robinson referred to the situation where g = gw =gn and the unemployment gap is zero as the "Golden Age" growth path, "thus indicating that it represents a mythical state of affairs not likely to obtain in any actual economy"

597. The book entitled, "Why Nations Fail; The origin of Power, Prosperity and Poverty" has been written by, *(JUNE 2023)*

(a) Abhijit Banerjee

(b) Daron Acemoglu and James A. Robinson

(c) Amartya Sen

(d) Joseph Stiglitz

Answer (b)

598. The components of services sector in Gross Value Added (GVA) are *(JUNE 2023)*

(A) Construction

(B) Trade, Hotels, Transport and Communication related to Broadcasting

(C) Electricity, Gas. Water supply and other utility services

(D) Public Administration, Defense and other services

(E) Financial, Real Estate and Professional services

Choose the correct answer from the option given below:

(a) B, C and E only

(a) A, B and C only

(a) A, B, D and E only

(a) A, B, C and E only

Answer (c) : The components in 'C' are part of manufacturing sector.

599. Given: *(JUNE 2023)*

I = 50+0.2Y

S = -150+0.4Y

G =50

Where I= investment, S =Saving, G =government expenditure, Y =National Income

What is the equilibrium level of national income?

(a) 1250 (b) 1500 (c) 250 (d) 2500

Answer: a

Solution:

I+G = S

50+0.2Y+50 = -150+0.4Y

100+0.2Y = -150+0.4Y

100+150 = 0.4Y -0.2Y

250 = 0.2Y

2500/2 =Y

1250

600. Given *(Year 2021)*

$Y = X^3 - 12X^2 + 36X + 8$, Identify which one of the following is correct?

(a) Y is maximum at X =6 and minimum at X =2

(b) Y is minimum at X =6 and maximum at X =2

(c) Y has two inflexion point at X =6 and X =2

(d) Y is maximum at X =2 and minimum at X =6

Answer: b

Solution:

$Y = X^3 - 12X^2 + 36X + 8$

$Y^1 = 3X^2 - 24X + 36 = 0$

$X^2 - 8X + 12 = 0$

$X^2 - 6X - 2X + 12 = 0$

$X(X-6) - 2(X-6) = 0$

X =6, 2

$Y^{11} = 6X - 24$

Put X=6

$Y^{11} = 8$(min)

Put X =2

$Y^{11} = -12$(max)

So Y is max at X=6 and min at X=2.

601. In random walk without drift,

(a) The effect of shock persist throughout the timeperiod.

(b) The effect of shock in the past dies out over time

(c) . The effect of shock drifts away quickly

(d) there is no effect of past shock

Answer (a)

Solution:

a) Random Walk without Drift

- The time series Y_t is said to be a random walk without drift, if

$$Y_t = Y_{t-1} + u_t \quad .... (4)$$

- Here, the value of Y at time **(t)** is equal to its value at time (t – 1) plus a random shock; thus it is an AR(1) model.
- Believers in the **Efficient Capital Market Hypothesis** argue that stock prices are essentially random and therefore there is no scope for profitable speculation in the stock market:
- If one could predict tomorrow's price on the basis of today's price, we would all be millionaires.

b) Random Walk with Drift

- Let's modify, $Y_t = Y_{t-1} + u_t$..............(4) as follows:

$$Y_t = \delta + Y_{t-1} + u_t \text{.....................(9)}$$

where δ is the drift parameter.

- The name drift comes from the fact that if we write the preceding equation as:

$$Y_t - Y_{t-1} = \Delta Y_t = \delta + u_t \quad .... \quad (10)$$

- It shows that Y_t drifts upward/downward, depending on δ being positive/negative.

DECEMBER 2023

1. Consider the payoffs of two players, who are close friends. They can either go for Diwali shopping or they can watch a World Cup cricket match.

		Player 1	
Player 2	Diwali shopping	(2,1)	(0,0)
	World cup	(0,0)	(1,2)

Identify which of the following is true for them:W

a. There is no Nash equilibrium for them

b. There is only one Nash equilibrium where player 1 goes for Diwali shopping and player 2 goes for a World Cup match.

c. Any of four combinations can be a Nash equilibrium

d. There are two Nash equilibrium.

Answer: (d)

Solution: Player 1 chooses '1' from '1' and '0' and will choose '2' from '0' and '2'. Strategies lie in different columns. So, it is not a dominant strategy. Player 2 chooses '2' from '2' and '0' and will choose '1' from '0' and '1'. Strategies lie in different rows. It also does not have a dominant strategy. **So, there are two Nash equilibriums (2,1) and (1,2).**

2. Suppose an economy is in medium-run equilibrium. Now the government enacts a law, making entry of new firms difficult, which increases the monopoly power the existing firms. Which of the following statements are true about this change?

(A) Output level will be lower in medium-run

(B) Output level will be lower in the short-run

(C) The Price level will be higher in the medium-run

(D) Price level will be higher in short run

Choose the correct answer from the options given below

(a) (A) and (C) Only

(b) (B), (C) and (D) Only

(c) (B) and (C) Only

(d) (A), (B) (C), and (D) Only

Answer: (d)

Solution: With the increase in monopoly power, the output level will be lower and the price level will be higher.

3.

. Suppose a cost function of producing q level of output in C(w,r,q) where $C(w,r,q) = q(\frac{w}{\alpha} + \frac{r}{\beta})$, where w and r are the wage cost and rental cost of 2 input capital (K) and labour (L) respectively. What will be the production function q of K and L?

1. $q=\alpha k+\beta L$
2. $q=[k^{\alpha}+L^{\beta}]^{r}$
3. $q=\min(\alpha l, K\beta)$
4. $q=A(k^{\alpha}.L^{\beta})$

Answer: 3

Solution:

$$C = q\left[\frac{w}{\alpha} + \frac{r}{\beta}\right] \text{ or } C = \left[\frac{qw}{\alpha} + \frac{qr}{\beta}\right]$$

$$\frac{\partial c}{\partial w} = L = \frac{q}{\alpha} \text{ or } q = \alpha L$$

$$\frac{\partial c}{\partial w} = K = \frac{q}{\beta} \text{ or } q = \beta K$$

Q is a function of αL and βK

4. If the average revenue function AR = 10+5q-q2, then the marginal revenue function is a:

(a) Convex function

(b) Concave function

(c) Can be both concave and convex function

(d) Weakly concave function

Answer: (b)

Solution: $AR = 10 + 5q - q^2$

$TR = 10q + 5Q^2 - Q^3$

$MR = 10 + 10Q - 3Q^2$

$\frac{\partial MR}{\partial q} = 10 - 6q$

$\frac{\partial^2 (AR)}{\partial^2 q} = -6 < 0$(maxima)

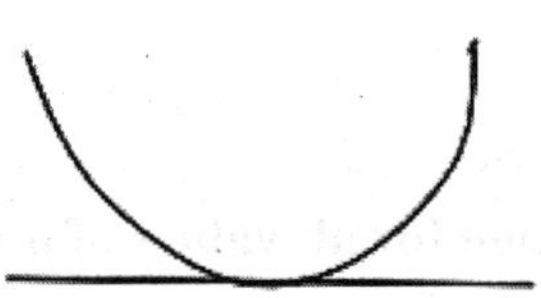

Minima, convex, 2nd derivation positive

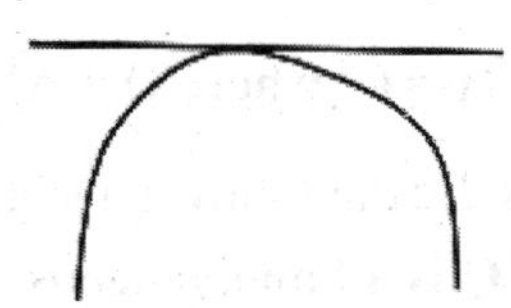

Maxima, concave, 2nd derivation negative

So, MR is concave.

5. In the case of two perfect complement goods, which of the following statements is not true?

a. The substitution effect is zero

b. The indifference curves are straight lines

c. The indifference curve are L shaped

d. The goods are always demanded in fixed proportions.

Answer: (b)

Solution:

(a) Substitutes

For perfect substitutes, MRS_{XY} = Constant and $E_S = \infty$ [infinity]

For perfect complements, MRS_{XY} = Zero and $E_S = 0$

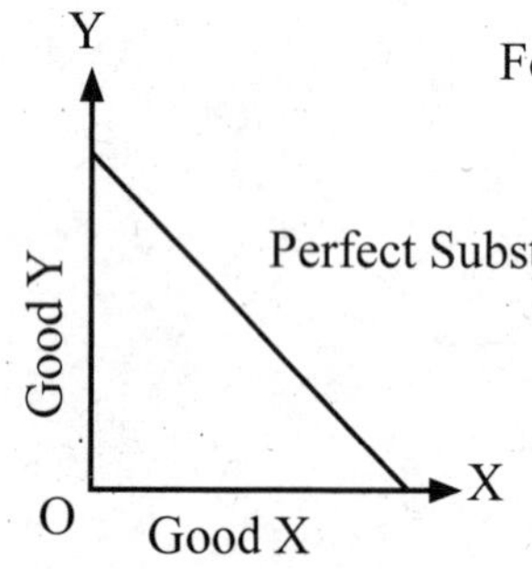

(b) Complements

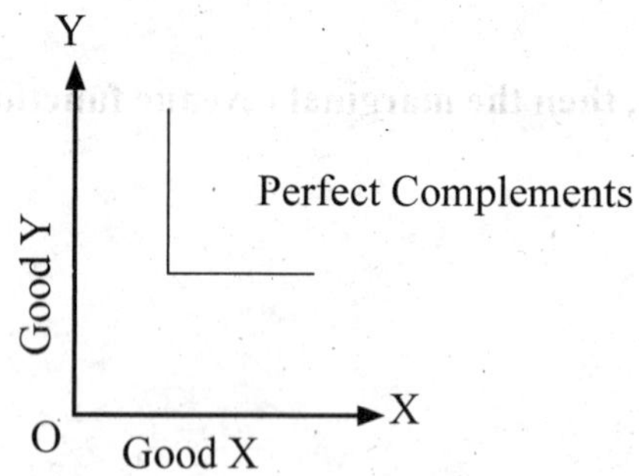

6. Let $H = e^Q$ where $Q = AX^{\alpha}Y^{\beta}$

Consider the following statements:

(A) Q is a homogeneous function for all values of α and β

(B) H is a homothetic function for all values of α and β

(C) Q is a homogeneous function only of α+β = 1

(D) H is not a homogeneous function

(E) Q is not a homogeneous function

Choose the correct answer from the options given below:

1. (A) and (B) only
2. (A) (B) and (D) only
3. (C) and (A) only
4. (E) and (D) only

Answer: 2

Solution:

A homogeneous function is a function of many variables such that if all variables of function multiplies by scaler then value of function multiplied by some power of same scaler.

For eg. $Y = X^2 + Z^2$

Multiplied with scaler λ

$=(\lambda X)^2 + (\lambda Z)^2$

$= \lambda 2(X^2+Z^2)$

$= \lambda^2 Y$

The degree of homogeneity is 2.

A function with degree n is called a homogeneous function. Homogeneous functions are a subset of set of homothetic functions.

All homogeneous functions are homothetic but not all homothetic functions are homogeneous.

Homogeneity of degrees 1 , 2 and less than 1 means constant returns to scale, increasing returns to scale, and decreasing returns to scale.

Therefore, in this question, $Q = AX^{\alpha}Y^{\beta}$ is homogeneous function and $H = e^Q$ is homothetic function H.

7. **Following are five statements about short run cost curves.**

(A) The Marginal Cost (MC) curve cuts both short run Average Cost (AC) curve and Average Variable Cost (AVC) curve at their lowest point

(B) The MC curve cuts AC curve from below, but nothing can be said about the AVC curve

(C) The distance between Total Cost (TC) curve and Total Variable Cost (TVC) curve gets reduced as quantity increases.

(D) The Average Fixed Cost (AFC) curve is asymptotic to the cost axis.

(E) The AC curve is u-shaped.

Choose the correct answer from the options given below:

(1) (A), (C) (D), (E) Only

(2) (B), (C), (E) Only

(3) (A), (E) Only

(4) (D) (E) (A) Only

Answer: 3

Solution:

- MC cuts both AVC and AC at their minimum points
- TC and TVC are parallel to each other
- AFC is asymptotic to both cost (y axis) and quantity (x axis).

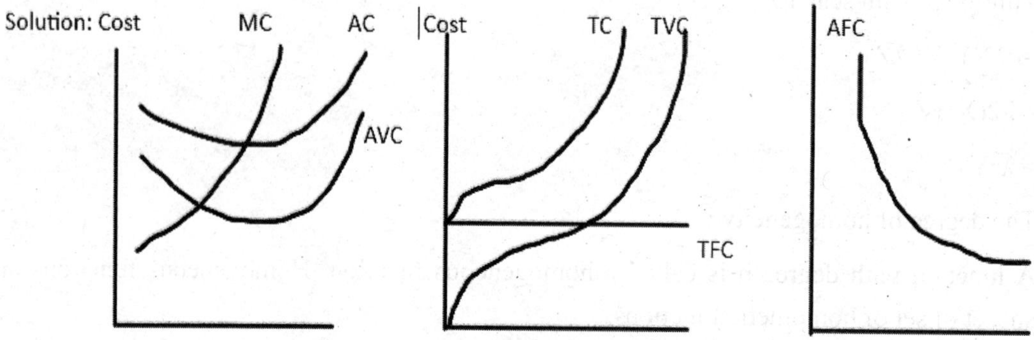

8. suppose production function q = f(K,L), is a homogeneous function of degree 1.

A. the marginal products of labor and capital $\frac{dQ}{dL}$ and $\frac{dQ}{dK}$ are homogeneous of degree 1.

B. the second order cross marginal product of k and L are equal $\left(\frac{d2Q}{dLdK} = \frac{d2Q}{dkdL}\right)$

C. By Euler's Theorem : $L\frac{dQ}{dL} + K\frac{dQ}{dK} = Q$

D. By Euler's Theorem : $L\frac{d^2Q}{dL^2} + K\frac{d^2Q}{dK^2} = 0$

Choose the correct answer from the options given below

1. A and B
2. A,B,C
3. A,C,D
4. B,C,D

Answer: 4

Solution:

If Q is a homogeneous function of degree n, then

$$\frac{dQ}{dL} + K\frac{dQ}{dK} = nQ$$

Euler's theorem is homogeneous of degree 1, so in this case

$$L\frac{dQ}{dL} + K\frac{dQ}{dK} = Q$$

Suppose homogeneous function of degree 1 is $Q = AL^{\alpha}K^{\beta}$

$$\frac{dQ}{dL} = \alpha AL^{\alpha-1}K^{\beta}$$

$$K\frac{dQ}{dK} = \beta AK^{\beta-1}L^{\alpha}$$

$$\frac{d2Q}{dKdL} = \alpha\beta AL^{\alpha-1}K^{\beta-1}$$

$$\frac{d2Q}{dLdK} = \beta\alpha AL^{\alpha-1}K^{\beta-1}$$

So, second order cross marginal products are equal.

9. Match list 1 with list 2

List 1		List 2	
a.	Shephard's lemma	i.	Hidden types of agent
b.	Adverse selection	ii.	envelop theorem
c.	Hotelling lemma	iii.	Indirect utility function
d.	Roy's identity	iv.	profit function

Choose the correct answer

1. a-iv,b-i,c-ii,d-iii
2. a-ii,b-i,c-iv,d-iii
3. a-ii,b-i,c-iii,d-iv
4. a-ii,b-iv,c-i,d-iii

Answer: 2

Solution:

1. **Shephard's lemma :** It is formula used to obtain Hicksian demand function for good X or Y directly from Expenditure function by forming the following ratio of partial derivatives.
   ∂ expenditure function/ ∂ price of good X
   Shephard's lemma is immediate application of Envelop theorem.
   Envelop theorem states that the change in optimal value of a function wrt the parameters of the function can be found by partially differentiating the objective function while holding X constant at its optimal value.

2. Adverse selection refers to a situation where sellers have more information than buyers have, or vice versa, about some aspect of product quality, although typically the more knowledgeable party is the seller. Adverse selection occurs when asymmetric information is exploited.

3. Hotelling's lemma is a result in microeconomics that relates the supply of a good to the maximum profit of the producer. It was first shown by Harold Hotelling, and is widely used in the theory of the firm.

4. A consumer's indirect utility function gives the maximum level of utility from a given set of prices and income, consistent with consumer's constrained optimization problem. It is a function of prices of goods and consumer's budget. It is denoted as V(p1,p2,m) where m is budget and p1, p2 are prices.
   Consumer demand function can be expressed as a ratio of derivatives of the indirect utility function, a result known as Roy's identity. i.e.

$$X = -\frac{\partial \text{ Indirect utility}/ \partial \text{ price of X}}{\partial \text{ Indirect utility}/ \partial \text{ income}}$$

10. In the given figure, DD is the demand curve and SS is the supply curve in a market. Choose the right answer from the following.

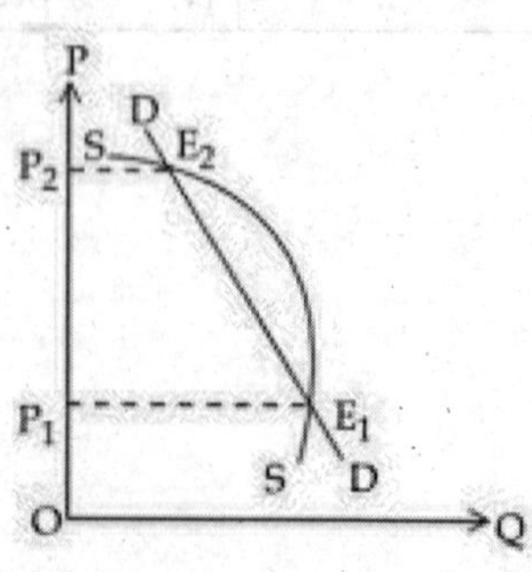

a. there is no stable equilibrium

b. E2 is the stable equilibrium, though E1 is an unstable equilibrium

c. E1 is the stable equilibrium, though E2 is an unstable equilibrium

d. Both E1 and E2 are stable equilibria

Answer: 3

Solution:

Stability of Equilibrium :-

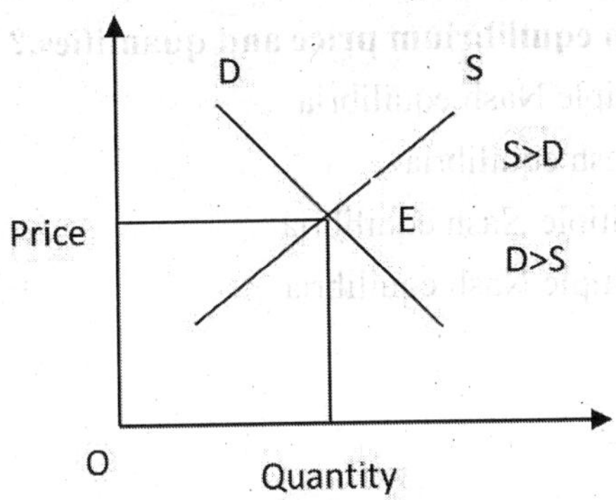

Stable equilibrium

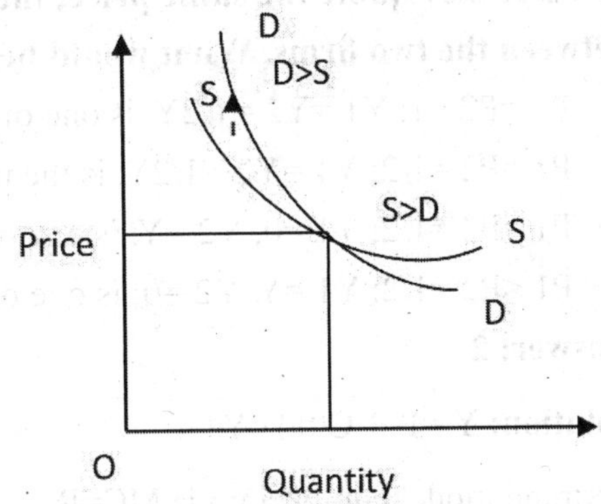

Unstable equilibrium

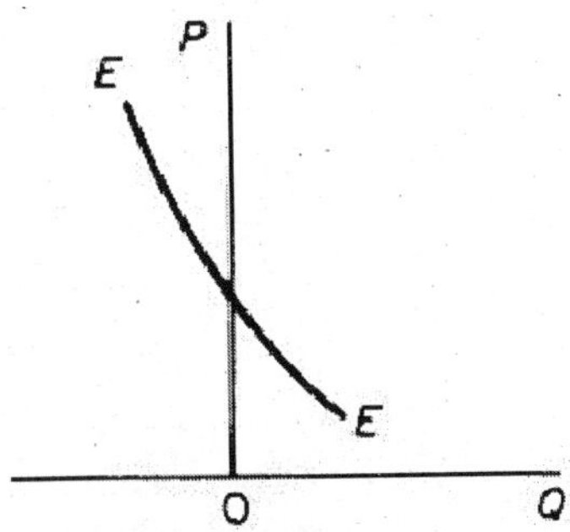

Stable equilibrium: slope of $E_{(P)} < 0$

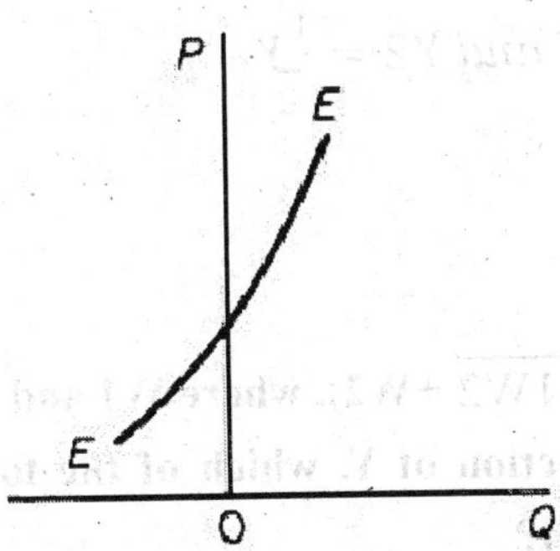

Unstable equilibrium: slope of $E_{(P)} > 0$

The equilibrium is stable if the slope of excess demand curve is negative at the point of intersection with the price axis.

The equilibrium is unstable if the slope of excess demand curve is positive at the point of intersection with the price axis.

11. **Consider a Bertrand duopoly where the 2 firms produce a homogeneous product. Assume the market demand curve is $y = y_1+y_2 = 1-p$, where p is the relevant market price, y is the total amount demanded at that price, y_1 and y_2 are the output levels of firms (1)and (2) respectively.**

Assume that the firms cost functions are C(yi) = ½ yi for I = 1,2. The rules of pricing game are as follows : each firm must simultaneously quote a price in the interval [0,1]. If the price are different, the firm with the lower price sells all the units demanded at that price. If they quote the same price, the amount demanded at that price is splited equally between the two firms. What would be the nash equilibrium price and quantities.?

a. P1 =P2 =1; Y1 =Y2 =1/2Y; is one of the multiple Nash equilibria

b. P1 =P2 =1/2; Y1 =Y2 =1/2Y; is the unique Nash equilibria

c. P1 >P2 =1/2; Y1 =0, Y2 =Y; is one of the multiple Nash equilibria

d. P1 <P2 =1/2; Y1 =Y, Y2 =0; is one of the multiple Nash equilibria

Answer: 2

Solution: Y =1-P, C = ½ Y

Bertrand model equilibrium is MC=P

MC= ½

P = 1-Y

½ = 1-Y

$Y = 1 - \frac{1}{2}$

$Y = \frac{1}{2}$

$P = 1 - \frac{1}{2} = \frac{1}{2}$

Quantity is split equally between two firms $Y1 = \frac{1}{2}Y$ and $Y2 = \frac{1}{2}Y$

i.e. $Y1 = Y2 = \frac{1}{4}$

12. **Suppose the cost function $C(W1,W2,Y)=Y(W1+\sqrt{W1W2}+W2)$, where W1 and W2 are the prices of 2 inputs which are used in the production of Y. which of the following properties of the cost function C(W1,W2,Y) is correct?**

(a) Cost function C(W1,W2,Y)is monotone, concave and continuous function in W1, W2.

(b) Cost function C(W1,W2,Y)is a non monotone, convex and continuous function in W1, W2.

(c) Cost function is continuous in W1 and W2 and discontinuous function in Y.

(d) Cost function is a continuous function and homogeneous function in degree 0.

Answer: (a)

Solution: Monotonic function is a function if it is increasing or decreasing. i.e.,

$Y=2x+3$

$Y=-x^5$

Function is non monotonic if it is both increasing and decreasing. i.e., $Y=X^2$

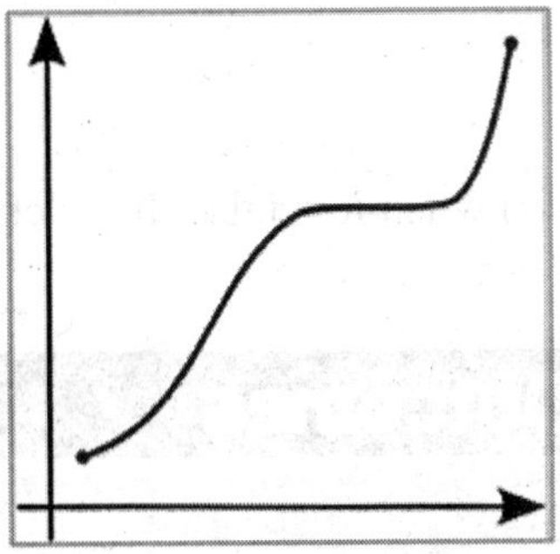

Figure 1 - A monotonically increasing function

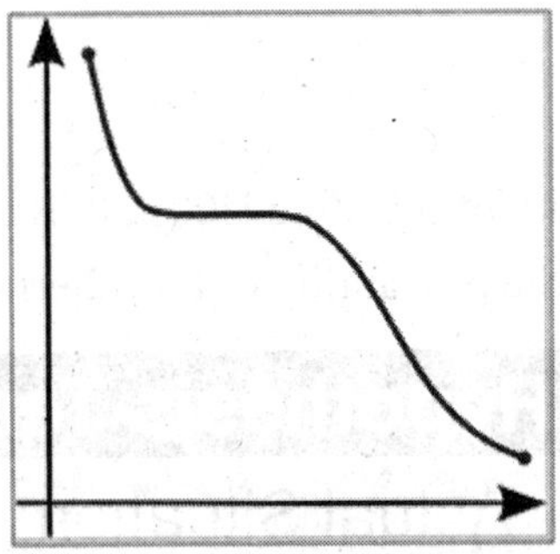

Figure 2 - A monotonically decreasing function

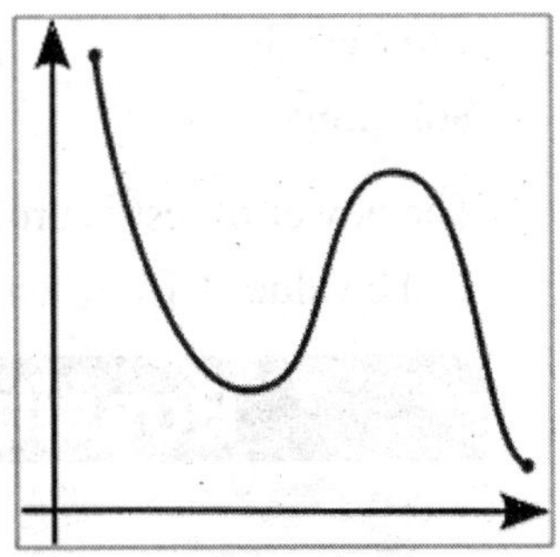

Figure 3 - A function that is not monotonic

$C = Y(W1+\sqrt{W1W2} + W2)$

2nd derivative of this function wrt w1 and w2 is -ve , so it is concave concave, maximise 2nd derivation

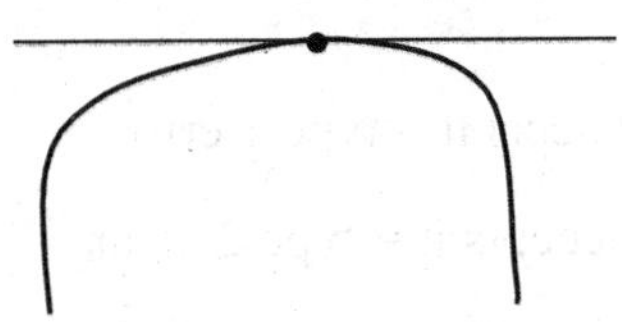

13. If the estimated slope coefficient in the regression of Y on X is β. What will be the estimated slope coefficient in the regression of 5Y on 10X.

1. 5β
2. 10β
3. 2β
4. 0.5β

Answer: 4

Solution:

Y=a+X/ β Slope of this line is β

5Y=a+10X/ β

Y=a/5+10X/5 β

Slope is 5 β /10

=0.5 β

14. The power of test refers to

a. Type 1 error

b. Type 2 error

c. 1-type 2 error

d. 1-type 1 error

Answer: 3

Solution:

The power of test is probability of rejecting H0 (null hypothesis) when it is false. It is defined as the value '1-β', when β is the probability of type 2 error.

Possible Hypothesis Test Outcomes		
	Actual Situation	
Decision	H0 True	H0 False
Accept H0	No error	Type II error
	Probability = 1 - α	Probability = β
Reject H0	Type I error	No error
	Probability = α	Probability = 1 - β

Hypothesis is true, but our test rejects it = type 1 error

Hypothesis is false but our test accepts it = type 2 error

- **Level of Significance -** The maximum size of Type I error, which we are ready to risk is called as level of significance. It can be 5% or 1 %. If we fix 5% level, it means we are 95% confident that our decision to reject null hypothesis is true.
- **Power of Test** – The probability of committing Type II error is denoted by β. It is defined as the value '1-β'. Our aim is to fix level of significance at 'α' and then maximize '1-β'.

15. Given the random sample of size n from the population with mean μ and variance σ2, the sample mean has the following expected value and variance:

1) $E(\overline{x}) = \mu$ $Var(\overline{x}) = \sigma^2$/n

2) $E(\overline{x}) = n\mu$ $Var(\overline{x}) = n\sigma^2$

3) $E(\overline{x}) = \mu$ $Var(\overline{x}) = \sigma^2$

4) $E(\overline{x}) = \mu$ $Var(\overline{x}) = n/\sigma^2$

Answer: 1

16. In a regression of the dependent variable on intercept and k other independent variable using n observation, what are respectively numerator and denominator degree of freedom for the F test for overall significance of the regression?

a. K-1, n-k

b. K,n-1-k

c. K-1, n-k-1

d. K, n-k

Answer:2

Solution: Formula to test overall significance of regression

$$F = \frac{MSR}{MSE} = \frac{RSS/K}{\frac{SSE}{n-k-1}}$$

Where, RSS = regression sum of squares

SSE = sum of squared errors

MSR = Mean regression sum of squares

MSE = mean squared errors

17. Given below are the two statements, one is labeled as assertion and the other is labeled as Reason (R)

Assertion (A): Given a random sample, the distribution of the sample mean tends to a normal distribution, as the sample size becomes very large.

Reason (R): Central limit theorem

In the light of the above statements, choose the most appropriate answer from the options given Below:

(1) Both (A) and (R) are correct and (R) is the correct explanation of (A)

(2) Both (A) and (R) are correct but (R) is not the correct explanation of (A)

(3) (A) is correct but (R) is not correct

(4) (A) is not correct but (IR) is correct

Answer: 1

Solution: The central limit theorem says that the sampling distribution of the mean will always be normally distributed as long as the sample size is large enough.

18. Match the following.

a.	sum of squares of n independent standard normal variables	1.	t distribution
b.	Ratio of a standard normal variate to square root of an independent, chi square variable(divided by its degree of freedom)	2.	f distribution
c.	Ratio of 2 independent chi square variables each divided by their respective degree of freedom	3.	standard normal distribution
d.	Normal variate minus its mean, divided by its standard deviation	4.	chi-square distribution

Choose the correct answer:

1. A-1, B-4, C-2, D-3
2. A-4, B-1, C-3, D-2
3. A-1, B-4, C-3, D-2
4. A-4, B-1, C-2, D-3

Answer: 4

Solution: A random variable has a Chi-square distribution if it can be written as a sum of squares of independent standard normal variables.

A t-distribution is the ratio of a Standard Normal divided by the square root of a Chi-square divided by it's degrees of freedom, e.g., Z / sqrt(C/c), where Z is a standard normal RV, C is the Chi-square RV, and c is the degrees of freedom.

An F distribution is the ratio of two Chi-square variables, each of which is divided its respective degrees of freedom. So (C1/c1) / (C2/c2), where the capital letters are the random variable (RV), and the lowercase are the degrees of freedom. Standard normal distribution formula

$z = (X - \mu) / \sigma$

where X is a normal random variable, μ is the mean of X, and σ is the standard deviation of X. You can also find the normal distribution formula here. In probability theory, the normal or Gaussian distribution is a very common continuous probability distribution.

19. Suppose you are testing a null hypothesis about the population mean, H0: μ= μ0, against H1: μ>μ0, with population variance given, the computed value of the test static is Zc. What is the p-value for this test, where ϕ () is the cumulative distribution function for the standard normal distribution?

1) Φ(Zc)
2) Φ(Zc/2)
3) 1 − Φ(Zc)
4) 1 − Φ(Zc/2)

Answer: 3

Solution:

To determine the p-value, you need to know the distribution of your test statistic under the assumption that the null hypothesis is true. Then, with the help of the cumulative distribution function (CDF) of this distribution, we can express the probability of the test statistics being at least as extreme as its value x for the sample:

Left-tailed test:

p-value = cdf(x).

Right-tailed test:

p-value = 1 - cdf(x).

Two-tailed test:

p-value = 2 × min{cdf(x) , 1 - cdf(x)}.

Generally, the level of statistical significance is often expressed in p-value and the range between 0 and 1. The smaller the p-value, the stronger the evidence and hence, the result should be statistically significant. Hence, the rejection of the null hypothesis is highly possible, as the p-value becomes smaller.

The p-value table shows the hypothesis interpretations:

P- value	**Decision**
P-value > 0.05	The result is not statistically significant and hence do not reject the null hypothesis
P-value < 0.05	The result is statistically significant and Generally, reject the null hypothesis in favour of the alternative hypothesis.
P-value < 0.01	The result is highly statistically significant and thus, reject the null hypothesis in favour of the alternative hypothesis.

20. The OLS regression output of wages on education (years of schooling S) and cognitive ability scores (CA) comes out to be:

$\widehat{wages}$ = -3.36+0.64S + 0.15 CA

(1.98) (0.12) (0.05)

With figures in parenthesis giving standard error.

The explained sum of square is 4745.75 with degree of freedom 2 and residual sum of square is 33651.28 with degree of freedom 567, which of the following statements are true?

A. **For one year increase in schooling, wage per hour increases by 640 rs. on the average, when CA is kept constant.**

B. **The value of t-statistic of CA is 3**

C. **The F statistic is given by** $F = \frac{4735.75/2}{33651.28/567}$

D. **The F statistic is given by** $F = \frac{33651.28/567}{4745.75/2}$

Choose the correct answer:

1. A,C
2. A,B,D
3. A,B,C
4. A, D

Answer: 3

Solution: Wages= -3.36+0.64s+0.15CA

Wages depend on schooling and cognitive ability scores.

0.64 means – for 1 year increase in schooling, wages increase by Rs. 640. When CA is held constant. (there is positive sign, so wages and S has positive relation)

Test statistic for CA = $\frac{\hat{\beta}-\beta}{SS(\beta)} = \frac{0.15}{0.05} = 3$

F statistic $= \frac{ESS/df}{RSS/df}$

$= \frac{4735.75/2}{33651.28/567}$

ESS- explained sum of square

RSS – residual sum of square

21.

List 1 -Model or method		**List 2**	
a.	Logit model	i.	Elasticities are constant
b.	Log-log model	ii.	binary dependent variable
c.	Auto regressive model	iii.	corrects for heteroscedasticity
d.	Weighted least squares	iv.	Includes lags of the dependent variable

1) (a-ii)(b-i)(c-iii)(d-iv)
2) (a-i)(b-ii)(c-iv)(d-iii)
3) (a-i)(b-ii)(c-iii)(d-iv)
4) (a-ii)(b-i)(c-iv)(d-iii)

Answer: 4

Solution: Weighted least square is a method used to correct heteroscedasticity in model.

Auto Regressive Model : A model is said to be auto regressive when the current value of dependent variable is a function of current value of independent variable and lagged value of dependent variable.

$$Y_t = \beta_0 + \beta_1 X_t + \beta_2 Y_{t-1} + u_t$$

Generalized least Square Model : The procedure of transforming the original variable in such a way that the transformed variables satisfy the assumption of the classical model and then applying OLS to it is known as the method of Generalised Least Square Model.

Discrete Choice Models:

Discrete choice model specifies the probability that an individual chooses an option among a set of alternatives. For eg. the choice of which car a person buys is statistically related to the person's income and age as well as to price, fuel efficiency, size and other attributes of available case.

Two types : 1) Binary Log it Model

2) Binary Probit Model

They are dummy dependent models in which dependent variable in considered dummy.

Model	Equation	Interpretation
Level-Level Regression	$Y = \alpha + \beta X$	One unit change in X leads to β unit change in Y
Log-Linear Regression	$log(Y) = \alpha + \beta X$	One unit change in X leads to $100 * \beta$ percent change in Y
Linear-Log Regression	$Y = \alpha + \beta \, log(X)$	One percent change in X leads to $\beta/100$ unit change in Y
Log-Log Regression	$log(Y) = \alpha + \beta \, log(X)$	One percent change in X leads to β percent change in Y

22. For a VAR model estimated using two variables X and Y. Lags of Y are jointly significant in the equation for X but Lags of X are jointly insignificant in the equation for Y. What can you conclude

(1) There is no Granger causality between X and Y

(2) There is bidirectional Granger causality between X and Y

(3) X Granger causes X but Y does not Granger cause X

(4) Y Granger causes X but X does not Granger cause Y

Answer: 4

Solution: Granger causality is a test to verify the usefulness of one variable to forecast other.

Equation of X

$X = \beta_0 + \beta_1 Y_t + \beta_2 Y_{t-1} + \beta_2 Y_{t-2} + \mu t$

Lags of Y are jointly significant.

Thus, Y granger causes X

Equation for Y

$Y = \beta_0 + \beta_1 X_t + \beta_2 X_{t-1} + \beta_2 X_{t-2} + \mu t$

Lags of X are jointly insignificant.

Thus, X does not Granger cause Y

23. Chow Test is normally run to understand if a single regression run on pooled data is more efficient to describe a relation between a dependent variable and a set of independent variables than the same regression being run separately on two subgroups of the sample. The steps involved in running the Chow Test are:

(A) Run the regression model on the pooled sample and calculate RSSp

(B) Run the same regression model on the two sub-samples separately and calculate RSS1 and RSS2

(C) Calculate the F statistic

(D) Check the critical F with related degrees of freedom and compare it with F calculated

(E) Do not reject H0 if Fcalculated <Fcritical

Choose the correct answer from the options given below:

(1) (A), (B), (C) (D) (E) (2) (A),(D),(C)(B),(E)

(3) (C),(A),(B),(D),(E) (4) (C),(B),(A),(D),(E)

Answer: 1

Solution:

- Sometimes your data will have a break point or structural point (a period of significant or violent change), splitting a data set into two parts. For example:Donations given to an organization before and after a natural disaster.Stock market prices before and after Black Friday.House prices before and after a significant interest change.Asset prices before and after civil war.

- ✧ If the two parts can be represented by one single regression line, we say that the regression can be "pooled."Let's say your linear regression analysis of two parts of a data set (shown on the right) resulted in the following two linear regression equations
- ✧ First part of the data: yt = X1*b1 + μ1Second part of the data: yt = X2*b2 + μ2
- ✧ The Chow test would tell you if the coefficients b1 = b2 and μ1 = μ2. If they are equal, the data set can be represented with a single regression line
- ✧ Running the Test
- ✧ The null hypothesis for the test is that there is no break point (i.e. that the data set can be represented with a single regression line).
- ✧ Run a regression for the entire data set (the "pooled regression"). Collect the error Sum of Squares data
- ✧ Run separate regressions on each half of the data set. Collect the Error Sum of Squares data for the two regressions.
- ✧ Calculate the Chow F statistic using the SSE from each subsample. The formula is: chow-test- formula

$$\text{Chow} = \frac{(RSSp-(RSS_1+RSS_2))/k}{(RSS_1+RSS_2)/(N_1+N_2-2k)}$$

where:

- RSSp = pooled (combined) regression line.
- RSS_1 = regression line before break.
- RSS_2 = regression line after break.
- Find the F-critical value from the F-table.
- Reject the null hypothesis if your calculated F-value falls into the rejection region (i.e. if the calculated F-value is greater than the F-critical value).

24. Given that Z_t is a zero mean white noise process with variance σ^2, which of the following are I(O) process?

a. $X_t = X_{t-1} + Z_t$

b. $X_t = \alpha X_{t-1} + Z_t$ (where $0<\alpha<1$)

c. $X_t = Z_t + Z_t-1$

d. $X_t = 8 + X_{t-1} + Z_t$

Choose the correct answer:

1. C only
2. B only
3. B and C
4. B, C and D

Answer: 3

25. Which of the following statements is not true for the Linear Probability Model (LPM) ?

(A) Conditional probability of occurrence of an event conditional on the value of explanatory variable X is a linear function of X

(B) Estimated value of the conditional probability of occurrence of the event lies between 0 and 1

(C) Error term is homoscedastic

(D) R^2 is a good measure of goodness of fit

Choose the correct answer from the options given below:

(1) (B) Only
(2) (B) and (C) Only
(3) (B), (C) and (D) Only
(4) (C) Only

Answer: 3

1. In LPM, There is nonfulfillment of $0<E(Yi|Xi)<1$
2. Error term is homoscedastic
3. R_2 may not be a measure of goodness of fit in such models.

26. Which of the following are features of a weakly stationary stochastic process?

(A) Mean is time varying

(B) Mean is constant

(C) Variance is constant

(D) Covariance is time invariant

Choose the correct answer from the options given below:

1. B and C only
2. B,C, D only
3. A,C,D only
4. A and C only

Answer: 2

Solution:

Features of weakly stationary stochastic process

1. Mean is constant
2. Variance is constant
3. Covariance is time invariant

Features of strict stationary stochastic process

1. Probability distribution does not change over time.

27. In the model In yi = α + βxi +ui, where In is natural log, the elasticity of y with respect to x is given by

a. β
b. βxi
c. β/yi
d. $\beta\frac{xi}{yi}$

Answer: 2

Solution: In yi = α + βxi +ui

$= \frac{1}{yi}\frac{\Delta y}{\Delta x} = \beta \ or \ \frac{\Delta y}{\Delta x} = \beta yi$

$= \frac{\Delta y}{\Delta x} \times \frac{\dot{x}}{yi}$

$= \beta yi \times \frac{xi}{yi}$

$= \beta xi$

28. Suppose Xi is the income of an individual I and Yi is the event that this individual owns a house, Pi = prob(Yi=1 | Xi) and Zi=β1+β2 Xi, which of the following is true for the logit model?

1)Pi = $\frac{1}{1-e^{-z_i}}$

2) Pi = $\frac{1}{1+e^{z_i}}$

3)Pi = $\frac{1}{1+e^{-z_i}}$

4)Pi = $\frac{1}{1-e^{z_i}}$

Answer:3

Solution: Logit, Probit and Tobit Mmodels

These are dummy dependent variables models

Logit Follows logistic distribution

$L_i = \ln(\frac{P_i}{1-P_i})$

Pi is probability of happening an event i.e. adoption of technology.

(1-pi) is probability of not happening an event.

P goes from 0 to 1, L from $-\infty$ *to* ∞

$Pi = \frac{1}{1+e^{-z_i}}$

where zi = $\beta_0 + \beta_1 x$

Pi=prob(yi=1 | Xi)

Means probability of y gives x.

29. Which of the following tests has stationary as null hypothesis?

a. **ADF test**

b. **Phillips perron test**

c. **ERS test**

d. **KPSS test**

Answer: 4

Solution: Tests of stationary in time series dicky fuller – for the first order autoregression model

Augmented dicky fuller – for the higher order autoregression model. It is used in the case of auto correlation in the model.

H_0 = series is non-stationary H1 = series is stationary

The Phillips–Perron test (named after Peter C. B. Phillips and Pierre Perron) is a unit root test. That is, it is used in time series analysis to test the null hypothesis that a time series is integrated of order.

KPSS(Kwiatkowski–Phillips–Schmidt–Shin) H_0 = series is stationary

H1 = series is non stationary

30.

	List 1		List 2
a.	Permanent income hypothesis of consumption	i.	T. Sargent and N, Wallace
b.	Life cycle hypothesis of consumption	ii.	Milton Friedman
c.	Real business cycle theory	iii.	Franco Modigliani
d.	Policy ineffectiveness proposition	iv.	F. Kydland and E.Prescott

(1) (a-iii)(b-ii)(c-i)(d-iv)
(2) (a-iii)(b-ii)(c-iv)(d-i)
(3) (a-ii)(b-iii)(c-iv)(d-i)
(4) (a-ii)(b-iii)(c-i)(d-iv)

Answer: 3

Solution:

Life cycle income hypothesis :-Given by Ando - Modi gilani in 1957.An individual will base his consumption on the lifetime income.

Real business cycle theory has developed rapidly after the initiation of Kydland and Prescott in 1982. It has grown substantially as an independent literature and served as a widely recognized framework for studies of the economy at business cycle frequencies.

policy ineffectiveness proposition is a new classical theory proposed in 1975 by Thomas J. Sargent and Neil Wallace based upon the theory of rational expectations.

Permanent income hypothesis:-given by Milton Friedman in 1957in his book "A theory of consumption function.

31. Among the new monetary aggregates suggested by the Third working group of RBI, which one/ ones include time deposits of term less than or equal to one year but do not include the time deposits with term more than one year?

(A) NM_0 **(B) NM_1**
(C) NM_2 **(D) NM_3**

Choose the correct answer from the options given below:

(1) (A) Only
(2) (C) Only
(3) (C) and (D) Only
(4) (B) and (C) Only

Answer: 2

Solution:

Weekly Compilation

- M0= Currency in Circulation + Bankers' Deposits with RBI + 'Other' Deposits with RBI*

Fortnightly

- M1 = Currency with the Public + Demand Deposits with the Banking System + 'Other' Deposits with RBI*=Currency with the Public + Current Deposits with the Banking System + Demand Liabilities Portion of Savings Deposits with the Banking System + 'Other' Deposits with RBI*
- M2=M1+ Time Liabilities Portion of Savings Deposits with the Banking System + Certificates of Deposit issued by Banks + Term Deposits of residents with a contractual maturity of up to and including one year with the Banking System=Currency with the Public + Current Deposits with the Banking System + Savings Deposits with the Banking System + Certificates of Deposits issued by Banks + Term Deposits of residents with a contractual maturity up to and including one year with the Banking System + 'Other' Deposits with RBI*.
- M3=M2+ Term Deposits of residents with a contractual maturity of over one year with the Banking System + Call/Term borrowings from 'Non-depository' financial corporations by the Banking System.
- **Note:** * 'Other' deposits with RBI comprise mainly: (i) deposits of quasi-government and other financial institutions including primary dealers, (ii) balances in the accounts of foreign Central banks and Governments, (iii) accounts of international agencies such as the International Monetary Fund, etc.

32. An economy characterized by huge involuntary unemployment would have an aggregate labour supply curve in a real wage labour supply plane that would be

a. Positively sloped

b. Vertical

c. Flat

d. Negatively sloped.

Answer: 3

Solution:

Keynesian involuntary underemployment equilibrium.

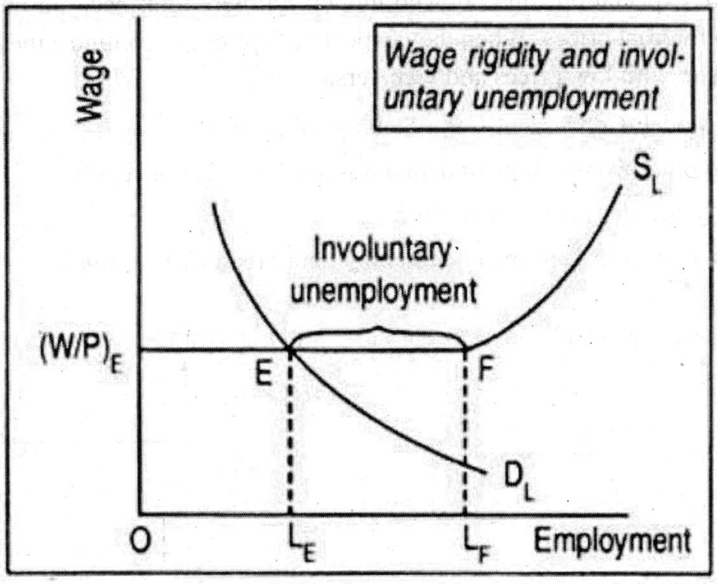

33. The demand and supply function for cobweb model are given as $Q_t^d=19-6P_t$ and $Q^s_t=6P_{t-1}-5$. Choose the right answer related to inter temporal equilibrium price and the nature of equilibrium:

1) $\overline{P} = 2$, explosive oscillation

2) $\overline{P} = 2$, uniform oscillation

3) $\overline{P} = 3$, damped oscillation

4) $\overline{P} = 3$, uniform oscillation

Answer: 2

Solution:

✧ **Cobweb phenomenon :** Cobweb phenomenon is economic theory stipulating that price fluctuations lead to fluctuations in supply, causing a cycle of rising and falling prices. For example, seeing higher prices, farmers sow the seeds for the crops to benefit from higher prices. This results in surplus production, more than the demand, resulting in a price crash, often referred to as the 'problem of plenty'. Seeing the low prices, farmers switch to different crops or produce less of the same crop, leading to lower than usual production for that particular crop. This increases the prices of crops, completing the cyclical variations in price and production.

✧ Adaptive expectations and cobweb model: Farmers look back on most recent prices in order to forecast prices. When they expect high prices to continue, they produce too much and end up with low prices and vice versa.

<u>Cobweb Model</u>:-<u>Convergent Case</u>:-Stable equilibrium

$E_d > E_s$. In other words, slope of demand is less than that of supply.

<u>Divergent Case</u>:-Unstable equilibrium

$E_d < E_s$. In other words, slope of demand is more than that of supply.

a) Cycle less growth path MPC= 0.5 Accelerator = 0

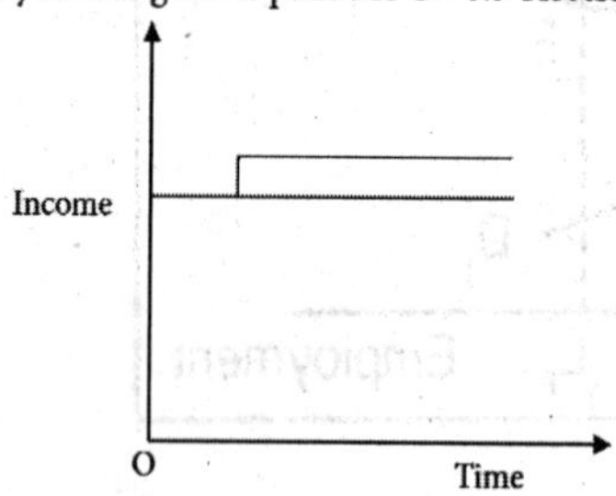

b) Dampened fluctuations MPC = 0.5 Accelerator =1

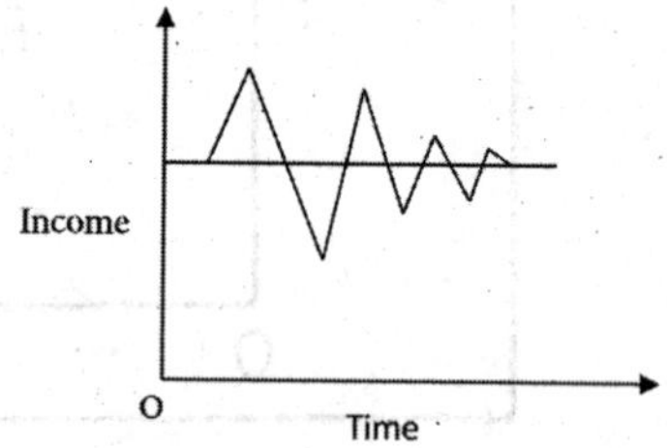

c) Constant Amplitude
Accelerator = 2

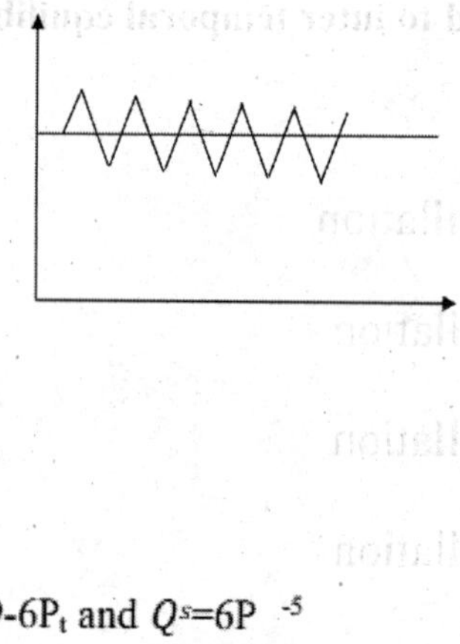

d) Anti-damped Cycles / Explosive Cycles
Accelerator = 3
MPC = 0.5

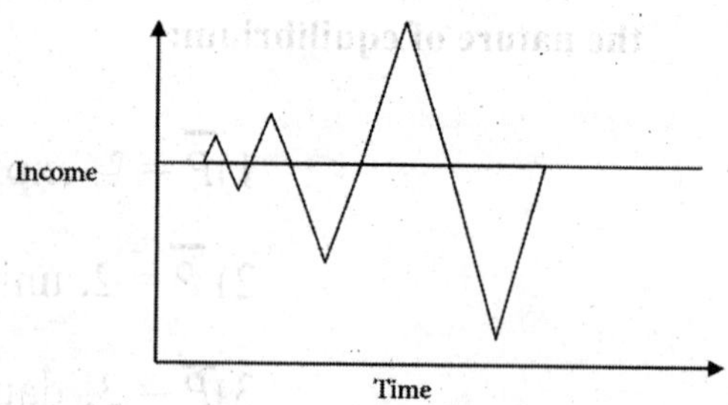

$Q^d_t = 19 - 6P_t$ and $Q^s_t = 6P_{t-1} - 5$

$Qd = 19 - 6P_t$

Slope = $\frac{1}{-6}$

Negative because of the relation between Q and P

$Qs = 6P_{t-1} - 5$

Slope = $\frac{1}{6}$

Here slopes are equal so there will be uniform oscillation.

Inter temporal equilibrium price

$Q^d_t = 19 - 6P_t$ and $Q^s_t = 6P_{t-1} - 5$

Qd=Qs

$19 - 6P_t = 6P_{t-1} - 5$

$19 - 6\acute{P} = 6\acute{P} - 5$

$19 + 5 = 6\acute{P} + 6\acute{P}$

$24/12 = \acute{P}$

$2 = \acute{P}$

34. In a market for labour's demand and supply, the equilibrium wage is w*. The government fixes a minimum wage at w'. Which of the following statements is true?

(1) There is a tendency of increased casualization of workers if w'> w*, where the workers would not receive lots of benefits.

(2) The market will now tend towards a new equilibrium at w', with no other changes, if w'> w*

(3) If w'< w*, there will be a tendency of increased casualization of workers.

(4) It will be impossible to administer such legislation unless w'= w*

Answer 1

Solution: pushing a wage above the equilibrium level raises the quantity of labor supplied and reduces the quantity of labor demanded.

SL>DL, leads to casualization

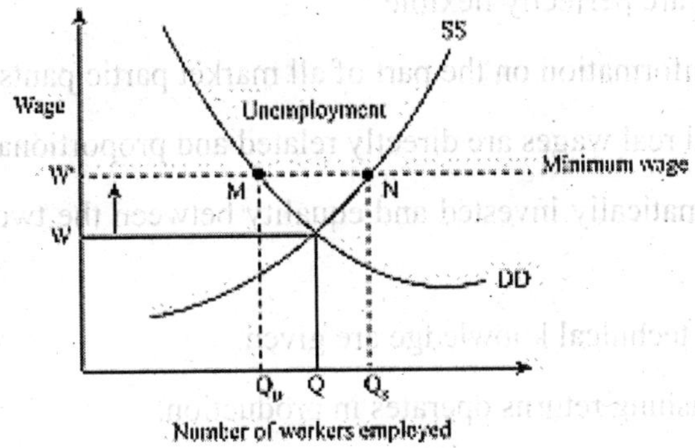

35. Given the following statements about major schools of thought in macroeconomics, state which ones are correct?

(A) The Keynesians believed in wage and price flexibility and highlighted the role of aggregate supply.

(B) The monetarists highlighted the importance of money in the economic system and that of expectations in the analysis of inflation.

(C) The classical school believed in the invisible hand and the efficiency of the market mechanism

(D) The new Keynesians make use of the assumption of imperfect markets in their frameworks.

Choose the correct answer from the options given below:

1. B,C,D
2. A,B,C,D
3. A,C,D
4. A,B,C

Answer: 1

Solution:

The classical theory of output and employment is based on the following assumptions :

1. There is the existence of full employment without inflation.
2. There is a laissez-faire capitalist economy without government interference.
3. It is a closed economy without foreign trade.
4. There is perfect competition in labour and product markets.
5. Labour is homogeneous.
6. Total output of the economy is divided between consumption and investment expenditures.
7. The quantity of money is given and money is only the medium of exchange.
8. Wages and prices are perfectly flexible.
9. There is perfect information on the part of all market participants.
10. Money wages and real wages are directly related and proportional.
11. Savings are automatically invested and equality between the two is brought about by the rate of interest
12. Capital stock and technical knowledge are given.
13. The law of diminishing returns operates in production.
14. It assumes long run.

UNEMPLOYMENT: KEYNES'S MONEY-WAGE RIGIDITY MODEL

1. Money Illusion. The first reason why firms fail to cut wages despite an excess supply of labour is that workers will resist any move for cut in money wages

   By money illusion it is meant that workers fail to realise that value of money, that is, its purchasing power in terms of commodities, changes when prices rise.

2. Wage fixation through contracts
3. Minimum Wage Laws
4. Efficiency Wages

New Keynesians: The term "New Keynesians" was coined by Parkin and Bade in 1982. The main aim of this school of thought was to improve upon the Keynesian theory. Keynes theory did not provide any rationale for the wage-price rigidity.

Therefore, their main aim was:

a. Provide a rationale behind wage-price rigidity.

b. Provide micro-foundations to macro theories.

Assumptions taken by New Keynesians were:

a. Involuntary unemployment is possible.

b. Imperfectly competitive market structures.

c. Considered both supply and demand shocks.

d. Considered asymmetric information and incomplete labour markets.

e. The New Keynesians have talked about nominal and real wage-price rigidity.

36.

	List 1		List 2
a.	Quantity theory of money	i.	Milton Friedman
b.	Involuntary unemployment	ii.	JM Keynes
c.	Randomised trial	iii.	Abhijeet V.Banerjee
d.	Relative poverty	iv.	A.K. Sen

1) (a-i)(b-ii)(c-iii)(d-iv)
2) (a-iv)(b-iii)(c-ii)(d-i)
3) (a-iii)(b-ii)(c-i)(d-iv)
4) (a-iii)(b-ii)(c-iv)(d-i)

Answer: 1

Solution: In response to the Keynesian view of the world, friedman made a restatement of the quantity theory in 1956 and used it as a cornerstone for monetarist thinking.

Friedman agreed that money could affect output in the short run. Indeed, he believed that monetary policy was much more powerful in this respect than fiscal policy.

According to Keynes, wage rigidity is the cause of involuntary unemployment. This means that a free enterprise capitalist economy always fails to reach full employment because of wage rigidity.

According to Sen, being poor does not mean living below an imaginary poverty line, such as an income of two dollars a day or less. It means having an income level that does not allow an individual to cover certain basic necessities, taking into account the circumstances and social requirements of the environment.

A randomized controlled trial is a type of scientific experiment mainly used in drugs trial. It is designed to identify the effectiveness of the treatment and eliminate certain kinds of bias. Subjects are randomly split into group that receives an intervention: the other the control group, which is left alone. The usefulness of the treatment is assessed in comparison to the control group.

37. Consider the following statements about the Aggregate Demand (AD) relation under price flexibilty and say which ones are correct?

(A) The AD curve will shift to the right if autonomous investment rises.

(B) The AD curve will shift to the right if net exports rise in an open economy.

(C) The AD curve will shift to the left if money supply contracts.

(D) As price rises, shifting the LM curve, the AD curve shifts to the left Choose the correct answer from the options given below:

(1) (A), (B), (C) Only
(2) (B), (C), (D) Only
(3) (A), (C), (D) Only
(4) (A), (B), (C), (D)

Answer: 1

Solution: Investment increases = AD will increase

So, AD shifts right

Exports will increase – income will increase – AD increase

So, AD will shift right

When the money supply decreases – purchasing power will fall- people will demand less

So, AD will shift left

With increase or decrease in prices, AD will not

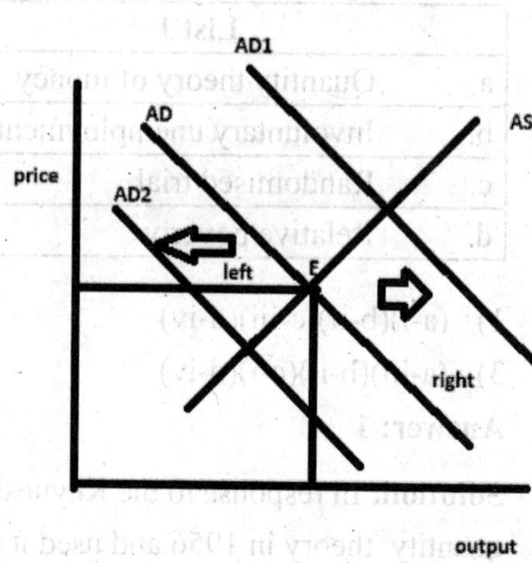

shift. Change in price leads to movement along demand curve.

38.

	List 1		List 2
a.	Investment is unresponsive to interest rates	i.	Relatively flat IS curve
b.	Money demand is perfectly elastic w.r.t. interest rates	ii.	vertical LM curve
c.	Money demand is completely inelastic w.r.t interest rates	iii.	Horizontal LM curve
d.	Investment is highly responsive to interest rates	iv.	Vertical IS curve

1) (a-iv)(b-iii)(c-ii)(d-i)
2) (a-iv)(b-ii)(c-iii)(d-i)
3) (a-i)(b-iii)(c-ii)(d-iv)
4) (a-iii)(b-iv)(c-i)(d-ii)

Answer: 1

Solution:

Slope of IS curve depends on

1) Interest elasticity of investment Demand Higher the elasticity of demand, flatter will be the IS curve and vice versa.

2) Size of the Multiplier More the size of the multiplier, flatter will be theIS curve and vice versa.

Slope of LM curve depends on

Income elasticity of demand for money :- More the income elasticity of demand for money, steeper will be the LM curve and vice versa.

Interest elasticity of demand for money :-

→Lesser the interest elasticity of demand for money, steeper the LM curve and vice versa.

39. If the interest rate is exogenously determined by the Central Bank of some country and the money supply is endogenously determined, the slope of the LM-curve in the interest rate-income plane would be

(1) Positively sloped
(2) Negatively sloped
(3) Horizontal
(4) Vertical

Answer: 3

Solution: Endogenous money is an economy's supply of money that is determined endogenously— that is, as a result of the interactions of other economic variables (Like interest rate and income), rather than exogenously (autonomously) by an external authority such as a central bank.

When we consider rate of interest to be exogenous , it means money supply is determined by other variable like income. So the curve will be horizontal. But if money supply is determined by rate of interest then endogenous money supply curve will upward sloping.

Exogenous money supply

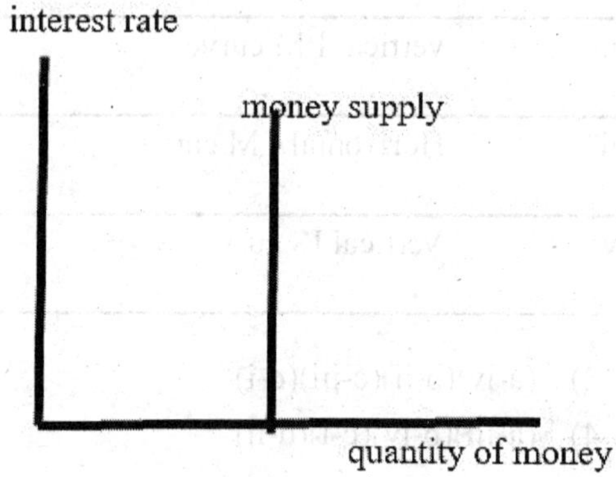

Endogenous money supply

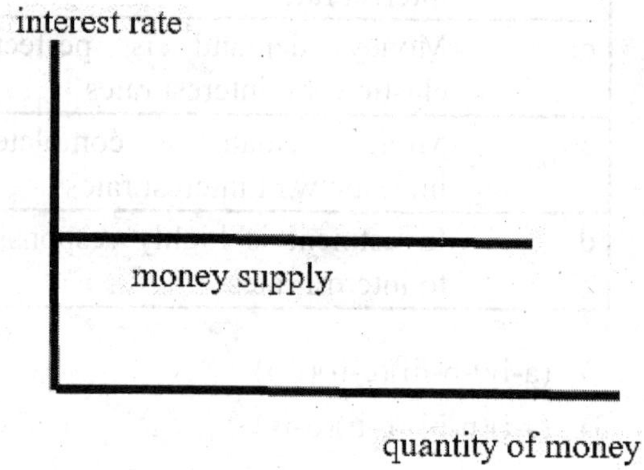

40. Arrange the given schools of thought in macroeconomics in chronological order, from the oldest to most recent one.

(A) The Keynesian school

(B) The new classical school

(C) The classical school

(D) The new Keynesian school

(E) The monetarists

Choose the correct answer from the options given below:

(1) (A), (D), (C), (B), (E) (2) (E). (C), (B) (A), (D)

(3) (C) (B) (A), (D), (E) (4) (C). (A), (E), (B), (D)

Answer: 4

41. Arrange the following steps of exchange rate channel of monetary transmission mechanism, in correct order, starting from first to last.

(A) reduction in policy rate

(B) capital outflows

(C) depreciation of the domestic currency

(D) rise in net exports

Choose the correct answer from the options given below:

(1) (A), (C) (D) (B) (2) (A), (D), (B), (C)

(3) (A), (B), (C), (D) (4) (A), (D), (C), (B)

Answer: 3

Solution: Reduction of domestic interest rate leads to capital outflow.

Capital outflow leads to a reduction in value of domestic currency

Due to this currency depreciates

Depreciation makes exports cheaper hence rise in net exports

42. In an economy real GDP has increased from \$ 990 PPP to \$ 1080 PPP during 2015 to 2020. The incremental capital-output ratio is 2.5. The rate of investment is:

(1) 27.8 Percent
(2) 22.5 Percent
(3) 3.9 Percent
(4) 19.5 Percent

Answer: 2

Solution:

GDP growth rate $= \frac{1080-990}{990} \times 100$

$= \frac{90}{990} \times 100$

$= \frac{capital}{output} = 2.5$

$= \frac{capital}{9.09} = 2.5$

Capital = 22.73

43. Suppose India is the home country and USA is the foreign country. The interest rates in India and USA are 6% and 4% respectively. The exchange rate of US Dollar is Rs. 80 today but is expected to rise to Rs. 84 in one year. Which of the following is true, according to the uncovered interest arbitrage parity condition?

(1) Capital will flow into the Indian economy

(2) Capital will flow out of the Indian economy

(3) No Capital flows

(4) Can't say on the basis of the information provided

Answer: 2

Solution: Interest arbitrage is international flow of short term liquid capital to earn higher returns abroad. If Foreign exchange risk is covered we have covered interest arbitrage , if it is uncovered we have uncovered interest arbitrage.

Interest rates in India are higher . USA investors can invest in India to take benefit of this 2% more interest. But depreciation of Indian rupee leads to loss in returns. Indian Currency is depreciated by 5%. ie. (84-80)/80*100 =5%

Investment in India will produce losses (2%-5%=-3%). So capital will flow out of Indian economy.

44. Suppose India is home country and USA is a foreign country. Interest rate in India is 3%, that in US is 1%. The Re-$ exchange rate is Rs. 80 per USD in the spot market and Rs. 81 per USD in the 3- month forward market. Which of the following are true for the resulting covered interest arbitrage flows?

(A) Indian Rupee will depreciate in spot market

(B) Indian Rupee will depreciate in forward market

(C) Interest rate will decline in India

(D) Interest rate will decline in US

Choose the correct answer from the options given below

(1) (A) and (B) Only
(2) (A) and (C) Only
(3) (A) and (D) Only
(4) (A) (B) (C) and (D)

Answer: 3

Solution: Covered interest arbitrage is spot purchase of foreign currency to make investments and simultaneous forward sale of foreign currency to cover foreign exchange risk.

Here interest rate in India is more. So to invest in India, Indian currency will be bought at spot rate, which will increase exchange rate , rupee will depreciate.

After maturity, through forward contract, US investor sold rupees to convert it into dollars and inflow of capital in USA leads to decrease in rate of interest in USA.

Hedge the currency risk by selling INR forward at Rs. 81/USD.

At maturity, receive INR, convert it back to USD at the forward rate, and repay the USD loan.

This process generates a risk-free profit due to the interest rate differential and the expected depreciation of the rupee.

Note : Students can watch youtube classes at MS STUDY GURU by Simranjit kaur mam for detailed explanations and practical examples of these concepts.

45. Consider the following statements about the Current Account of the balance of payment and Indicate which statements are true

(A) Current Account deficit equals excess of imports over sum of exports and net transfers received by a country.

(B) Current Account deficit may be covered by borrowing from foreigners.

(C) Current Account deficit may be covered by buying assets from foreigners.

(D) If India's Current Account deficit in a particular period is $ 50 million, it can be financed by net capital inflows amounting to $50 million

Choose the correct answer from the options given below:

(1) A, B, C, D (2) A, B, D only

(3) A, C, D only (4) B, C, D only

Answer: 2

Solution

- Current account deficit is financed by capital inflows.Borrowing is a capital inflow.
- Current account deficit= debit side of current account is more than credit side of current account.

46. The current account deficit of BOP may be financed in many ways. Which of the following are correct?

A. **FDI inflows**

B. **Inflow of foreign portfolio investment**

C. **Borrowing from IMF or World Bank**

D. **Drawing down foreign exchange reserves**

Choose the correct answer from the option given below

1. A, B, C 2. B, C, D

3. A, B, C, D 4. A, C, D

Answer: 3

Solution:

1. **FDI inflows (Foreign Direct Investment):** When foreign companies invest directly in businesses or projects in the domestic economy, they bring in foreign currency, helping to finance the deficit.
2. **Inflow of foreign portfolio investment:** When foreign investors purchase domestic assets like stocks or bonds, they also bring in foreign currency, contributing to the financing of the deficit.
3. **Borrowing from IMF or World Bank:** These international financial institutions can provide loans to countries with current account deficits, offering another source of financing.
4. **Drawing down foreign exchange reserves:** Countries can use their existing foreign

exchange reserves to temporarily cover the deficit. However, relying heavily on this method is not ideal for long-term sustainability.

5. Current account deficit is financed by capital inflows.

47. Consider the following statements about the Specific Factors model of International Trade and say which ones are correct?

(A) Factor specific to the export sector in each country gain from trade.

(B) Factor specific to the import competing sectors in each country lose from trade

(C) Mobile factors that can work in either sector may gain from trade

(D) Mobile factors that can work in either sector may lose from trade Choose the correct answer:

1. A, C, D
2. B, C, D
3. A, B, C
4. A, B, C, D

Answer: 4

Solution:

In specific factor model, trade will have an ambigious/uncertain(gain or loss) effect on the nation's mobile factors, benefits the immobile factors specific to the nation's export commodities and harm the immobile factor specific to the nation's import competing commodities.

The model's name refers to its distinguishing feature—that one factor of production is assumed to be "specific" to a particular industry. A specific factor is one that is stuck in an industry or is immobile between industries in response to changes in market conditions. A factor may be immobile between industries for a number of reasons. Some factors may be specifically designed (in the case of capital) or specifically trained (in the case of labor) for use in a particular production process. In these cases, it may be impossible, or at least difficult or costly, to move these factors across industries.

48. Under the flexible exchange rate, if the current account deficit increases and the capital account surplus increases for an economy, the exchange rate (domestic currency per US dollar) would:

1. Appreciate
2. Depreciate
3. Depends on which one is higher
4. Not depend on the BoP situation

Answer: 3

Solution:

- ✧ If current account deficit more than capital account surplus then it leads to total BOP deficit

.A deficit in BOP leads to a higher demand for foreign currency, then national currency depreciates.

- ✧ If current account deficit less than capital account surplus then it leads to total BOP surplus .A surplus in BOP leads to a higher supply for foreign currency, then national currency appreciates.
- ✧ So it depends on which one is higher.

49. Consider an economy with perfect capital mobility, fixed price level and flexible exchange rate. Starting from equilibrium, suppose there is a monetary expansion.

Which of the following are true for the new equilibrium, as compared to the initial equilibrium?

(A) Output will be higher

(B) Contumption will be higher

(C) Interest rate will be lower

(D) Interest rate will be higher

Choose the correct answer from the options given below:

(1) (A) Only	(2) (B) Only
(3) (A) and (B) Only	(4) (A) and (C) Only

Answer: 3

Solution:

Consider monetary expansion.

1. An increase in Money supply shifts the LM curve downward and to the right.
2. This puts a downward pressure on the domestic interest rate ($i < i^*$).
3. But this immediately invites a massive capital outflow.
4. This depreciates the nominal exchange rate E as well as the real exchange rate q.
5. This improves the trade balance T.

Again, the whole sequence is assumed to take place in an instant. Compared with the domestic version of IS-LM, monetary policy is more powerful because the outward shift of LM invites an additional outward shift of IS. Both LM and IS cooperate to increase income. The conclusion is that under a floating exchange rate and perfect capital mobility, monetary policy is very effective.

Monetary policy is effective in that case. So output and employment will increase.

Monetary Expansion

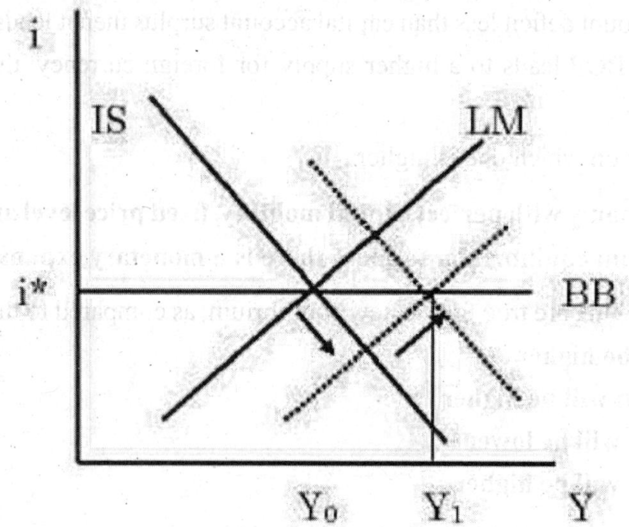

Consider fiscal expansion.

1. An increase in G shifts the IS curve upward and to the right.
2. This puts an upward pressure on the domestic interest rate (i > i*).
3. But this immediately invites a massive capital inflow.
4. This appreciates the nominal exchange rate E as well as the real exchange rate q.
5. This worsens the trade balance T.

As the model is constructed, no gradual adjustment is allowed; these events are supposed to take place instantaneously. The exchange rate appreciates and the trade balance worsens until the initial increase

in G is completely offset. The IS curve is pushed back to the original position, and Y cannot increase at all.

What happened is that, in Y = A + T, as A is increased by fiscal spending, T is reduced by exactly the same amount. Y is unchanged, and only the relative composition of Y is changed. The conclusion is that under a floating exchange rate and perfect capital mobility, fiscal policy is ineffective. Here, "ineffective" means unable to increase Y.

Fiscal Expansion

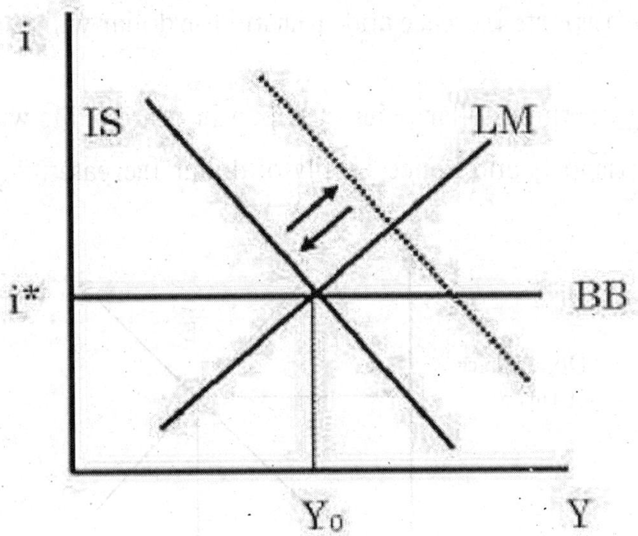

50. **The Central Bank of a country maintains a fixed exchange rate, which is defined as the number of units of domestic currency per unit of foreign currency. Currently the domestic currency is overvalued against the foreign currency. In this context, indicate the kind of intervention required by the Central Bank to maintain the parity, by putting the following statements in correct order.**

(A) The demand for foreign currency exceeds its supply

(B) The exchange rate is lower than the market clearing exchange rate

(C) The gap between supply and demand for foreign currency is equalized

(D) The Central Bank's stock of foreign currency is depleted

(E) The Central Bank sells foreign currency from its stock of reserves Choose the correct arawer from the options given below:

(1) (B), (E), (A), (D),(C)
(2) (B). (A),(E), D) (C)
(3) (B), (E)(A),(C),(D)
(4) (B) (A),(E),(C),(D)

Answer: 4

Solution

Exchange Rate Determination

Demand for dollars :- When dollar price of rupee falls implying that rupee appreciate, then imports increase and demand for dollar will increase.

Supply of dollars :-when dollar price of rupee increases, this will discourage the imports and hence supply of dollar increases.

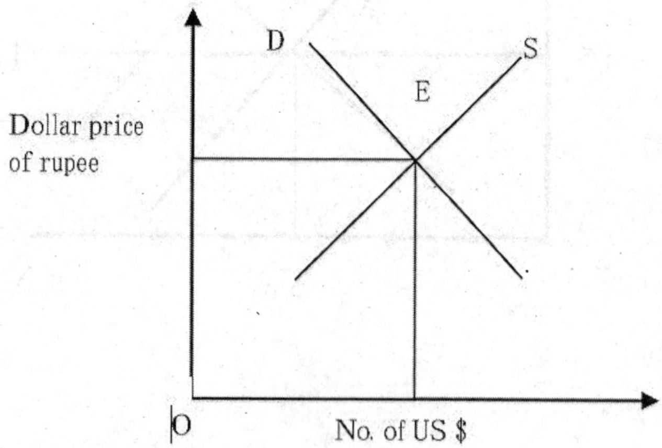

When The exchange rate is lower than the market clearing exchange rate, demand of dollars (foreign currency) increases as can be seen ion fiqure . when demand of dollars increases, central bank sells foreign currency from its stock then again equilibrium in diagram achieved.

51. Arrange the following chronologically starting from the oldest.

(A) Theory of big push

(B) The accumulation of capital

(C) Theory of cumulative causation

(D) Unbalanced growth

(E) Development with unlimited supplies of labour

Choose the correct answer from the options given below:

1. E A C B D
2. A E B C D
3. E B A D C
4. A B E C D

Answer: 2

Solution:

The major contributions to the concept of the Big Push were made by Paul Rosenstein-Rodan in 1943

Lewis theory of development :- given by Arthur Lewis in 1954. Also known as "Model of unlimited supply of labour."

The accumulation of capital by Jaon Robinson in 1956.

The theory of cumulative causation is developed by Swedish economist Gunnar Myrdal in rich lands and poor, published in 1957.

Unbalanced Growth :- propounded by 'Hirschman' in his work 'The strategy of economic development' (1958).

52.

List 1		List 2	
a.	Unequal exchange	i.	A.Hirshman
b.	The development ofunderdevelopment	ii.	G.Myrdal
c.	Backward and forward linkage effect	iii.	A.Emmanuel
d.	Backwash effect	iv.	G.Frank

1) (a-ii)(b-iii)(c-i)(d-iv)
2) (a-iii)(b-i)(c-iv)(d-ii)
3) (a-iii)(b-iv)(c-i)(d-ii)
4) (a-ii)(b-iv)(c-iii)(d-i)

Answer: 3

Solution:

Emmanuel gives unequal exchange theory.

'The Development of Underdevelopment' is article by G. Frank.

Hirschman introduces the concept of backward and forward linkages. A forward linkage is created when investment in a particular project encourages investment in subsequent stages of production. A backward linkage is created when a project encourages investment in facilities that enable the project to succeed.

Spread-backwash effects were outlined by G. Myrdal (1957) and A. Hirschman (1959) in the late 1950s. 'Generally, spread effects are the positive effects of urban proximity for communities, and backwash effects are the negative consequences of proximity.

53. The Solow residual is

a. The difference between the rate of growth of productivity and the rate of growth of inputs
b. The difference between the rate of growth of output and the rate of growth of saving
c. The difference between the rate of growth of output and the rate of growth of inputs
d. The difference between the golden rule level of consumption and the steady state level of consumption

Answer: 3

Solution: The Solow residual is the portion of an economy's output growth that cannot be attributed to the accumulation of capital and labor, the factors of production. The Solow residual represents output growth that happens beyond the simple growth of inputs.

54. Endogenous growth theory assumes

1. Increasing return to scale and perfect competition.
2. Decreasing return to scale and perfect competition.
3. Increasing return to scale and imperfect competition.
4. Decreasing return to scale and imperfect competition.

Answer: 3

Solution:

Endogenous growth theory is an economic theory that contrasts with the traditional neoclassical growth theory by emphasizing that economic growth is not only influenced by external factors such as technology or population growth but is also determined by factors within the economic system itself. The term "endogenous" means that the factors driving economic growth are internal or inherent to the economic system.

Key features and concepts of endogenous growth theory include:

1. **Human Capital and Knowledge Accumulation:** Endogenous growth theory highlights the role of human capital and knowledge accumulation as key drivers of economic growth. Investments in education, training, and research and development are seen as essential for sustained growth.
2. **Increasing Returns to Scale:** Unlike neoclassical growth theory, which often assumes constant returns to scale, endogenous growth theory often incorporates increasing returns to scale. This implies that as more inputs (capital, labor, etc.) are added to the production process, the efficiency and productivity of those inputs increase, leading to positive feedback loops and sustained growth.
3. **Technological Progress as an Endogenous Variable:** In traditional growth theories, technological progress is often treated as an exogenous variable. Endogenous growth theory, on the other hand, considers technological progress as an endogenous outcome of factors such as research and development activities and human capital accumulation.
4. **Imperfect Competition:** Endogenous growth models often involve imperfect competition, suggesting that firms have some degree of market power. This market power can encourage innovation and investment in human capital, contributing to economic growth.
5. **Externalities:** The theory recognizes the importance of positive externalities, where the actions of one economic agent benefit others. For example, knowledge spillovers from

research and development activities can have positive effects on the overall economy. Prominent economists associated with the development of endogenous growth theory include Paul Romer and Robert Lucas. Romer's work, in particular, has been influential in shaping the understanding of how factors such as knowledge, human capital, and increasing returns contribute to long-term economic growth.

55. Gini-coefficient , a widely used measure of inequality in income is defined as

1. $\frac{1}{n^2 \mu} \sum_i^n \sum_{j \leq 1} (yi - yj)$

2. $\frac{2}{n^2 \mu} \sum_i^n i\, yi - [\frac{n+1}{n}]$

3. $\frac{2}{n\mu} \frac{\sum_i^n i\, yi}{\sum_i^n \dot{y}} - [\frac{n+1}{n}]$.

4. $\frac{1}{n^2 \mu} \sum_{i=1}^{n} \sum_{j=1}^{n} |(y_i - y_j)|$

Answer: 2

In 2nd formula, yi=(xi- $\bar{x}$)

xi=observed values

i=rank of values

n=number of values

56.

	List 1		List 2
A.	Kenneth Arrow	i.	Analysis of causal relationship
B.	Robert Solow	ii.	fundamental contribution in behavioural economics
C.	Daneal Kanheman	iii.	fundamental contribution in welfare economics
D.	Joshua Angrist	iv.	fundamental contribution in growth theory

1) (a-iii)(b-iv)(c-i)(d-ii)
2) (a-ii)(b-i)(c-iii)(d-iv)
3) (a-iii)(b-iv)(c-ii)(d-i)
4) (a-i)(b-iv)(c-iii)(d-ii)

Answer: 3

Solution:

In 1951, Arrow presented the first and second fundamental theorems of welfare economics and their proofs without requiring differentiability of utility, consumption, or technology, and including corner solutions. He was an American economist known for his contributions to welfare economics and to general economic equilibrium theory. He was cowinner (with Sir John R. Hicks) of the Nobel Prize for Economics in 1972.

Robert Solow, In the 1950s, he developed a mathematical model illustrating how various factors can contribute to sustained national economic growth. From the 1960s on, Solow's studies helped persuade governments to channel funds into technological research and development to spur economic growth. Solow also was the first to develop a growth model with different vintages of capital. The idea was that because capital is produced based on known technology, and because technology is improving, new capital is more valuable than old capital.

Daniel Kahneman won the Nobel Prize in Economic Sciences in 2002 for integrating psychological insights into economics. He is primarily known for demonstrating how humans make decisions, particularly in situations of uncertainty, which can be seen in the phenomenon of loss aversion. Daniel Kahneman and Amos Tversky are often referred to as the fathers of behavioral economics, for demonstrating that the human brain relies on mental shortcuts and biases in decision-making, which often leads people to irrational ends.

Joshua Angrist, Israeli-American economist who, with the Dutch-American economist Guido Imbens, was awarded one-half of the 2021 Nobel Prize for Economics for his "methodological contributions to the analysis of causal relationships" in labour markets.

57. Given below are two statements:

Statement (1): Human Development is a process of enlarging peoples choices

Statement (II): Human Development Index (HDI) is based on the following indicators: Life expectancy at birth, expected years of schooling, mean years of schooling & Gross domestic product per capita at dollar PPP.

In the light of the above statements, choose the most appropriate answer from the options given below:

(1) Both Statement 1 and Statement II are correct

(2) Both Statement 1 and Statement Il are incorrect

(3) Statement I is correct but Statement II is incorrect

(4) Statement 1 is incorrect but Statement Il is correct

Answer: 3

Solution: The health aspect of the HDI is measured by the life expectancy, as calculated at the time of birth, in each country, and normalized so that this component is equal to 0 when life expectancy is 20 and equal to 1 when life expectancy is 85

Education is measured on two levels: the mean years of schooling for residents of a country, and the expected years of schooling that a child has at the average age for starting school.

The economic metric chosen to represent the standard of living is GNI per capita based on purchasing power parity (PPP), a common metric used to reflect average income.

58. Which of the following dimensions is included in HPI-2 (Human Poverty Index - 2)

(1) Gender Inequalities

(2) Financial Inclusion

(3) Social Inclusion

(4) Economic Inclusion

Answer: 3

Solution:

The Human Poverty Index is an indicator of the standard of living in a country, developed by United Nations (UN) to complement the Human Development Index (HDI) and was first reported as part of Human Development report in 1997. It was considered to better reflect the extent of deprivation in developed countries compared to HDI. In 2010 it was supplanted by the UN's Multidimensional Poverty Index.

The HPI concentrates on the deprivation in the three essential elements of human life already reflect in the HDI: Longevity, Knowledge and a decent Standard of Living

The Human Poverty Index for developing countries (HPI-1)

While the HDI measures average achievement, the HPI-1 measures deprivations in three basic dimensions of human development captured in the HDI:

1. A long and healthy life - vulnerability to death at a relatively early age, as measured by the probability at birth of not surviving to age 40.
2. knowledge - exclusion from the world of reading and communications, as measured by the adult literacy rate.
3. A decent standard of living lack of access to overall economic provisioning, as measured by the unweighted average of two indicators, the percentage of the population not using an improved water source and the percentage of children under weight-for-average.

Calculating the HPI-1 is more straightforward than calculating the HDI. The indicators used to measure the deprivation already normalized between 0 and 100 (because they are expressed in percentages), so there is no need to create dimension indices as for the HDI.

The Human Poverty Index for OECD countries (HPI-2)

The HPI-2 measures deprivations in the same dimensions as the HPI-1 and also captures social exclusion. Thus it reflects deprivation in four dimensions:

1. A long and healthy life vulnerability to death at a relatively early age, as measured by the probability at birth of not surviving to age 60.
2. Knowledge-exclusion from the word of reading and communications, as measured by the percentage of adults (ages 16-65) lacking functional literacy skills.
3. A decent standard of living as measured by the percentage of people living below the income poverty line (50% of median adjusted household disposable income)
4 Social exclusion-as measured by the rate of long-term unemployment (12 months or more)

59. World Hunger Index includes:

(A) Child mortality with weight 1/3

(B) Child stunting with weight 1/3

(C) Undernourishment with weight 1/3

(D) Child wasting with weight 1/6

(E) Child mortality with weight 1/6

Choose the correct answer from the options given below:

(1) (A), (B) and (C) Only (2) (A), (C) and (D) Only

(3) (B), (C) and (E) Only (4) (D) and (E) Only

Answer: 2

Solution:

✧ The GHI combines 4 component indicators:

✧ Undernourishment: share of the population with insufficient caloric intake.

✧ Child stunting: share of children under age five who have low height for their age, reflecting chronic undernutrition.

✧ Child wasting: share of children under age five who have low weight for their height, reflecting acute undernutrition.

✧ Child mortality: share of children who die before their fifth birthday, reflecting in part the fatal mix of inadequate nutrition and unhealthy environments.

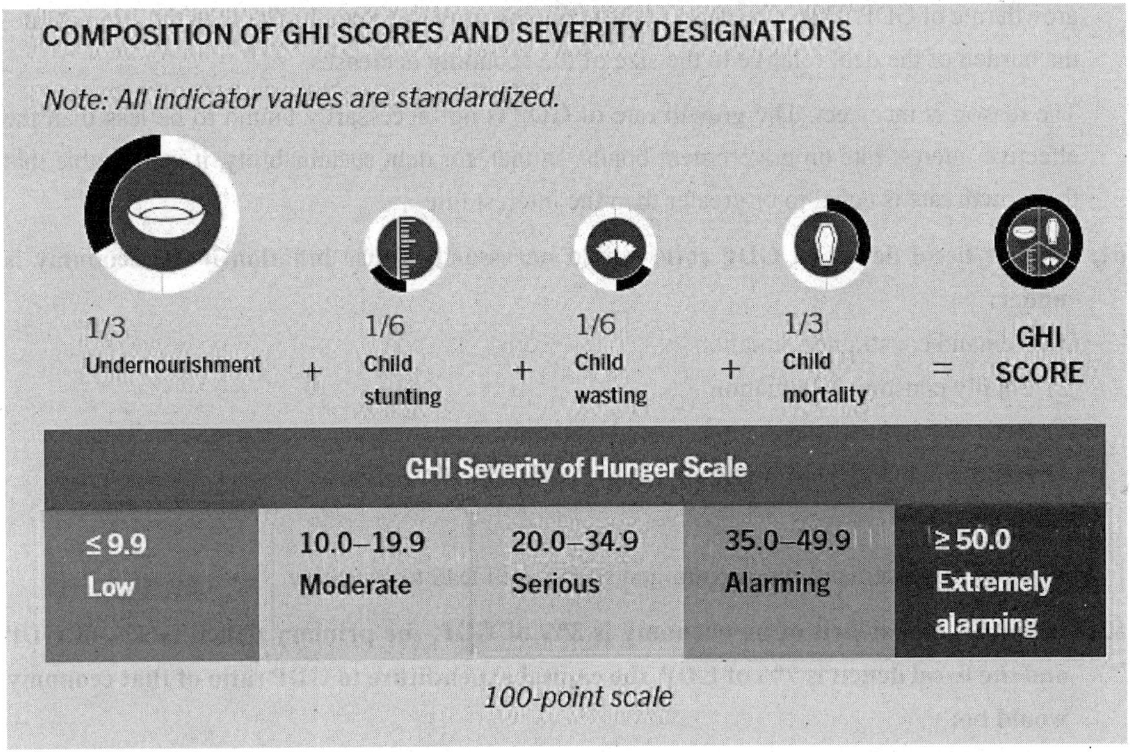

60. Given below are two statements: one is labeled as Assertion (A) and the other is labelled as Reason (R).

Assertion (A): According to the Domar condition of debt sustainability, the public debt would not rise as a proportion of GDP if the effective interest rate on government liabilities happens to be less than or equal to the growth rate of GDP at current price.

Reason (R): Growth rate of GDP of an economy at current price is bound to be less than the effective interest rate on the government bonds.

In the light of the above statements, choose the most appropriate answer from the options given below:

(1) Both (A) and (R) are correct and (R) is the correct explanation of (A)

(2) Both (A) and (R) are correct but (R) is not the correct explanation of (A)

(3) (A) is correct but (R) is not correct

(4) (A) is not correct but (R) is correct

Answer: 3

Solution: The Domar condition of debt sustainability states that for the debt-to-GDP ratio to remain stable, the effective interest rate on government debt should be less than or equal to the growth rate of GDP. This is because, if the economy grows at a rate higher than the interest rate, the burden of the debt relative to the size of the economy decreases.

The reason is incorrect. The growth rate of GDP is not necessarily bound to be less than the effective interest rate on government bonds. In fact, for debt sustainability, it is desirable that the growth rate is equal to or greater than the interest rate

61. Higher fiscal deficit to GDP ratio would necessarily cause inflation if the economy is under:

(1) Demand constrained situation

(2) Supply constrained situation

(3) Both demand and supply constrained situation

(4) Neither demand constrained nor supply constrained situation

Answer: 2

Solution: High demand and constrained supply will lead to price rise.

62. If the revenue deficit of an economy is 3% of GDP, the primary deficit is 2% of GDP and the fiscal deficit is 7% of GDP, the capital expenditure to GDP ratio of that economy would be:

1. 5% of GDP
2. 1% of GDP
3. 4% of GDP
4. 2% of GDP

Answer: 3

Solution: Fiscal Deficit = total expenditure -total receipts(excluding borrowings, because borrowings are the capital receipts)

FD = (capital expenditure + revenue expenditure) – Revenue receipt

FD Capital expenditure+ revenue deficit

7 = CE +3

7-3 =CE

4%=CE

63.

List 1		List 2	
a.	Ramsar convention	i.	ozone layer depletion
b.	Basel convention	ii.	reduction of greenhouse gas emission
c.	Montreal protocol	iii.	conservation of wetlands
d.	Paris agreement	iv.	control of trans-boundary movement of hazardous wastes and disposal

1) (a-i)(b-iv)(c-iii)(d-ii) 2) (a-iii)(b-i)(c-ii)(d-iv)
3) (a-iv)(b-i)(c-iii)(d-ii) 4) (a-iii)(b-iv)(c-i)(d-ii)

Answer: 4

Solution:
Montreal Protocol: The Montreal Protocol, agreed upon in 1987, is an international treaty aimed at protecting the ozone layer by phasing out the production and consumption of ozone-depleting substances. It has been successful in reducing the use of harmful substances like chlorofluorocarbons (CFCs).

Ramsar Convention on wetlands was initiated in 1971, serves as a framework for the conservation and wise use of wetlands and their resources. It aims to maintain the ecological character of wetlands, promote their sustainable utilisation, and protect the important function they provide.

Paris Agreement: The Paris Agreement aims to enhance the global response to the threat of climate change by ensuring that the increase in global temperature is kept well below 2 degrees Celsius above pre-industrial levels. It was signed in 2015 as an action plan under the United Nations Framework Convention on Climate Change (UNFCCC).

Basel Convention: The Basel Convention, adopted in 1989, aims to reduce the movement of hazardous waste between countries. It promotes environmentally sound management and disposal of hazardous wastes and controls their transboundary movements to protect human health and the environment.

64.

List 1	List 2
A. Coase theorem	i. property right, victim's pay and polluter paypriniciple
B. Climate change	ii. lax environmental regulation, hidden subsidy
C. Ecological dumping	iii. quantity restriction
D. Tradable emission permit	iv. global externality

1) (a-iii)(b-iv)(c-ii)(d-i) 2) (a-i)(b-iv)(c-ii)(d-iii)
3) (a-ii)(b-i)(c-iii)(d-iv) 4) (a-iii)(b-iv)(c-i)(d-ii)

Answer: 2

Solution: The Coase Theorem argues that under the right conditions parties to a dispute over property rights will be able to negotiate an economically optimal solution, regardless of the initial distribution of the property rights.

The Coase Theorem offers a potentially useful way to think about how to best resolve conflicts between competing businesses or other economic uses of limited resources.

In order for the Coase Theorem to apply fully, the conditions of efficient, competitive markets, and most importantly zero transaction costs, must occur.

In the real world, it is rare that perfect economic conditions exist, making the Coase Theorem better suited to explaining why inefficiencies exist as opposed to a way to resolve disputes.

Global environmental externalities" is an umbrella term that refers to the negative environmental consequences of direct natural resource use and human production and consumption activities arising in broad spatial settings in the presence of incomplete property rights. GHG emissions represent a truly global externality.

Ecological dumping refers a situation where national governments choose less strict environmental standards.

Tradable emissions permits are used in an environmental regulatory scheme where the sources of the pollutant to be regulated (most often an air pollutant) are given permits to release a specified number of tons of the pollutant.

65.

List 1		List 2	
A.	Demographic transition	i.	Dualism
A.	Stages of growth	ii.	take off
B.	Rural urban migration decision	iii.	replacement rate
C.	Female labour force participation rate	iv.	Backward bending labour supply curve

1) (a-i)(b-ii)(c-iii)(d-iv) 2) (a-iv)(b-i)(c-iii)(d-ii)

3) (a-iii)(b-ii)(c-i)(d-iv) 4) (a-iv)(b-i)(c-ii)(d-iii)

Answer: 3

Solution:

1. Replacement level fertility is the level of fertility at which a population exactly replaces itself from one generation to the next. In developed countries, replacement level fertility can be taken as requiring an average of 2.1 children per woman.

   Demographic transition is a phenomenon and theory which refers to the historical shift from high birth rates and high death rates in societies with minimal technology, education (especially of women) and economic development, to low birth rates and low death rates in societies with advanced technology, education and economic development, as well as the stages between these two scenarios.

2. The 5 stages of Rostow's model are:
   - Stage 1: Traditional Society.
   - Stage 2: Preconditions for Take-off.
   - Stage 3: Take-off.
   - Stage 4: Drive to Maturity.
   - Stage 5: Age of High Mass Consumption.
3. Economic dualism, most broadly defined, refers to the coexistence of two or more economic systems.
4. A backward-bending supply curve of labour, or backward-bending labour supply curve, is a graphical device showing a situation in which as real (inflation-corrected) wages increase beyond a certain level, people will substitute time previously devoted for paid work for leisure (non-paid time) and so higher wages lead to a decrease in the labour supply and so less labour-time being offered for sale.

66. Read the following statements regarding demography across India's major states

(A) Kerala pioneered fertility transition in India.

(B) Bihar has high IMR, as well as low reporting of morbidity.

(C) Orissa records the highest share of immunized children as per NFHS-5 round.

(D) Tamil Nadu has the highest share of old age population as per Census 2011.

(E) Madhya Pradesh has the highest share of stunted children as per NFHS-5

Choose the correct answer from the options given below:

1. (A), (D) Only
2. (A) (B) (E) Only
3. (A)(D) (E)Only
4. (A) (B) (C) Only

Answer: 4

67. According to the Census 2011, which major Indian state is the most urbanized ?

(1) Maharashtra
(2) Punjab
(3) Karnataka
(4) Tamil Nadu

Answer: 4

68. Under the flexible inflation targeting framework of monetary policy adopted by the RBI in 2016, what is the target range of rate of inflation?

(1) (4±2)%
(2) (5±2)%
(3)(3±2)%
(4) (2±2)%

Answer: 1

Solution: The RBI has been mandated by the government to ensure the consumer price index (CPI)- based inflation remains at 4 per cent, with a margin of 2 percent on either side.

69. Which one of the following are money market instruments ?

(A) 91-day Treasury bill

(B) Commercial paper

(C) Certificate of deposit issued by banks

(D) 5-yr government bond

Choose the correct answer from the options given below:

(1) (A) Only (2) (A) and (B) Only

(3) (A), (B) and (C) Only (4) (B) and (C) Only

Answer: 3

Solution:

Money Market → deals with short term funds.

Instruments of MM →

Treasury Bills → Issued by the central government on behalf of the government, to curb temporary liquidity shortfalls. They not yield interest but issued at redemption price.

Repo → From seller's point of view . Commercial banks take loans from RBI at repo rate.

Reverse repo → from buyer's point of view. Commercial banks lends to RBI at reverse repo rate.

Commercial papers → They are short-term unsecured, promissory notes issued by the corporations and Financial Institutions are some discounted value.

Bills of exchange → a return order to a person requiring them to make aspecified payment to the signatory.

Certificate of deposits → It is type of federally insured savings account that has a fixed interest rate and fixed date of withdrawal known as maturity date.

Call money market → Market for extremely short period loans i.e. One to fourteen day

70. Arrange the following events in Indian Financial System in correct chronological order, starting from earliest to latest

(A) Setting up of PFRDA

(B) Setting up of UTI

(C) Nationalisation of 14 commercial banks

(D) Implementation of IBC

Choose the correct answer from the options given below

(1) (A)(B)(C)(D)

(2) (C)(A), (B), (D)

(3) (B)(C), (A), (D)

(4) (A)(C), (B), (D)

Answer: 3

Solution:

(A) Setting up of PFRDA (Pension Fund Regulatory and Development Authority): PFRDA was established on August 23, 2003.

(B) Setting up of UTI (Unit Trust of India): UTI was established on February 1, 1964.

(C) Nationalisation of 14 commercial banks: The nationalization of 14 major banks in India took place on July 19, 1969.

(D) Implementation of IBC (Insolvency and Bankruptcy Code): The Insolvency and Bankruptcy Code was enacted in 2016 and came into effect on December 1, 2016.

71. Repo rate is the interest rate at which:

(1) The commercial banks borrow from the RBI

(2) The commercial banks borrow from the other commercial banks

(3) The commercial banks deposit money to the RBI

(4) The common people deposit money to the RBI

Answer: 1

Solution: Repo Rate :-RBI charges to commercial banks for short term loans.↑ in repo rate leads to ↓ in money supply. Repo rate is technically a repurchase agreement in which the commercial banks offer securities such as Treasury Bills to the RBI in return for short term funds.

72. Given below are two statements:

Statement (1): Agricultural GDP constitutes less than 16% of aggregate GDP at 2011-12 constant prices and less than 20% of the aggregate GDP at current prices in 2022-23 (PE) in India.

Statement (II): Service sector GDP constitutes less than 16% of aggregate GDP at 2011-12 constant prices and less than 20% of the aggregate GDP at current prices in 2022-23 (PE) in India.

In the light of the above statements, choose the most appropriate answer from the options given below:

(1) Both Statement I and Statement II are correct

(2) Both Statement I and Statement II are incorrect

(3) Statement I is correct but Statement II is incorrect

(4) Statement I is incorrect but Statement II is correct

Answer: 3

Solution:

Sector wise GDP in India (2022-23) at current price		Sector wise GDP in India (2022-23) at constant price	
Agriculture sector	18.42%	Agriculture sector	15.13%
Industrial sector	28.25%	Industrial sector	30.66%
Service sector	53.34%	Service sector	54.19%

73. In March, 2023 the consumer price index (CPI) of a country with a 1982 base index of 100, was 234.7. This means the cost of purchasing the market basket of goods and services:

(1) has decreased by 134.7% since 1982

(2) has increased by 34.7% since 1982

(3) has increased by 234.7% since 1982

(4) has increased by 134.7% since 1982

Answer: 4

Solution: let x% increase is 100

Percent increase is

$100 \times \frac{x}{100} + 100 = 234.7$

X+100 = 234.7

X = 234.7-100

X = 134.7

74. Arrange the following names of former governors of RBI in the sequence in which they held the post starting from the earliest to latest.

(A) Y.V. Reddy **(B) D Subbarao**

(C) Raghuram Rajan **(D) Urjit Patel**

Choose the correct answer from the options given below:

(1) (C) (B) (D). (A) (2) (C) (A) (D) (B)

(3)(A)(B)(C) (D) (4) (D) (C) (A) (B)

Answer 3

Solution:

1. Bimal Jalan: Served as RBI Governor from November 22, 1997, to September 6, 2003.
2. Y. V. Reddy: Served as RBI Governor from September 6, 2003, to September 5, 2008.
3. Duvvuri Subbarao: Served as RBI Governor from September 5, 2008, to September 4, 2013.
4. Raghuram Rajan: Served as RBI Governor from September 4, 2013, to September 4, 2016.
5. Urjit Patel: Served as RBI Governor from September 4, 2016, to December 10, 2018.
6. Shaktikanta Das: Appointed as RBI Governor and assumed office on December 12, 2018. He was in office as of my last knowledge update in January 2022.

75. Arrange the following in order of their year of establishment starting from the oldest.

(A) Lakdawala Committee

(B) Khusro Committee

(C) Alagh Committee

(D) Nayak Committee

(E) Tendulkar Committee

Choose the correct answer from the options given below:

(1) (D) (B) (C) (A) (E) (2)(C) (D) (B), (A) (E)

(3) (C)(B) (D) (A) (E) (4) (B)(C) (D) (E) (A)

Answer: 3

Solution:

Alagh Committee (1979): Task force constituted by the Planning Commission under the chairmanship of YK Alagh, constructed a poverty line for rural and urban areas on the basis of nutritional requirements and related consumption expenditure.

Poverty estimates for subsequent years were to be calculated by adjusting the price level for inflation.

Khusro Committee is also known as Agricultural Credit Review Committee which was established in 1989.

Nayak Committee: The Reserve Bank of India constituted on 9 December 1991, a Committee under the Chairmanship of Shri P.R. Nayak, Deputy Governor to examine the difficulties confronting the small scale industries (SSI) in the country in the matter of securing finance.

Lakdawala Committee (1993): Task Force chaired by DT Lakdawala, based on the assumption that the basket of goods and services used to calculate Consumer Price Index- Industrial

Workers (CPI-IW) and Consumer Price Index- Agricultural Labourers (CPI-AL) reflect the consumption patterns of the poor, made the following suggestions:

Consumption expenditure should be calculated based on calorie consumption as earlier.

State specific poverty lines should be constructed and these should be updated using the CPI-IW in urban areas and CPI-AL in rural areas.

Discontinuation of scaling of poverty estimates based on National Accounts Statistics.

Tendulkar Committee (2009)

Expert group constituted by the Planning Commission and, chaired by Suresh Tendulkar, was constituted to review methodology for poverty estimation and to address the following shortcomings of the previous methods:

Obsolete Consumption Pattern: Consumption patterns were linked to the 1973-74 poverty line baskets (PLBs) of goods and services, whereas there were significant changes in the consumption patterns of the poor since that time, which were not reflected in the poverty estimates.

Inflation Adjustment: There were issues with the adjustment of prices for inflation, both spatially (across regions) and temporally (across time).

Health and Education Expenditure: Earlier poverty lines assumed that health and education would be provided by the state and formulated poverty lines accordingly

76. The expert committee set up by RBI in 2013 to revise and strengthen the monetary policy frame work in India was chaired by:

(1) Raghuram Rajan (2) Urjit Patel

(3) Deepak Mohanty (4) Michael Patra

Answer: 2

Solution: The expert committee set up by the Reserve Bank of India (RBI) in 2013 to revise and strengthen the monetary policy framework in India was chaired by Dr. Urjit R. Patel. The committee is commonly known as the Urjit Patel Committee.

77. Consider the following centrally sponsored schemes in India and choose the right sequence of time (year) when they were launched, from earliest to latest.

(A) Beti Bachao Beti Padhao

(B) Ujjwala

(C) Swach Bharat Abhiyan

(D) Ayushman Bharat

(E) Right to Education

Choose the correct answer from the options given below:

(1) (E), (A), (C. (B) (D)
(2) (E) (C) (A), (B). (D)
(3) (A), (E), (C), (B). (D)
(4) (A), (C), (E). (D) (B)

Answer: 2

Solution:

(A) Beti Bachao Beti Padhao: Launched in 2015.

(B) Ujjwala: Pradhan Mantri Ujjwala Yojana (PMUY) was launched in 2016.

(C) Swachh Bharat Abhiyan: Launched on October 2, 2014.

(D) Ayushman Bharat: Launched in 2018.

(E) Right to Education (RTE): The Right to Education Act came into effect on April 1, 2010

78. Given below are two statements:

Statement (I): The Government's spending on social services as a percentage of GDP has been rising since 2017-18.

Statement (II): The Government's spending on social services as a percentage of total expenditure has also been continuously rising since 2017-18. In the light of the above statements, choose the most appropriate answer from the options given. below:

(1) Both Statement 1 and Statement II are correct

(2) Both Statement I and Statement II are incorrect

(3) Statement I is correct but Statement II is incorrect

(4) Statement I is incorrect but Statement Il is correct

Answer: 3

Comprehensive

Assume that there are 2 firms producing steel. There is a negative externality due to production causing pollution. Firm I's output is q1, and Firm 2's is q2, Assume that the market price for steel is Ps=1 Now consider two scenarios:

Scenario 1: firm I's cost function is $C1(q1)=q1^2$ and firm 2's cost function is $C2(q1,q2)=(q2+0.75\ q1)^2$. In short, firm I's production is not affected by firm 2 but firm 2's production is affected by firm 1, i.e., Firms 1's operation causes firm 2's costs to rise.

Scenario 2: Assume that negative externality works both ways i.e., both the firms face the adverse impact. So assume: $C1(q1,q2) = (q1+0.75q2)^2$ and $C2(q1,q2) = (q2+0.75q1)^2$, i.e., Firms 1's operation causes firm 2's costs to rise and vice versa.

Sub-questions

79. What is the equilibrium profit of firm 2 (π2) in the short run, in scenario 1?

1. $\pi2 = 0.025$
2. $\pi2 = 0.125$

3. $\pi2 = -0.125$ 4. $\pi2 = 0.75$

Answer: 3

Profit = revenue -cost and revenue =price *quantity.

For profit maximization quantities, do first derivative of profit functions, put them equal to zero and find

q1 ,q2

$\pi1 = Pq1-(q1^2)$ (p=1 given)

$\pi'1 = 1-2q1 = 0$

q1=0.5

$\pi2 = Pq2-(q2+0.75\ q1)^2$

$\pi'2 = 1-2(q2+0.75q1) = 0$

by solving, q2=0.125

now put q1 and q2 in $\pi2 = Pq2-(q2+0.75\ q1)^2$

$\pi2$ will be -0.125.

Firms 1's operation causes firm 2's costs to rise.

So firm 1 profits will be + 0.125

80. What is the long run profit of firm 1 ($\pi1$), in scenario 1?

1. $\pi1 = 0.025$ 2. $\pi1 = 0$

3. $\pi1 = 0.25$ 4. $\pi1 = 0.125$

Answer: 4

81. do you think that the equilibrium outcome for scenario 2 is inefficient? How would be the efficiency be resolved?

1. No, the equilibrium outcome of the firms are profit minimising outcome.
2. The externality can be resolved by closing down both the firms is $\pi1 = \pi2 = 0$
3. If one of the firm is forced to close down, the externality will be reduced and their joint profit is $\pi1 + \pi2 = 0.071$.
4. If one of the firm is forced to close down, the externality will be reduced and their joint profit is $\pi1 + \pi2 = 0.109$.

Answer: 4

If one firm is forced to shut down, put its quantity as 0.

$\pi1 = Pq1-((q1+0.75q2)^2)$ put q2=0

=q1-q12

π'1=1-2q1=0

q1=0.5

put q1=0.5 and q2=0 in π1=Pq1-((q1+0.75q2)^2) , profits of firm 1 will be 0.25

now put q1=0.5 and q2=0 in π2=Pq2-(q2+ 0.75 q1)^2, profits of firm 2 will be -0.140625

joint profits= 0.25-0.1406=0.109

82. What is the long run profit of firm 2 (π2), in scenario 1?

1. $\pi 2 = 0.125$
2. $\pi 2 = 0.120$
3. $\pi 2 = 0.5$
4. $\pi 2 = 0$

Answer: 4

Solution:

In long run P =AC, price = 1

AC2 = (q2+0.75q1 / q2)^2

=q2^2 + (0.75)^{2}q1^2 + 2(0.75)q1q2 / q2^2

= q2+ (0.75)^2 q1^2 / q2+ 1.5 q1

= q2 + (0.75)^2 (0.5)^2 /q2+ 1.5 (0.5)

= q2+ 0.140625 / q2 + 0.75

= q2+0.140625+0.75q2 = q2

= 0.75q2 = -0.140625

Output can't be negative Firm 2 will shut down

= π2 is 0 in long run.

83. What would be the market equilibrium profit of 2 firms, in scenario 2?

1. $\pi 1 = 1/28$, $\pi 2 = 1/28$
2. $\pi 1 = 2/7$, $\pi 2 = 2/7$
3. $\pi 1 = 1/14$, $\pi 2 = 1/14$
4. $\pi 1 = \pi 2 = 0$

Answer: 1

Solution:

Scenario 2:

Market equilibrium profit

C1 = (q1+0.75q2)^2

C2 = q2+0.75q1)^2

$MC1 = 2(q1+0.75q2)$

$MC2 = 2(q2+0.75q1)$

$MR1 = MC1$

$1 = 2(q1+0.75q2)$---------------1

$MR2 = MC2$

$1 = 2(q2+0.75q1)$---------------2

By solving equation 1 and 2

1. $q1+0.75q2 = ½$

$q1+3/4q2 = ½$

$4q1+3q2 = 2$

2. $0.75q1 + q2 = ½$

$3/4q1+q2 = ½$

$3q1 + 4q2 = 2$

$[4q1+3q2 = 2] \times 3$

$[3q1+4q2 = 2] \times 4$

$12q1+9q2 = 6$

$12q1 + 16q2 = 8$

$q2 = 2/7$

$4q1 + 3 \times 2/7 = 2$

$4q1 = 2 - 6/7$

$4q1 = 14-6 /7$

$q1 = 8/7 \times 4$

$q1 = 2/7$

$\pi1 = pq1 - (q1 + 0.75q2)^2$

$= 2/7 - (2/7 + ¾ \times 2/7)^2$

$= 2/7 - (4+3 / 14)2$

$= 2/7 - ¼ = 8-7 / 28 = 1/28$

Similarly, $\pi2 = 1/28$

Comprehension: 2

According to the NSO, MOSPI press release dated 31 May 2023, the revised estimate of GDP at the current price for the year 2021-22 was Rs. 2,34,71,012 crores and that for 2020-21 was Rs. 1,98,29,927 crores. The GDP at 2011-12 constant prices for the year 2020-21 and 2021- 22 were Rs. 1,36,87,118 crores and Rs. 1,49,25,840 crores respectively. At the current prices, the net taxes on products were Rs. 20,32,128 crores in 2021-22(RE). The PFCE, GFCE, GFCF in 2021-22 were Rs. 1,43,44,336 crores, Rs. 26,25,361 crores and Rs. 67,86,391 crores respectively. Change in stocks (CIS), valuables, and discrepancies in 2021-22 were Rs.

1,63,438 crores, Rs. 3,79,112 crores and Rs. (-) 208,247 crores (negative) respectively in current prices.

84. If the value of exports in 2021-22 at current price be Rs. 50,49,645 crores, the import in 2021-22 at current prices in India was:

(1) Rs. 56,69,024 crores

(2) Rs 6,19,378 crores

(3) Rs. 1,17,18.975 crores

(4) Ra. 94,11,752 crores

Answer: 1

GDP=PFCE+GFCE+GFCF+Change in Stocks+Valuables+Discrepancies + (Exports - Imports)

2,34,71,012 =1,43,44,336, + 26,25,361 + 67,86,391+1,63,438 + 3,79,112 + (-) 208,247

+(50,49,645 - imports)

Imports = 5669024

85. The current account deficit to GDP ratio (both at current prices) in 2021-22 for India was:

(1) 1.75%

(2) 3.53%

(3) 4.06%

(4) 2.64%

Answer: 4

Solution:

As exports are given in above question 83 = 5049645

And imports are 56,69,024

CAD = Exports- imports

=5049645 – 5669024

=619379

CAD to GDP ratio =

Nominal GDP at 2021-22 = 23471012

Ratio = 619379/23471012 x 100

= 2.64%

86. The Gross Value Added (GVA) at basic prices in 2021-22 was:

(1) Rs. 2,55,03,140 crore
(2) Rs. 2,14,38,884 crore
(3) Rs. 2,34,71,012 crore
(4) Rs. 1,49,37,569 crore

Answer: 2

Solution:

GDP= GVA+TAXES-SUBSIDIES

GDP at the current price for the year 2021-22 was Rs. 2,34,71,012 crores

The net taxes on products were Rs. 20,32,128 crores in 2021-22

GVA at basic price is = 2,34,71,012 – 20,32,128

=2,14,38,884 crore.

87. What was the inflation rate in India based on GDP deflator?

a. 4.5%
b. 6.6%
c. 9.3%
d. 10.2%

Answer: 3

GDP Deflator for year 2020-21 = Nominal GDP/Real GDP x 100

= 1,98,29,927/13687118 x 100

= 144

GDP deflator for 2021-22 = 23471012/14925840 x 100

= 157

Inflation Rate = 157-144 / 144 x 100

=9.0277

Hence, option 3 is nearest and correct.

88. In 2021-22, the investment GDP ratio in India was?

a. 31.2%
b. 90%
c. 40.1%
d. 42.2%

Answer: 1

Solution:

Investment = GFCF + Change in Stock + valuables

= 6786391 + 1,63,438 + 3,79,112

= 7328941

Nominal GDP at 2021-22 = 23471012

Ratio = 7328941 / 23471012 x 100

=31.2%

89. Consider a consumer's choice based on only 2 commodities ie., X∈ R^2_+, where X is a set of all commodity bundles which the consumer can conceive of. Suppose x and y are the 2 different commodity bundles and the budget set B of the consumer can be written as B ={(x,y):$P_1x+P_2y \leq M$}; $x_i > 0$, i=1, 2. Which of the following statement is true?

1)the budget set is an open, bounded and convex set

2) the budget set is not a bounded set

3) the budget set is closed and non convex set

4) the budget set is closed, bounded and convex sets

Answer 4

Solution: If all the boundary points are included in the set, then it is a closed set. If all the boundary points are not included in the set then it is an open set. For example, x+y>5 is an open set whereas x+y>=5 is a closed set. set x>=5 and y<3 is neither as boundary x=5 included but y=3 is not included.

$$\text{Concavity: } f(k) \geq m$$
$$\text{Convexity: } f(k) \leq m$$
$$\text{Linear: } f(k) = m$$

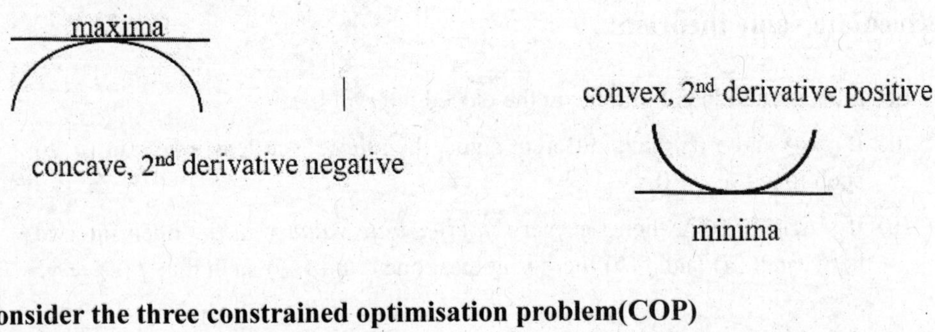

90. Consider the three constrained optimisation problem(COP)

a. Maximize z= In x, subject to x>1

b. Maximize z= In x, subject to x<1

c. Maximize z= In x, subject to 1<x<2

1. a and b have no solution but c has solution
2. a and b have solution but c has no solution
3. a, b and c have no solution
4. a and c have no solution but b has solution

choose the correct answer from the options given below

1. only 1 is correct
2. only 2 is correct
3. only 3 is correct
4. only 4 is correct

Answer: 3

derivate z wrt x and put it equal to 0, according to maxima rule

z=lnx

z'=1/x=0

1=0

hence, it has no solution.

91. suppose f(.) is a continuous function over a closed and bounded interval (a, b). Then there exists a point d in (a, b) where f(.) has a minimum, and a point c in (a, b) where f(.) has a maximum, so that f(d)≤f(x)≤f(c) for all x in (a, b). the statement is derived from:

1. Intermediate value theorem
2. Rolle's theorem
3. Mean value theorem
4. Extreme value theorem

Answer: 4

Solution:

Intermediate value theorem:

> Let f be a function continuous in the closed interval $[a, b]$.
>
> (i) If $f(a)$ and $f(b)$ have different signs, then there is at least one c in (a, b) such that $f(c) = 0$.
>
> (ii) If $f(a) \neq f(b)$, then for every *intermediate value* y in the open interval between $f(a)$ and $f(b)$ there is at least one c in (a, b) such that $f(c) = y$.

Mean value theorem:

If f is continuous in the closed bounded interval $[a, b]$, and differentiable in the open interval (a, b), then there exists at least one interior point x^* in (a, b) such that

$$f'(x^*) = \frac{f(b) - f(a)}{b - a}$$

Rolle's theorem:

If f is continuous in closed interval [a,b] and differentiable in open interval [a,b]; and f(a)=f(b),then there exists at least one c in [a,b] such that f'(c)=0.

The Extreme Value Theorem :

Suppose the function $f(x, y)$ is continuous throughout a nonempty, closed and bounded set S in the plane. Then there exists both a point (a, b) in S where f has a minimum and a point (c, d) in S where f has a maximum—that is,

$$f(a, b) \leq f(x, y) \leq f(c, d) \qquad \text{for all } (x, y) \text{ in } S$$

Now, the statement you provided says that if f(x) is a continuous function over a closed and bounded interval (a,b), then there exists a point d in (a,b) where f(x) has a minimum, and a point c in (a,b) where f(x) has a maximum, so that f(d)≤f(x)≤f(c) for all x in (a,b).

This matches the conditions of the Extreme Value Theorem.

92. If f(x,y) is a homogeneous function of degree 2 with f'(2,3) = 4 and f' (4,6) = 12, find f(6,9) =?

1. 117 2. 234 3. 115 4. 243

Answer: 1

Solution:

Let $f(x,y) = ax^2+by^2$

$f(\lambda x, \lambda y) = a\,\lambda^2x^2 + b\,\lambda^2y^2$

$= \lambda^2\,(ax^2+by^2)$

$= \lambda^2\,f(x,y)$

It is homogeneous of degree 2

Now, $f'1(x,y) = \frac{d}{dx}(ax^2+by^2)$

$= 2ax$

Given that, f (2,3) = 4

$f'1\ (2,3) = 2a(2) = 4$

$4a = 4$

$a = 1$

$f'2(x,y) = \frac{d}{dx}(ax^2+by^2)$

$= 2by$

$f'2\ (4,6) = 2b(6) = 12$

$12b = 12$

$b=1$

Given that f (4,6) = 12

$f'2\ (6,9) = (ax^2+by^2)$

$= (1)36 + (1)\ 81 = 117$

93. Consider a matrix $A = \begin{bmatrix} 3 & 5 \\ -2 & -4 \end{bmatrix}$

Consider the following statements on characteristic polynomial, Eigen Values and Eigen Vectors.

(A) The characteristic polynomial is $\lambda^2 + \lambda - 2$

(B) The characteristic polynomial is $\lambda^2 - 2\lambda - 4$ and the characteristic root or Eigen values are $\lambda* = 2$ *and* 1

(C) The characteristic polynomial is $\lambda^2 - \lambda + 2$ and the characteristic root or Eigen values are $\lambda* = 1$ *and* 2

(D) The characteristic root or Eigen Values are $\lambda* = -2$ *and* 1

Choose the correct options:

1. A,C and D only
2. C only
3. B and D only
4. A and D only

Answer;4

Solution:

$$A = \begin{bmatrix} 3 & 5 \\ -2 & -4 \end{bmatrix}$$

Eigen Values

$$A-\lambda^{I} = \begin{bmatrix} 3-\lambda & 5 \\ -2 & -4-\lambda \end{bmatrix} = 0$$

$(3-\lambda)(-4-\lambda) + 10 = 0$

$-12 - 3\lambda + 4\lambda + \lambda^2 + 10 = 0$

$\lambda^2 + \lambda - 12 + 10 = 0$

$\lambda^2 + \lambda - 2 = 0$

$\lambda^2 + 2\lambda - \lambda - 2 = 0$

$\lambda(\lambda + 2) - (\lambda + 2) = 0$

$= \lambda = -2, and\ 1$

94.

If A = A = $\begin{bmatrix} 2 & 3 \\ 0 & 4 \end{bmatrix}$ *and* $B = \begin{bmatrix} 2 & 0 \\ 1 & 5 \end{bmatrix}$ which of the following is not correct?

1) $A^TB. = \begin{bmatrix} 4 & 0 \\ 10 & 20 \end{bmatrix}$

2) $(A + B)^T = \begin{bmatrix} 4 & 1 \\ 3 & 9 \end{bmatrix}$

3) $A^TB. = \begin{bmatrix} 0 & 4 \\ 10 & 20 \end{bmatrix}$

4) $A^TB^T = \begin{bmatrix} 4 & 2 \\ 6 & 23 \end{bmatrix}$

Answer: 3

Solution:

$$A = \begin{bmatrix} 2 & 3 \\ 0 & 4 \end{bmatrix} \; B = \begin{bmatrix} 2 & 0 \\ 1 & 5 \end{bmatrix}$$

$$A^T = \begin{bmatrix} 2 & 0 \\ 3 & 4 \end{bmatrix} \; B = \begin{bmatrix} 2 & 0 \\ 1 & 5 \end{bmatrix}$$

$$A^TB = \begin{bmatrix} 2\times 2 & 0\times 1 & 2\times 0 & 0\times 5 \\ 3\times 2 & 4\times 1 & 3\times 0 & 4\times 5 \end{bmatrix}$$

$$= \begin{bmatrix} 4 & 0 \\ 10 & 20 \end{bmatrix}$$

$$A^T = \begin{bmatrix} 2 & 0 \\ 3 & 4 \end{bmatrix}$$

$$B^T = \begin{bmatrix} 2 & 1 \\ 0 & 5 \end{bmatrix}$$

$$A^TB^T = \begin{bmatrix} 2\times 2 & 0\times 0 & 2\times 1 & 0\times 5 \\ 3\times 2 & 4\times 0 & 3\times 1 & 4\times 5 \end{bmatrix}$$

$$= \begin{bmatrix} 4 & 2 \\ 6 & 23 \end{bmatrix}$$

$$A + B = \begin{bmatrix} 4 & 3 \\ 1 & 9 \end{bmatrix}$$

$$(A + B)^T = \begin{bmatrix} 4 & 1 \\ 3 & 9 \end{bmatrix}$$

95. $A=\begin{bmatrix}3 & 2\\8 & 2\\2 & 0\end{bmatrix}$ $B=\begin{bmatrix}5\\9\end{bmatrix}$

(A) AB is given by = $\begin{bmatrix}3 & 2\\8 & 2\\2 & 0\end{bmatrix}$

(B) BA is given by [32 82 20]

(C) AB is not defined

(D) BA is not defined

(E) A B is defined

Choose the correct answer from the options given below

1. C and B
2. A, D, E
3. Only A
4. A and D

Answer: 4

Solution:

Rule for Matrix Multiplications:-

No. of Col. Of Matrix A → Must be equal to → No. of Rows of Matrix B

1st Row is multiplied with 1st coloumn.

$A=\begin{bmatrix}1 & 2\\4 & 6\end{bmatrix}$ $B=\begin{bmatrix}3 & 1\\2 & 5\end{bmatrix}$

$A=\begin{bmatrix}1\times3+2\times2 & 1+5\times2\\4\times3+6\times2 & 4\times1+6\times5\end{bmatrix}$

$A=\begin{bmatrix}1 & 3\\2 & 8\\4 & 0\end{bmatrix}$ $B=\begin{bmatrix}5\\9\end{bmatrix}$

Number of columns of A is equal to number of rows of B. So multiplication is possible

$$AB=\begin{bmatrix}1\times5 & 3\times9\\2\times5 & 8\times9\\4\times5 & 0\times9\end{bmatrix}=\begin{bmatrix}32\\82\\20\end{bmatrix}$$

Number of columns of B is $\neq$ to number of rows of A. So multiplication is not possible.

96. Consider the following statements

a. **The union of finite numbers of a closed set is a closed set**

b. **The empty set is an open set but not a closed set**

c. **Every infinite set is a open set**

d. **The intersection of finite numbers of open sets is an open set**

Choose the correct answer from the options given below:

1. A and B
2. B and C
3. A and D
4. A , B, and C

Answer: 3

Solution:

✧ If all the boundary points are included in the set, then it is a closed set. If all the boundary points are not included in the set then it is an open set. For example, x+y>5 is an open set whereas x+y>=5 is a closed set. set x>=5 and y<3 is neither as boundary x=5 included but y=3 is not included.

✧ A finite set in mathematics is a set that has a finite number of elements. In simple words, it is a set that you can finish counting. For example, {1,3,5,7} is a finite set with four elements. The element in the finite set is a natural number, i.e. non-negative integer.

97. In a negatively skewed distribution, which among the following would be true?

a. Mean> mode

b. Mean<mode

c. Median<mode

d. Mode>mean

Choose the correct answer from the options given below:

1. a and b
2. b and c
3. b and d
4. a and c

Answer: 2 and 3 both options are correct i.e, statement b, c and d

Solution: Skewness: measure the direction in which the values are dispersed. It means degree of symmetry or asymmetry of the series. For a series to be symmetrical, the sum of positive deviation from median should be equal to the sum of negative deviation from the median.

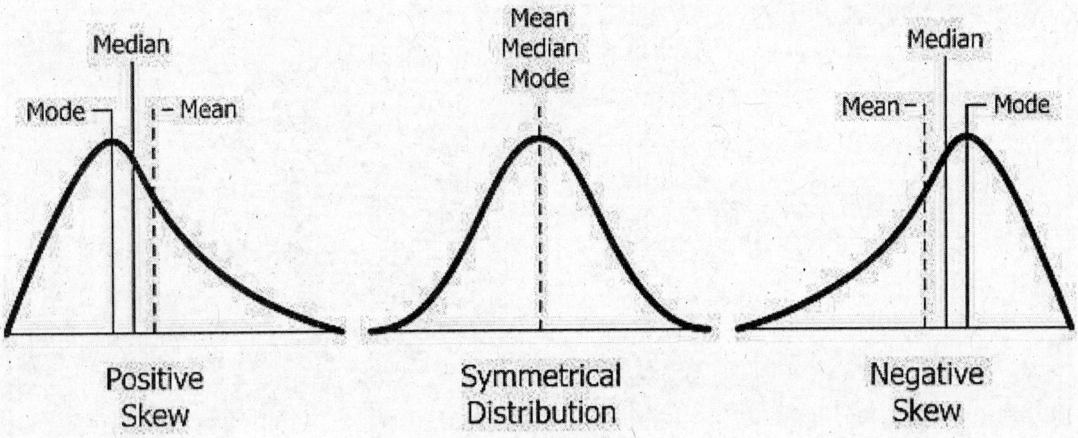

$\bar{x} > M > Z$ $\bar{x} = M = Z$ $\bar{x} < M < Z$